F
1528
,N498
1982

NICARAGUA IN REVOLUTION

Edited by
THOMAS W. WALKER

PRAEGER SPECIAL STUDIES • PRAEGER SCIENTIFIC

GOSHEN COLLEGE LIBRARY
GOSHEN, INDIANA

Library of Congress Cataloging in Publication Data

Main entry under title:

Nicaragua in revolution.

    Includes index.
    1. Nicaragua—History—Revolution, 1979.
I. Walker, Thomas W.
F1528.N498   972.85′052   81-17746
ISBN 0-03-057972-4 (hbk.)   AACR2
ISBN 0-03-057971-6 (pbk.)

Published in 1982 by Praeger Publishers
CBS Educational and Professional Publishing
A Division of CBS, Inc.
521 Fifth Avenue, New York, New York 10175 U.S.A.

© 1982 by Praeger Publishers

All rights reserved

23456789 145 987654321
Printed in the United States of America

TO THAT NOBLE ASPECT OF THE HUMAN SPIRIT
WHICH SUCCEEDED IN FLOWERING
SO BRIGHTLY
IN THE LAND OF SANDINO

CONTENTS

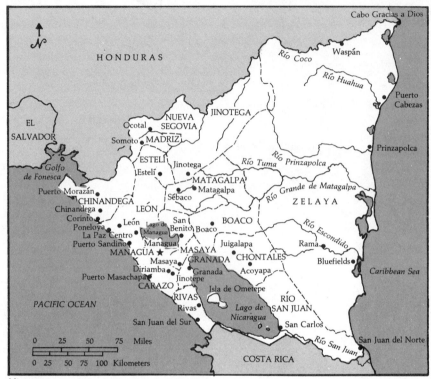

Nicaragua

Map from Thomas W. Walker, *Nicaragua:The Land of Sandino* (1981)

By permission of Westview Press

PART I

INTRODUCTION

THOMAS W. WALKER

This book was conceived with the purpose of providing the reader with a systematic and detailed examination of the Nicaraguan Revolution through its first year and a half in power.* In pursuit of this objective, an outline was prepared in the winter of 1979-80 and a group of scholars was contracted to research and write chapters on each of the major topics. As word of the project spread, other scholars with additional pertinent topics contacted the editor and were integrated into this collective effort. In the end, some two dozen individuals—of various nationalities—came to participate as chapter authors or co-authors.

In order to allow maximum space for the findings of these authors, this introduction will be short. Its objective is simply to set the Revolution in perspective (1) by discussing the concept and historical experience of "revolution" in Latin America and, (2) by tracing the social, economic, and political history out of which the Nicaraguan Revolution flowed.

Revolution
As the term is commonly used by social scientists, "revolution" implies a process of rapid social, economic, and political change which normally entails physical violence and results in a restructuring of the relationship between classes. The old privileged class, or classes, is displaced by a formerly subservient class. A common symptom of real revolution is a massive outflow of emigrés composed largely of individuals from the former privileged class.

If one employs this definition in examining the history of Latin America, one quickly arrives at the conclusion that, contrary to popular belief, "revolution" is a very rare phenomenon indeed in that part of the world. Though many Latin American countries have undergone frequent extra-legal changes in government via successful revolts, *coups d'etat*, *golpes de estado*, and the like, few have subsequently experienced any

* The editor would like to thank the Department of Political Science, the College of Arts and Sciences, and the Office of Research and Sponsored Programs at Ohio University for crucial and significant financial support which greatly facilitated the coordination of this collective effort. Among other things, this funding allowed the editor to travel to Nicaragua on four separate occasions following the Sandinist victory of July 19, 1979.

serious attempt at the reordering of social and economic structures. Even if one accepts incomplete or abortive efforts, it is clear that real revolution has never even been tried in most of the Latin American countries. Even in the supposedly turbulent twentieth century, only a handful of countries have witnessed the coming to power of avowedly revolutionary groups that subsequently embarked on programs of real revolutionary change. Generously, one might include seven in this category: Mexico, 1911—1940; Guatemala, 1945-1954; Bolivia, 1952-1964; Cuba, 1959 to date; Peru, 1968-1975; Chile, 1970-1973; and Nicaragua, 1979 to date. Of these would-be revolutions, five eventually died, were crushed, or were transformed into non-revolutionary systems before significant social and economic restructuring could be completed.

Why, one might ask, given the record to date, did Latin American revolutionaries persist? Part of the answer is that for many Latin Americans who were sincerely concerned about the terrible social condition of the bulk of the peoples of the region, a violent approach to structural change seemed to be the *only* viable solution. By the late twentieth century, it was fairly obvious, to those who cared to see, that very basic structural impasses stood in the way of human development for the vast majority of the people of Latin America. Furthermore, these blockages did not appear amenable to gradualist, nonviolent reforms such as those advocated by the United States from the time of the ill-fated "Alliance for Progress" in the early 1960s through the equally ineffective "human rights campaign" of Jimmy Carter late in the next decade. Quite simply, as gross national product (GNP) grew in most countries and a tiny privileged middle sector and upper class became increasingly affluent, the human condition of the vast majority of the people of Latin America either improved hardly at all, stagnated, or actually declined. And, this pattern seemed stubbornly to persist whether the political form of the moment was liberal "democracy" (*a la* Colombia from the late 1950s onward), one-man dictatorship (Paraguay under Alfredo Stroessner or Haiti under the Duvaliers), or military rule (Brazil from 1964 onward and Chile after 1973).

The roots of the problem seemed to lie in a complex of social, economic, and political factors which many Latin American scholars and, later, an increasing number of North Americans and Europeans, came to refer to as "dependency."[1] Though the *dependistas* (as the writers who examined this subject were called) often disagreed with each other on specifics, a general consensus began to emerge to the effect that the social stagnation of Latin America was due in large part to the combination of an income-concentrating, externally-oriented and conditioned form of capitalism with political systems controlled by the same minority classes which were receiving the bulk of the benefits from the distorted economic growth taking place.

Under these conditions, capitalist "development" in Latin America clearly was not following the pattern set by the industrialized countries. In the so-called "developed" world, the common man had attained a crucial economic (and therefore political) role as a consumer. Therefore, even if there was such a thing as a "ruling class," it was not in that group's interest to use its political power to exploit the common citizen to the extent that he could no longer consume. However, this was not true of Latin America, where capitalist economics were heavily externally oriented. There the tiny middle and upper classes which controlled the political systems derived most of their income directly or indirectly from export or from the local MNC-dominated manufacture of products which they, not the masses, consumed. Under these conditions, the common citizen was important not as a consumer but rather as an easily exploitable source of cheap labor. Therefore, there was little or no economic incentive for the elite-dominated governments of Latin America to call upon their own class or classes to make the very real sacrifices necessary to improve the lot of the vast majority of the people.

Nor was there much apparent political incentive for such reforms. One of the most basic principles of politics is that benefits flow to groups in society more or less in direct proportion to their ability to exert pressure or to exercise power. Although the United States at the beginning of the Alliance for Progress solemnly admonished the ruling classes of Latin America to implement reform or suffer the consequences of Castro-like revolution, Washington quickly made such reforms appear to be politically unnecessary by providing Latin America's military establishments with so much "counter-insurgency" military aid that the privileged elites actually came to feel quite immune from the coercive power of the mass of the people. As a result, paradoxically, social injustice and exploitation were allowed to mount to the point where violent revolution would eventually be the only hope or option for most Latin Americans.

Another reason that Latin American revolutionaries did not give up is that they were increasingly convinced that history was on their side. They drew confidence from the fact that each previous revolutionary attempt—successful or not—had added to the "technology" of revolution. Though the United States Department of State and the popular press were fond of depicting Latin American revolutionaries as sinister "terrorists" and thugs bent on delivering their countries into the hands of the Soviet Union, that picture was far from accurate. If we can generalize from the Nicaraguan experience and from scattered information from other countries, these people tended to be highly motivated and patriotic young men and women drawn disproportionately from the ranks of high school and university teachers and students. As such, they were intellectually active people with a much better than average awareness of national and regional history. Clearly, they felt that the history of revolution in Latin America held valuable lessons.

One of the insights which history seemed to offer was that there are no peaceful shortcuts to "revolution." Of the seven revolutionary experiments mentioned above, the three which came to power without violent struggle and therefore without either mass mobilization or the dissolution of the conventional military establishment were eventually overthrown with little difficulty by the military. Here we refer not only to the democratically-elected revolutionary governments of Guatamala (1954) and Chile (1973), but also to the Peruvian revolution which was strangled in 1975 by the same military institution that had given it birth in the first place.

On the other hand, the Latin Americans had also learned that guerrilla warfare could not succeed without mass support. Such backing had been a major key to the success of the guerrillas in Cuba in 1959. Fidel Castro and his comrades had purposely cultivated a mass following not only through the clandestine broadcasts of "Radio Rebelde," but also by treating peasants with respect and by implementing social reforms in liberated areas. Yet, by the same token, guerrilla movements in the 1960s and early 1970s had met with a series of defeats due largely to their relative isolation from the people. For some reason, Ché Guevara in Bolivia, the Tupamaros of Uruguay, Carlos Marighela in Brazil, the Colombian FARC, and so on—highly motivated though they may have been—had failed to win the "hearts and minds" of the local populaces. Undoubtedly, some of their lack of success could be attributed to the façade of legitimacy of the elite regimes they were opposing. But much of it could be credited to their failure to communicate effectively with the masses.

Latin American revolutionaries had also learned much about what to do once in power. There was a growing awareness that the challenge of running a revolutionary system is as great as, or greater than, that of seizing power in the first place in that it requires sweeping and effective innovation on a number of fronts simultaneously. For many observers, the failure of the Mexican, Guatemalan, Bolivian, Chilean, and Peruvian revolutionary experiments was attributable, at least in part, to a relative lack of bold, unified, and decisive actions. In some cases, the revolutionary leaders were stymied by obstacles beyond their control (unreconstructed military institutions, constitutional constraints, and so on), but in others, they appear to have been unnecessarily timid.

It was clear that if a "revolution" is, indeed, to be "revolutionary," it must immediately embark on a number of social programs designed to improve the human condition of the previously exploited majority. These would include some variant of agrarian reform; projects and legislation designed to advance public health, education, and housing; increased emphasis on the rights of rural and urban workers; and an effort to resurrect and nourish popular, "native" culture.

Each of the revolutionary experiments mentioned earlier featured most, if not all, of these types of reform. From these experiences, much had been learned about what "worked" and what did not. This was especially true in the areas of agrarian reform and education. In the former, some revolutionary governments had simply redistributed land without much technical followup (Bolivia being an excellent example), while others (such as Cuba) had opted for collectivized utilization and extensive state control. There were advantages and disadvantages to both approaches.

In education, the problem to be tackled first in most countries was mass illiteracy. In the elite-oriented systems of prerevolutionary Latin America, an aware and well-educated citizenry, if not seen as downright dysfunctional, was certainly never a high-priority goal. Quite the reverse is true in a real revolution, where a literate and involved populace is viewed as the focal point and motor of development as well as the principal guardian of the revolutionary system. From the Mexican Revolution through its Cuban successor, literacy campaigns were often the centerpieces of revolutionary social policy. In Mexico in the 1920s, José Vasconcelos, the country's first Minister of Education, embarked on a sweeping program of revolutionary public education, including a literacy campaign. Through this program, poor Mexicans not only learned to read and write, but also developed a renewed pride in Mexican culture and a sense of the basic goals of their revolution. While the Mexican campaign was relatively primitive—informally organized, it suffered from a very unfavorable student-teacher ratio—it *did* contain a very important idea: that literacy training should involve not only the teaching of reading and writing, but also a deliberate program of political and social consciousness-raising. This idea applied in the more ambitious and better organized literacy campaigns of Cuba (1961) and Nicaragua (1980) would bear remarkable fruit.

Another lesson of history was that mass mobilization is extremely important to the survival and success of any revolution. Each of Latin America's revolutionary experiments involved some emphasis on the development of mass organizations. In the more primitive cases, this amounted to little more than formal constitutional protection for the worker's right to organize and some governmental support for unions in their claims against private businesses, particularly foreign businesses. The Cuban Revolution, however, added a new dimension to the concept of mass mobilization. In addition to mobilization through specific organizations for rural and urban labor, students, women, and so on, the Cubans also created a vast network of grass-roots neighborhood groupings called the Committees for the Defense of the Revolution (CDRs). Organized late in 1960 with the initial purpose of mobilizing the Cuban people to guard against mounting counter-revolutionary activity, the CDRs eventually took on a variety of additional important functions. By mobilizing volunteer labor at the local level, they helped cut the cost of government programs. They served as two-way conduits of communication between the government and the people. And they were important devices for political socialization in that they gave the Cuban people an opportunity to become involved in, and therefore more aware of, and committed to their revolution. For a short while, the Cuban example appeared to have been transplanted to Peru, where the leaders of that country's military revolution created an agency titled "The National System to Support Social Mobilization" (SINAMOS) for the explicit purpose of building a mass base for that otherwise elite-run "revolution." Eventually, however, when the popular pressures created by SINAMOS came to threaten the military's sense of order, the whole idea was modified and then scrapped. Though it had failed in Peru, the Cuban concept of mass mobilization would eventually come to play an even more important and innovative role in the Nicaraguan Revolution.

History also demonstrated that another important ingredient in successful revolution is political socialization. Of course, every society engages in political socialization—the transmission from one generation to the next of values and patterns of behavior supportive of its political system. In the United States, children are taught in the schools and in voluntary organizations to salute the flag, to recite the Pledge of Allegiance, to venerate national heroes and traditions, and generally to be good U.S. citizens. In a revolutionary society, political socialization is even more important since, in such a setting, there is an immediate need both to dismantle elitist, dysfunctional, prerevolutionary values and to build a new sense of nationhood and citizenship consonant with a more egalitarian system. An early example in revolutionary political socialization was set by Mexico's José Vasconcelos. His programs in public education (the literacy campaign, for instance) and popular art and culture (the famous revolutionary muralists)—heavily laced, as they were, with a nationalist and revolutionary message—served as an example for similar or more sophisticated programs adopted elsewhere. In addition, from Cuba onward, the much expanded concept and practice of mass mobilization provided new vehicles for the massification of revolutionary values. Finally, the technological revolution in the mass media made it possible for revolutionary leaders to speak directly and frequently to their people.

Over the decades, Latin Americans had also learned much about regional economics. Frustrated in the late 1950s and 1960s by the total inadequacy of "gringo" theories of development in explaining the continuing and, in some cases, deepening misery of most of the people in most Latin American countries, they generated their own theories of "dependency" which seemed to them, and later to many U.S. scholars, to relate more closely to reality. Armed with these perceptions, they then felt better able to cope with the designing and running of a revolutionary economy. Though, for small states, economic *dependence* on external commerce and technology would continue to be a fact of life, the socially regressive variant, *dependency*, might be eliminated if the state would take over the "commanding heights" of the economy and reorient productive capacity and excess profit in a socially responsible direction. This might not even involve total socialization of the economy. Indeed, Fidel Castro, apparently regretting his nationalization of most of the Cuban economy, is said to have advised the Nicaraguans to try to preserve "responsible" private enterprise. "Responsible" businesses presumably would maintain full production, not export capital, refrain from exploiting workers, and pay their fair share in taxes.

In addition, revolutionary economic planners would have to take into consideration the U.S. "track record" in using economic destabilization as a way of destroying populist or revolutionary governments (Brazil, 1964; Chile, 1973; Jamaica, 1980). Accordingly, any revolutionary government would naturally seek to diversify its external commercial ties so as not to be excessively vulnerable to the very real possibility of destabilization orchestrated from Washington. This does not mean that a revolutionary regime would necessarily want completely to sever its ties with the United States. Much of Cuba's economic difficulties can be attributed to its isolation from U.S. markets and technology. However, given past experience, it would simply be prudent to avoid overdependence on any one country—especially one which had a tendency to interpret national revolution rather consistently from a myopic cold-war perspective.

Finally, some revolutionary experiences, notably those of Bolivia and Cuba, underscored for many Latin Americans the need to avoid excessive indebtedness. In Bolivia, it could be argued that the United States had coopted and eventually derailed the revolution through its role as creditor. Perhaps sensing that the revolution could be destroyed from within, Washington was quite willing in the late 1950s and early 1960s to underwrite the Bolivian government with large loans. Having done so, it then was in a position to offer advice on how to run the economy. When following this advice led to labor unrest, the United States helped retrain and equip the "revolutionary" armed forces to deal with these "threats to stability." Eventually, in 1964, the by-then quite reactionary military overthrew what was left of the "revolution." In Cuba, on the other hand, the U.S. move to isolate the revolutionary government from Western markets and financial sources drove it into an increasing economic and therefore political dependence on the Soviet Union. This dependence was then augmented by the low productivity of a heavily socialized economy and the high cost of maintaining an armed force adequate to defend Cuba's sovereignty against the proven aggressiveness of its neighbor to the north while at the same time carrying out badly needed social programs. The obvious lesson from both of these cases was that future revolutionary governments should mobilize the material and human productive capacity of the nation more efficiently so as to make high foreign debts less necessary. A state-controlled, but not totally nationalized economy might be one answer. A greater reliance on self-help and voluntary labor might be another. Both of these were to be tried in Nicaragua.

Yet another major lesson of history was that any revolution should be prepared to defend itself from inevitable counterrevolution, domestic, international, or both. In the first place, it had long been obvious that any genuinely progressive or revolutionary government would be foolish to *assume* friendly behavior on the part of the United States government. The United States had made incursions into Mexico during the early years of its populist revolution. It had recruited and prepared surrogate exile invasion forces for Guatemala (1954) and Cuba (1961). It had trained the local military establishment which quashed the revolutionary experiment in Bolivia (1964). It had sent U.S. Marines into the Dominican Republic in 1965 to block the return to power of social democratic forces which it had mistaken for "communist." And, it had used economic destabilization and CIA covert action to prepare the "ambient" for the Chilean military coup of 1973.[2] And, if externally-generated counterrevolutionary activity was to be expected, so too was its domestic counterpart. An authentic revolution involves the reallocation of scarce resources in behalf of the hitherto exploited majority. Luxury for the few is sacrificed in the name of social justice for the many. This, of course, represents a real threat to the middle-sector and upper-class minorities. For this reason, it is fully predictable that these elite minorities will eventually regroup their forces—political, economic, intellectual, and military—and channel them into counterrevolutionary activities.

But Latin American revolutionaries had also learned a great deal about tactics of defense against counterrevolution. A first obvious lesson was that no revolution can survive the counter-revolution as long as the traditional military establishment remains intact. The cases of Guatemala, Chile, and Peru had demonstrated that such military organizations would inevitably turn to counter-revolution in behalf of the privileged sectors.[3] Furthermore, it was also obvious that U.S. influence within a supposedly "revolutionary" armed force could have the same disastrous result (Bolivia, 1964). What was needed instead, was the creation of a loyal and politically and socially conscious revolutionary armed institution. This would require an emphasis on literacy for the troops as well as political and social education at all levels. And it would necessitate a firm rejection of all military aid from nonrevolutionary countries when such aid was tied to the acceptance of officer and (or) troop training programs. The Cuban Revolution followed these tactics; the Peruvian one did not.

And there were other measures which a revolutionary government could take to prepare itself for the inevitable counterrevolution. The Cuban experience, for instance, had demonstrated that it was useful to augment the strength of the regular armed forces by creating a mass volunteer militia. While the latter cost relatively little, it provided a margin of preparedness which proved useful in times of danger such as during the Bay of Pigs Invasion in 1961. In addition, nonmilitary mobilization through grass-roots organizations such as the neighborhood defense committees could help a revolution defend itself, especially against domestic counterrevolution. The CDRs in Cuba played a crucial role in preventing domestic collaboration with the Bay of Pigs invaders. But, in the long run, the best defense against counterrevolution had been, and always would be, the quick and effective implementation of a revolutionary social program designed to uplift the condition of the masses. In positively affecting the lives of the poor, the revolution could build a bulwark of popular support which could withstand the attacks of the former privileged minority and its traditional international protector.

Latin Americans also had learned much about the concept and practice of "democracy." Over the years, it had become quite clear that liberal democracy in any society tends to protect and preserve the social status quo. In those few "developed" countries where *relatively* high levels of social justice exist—England, Sweden, the United States, and so on—this type of democracy serves to reinforce *relative* equality. By the same token, however, in the very inegalitarian societies of Latin America, it was clear that the tiny privileged elites rarely had much difficulty in manipulating ostensibly "democratic" systems to produce governments and public policy which actually reinforced and perpetuated inequality. This was not surprising given the fact that such elites enjoyed tremendous economic resources, a vast advantage in education and control of most of the mass media. In prerevolutionary Latin America, liberal democracy, then, was an empty ritual and a real obstacle to social change.

But, even in a revolutionary setting, liberal democracy had proven to have its drawbacks. In Bolivia and Mexico, it had helped cause the revolutionary systems to degenerate into a sort of directionless populism in which politicians, while promising benefits for everyone, were afraid to call for needed sacrifices. In addition, it was clear that the holding of national elections could increase a revolutionary system's vulnerability to international political manipulation via the tactic of economic destabilization.

These perceptions of democracy posed a real dilemma. While most were deeply committed to democracy in theory, Latin American revolutionaries had become highly skeptical of the narrow *liberal* definition and practice. Many Latin Americans felt that "democracy" ought, first of all, to include social and economic dimensions. It was predictable, therefore, that social revolutionaries in the late twentieth century would be wary of implementing political democracy of a type which either would block major social restructuring or could be manipulated from abroad in a counter-revolutionary direction via the tactic of economic destabilization. The building of democracy from below by means of mass mobilization through grass-roots functional and neighborhood organizations would be stressed instead. The revolutionaries would argue that whereas liberal democracy had allowed the people only a ritualistic and ineffective role every few years, "popular democracy" gives the common citizen political participation on a continuous and meaningful basis.

Of course, there were many other lessons which revolutionaries could, and did, draw from the history of twentieth-century Latin America. No short introduction can adequately describe the various facets of this growing awareness. Suffice it to say that many Latin Americans were fortified in their revolutionary purpose both by their awareness of history and by the growing conviction that there was no nonviolent way out of the structural impasse which held the vast majority of their fellow countrymen in misery.

Nicaragua: A Basic Description

Nicaragua is, and always has been, a land of considerable potential.[4] She resembles the state of Iowa in extension (57,143 square miles as opposed to 56,290), population (2.5 and 2.9 million, respectively), and the unusually high quality of much of her land. She also has considerable potential for geothermal and hydroelectric energy, significant lumber and mineral resources, and rivers and lakes positioned in such a manner as to make her an ideal site for an interoceanic waterway. In addition, her people are relatively homogeneous and culturally integrated. Practically all Nicaraguans are mestizo—a mixture of Caucasian and Indian—and share an Hispanic culture. Little racial prejudice exists. Finally, Nicaraguans are a friendly, outgoing people with ample cause to be proud of things *Nica* such as their distinctive cookery, music, dialect, literary heritage, and sense of humor.

Ironically, however, when the popular forces finally achieved power in 1979, most Nicaraguans were still living in abject poverty. Though the annual gross national product (GNP) had reached a little over $800 U.S. per capita, it was very poorly distributed. Until the Sandinist revolution, over half of all Nicaragua's citizens had been expected to make do on between $200 and $300 per person per year in a country where the cost of food, clothing, and so on, was almost as high as in the United States. Not surprisingly, most Nicaraguans lived in inadequate housing, dressed and ate poorly, and had little or no access to education, health care, and other public services. The average life expectancy at birth in 1979 was 53 years, ten years shorter than that for Middle America as a whole and a full eighteen years short of the equivalent statistic for Cuba, at the time Latin America's leader in that respect.[5]

This ironic condition of mass misery in a land of natural riches is best understood in terms of the concept of dependency discussed earlier. Quite simply, since the arrival of the Spaniards in the sixteenth century, Nicaragua's human and material resources had been used consistently for the benefit of a small, privileged, export-oriented minority. Frequently, the domestic system of exploitation had been reinforced by the country's relationship with foreign powers. Throughout this sad history, however, there also ran a long and inspiring tradition of popular resistance which was to culminate in 1979 in the triumph of the Sandinist Revolution.

The Colonial Period

When Spaniards under the command of Gil Gonzalez first arrived in western Nicaragua[6] in 1522, they encountered a fairly advanced agrarian society. The approximately one million native inhabitants of the region—decendants of immigrants and refugees from the Maya and Aztec civilizations to the north—lived in numerous cities and villages ranging in population from a few hundred to tens of thousands. Though society was organized along feudal lines, land was held communally, with each family having access to a designated plot. On these parcels, the people grew corn, cassava, chili, beans, tobacco, and vegetables. While some of what they produced went in tribute to the local chiefs, the rest could be consumed by the family or sold in local markets. Though the people undoubtedly suffered occasional hardships as a result of intertribal warfare and periodic crop failure, this was a relatively self-contained system which appears generally to have functioned adequately in satisfying the basic human needs of even the common citizen.

The Spanish conquest appears to have had an immediate and devastating impact on the Indian civilization of the area. After some initial resistance led by Chiefs Diriangén and Nicarao, the *Conquistadores* were eventually able to consolidate Spanish control over the region. Superimposing themselves on the pre-existing feudal structure, they demanded tribute in gold and, when that was depleted, Indian slaves. Both "commodities" were exported, the gold to Spain and the slaves to other colonies where they normally perished within a few months or years. By the 1540s, the lucrative export of slaves and widespread death through contact with common European diseases, against which local natives had no natural immunity, caused the Indian population of the region to plummet to a few tens of thousands.[7] This holocaust also had an equally striking impact on the economy in that it all but destroyed the region's labor-intensive agricultural system. Though some traditional farming persisted here and there, most of the rich lands of Nicaragua soon reverted to jungle or were exploited less intensively for the raising of cattle to produce hides, tallow, and salted meat for sale to other colonies. The process of dependent underdevelopment had begun.

After the gold and slave "booms" of the early colonial period had subsided, Nicaragua became a sleepy backwater of Spain's colonial empire. Monopolizing the colony's human and material resources, the tiny Spanish elite accrued wealth through ship-building, intermittent gold-mining and the export of agricultural and cattle products. A state of mutual suspicion and rivalry developed and festered between the cattle-based, self-styled "aristocrats" of the city of Granada on Lake Nicaragua and the more commercially-oriented elites of the administrative capital, León, to the northwest. To make matters worse, from the middle of the seventeenth century onward, the underpopulation of the colony and the ostentatious concentration of wealth in the hands of a privileged minority also made Nicaragua a prime target for attacks from pirates from Northern Europe, especially England.

The First Century of "Independence"

In the early nineteenth century, Nicaragua achieved her independence in three stages, first as part of the Mexican Empire of Agustín de Iturbide in 1821, then as a member of the Central American Federation in 1824, and finally as a technically sovereign state in 1838. During most of the next nearly one hundred years, the country was to be buffeted by foreign intrigue and intervention and torn by intra-elite conflict.

Both of these themes came into play during the first two decades after "independence." During this time, the privileged classes of León and Granada (who eventually came to call themselves "Liberals" and "Conservatives" respectively) sent rag-tag armies into battle with each other to determine which city and elite was to enjoy the spoils of running the country. Meanwhile, the discovery of gold in California in 1848 and therefore renewed interest in Nicaragua's potential as a site for a transoceanic waterway drew Britain and the United States into intermittent competitive meddling in the area.

Eventually, the whole process came to a climax in 1855, when the Liberals invited an American soldier-of-fortune, William Walker, to help them defeat the Conservatives. Not long after bringing them to power, however, Walker pushed his Liberal allies aside and declared himself president. Slavery was legalized and English became the official language. This bizarre turn of events not only catalyzed both parties and all of the other Central American republics into a virtual holy war against the Yankee interloper, but also so discredited the Liberals that the Conservatives were able to rule Nicaragua with little opposition for the next third of the century.

From then until the last decade of the century, Nicaragua enjoyed relative political calm under a series of regularly "elected" Conservative presidents. A new constitution was adopted in 1858, a coffee "boom" began, and Managua, which had become the compromise capital in 1851, grew and prospered.

Under this superficial calm, however, economic changes were taking place which were to have a profoundly adverse effect on Nicaragua's common citizens. In the turmoil and confusion of the first half of the nineteenth century, Nicaragua's international dependency relationship had been temporarily disrupted. During this period, a small independent peasantry began to flourish again and the rudiments of an internal marketing system began to develop. The sudden world demand for coffee in the second half of the century, however, provided a powerful incentive for the traditional elites to seek new land and cheap exploitable labor. The Conservative governments, therefore, passed a series of laws which effectively drove peasants and Indian communal land holders off their land and turned them into an impoverished and dependent rural proletariat. Though the rural poor rose up against their oppressors in the "War of the *Comuneros*" in 1881, the government enforced the new "order" at a cost of about 5,000 dead.[8]

In 1893, conservative hegemony finally came to an end in a successful uprising which eventually elevated a Liberal, José Santos Zelaya, to the presidency. Zelaya, who held power as dictator-president for the next seventeen years, was certainly no great champion of social justice. He continued to open up "new" lands to the coffee growers. However, he was a modernizer and nationalist. He reorganized the military and the government, forstered public education, separated Church and State, and so on. As a nationalist, he defied the British by reasserting full sovereignty over Nicaragua's Atlantic coast, championed Central American integration, and firmly rejected a canal treaty proposal by the United States which he viewed as potentially injurious to Nicaraguan sovereignty

Zelaya's nationalism, however, eventually got him into trouble. The United States, which had become a colonial power as a result of the Spanish American War of 1898, resented the independent spirit of this Central American leader. Decision-makers in Washington felt that they knew best what was good for these "backward" countries. Therefore, late in the first decade of the twentieth century, when Zelaya began negotiating with other foreign powers for the building of a Nicaraguan canal, which would have competed with the U.S. waterway at Panama, the United States encouraged the Conservatives to rebel. When they did so in 1909, Washington sent a military force to Bluefields on Nicaragua's Atlantic coast to see to it that the rebellion not be put down. Zelaya himself resigned in 1909 and the Conservatives took power in 1910.

One last spark of Liberal nationalism flared up in 1912, when Liberals and dissident Conservatives led by Benjamín Zeledón attempted to overthrow the palpably corrupt and inept Conservative government. Just as Zeledón's forces were on the verge of victory, U.S. Marines were sent in to restore "order." Ordered by U.S. officials to cease his rebellion, Zeledón fought on, warning the U.S. commander that he and his country would bear the "tremendous responsibility and eternal infamy that history would attribute to you for having employed your arms against the weak who have been struggling for the reconquest of the sacred rights of [their] fatherland."[9] The young Liberal patriot was soon defeated and, with apparent U.S. acquiescence, executed by the Conservatives.

For most of the period from 1912 to 1933, Nicaragua was physically occupied by U.S. troops in an apparent effort to achieve some sort of pro-U.S.

stability. During the first occupation, from 1912 to 1925, the United States ran Nicaraguan affairs through a series of Conservative presidents. It was a symbiotic relationship. The Conservatives could not have held power without U.S. help and Washington could now ask for certain favors from their clients. The most important of these was the signing in 1914 and ratification in 1916 of the Bryan-Chamorro Treaty which gave the United States the same sort of canal building rights that Zelaya had withheld years earlier. It was not that the United States actually intended to build a Nicaraguan canal. Rather, this was simply a way of preventing any other country from doing so.

By the mid-1920s, U.S. decision-makers had convinced themselves that the Conservatives were now ready to carry on without the presence of U.S. troops. They were wrong. Within a few months of the first U.S. withdrawal in 1925, fighting broke out between Liberals and Conservatives and, late in 1926, Marines landed in Nicaragua again.

This time Washington arranged a peace settlement between the leaders of the traditional parties which allowed the Liberal elite a place at the table. Indeed, as a result of the U.S.-supervised elections of 1928 and 1932, Liberals were elected president. The Americans, however, were the *real* rulers of Nicaragua. As one U.S. scholar commented in reference to the powers of the first elected Liberal, the United States "controlled his regime from a number of points: The American Embassy; the Marines...; the Guardia National, with its United States Army officers; the High Commissioner of Customs; the Director of the Railway; and the National Bank."[10] It was in this period that Nicaragua signed with Colombia the very concessionary Barcenas Meneses Esguerra Treaty of 1928. As a result of this treaty, she gave up her claim to the Providencia and San Andrés Islands directly off her Atlantic coast. Though clearly not in Nicaragua's interest, this treaty helped assuage Colombian anger over the U.S.-engineered loss of her province of Panama in 1903 while it voided additional Colombian claims which tended to cloud the validity of some U.S. rights under the Bryan-Chamorro Treaty.

Probably the two most important features of the second occupation, however, were (1) a prolonged and rather successful guerrilla war which Augusto César Sandino waged against the American occupiers, and (2) the creation of the U.S.-trained and equipped Nicaraguan National Guard. Sandino and his tactical and ideological legacy are covered in chapter 2. Suffice it to note here that Sandino was the one Liberal officer who refused to sign the U.S.-sponsored peace treaty of 1927, choosing instead to fight on against the Yankee occupiers. "The sovereignty and liberty of a people," he proclaimed, "are not to be discussed but rather to be defended with weapons in hand." He and his small army of peasants and workers quickly learned the tactics of guerrilla warfare and, in spite of such U.S. tactics as the aerial bombardment of "enemy" population centers and the forced relocation of peasants, the guerillas were able to harass the Americans with relative impunity until the foreign troops finally left in 1933.[11]

The creation of a national constabulary to maintain pro-American stability in Nicaragua had long been a dream of U.S. officials. [12] During the second occupation, the "threat" posed by the "bandit" Sandino gave the project additional urgency. The development of a powerful and professional National Guard would, it was hoped, "Nicaraguanize" (if you will) a war which had become so unpopular in the U.S. that Congress eventually voted to cut off all funding for it. From the vantage point of history, however, what was really important about the Guard was that it created a new, powerful, and uncontrollable factor in Nicaraguan politics. Its first Nicaraguan commander, Anastasio Somoza García, appointed as the Americans prepared to leave the country, was to use the Guard as the central factor in fashioning and maintaining a dynastic dictatorship which would oppress and abuse the Nicaraguan people for well over four decades.

The Somoza Period
Though, in all fairness, such an outcome was probably not foreseen at the time by most U.S. policymakers, the transition from Yankee occupation to Somoza dictatorship took place fairly rapidly. The son of a medium-scale coffee farmer, Anastasio Somoza García had worked his way into the top position in the Guard largely through his ability to ingratiate himself with the Americans. A graduate of the Pierce School of Business Administration in Philadelphia, he spoke fluent English and knew how to make himself "one of the boys" when around Americans. After the U.S. troops left, he worked quickly to consolidate his power by purging all Guard officers who might have stood in his way; by ordering the capture and murder of Sandino in 1934 (even though Sandino had formally signed a peace agreement in which his safety and that of his men had been explicitly guaranteed); and by cultivating the loyalty of the Guard by allowing officers and men alike to engage in various corrupt activities. In a short while, he began by openly defying the elected president and, in 1936, he dropped all pretenses, staged a *coup*, and had himself "elected" president. He was inaugurated on New Year's Day, 1937.

The Somozas were to run Nicaragua virtually as a private estate until the Sandinistas drove them from power in 1979. Anastasio Somoza García ruled directly as president or indirectly through puppet presidents from 1937 until 1956, when a young poet-patriot, Rigoberto López Pérez, carried out a suicidal but successful assassination attempt. After the *ajusticiamiento*, or "bringing to justice" as Nicaraguans call it, Somoza's sons, Luis Somoza Debayle and Anastasio Somoza Debayle took over. Luis was president from 1956 to 1963. The Family then ruled through puppet presidents until 1967, when Anastasio Jr. had himself "elected" president for a term which was to have lasted until 1971. Once in office, however, he amended the constitution to allow himself another year in the presidency, and then stepped down for two years while a puppet Triumvirate oversaw the writing of another constitution which allowed him to be re-elected in 1974 for another term scheduled to have lasted until 1981.

There were differences in style among the Somozas. Luis, for instance, stood out from the other two in that he *seemed* to be less personally greedy and more concerned with improving the Dynasty's "democratic" and developmentalist image. Of course, this style fit nicely with the proclaimed goals of the Alliance for Progress, begun during Luis' presidency. But, in reality, all three Somozas were dictators who ran the affairs of their country to their personal benefit and against the interests of the vast majority of their countrymen.[13]

The Somoza formula for rule was simple and effective: (1) appease and co-opt "important" domestic power contenders, and (2) cultivate the "friendship" of the United States. In the very unequal society of prerevolutionary Nicaragua, the major domestic power contenders were the Church; the agricultural, industrial, and commercial elites; the leadership of the traditional parties; and the military. Though originally identified with the Conservatives, the Church hierarchy switched its allegiance to the Somozas during the presidency of the first Somoza and continued to support the Dynasty until the late 1960s. The monied elite benefited from the family's *laissez-faire*, income-concentrating economic philosophy and from the nearly total absence of governmental interest in protecting the rights of urban and rural workers. The majority segment of the Liberal Party supported the Dynasty simply because the Somozas were, after all, "Liberals." And, in order to maintain a facade of democracy, the Somozas even saw fit frequently to buy Conservative "opposition" participation in electoral campaigns by offering the leaders of that party various benefits ranging from bribes to minority participation in government.

The most important domestic power factor, however, was the military. The Somoza family employed two tactics in maintaining its loyalty. First, they made sure that the top command of the Guard remained at all times in the hands of a family member. Equally important, they consciously worked to isolate the military psychologically from the Nicaraguan people by allowing it to become a sort of Mafia in uniform which controlled the rackets and took kickbacks and bribes for a variety of activities—legal and illegal. Since Nicaraguans of all classes hated the Guard, the Somozas could always remind them that if the family were ever overthrown, the Guard would be in grave trouble.

The second major tactic of the Somozas was the careful cultivation of the United States. This was accomplished through personal as well as political means. On the personal plane, all of the Somozas were educated in the United States, spoke fluent English, could turn on U.S. mannerisms at will, and were skilled at manipulating Americans. At the same time, in the realm of international politics, the Somozas were always obsequiously "pro-American." The enemies of the United States were automatically their enemies, be they the Axis Powers during the Second World War or the Communists thereafter. Accordingly, Nicaraguan territory was used by the United States for military bases during the Second World War and for the training of CIA surrogate invasion forces for Guatemala (1954) and Cuba (1961). Nicaraguan troops joined U.S. forces in the occupation of the Dominican Republic in 1965 and were offered, but politely refused, during the Korean and Vietnam "conflicts." In return, the United States sent ambassadors to Managua who were usually enthusiastically friendly to the Somozas. In addition, especially in the 1960s and 1970s, U.S. foreign aid—economic, "social," and military—poured into Nicaragua, and more membersof Somoza's National Guard received training in the United States or at U.S. bases in Panama than was true of any other Latin American military establishment.[14]

The social impact of Somoza rule was profound and generally negative. Though a large and entangled social-service bureaucracy was created in the early 1960s in order to take advantage of opportunities provided by the Alliance for Progress, few benefits "trickled down" to the mass of the people. The new programs served largely as a way of providing employment and opportunities for the personal enrichment for the Somoza elite and its middle-class allies. Meanwhile, the developmentalist economic policies of the regime were causing very real hardship for the common citizen. As the international demand for additional products such as cotton grew, "new" lands were opened to the monied elite. As in the days of the coffee "boom" almost a century before, individual peasants once again were driven from the land—this time primarily from the Pacific lowlands. This process of rural dislocation contributed in turn to an accelerated rate of urbanization, especially in the late 1960s and 1970s. Unfortunately, by this time, the social-service bureaucracy, which might have helped ease the suffering of the rural-urban migrants, was so hopelessly corrupt and inept that the problems of the poor were, in fact, largely neglected.

The disintegration and collapse of the Somoza system began in the early 1970s under Anastasio Somoza Debayle. During this period, Nicaraguans of all classes became increasingly alienated by the intemperate dictator's growing greed and brutality. Two major events accelerated the process of popular disaffection. The first was the "Christmas" earthquake of 1972, which destroyed most of the capital city, Managua. In the wake of this disaster, Somoza and his accomplices used their control of the government to funnel international relief funds into their own pockets. Very little was done for the disaster victims and, until the Sandinist victory, most of Managua remained an unreconstructed moonscape. Two years after the quake, when the Sandinist Front of National Liberation pulled off a very successful hostage-ransom operation, Somoza again reacted with intemperance. Humiliated and enraged by the FSLN's success, the dictator declared a state of seige, instituted full censorship of the press and launched the Guard on a campaign of terror in rural areas where FSLN guerrillas were believed to be operating. Hundreds of peasants were raped, tortured, and (or) murdered outright; many others were taken away never to be heard from again.[15]

By the mid-1970s, Somoza was in serious trouble. His excesses had generated opposition from such widely diverse groups as labor, the Church hierarchy, and a large segment of the commercial and industrial elite. Furthermore, the dictator's flagrant disregard for human rights won him considerable international notoriety. In 1977, with the inauguration of human rights advocate Jimmy Carter, even the "friendship" of the Somozas' long-term protector, the United States, became less certain.

Though there was a tendency in the United States following the Sandinist victory to either blame or praise the Carter Administration for consciously promoting the downfall of the Somoza system, such assertions are quite unwarranted. It is highly doubtful that the Carter Administration ever desired the overthrow of the Somoza system, much less the coming-to-power of the popularly-based FSLN. The decision to push "human rights" in Nicaragua seems to have been based on profound misperceptions of Nicaraguan reality. Apparently it was felt that Nicaragua would be a good, low-risk testing ground for the human rights policy. Not only was Somoza sure to follow orders, but also the Administration had received assurance from U.S. military attachés working with Somoza's Guard that the guerrilla "threat" had been wiped out during the rural "counter-insurgency" operations of the previous two years. In fact, almost immediately after Somoza, under heavy pressure from Washington, lifted the state of siege and reinstated limited freedom of the press in September 1977, popular opposition to the tyrant and the system he headed began to mount. The leading opposition daily, La Prensa, was filled with reports of the corruption and brutality of the Somoza regime. In October, the FSLN demonstrated that it was alive and well by attacking National Guard outposts in several provincial capitals. Simultaneously, "The Twelve," a group of prominent business, religious, and professional leaders, denounced the regime and called for a solution which would include the FSLN. In sum, the United States had failed to perceive that an artificial injection of civil and political liberties into a system built on the denial of basic social and economic justice can have a highly destabilizing effect.

Within a couple of months, the struggle which many Nicaraguans refer to as the "War of Liberation" had begun. The United States now worked with greater urgency to arrange a political compromise between Somoza and his traditional opposition in order to preserve the Guard and Somoza's Liberal Party and, at the same time, exclude the Popularly-based FSLN. But most Nicaraguans rejected these schemes for what they contemptuously

called "*Somocismo* without Somoza"—and the revolutionary process moved inexorably toward its final outcome.

The catalyst which triggered the War of Liberation was the murder on
January 10, 1978, of beloved *La Prensa* editor, Pedro Joaquín Chamorro.
This and the very clumsy government coverup which followed led that
month to riots and a nationwide general strike. Though these failed to topple the dictatorship, popular discontent boiled over once again in February,
when the inhabitants of an Indian *barrio* called Monimbó in the city of
Masaya rose up against the National Guard and held government troops at
bay with an assortment of pathetic hand weapons and home-made contact
bombs for almost a week. Though this prototype insurrection was bloodily
suppressed, student strikes and other acts of defiance continued into the
summer.

In August 1978, Nicaraguans were stunned by the disclosure of a
"secret" letter from Carter to Somoza congratulating the latter for his promise to improve the human rights situation in Nicaragua. Exasperated by
this news and wanting to recapture the initiative, the FSLN later that month
carried out their famous "Operation Pigpen," in which a small group of
commandos seized the national legislative palace and held over 1,500
hostages until the dictator once again agreed to meet a series of stinging
demands. Next came another prolonged businessmen's strike and the
famous "September Uprisings" in which young people ("Los Muchachos")
in most of the cities of Nicaragua, assisted by FSLN regulars, rose up—
Monimbó style—against the dictator. Poorly armed, the insurgents were
eventually forced to withdraw from one city after another, leaving
Somoza's troops to carry out a bloody and indiscriminate "mop-up"
operation against the civilian population, bringing the death toll to over
5,000.[16]

From October to the following June, both sides prepared for the future.
Somoza bought the time he needed to finish liquidating his immense assets
and to transfer capital abroad by craftily negotiating with the traditional
opposition and the Americans who were still pursuing the phantom of a
peaceful elite-based "solution." Meanwhile, with the financial help of
various groups including the Social Democratic Parties of Western Europe,
and the logistical support of such widely disparate governments as those of
Costa Rica, Panama, Venezuela, and Cuba, the FSLN rearmed itself with
light weapons purchased on the international arms market. The regular
FSLN army was expanded from a few hundred to several thousand and,
throughout the country, neighborhood "Civil Defense Committees" worked
feverishly to prepare for the next insurgency.

The "Final Offensive" was announced early in June 1979. Barricades
were erected in working-class neighborhoods throughout the country and,
one by one, Somoza's garrisons were overcome. Alarmed by the near certainty, now, of a popular victory, the United States asked the Organization

of American States to send a "peacekeeping force" to Managua, a transparent attempt to preserve the old system. This proposal was unanimously rejected by the OAS. On July 17, Somoza fled the country and, two days later, the FSLN entered Managua and accepted the surrender of what was left of the Guard.

The War of Liberation had cost Nicaragua around 50,000 lives, or approximately 2 percent of her population. In the United States, that would be the equivalent of a loss of around 4.5 million people, or over 75 times the U.S. death toll in the entire Vietnam conflict. But as Nicaraguans reminded the author on his trip there a few days later, freedom, justice, and national dignity are sometimes worth such a price.

The Revolutionary System
With the victory of the FSLN, the social configuration of political power in Nicaragua changed abruptly. Unlike the Somozas, who had based their power in a corrupt, foreign-trained military establishment and in a small internationalized economic elite, the *Sandinistas* drew their strength—and their revolutionary mandate—from the mass of the people. The system of government which took shape in the next one and a half years reflected this reality. On the one hand, the formal structures of government—the Governing Junta of National Reconstruction, the Council of State and the various ministries—reflected a genuine and pragmatic desire on the part of the revolutionary leadership to maintain a pluralistic, multiclass approach to revolution. Yet on the other hand, it was clear from the start that these formal organs were ultimately responsible to the National Directorate of the FSLN which had created them in the first place. The nine-man Directorate, in turn, drew its political strength from its direct control of the armed forces (the Sandinist People's Army, the Sandinist Police, and the Sandinist Popular Militias) and from the people themselves, hundreds of thousands of whom had mobilized during the war and afterwards into various Sandinist mass or popular organizations.

Given these realities, the personnel who comprised the formal apparatus of government had wide freedom in designing and implementing revolutionary reform but no option whatsoever to betray the humanistic goals for which so many people had given their lives. Accordingly, as will be shown in the chapters on revolutionary programs and policy, the government, in its first one and a half years in power, worked effectively, imaginatively, and with great dedication to implement a wide variety of changes designed to uplift the human condition of the mass of the people.

Almost immediately after the FSLN victory, and without waiting to examine the reality of the situation, conservative ideologues in the United States began painting the Nicaraguan Revolution as "another Cuba," and a dangerous extension of Soviet influence. They pointed to the (actually, rather minor) assistance the Cubans had given the Nicaraguans during the war and the presence of Marxists in the FSLN. They also expressed their alarm that the new government was accepting Cuban social and technical assistance.

In reality, however, although they logically felt a bond of friendship and found much in common with the only other real revolutionary government in Latin America, the Nicaraguan revolutionaries, above all, were nationalists. Their revolution would reflect an unusual and original blend of pragmatic Marxism and progressive Catholic thought. Naturally, Nicaraguan revolutionaries would draw on the experiences of other revolutions. And, of course, they would find much to be learned from the example of Cuba. Yet at the same time, they quickly demonstrated that they would be quite selective in adopting or modifying ideas which seemed to show promise for Nicaragua while rejecting others which did not. There would be no mass executions of former *Somocistas*. A concerted effort would be made to avoid personalistic, one-man rule; to protect individual liberties; to preserve a "responsible" private sector; and to maintain friendly, or a least formally correct, relations with the United States. And practically everyone, including the Marxists, seemed to agree that the Church—which had changed greatly in a little over a decade and had eventually contributed significantly to the popular victory—should be integrated into the revolutionary process and allowed to live the revolutionary and humanistic message which many felt was the heart of the teachings of Christ. In sum, this was a revolution of, by, and for Nicaraguans.

Notes

[1] For a useful discussion of "dependency," see Ronald H. Chilcote and Joel C. Edelstein, eds., *Latin America: The Struggle with Dependency and Beyond* (New York: John Wiley and Sons, 1974); and Richard R. Fagen, "Studying Latin American Politics: Some Implications of a *Dependencia* Approach," *Latin American Research Review*, Vol. XII, No. 2 (1977), pp.3—26

[2] For ample documentation of the successful U.S. destabilization of Chile, see United States Senate, Staff Report of the Select Committee to Study Governmental Operations with Respect to United States Intelligence, *Covert Action in Chile* (Washington, D.C.: U.S. Government Printing Office, Dec. 18, 1975).

[3] This, by the way, is the reason many observers were so deeply skeptical about the U.S.-sponsored experiment in "moderate" civilian-military "revolution" which came to power in El Salvador on October 15, 1979.

[4] For a more adequate introduction to Nicaragua than can be provided in the space allowed for this chapter, see Thomas W. Walker, *Nicaragua: The Land of Sandino* (Boulder, Colorado: Westview Press, 1981).

[5] 1979 World Population Data Sheet (Washington, D.C.: The Population Reference Bureau, 1979).

[6] The inhabitants of the sparcely-populated eastern half of Nicaragua tended to be hunters or gatherers of South American origin.

[7] This amazing process of depopulation is quite well documented. For a sound and scholarly examination of the subject see: David Richard Radell, "Native Depopulation and the Slave Trade: 1527—1578," in his *An Historical Geography of Western Nicaragua: The Spheres*

of Influence of León, Granada, and Managua, 1519-1965 (Berkeley: University of California, Ph.D dissertation, 1969), pp. 66—80.

[8] For a good account of the process of social dislocation caused by the coffee "boom," see Jaime Wheelock Román, *Imperialismo y Dictadura: Crisis de una Formación Social* (México: Siglo Veintiuno Editores, 1975).

[9] From a handwritten letter from Zeledón to Col. J. H. Pendleton, Masaya, Nicaragua, October 3, 1912. Fascimile copy courtesy of Zeledón's grandson, Sergio Zeledón.

[10] Ralph Lee Woodward, Jr., *Central America: A Nation Divided* (New York: Oxford University Press, 1976), p. 200.

[11] Two of the better books on Sandino are Neil Macaulay, *The Sandino Affair* (Chicago: Quadrangle Books, 1967) and Gregorio Selser, *Sandino* (New York: Monthly Review Press, 1981).

[12] For an excellent study of the relationship between the United States, the Nicaraguan National Guard and the Somoza dynasty, see Richard Millett, *Guardians of the Dynasty: A History of the U.S.-Created Guardia Nacional de Nicaragua and the Somoza Family* (Maryknoll, N.Y.: Orbis Books, 1977).

[13] During their long domination of Nicaragua, the Somozas accrued massive holdings in virtually every sector of the economy. By 1956, when Anastasio Somoza García was killed, the family was worth around $50 million. By the time Anastasio Jr. was "elected" a decade later, this fortune had tripled to around $150 million. At the time of the 1972 earth quake, it was commonly estimated at $300 million. And, when Somoza was overthrown, he was believed to have been worth well in excess of a half a billion dollars—no one knows for sure.

[14] Millett, *Guardians*, p. 252.

[15] Amnesty International, *The Republic of Nicaragua: An Amnesty Report* (London: Amnesty International, 1977).

[16] For a remarkably frank discussion of this grisly operation, see Inter-American Commission on Human Rights. Organization of American States, *Report on the Situation of Human Rights in Nicaragua* (Washington, D.C.: General Secretariat of the OAS, 1978).

PART II

THE INSURRECTION

Authentic social revolution involves two major phases: (1) the insurrectionary period, in which the *ancien regime* is overthrown, and (2) the post-insurrectionary era featuring a process of sweeping social, economic, and political change. The nature of the insurrectionary phase is of crucial importance in determining the success or failure of post-liberation efforts to create a new and more just system. Ironically, if the overthrow of the old regime is accomplished easily with neither popular mobilization nor the defeat and dismantling of the traditional armed forces, the likelihood that the new political system will be able to effect significant change and defend itself from counterrevolution will be very limited.

The three chapters in this part relate to Nicaragua's insurrectionary experience, an exceedingly difficult struggle indeed. Ricardo Chavarría examines the history of the insurrection, comparing and contrasting it with that of Cuba two decades earlier. He demonstrates that the Nicaraguan experience was *qualitatively* different from that of Cuba because of the more entrenched and stubborn nature of the Nicaraguan dictatorship and the more active pro-status-quo machinations of the United States. The Nicaraguans had a much more difficult challenge than did the Cubans, and they were, therefore, forced to employ an original technique, mass "popular insurrection." William LeoGrande discusses the U.S. reaction to the revolution and the various policies the Carter Administration employed in its effort to arrive at a "solution" which would have preserved Somoza's National Guard and Liberal Party while essentially excluding the FSLN. Harry E. Vanden examines the ideology of the insurrection and concludes that it was *"very much Nicaraguan and was not a copy or imitation of any other nation."*

Chapter 1

The Nicaraguan Insurrection:
An Appraisal of its Originality

RICARDO E. CHAVARRÍA

For nearly two decades after the fall of the Batista dictatorship in Cuba and the installation there of the first socialist regime in Latin America, it seemed unlikely that a revolutionary event of great consequence could be repeated in the region. The failure of Ché Guevara in Bolivia and the apparent annihilation of the various armed movements in neighboring countries underscored the improbability of such a revolution taking place. In Chile the attempt to implement revolutionary social change through peaceful, electoral means also failed dramatically with the overthrow of Salvador Allende in September 1973. Neither the guerrilla strategy of Cuba nor the electoral strategy followed in Chile seemed to offer an avenue to power for revolutionaries in Latin America.[1] However, the success of the war of liberation in Nicaragua in July of 1979 not only shattered this assumption but also presented an original revolutionary model, the popular insurrection.

Armed popular insurrection became the most mature form of political struggle in Nicaragua, and its most mature expression took shape in the events of May-July 1979. Moreover, the extensiveness and intensity of the fighting meant that the revolutionary process, prior to the taking of power, developed more fully in Nicaragua than in Cuba. In Cuba "the fall of Batista was not the same thing as the coming of the revolution."[2] In contrast, the insurrection in Nicaragua was accompanied by a revolutionary crisis which resulted not only in the fall of the dictator but also in the inauguration of a revolutionary regime. Of necessity, this difference affected the subsequent development of both revolutionary experiences, at least during their first year of existence.[3] Let us briefly review Cuba's guerrilla strategy in order later in the chapter to discuss the originality of Nicaragua's insurrectionary model.

Cuba and the Guerrilla Strategy
The initial struggle of Fidel Castro and his followers against the Batista regime in July 1953 had the characteristics of a *putsch*. Later on, in December 1956, the Fidelista strategy was primarily conceived in terms of a

general uprising to take place in Santiago upon the arrival of the expeditionaries aboard the yacht *Granma*. As it turned out, however, guerrilla strategy became not only a contingency plan put into action but also the only real alternative to survive. Parallel to the events affecting the *Sierra* (the mountain forces), the *Llano* (urban underground) remained fragmented into at least four different groups, broken into two main groups, namely the *Directorio Revolucionario* (Revolutionary Directorate, or simply DR) and the *Movimiento 26 de Julio* (26th of July Movement, or M-26-7); and other secondary groups such as the Triple A (AAA) and Organización Auténtica (Organization of Authentics, or OA). Aside from the tactical discrepancies between DR, which emphasized the importance of Havana and the university; and M-26-7, which concentrated its efforts in the city of Santiago and the mountains in Oriente province, the interrelationships of these four movements oscillated through time. Some tactical errors of the urban underground as well as the particular conditions in which the struggle took place in the cities, weakened the position of the DR, and this in turn resulted in a process of leadership articulation around the person of Fidel Castro, a prominent member of the M-26-7. By August of 1957, the urban underground of the M-26-7 itself was assigned one specific role, namely, to sustain Fidel Castro's guerrillas.[4] This was crucial for the very development of the so-called Sierra strategy (guerrilla), at least during the "nomade phase" of it.[5]

Insurrectionists in the cities gradually ventured into the mountains, and several guerrilla groups emerged independently from Castro early in 1958: the DR guerillas, the Second National Front of Escambray (a splinter of DR), the Auténtícos and the Ortodoxos guerrillas. All of them went into the mountains of Central Cuba. The opening of the Second Front in northern Oriente province, Sierra Cristal, occurred in March, 1958, under the command of Raúl Castro. By April, no more than 400 adequately armed men and some 500 unarmed volunteers were in the mountains of Oriente province.[6] In late 1958, a few forces from the Catholic University, the Fourth Guerrilla Front, went into Pinar del Rio mountains; and a small group of the Popular Socialist Party guerrillas (communist) participated in the last battles of 1958.[7] In spite of all this, some discrepancies still persisted between the Sierra and the Llano. In Ché Guevara's words:

> The *Sierra* was already certain to have the ability to develop guerrilla strategy, to transfer it to other locations in a way which would encircle the cities under tyranny, and ultimately explode the whole apparatus of the regime by means of a struggle of strangulation and exhaustion:... The *Llano* was adopting a position which was apparently more revolutionary, one of urban armed struggle to converge into a general strike that would be capable of toppling Batista and taking power within a short period of time.[8]

Although there exists some doubt about Fidel Castro's responsibilities for the idea of the general strike of April, 1958, and its failure, the movement in the Llano suffered a tremendous blow, and ultimately, the Sierra was confirmed as the most critical factor for the movement to succeed.[9] The concept of general strike as sanctioned by the fellow comrades of the Llano was too narrow and subjective because very little insurrectionary preparation existed throughout the island.[10] And, of course, no urban insurrection is feasible without the political mobilization of the masses.

Territorial consolidation of the guerrilla strategy was preceded and accompanied by the organization of the rural population through the carrying out of some educational and agricultural projects as well as the setting up of several small campaign hospitals and a few industrial facilities. During the "Summer Offensive" in which the regular army committed some 12,000 troops, guerrilla resistance turned into a war of columns and positions that ultimately became a frustrating experience for the army. The rebels assumed the initiative, and as of September, they were ready to come out of the hills to launch the final offensive, which actually began in November.

Since the Oriente province produced as much as three quarters of the entire Cuban sugar crop and much of the coffee, gaining control of the region was crucial for the rebels' ultimate success. In the process of assuming control of the central highway, they were able to isolate the army, and force it back into big garrisons. One by one, and also in simultaneous operations, urban areas were occupied. This strategy was developed around two principal capitals, namely, Santiago and Santa Clara.

The fall of Santa Clara cut the island in half, leaving the field open for an attack on Santiago. The Battle of Santa Clara was the decisive military operation of the campaign. At that point in time, political hegemony depended on military supremacy, and this explains why the Camilo Cienfuegos column was allowed to become the vanguard of the march toward Matanzas and Havana. Otherwise, the Fidelistas could not have prevented a *coup d'état* or some other sort of power grab from happening.[11] At that point in time, the problem was essentially political in character.

The Nicaraguan Model

On July 19, 1979, one of the most sanguinary dictatorships in Latin America was finally demolished by a popular revolutionary insurrection. The Sandinista victory was the culmination of a long history of popular struggles in Nicaragua. Within this tradition, the figure of Augusto C. Sandino emerged not only as the popular hero but also as the champion of nationalism. In a heroic guerrilla war which lasted from 1927 to 1933, Sandino and his peasant army, backed by patriotic sectors in the cities, had resisted the occupying forces of the United States. Before withdrawing its troops, the U.S. had developed a new plan of political stabilization in which the creation of a Nicaraguan National Guard was the key factor. However, by substituting

Nicaraguans for U.S. Marines, the U.S. government set the basis of a fratricidal struggle. From its very foundation, the National Guard served elite interests and its members gradually became the "Guardians of the [Somoza] Dynasty."[12]

The success of guerrilla warfare in Cuba inspired sporadic and isolated attempts to adopt a similar strategy in Nicaragua, but these attempts lacked a common ideological basis. The Sandinista Front for National Liberation (FSLN) was founded in 1961 in Honduras by Carlos Fonseca, Silvio Mayorga, and Tomás Borge, but it was Fonseca who provided ideological unity for the first guerrilla focus. This operated in 1963 in the mountains of the Coco River and the Bocay region, along the Honduran-Nicaraguan border. It ended in a military defeat in which Fonseca was captured by the Honduran army and sent to prison in Tegucigalpa.

After an interlude of political agitation within the student movement, in alliance with the traditional left, the FSLN returned to the mountains in 1967. The guerrilla group called Pancasán was the "first serious attempt to intimately tie the FSLN with the backward and poor peasants of the mountains."[13] With a few exceptions, however, rural folk were not enthusiastic about the guerrillas, and the strategy once again ended in military failure.

Returning to the cities, the FSLN began building a political structure in which several intermediate organizations served as links between the Sandinista movement and the people. The period from 1967 to 1974 was characterized as a phase of "accumulation of forces in silence."[14] At this time, sporadic armed assaults on banking and commercial institutions were carried out by FSLN militants to help finance the struggle and to let people know about their popular demands. During this period, several important leaders of the FSLN were lost to official repression.[15]

The aftermath of the devastating Managua earthquake of December 1972 facilitated the political mobilization of the labor movement. Construction workers subsequently won a tremendous victory in a prolonged strike and hospital workers followed suit. Meanwhile, an electoral formula of conciliation was articulated by Unión Democrática de Liberación (Democratic Union for Liberation [UDEL]), a pluralist and progressive organization. The FSLN attack on the residence of a notorious Somocista bureaucrat on December 27, 1974, broke the silence. Kidnapping some of the most influencial members of the regime was a qualitative step forward for the "Juan José Quezada" commando group and the inauguration of a new phase in the struggle against the dictatorship, which amounted to an open declaration of war.[16] Never before had the regime been so humiliated. The FSLN claimed for itself the right to "legitimately interpret the interest of the revolutionary classes in Nicaragua" and declared that it was the people's representative and depositary.[17]

As a result of the December action, the Somoza regime unleashed a wave of repression through a state of siege which was not lifted until

September 1977. Though many guerrilla combatants were recruited during this period, rapid expansion also became the occasion for the emergence of three factions within the FSLN. In 1975, an internal split developed between the original Prolonged Popular War tendency (GPP) and the Proletarian tendency (TP), which ultimately materialized into a third faction in exile, called the Insurrectionalist tendency, or Tercerista (Third Way [TT]).[18] Factionalism was more a matter of partial and temporary disagreement concerning political analysis and military strategy than a real struggle for power within the FSLN. Each tendency continued to consider itself to be structurally part of the FSLN. Therefore, no real split occurred beyond the practical division of revolutionary labor.[19] Four issues of partial disagreement were identified:

1. Whether to concentrate on rural guerrilla warfare (GPP) or on organizing among the working class (TP). (Not necessarily mutually exclusive.)
2. Military (GPP) vs. political priority (TP). (In practice, both tactics adopted during 1974-75.)
3. How best to coordinate efforts, if at all, with the bourgeois oppositon.
4. The timing of the revolution.

In October 1975, the members of the GPP tendency within the FSLN National Directorate condemned the Proletarian tendency, a disciplinary action which was refused not only by the affected but also by the emerging Insurrectionalist tendency in exile. In turn, the TT developed a new interpretation, which ultimately contributed a broader perspective. It held that: (1) the National Guard was not as efficient as publicized, (2) popular uprisings were feasible, and (3) a pluralistic political position would be more effective in winning national and international support.

Mounting repression by Somoza's National Guard and its external allies, namely the CONDECA forces (Council for the Defense of Central America),[20] resulted in the death of many armed FSLN units in northern Nicaragua. According to Lt. Gen. William P. Yarborough, visiting with the U.S. military mission in rural Nicaragua, Somoza had apparently won a military victory in the countryside.[21] The cost of such an alleged victory was the disappearance of hundreds of *campesinos*. These were denouced by Catholic Church leaders and members of the opposition in a nationwide campaign which eventually resulted in hearings in the U.S. House of Representatives on June 8 and 9, 1976. After the inauguration of Jimmy Carter in 1977, and threats by the U.S. Congress to cut off $3.1 million in military aid, Somoza grudgingly lifted the state of siege that September.

The heavy blows suffered by the rural guerrilla organization as well as the lifting of the state of siege indirectly made the Insurrectionalist tendency the most attractive alternative to adopt. As a matter of fact, the FSLN reappeared in October 1977, operating with more modern weapons and carrying out hit-and-run raids throughout the country. Meanwhile, a new political organization, "The Twelve," a highly respected group of business, professional, and religious leaders, demanded substantial changes in the government. They argued that the FSLN had matured politically and should be considered a legitimate political force.

The year 1978 was filled with dramatic and spectacular events. From January to September, four major events marked the rising societal crisis: (1) the assassination of Pedero Joaquín Chamorro, (2) the Monimbó Popular Armed Rebellion, (3) the Attack on the National Palace, and (4) the September Insurrection. All of this converged into a mood of national mobilization, an increasing potential for success.

The Assassination of Pedro Joaquín Chamorro

The assassination of Pedro Joaquín Chamorro, a courageous journalist who had long opposed the Somoza dynasty, was a serious political mistake apparently committed by people high in the Somoza regime. It also spelled trouble for the Nicaragua upper class. As a result, UDEL withdrew from the "National Dialogue" that Archbishop Miguel Obando had called late in 1977, and Somoza was left with virtually no political resource other than his own Nationalist Liberal Party.

The reaction of the Nicaraguan people was massive and immediate. Angry crowds attacked Somoza-owned business establishments and burned several buildings in Managua. And the business community conducted an 85 percent effective "general strike", or business work stoppage which lasted for two weeks beginning January 22. Somoza's strategy was to wait it out. At the same time, he brutalized protestors when street barricades began to appear throughout Nicaragua. The financial oligarchy did not support the stoppage, and when the business community put an end to it, the popular sector became more aggressive in acting on its own. Similarly, the FSLN assumed the initiative by attacking National Guard outposts in the cities of Rivas and Granada.[22]

In the context of mounting repression, the Archbishop began to qualify the Church's nonviolent position, stating that there were circumstances when armed resistance might be legitimate.[23] He was paraphrasing a traditional teaching of the Church. Curiously, it was at this point that U.S. Ambassador, Mauricio Solaún, stated that in order to restore peace it was necessary for everyone to refrain from violence and pacifically discuss the crisis.[24]

The Armed Rebellion at Monimbó and Its Aftermath

The name Somoza was a morbid shadow which surrounded the death of both Sandino and Chamorro. The forty-fourth anniversary of Sandino's assassination was marked by a Catholic celebration by the Indian community of Monimbó, located on the southern edge of Masaya. Upon leaving the ceremony, people found themselves surrounded by National Guard troops who opened fire and threw several tear gas bombs into the crowd. That night the residents of the neighborhood closed off the main street entrance with a large FSLN banner and the conflict escalated into an all-out rebellion. With home-made weapons, machetes, clubs, and paving block barricades, the Monimboseños forced the Guard out of their *barrio*, and from February 22 to February 27, held out against 600 soldiers with tanks, machine guns and helicopters under the command of the dictator's oldest son, Anastasio III. The losses in Monimbó amounted to at least 200 people, but Monimboseños had let the whole country know that they were more determined than ever to oust Somoza. Their rebellion had illustrated one of the secrets of the Nicaraguan popular insurrection: neighborhood organizations are the backbone of revolutionary societies.[25]

The events at Monimbó led other groups to defy the dictatorship. On April 6, more than 60,000 students became directly involved in the most massive and prolonged student strike in the history of Nicaragua. The student leadership now became the vanguard of the urban struggle. In July, another nationwide strike of hospital workers erupted. At the same time, women's and human-rights issues were heralded by AMPRONAC (The Association of Women Confronting the National Problem). Thus the political mobilization of the popular sectors was converging into the events which would take place in August.

The Attack on the National Palace
In July, President Carter sent Somoza a personal letter congratulating him on his "concern to improve human rights in Nicaragua." The insurrectionalist group, outraged that the U.S. had apparently decided to support Somoza while the people of Nicaragua were being massacred, decided to act. The target of their next operation would be the National Palace, which housed Somoza's onerous rubber-stamp congress.

The plan which the Insurrectionalists adopted was the most audacious and spectacular in the history of the FSLN. Acting as if they were the special security guard assigned to Somoza's oldest son, they abruptly entered the Palace on August 22. With only 25 guerrillas the FSLN quickly took as hostage most of the members of the Chamber of Deputies and some 2,000 public employees. Archbishop Obando and the bishops of León and Granada acted as intermediaries. After forty-five hours of frantic negotiations, Somoza gave in to most of the Sandinista demands: the release of 59 prisioners from all three FSLN tendencies (including Tomás Borge); the donation of a huge amount of cash; the airing of an FSLN pronouncement; safe pasage out of Nicaragua for the liberated FSLN prisoners and the commandos; and the resolution of the hospital workers strike. Unusual publicity was given to this event in the international arena, and the FSLN captured the popular imagination. From then on, many people in Nicaragua were convinced of the real possibility that the FSLN would topple Somoza.[26]

The September Insurrection

The success of the attack on the National Palace was crucial in the development of a *sandinista*, as opposed to a mere anti-Somoza movement. Simple anti-Somoza objectives had typified the National Democratic Movement (MDN), which had emerged as an outgrowth of the business-organized work stoppage of late January. Later, a Broad Opposition Front (FAO) had been founded as an alliance between the old UDEL, the MDN, The Twelve, and several labor unions. The arrival of The Twelve in late July was a turning point in the political struggle against Somocismo. The Sandinista appeal to the masses was substantially enhanced because The Twelve were identified with the most conciliatory sector of the FSLN, namely, the Tercerista or Insurrectionalist. On July 17, a popular alternative to FAO was formed into a single block called the United People's Movement (MPU). Initially, twenty-two organizations were integrated into the MPU coalition and three principal objectives were defined: (1) to mobilize the population for the popular overthrow of Somoza; (2) to expand the coalition and unify broad popular sectors; and (3) to contribute to the process of unification of the revolutionary forces.[27]

Late in August, the business-oriented FAO sponsored a new general strike designed at least in part to steal the initiative from the FSLN and the MPU. However, this was not a significant political move since August is an idle period in the agricultural cycle. In the long run, the work stoppage simply served the economic interests of the business community. It did little to deflect or defuse the combative attitude which prevailed within the popular sectors.

On August 28, a Monimbó-style popular insurrection erupted in the city of Matagalpa. This was a spontaneous action carried out by youngsters armed only with pistols, rifles, and home-made contact bombs, their faces covered with black and red bandanas. Forcing the troops back to their barracks, *los muchachos* held out against them for two weeks. The alternatives for the FSLN were either to stop such insurrectionary tactics or to lead them.[28] The Front decided to respond positively to the popular initiative. On September 9, integrated uprisings erupted in four other cities: León, Masaya, Chinandega, and Managua, and the following day, Estelí joined the insurrectionalist movement. These cities are located in the western half of Nicaragua, where the great majority of the population live. It was anticipated that the National Guard would attempt to retake these positions all at once, thus overextending their forces. With most of its headquarters surrounded by the civilian forces and FSLN combatants, the Guard initially adopted a defensive tactic. Later, however, Somoza's air force submitted the cities to massive bombing before ground forces retook them one at a time. The FSLN fighters then retreated into the hills accompanied by thousands of youngsters and townspeople. Finally, tanks and troops went from house to house to subject those who remained to a genocidal "Operation Cleanup."

September's death toll was calculated at 5,000; more than 10,000 were injured; 25,000 were left homeless; and more than 60,000 sought asylum in other Central American countries, particularly Costa Rica. The Human Rights Commission of the Organization of American States was sent to Nicaragua to carry out investigations *in loco,* and its conclusions clearly condemned the Somoza regime.[29]

Many of the September casualties resulted from a lack of coordination within neighborhoods and from the fragmentation of FSLN leadership. In order to overcome these defects and to prepare civilians to resist the National Guard, the MPU subsequently set up the Civilian Defense Committees. These committees were organized block by block and coordinated by neighborhood and zonal steering committees. Underground preparations were conducted and several tasks were accomplished by CDC's members: the collection of medicines and first aid supplies; training in rudimentary first aid skills; storing of basic foodstuffs; surveillance of National Guard movements and of the activities of Somoza's spies; the maintenance of constant communication with the FSLN; the storage of ammunitions and preparation of home-made weapons; the building of evacuation passageways in the form of hidden wall openings and tunnels; and so on.

Whereas Somoza's genocidal tactics had tended to deplete his resources, the people were now ready to convert their military defeat into a definite victory, both militarily and politically. Somoza and his Guard had become the principal enemies of the People of Nicaragua.

The Final Offensive

Alarmed by the strength and determination demonstrated by the popular forces during the September uprisings, the United States now attempted to mediate a nonviolent accomodation between Somoza and his traditional elite opposition. The U.S. initiative within the Organization of American States materialized into a "Trinational Commission for Friendly Cooperation" involving Guatemala, the Dominican Republic, and the United States. In Nicaragua, the FAO encouraged support for the mediation effort, but its leadership sought little more than a reform of the Somoza regime. Though the Carter strategy included the application of both pressure and incentives, Somoza's obstinancy frustrated the U.S. effort. Moreover, U.S. support of the conservative sector within FAO exacerbated the situation and its liberal factions withdrew one by one from the mediation process, charging that the Commission only wanted to establish a *Somocismo sin Somoza* (Somozaism without Somoza). At this stage, Somoza's suggestion to hold a plebiscite was immediately encouraged by the U.S.[30] This option, however, fell through because of conflicting conditions demanded by both sides. As a result, bourgeois unity disintegrated and the proletarian forces consolidated on a strategy of "parallel power."[31] This amounted to what Charles Tilly calls "multiple sovereignty," the identifying feature of any revolutionary situation.[32] In his words, a revolutionary situation

> begins when a government previously under the control of a single, sovereign polity becomes the object of effective, competing, mutually exlusive claims on the part of two or more distinct polities. It ends when a single sovereign polity regains control over the government.[33]

In terms of Tilly's formulation, three proximate causes of multiple sovereignty existed: (1) the appearance of contenders advancing exclusive alternative claims to the control over the government; (2) commitment to those claims by a significant segment of the subject population; and (3) Governmental insufficiency and inefficiency to suppress (1) and/or (2).[34] This formulation is more than adequate to indicate why and how a revolution took place in Nicaragua.

The strategy of "parallel power" sprang out of the creation of the National Patriotic Front (FPN) in January, 1979, which united the FSLN, the MPU and the progressive sectors of the FAO. This unification of most of the anti-Somoza forces openly challenged the bourgeois opposition as various commissions began organizing within the FPN to pressure the system when it was least able or willing to make social concessions. Within the FPN, the FSLN used the MPU as its basic support structure to reorganize the masses. Meanwhile, since late in 1978 the leaders of FSLN tendencies had been involved in an effort to unify themselves. Finally, on March 8, 1979, the "Joint National Leadership of the Sandinista Front for National Liberation," composed of all three factions, announced the final reunification and issued their "program of national unity."

Fortunately, as the opposition was unifying itself and preparing for the final offensive, Somoza found himself facing several crises. A military crisis had forced him to beef up his Guard from 7,500 to some 10,000[35] and then increasingly to militarize the state apparatus. An economic crisis took place when the International Monetary Fund forced him to devaluate the currency. The unification of the revolutionary front then, simply lent the political, military and economic crises out of the Somoza regime the nature of a revolutionary crisis.

By early 1979, the FSLN had increased its forces to around 2,500 and was ready to unleash the final offensive. To win a definite victory it had to coordinate and simultaneously use three tactics: (1) a national strike, (2) popular insurrection, and (3) military attacks. The central focus of the FSLN strategy sprang from "the dynamic unity which had developed between the FSLN vanguard and the popular forces."[36]

Two joint guerrilla operations took place in late March and early April. These were diversionary in nature, designed to draw Guard troops into the mountain stronghold of the FSLN in the north. The April attack on Estelí was followed by an unexpected uprising of the population, which forced the FSLN in solidarity to commit up to two contingents of some 200 guerrillas each. The latter held the city for a week and then withdrew in an orderly retreat.In that operation the Guard committed 2,000 well-equipped troops. Late in April, some 150 guerrillas were trapped east of Lake Nicaragua while opening up a front which was supposed to draw the Guard out of its heavy concentration in the area along the Costa Rican border. This "Nueva Guinea Operation" failed dramatically when some 100 guerrilla combatants were killed.

Strategically, the Master Plan of the Insurrection gave the "Carlos Fonseca Amador"Northern Front the most important mission, namely, the wearing out of the enemy. In addition, popular uprisings were anticipated in connection with the "Benjamín Zeledón" Southern Front offensive which was supposed to bottle up a large contingent of the Guard.[37] Although the efforts on the Northern Front were severely limited by a substantial rein-forcement of regular troops mobilized from the southern region, this did release pressure on the FSLN on the Southern front which launched a coor-dinated attack along the entire region with some 600 combatants led by the already legendary Edén Pastora (Commander "Zero"). This was the prelude of the general insurrection.

On June 4, the FSLN Joint National Leadership called for a general strike, effective June 5, and announced the beginning of the final offensive. This paralyzed the country. The so-called "Internal Front" took on central importance in this last stage of the war because of the fact that only the popular forces could lead the urban insurrection. The Internal Front was composed of MPU-CDCs, or popular insurrection forces, in each city, par-ticularly in Managua, in coordination with the FSLN leadership. The "Rigoberto López Pérez" Western Front entered León, Nicaragua's second largest city, on June 2, and in two days of intense fighting assumed virtual control of the city. Beginning June 6, the Northern Front aimed its main of-fensive at Matagalpa. In order to concentrate its columns and coordinate simultaneous operations in all Fronts, the FSLN high command needed to implement a strategy to win time. It was decided to bottle up the Guard in Managua and cut its lines of supply. At this point, on June 9, the Battle of Managua began with the original plan of holding the city for only three days.[38] As it turned out, however, the Sandinistas held Managua for seven-teen days.

By mid-June, the whole FSLN military organization had launched simultaneous operations. Whereas some units attacked the border towns of Peñas Blancas in the south and Las Manos in the north, the "Carlos Roberto Huembres" Eastern Front took Juigalpa, and the "Camilo Ortega" Central Front moved on Masaya. The principal roads leading into and out of the most important cities were controlled by the insurgents and most of the Guard units were either confined to their own barracks or forced into merely defensive positions. León and Matagalpa illustrated this. By June 16, the former was under FSLN control, and in the latter only a few pockets of Guard units were still resisting. Somoza was unable to counter the extensiveness of the FSLN offensive. In spite of the fact that he did submit the principal cities of Nicaragua to intense and indiscriminate aerial bombardment, Somoza was no longer able to employ his "September strategy" of retaking towns one by one. The Guard was now largely unable to supply relief forces either inside the cities or to the field.

On June 16, the Sandinista radio station announced the creation of the Provisional Government, a move which resulted in the decision by the Andean nations to award belligerency status to the FSLN, and in the OAS's dismissal of a Somoza request aimed at investigating the Nicaraguan-Costa Rican border. Later on, Panama granted diplomatic recognition to the Provisional Government, amid the OAS deliberation regarding a U.S. proposal calling for an inter-American peace keeping force to be sent to Nicaragua. On June 23, the U.S. suffered an unprecedented defeat in the OAS when the Andean proposal was voted 17-2, demanding Somoza's unconditional resignation and upholding the principle of nonintervention.

Plans for the Managua operations were basically defensive, just to win time in order to coordinate simultaneous operations elsewhere. With only 150 combatants and a few hundred popular militiamen, taking over Managua was unthinkable.[39] After nine days of heroic resistance, a shipment of ammunition was dropped from a Navajo plane in Bello Horizonte, a neighborhood in eastern Managua. At that point, barricades no longer appeared to be the best way to stop the Guard, and a new tactic was adopted. The Sandinistas retreated in order to produce an effect of "invisibility" and take the Guard by surprise. This worked for a while.[40] However, the resulting house-to-house tactic also had its limitations. Meanwhile, a stalemate had developed on the Southern Front, with the National Guard elite forces holding some territory while FSLN and militia units resisted in Rivas. As the Northern and Western Front were consolidated, the only real option for the forces in Managua was to engage in a tactical retreat toward Masaya. This was successfully carried out from June 25 to June 27.

The tactical retreat toward Masaya meant a qualitative step forward because it reinforced FSLN forces in that region, giving them a total of some 6,000 people (3,000 guerrillas and militia, and 3,000 muchachos and civilians). This permitted the consolidation of the entire Carazo region, leaving Somoza's troops in the southern areas with little or no chances to retreat back to Managua. As a result, the rebels took Jinotepe on July 5, the first territory to be liberated in Nicaragua. Two days later, León was liberated as Fort Acosasco, six kilometers south of the city, was taken by the insurgents. In a short while, the FSLN was in control of twenty-three cities and towns throughout Nicaragua, and several popularly elected town councils came into being.

Politically, the Somoza regime was isolated, both internally and internationally. The dictator misread the situation and tried to resolve a societal crisis by adopting exclusively military means. On June 24, he called a meeting of his sixteen regional military chiefs and had them swear loyalty to him. He had also relied on Salvadorean and Honduran troops and unreported numbers of foreign mercenaries. His air force napalmed the FSLN strongholds in Managua, and then Masaya. The National Guard was an army of occupation operating in enemy territory, and in spite of the "efficiency, professionalism, and reponsiveness to its chain of command"[41] that most of its officers had learned from U.S. Military training schools, their efforts were doomed.

The Guard failed to penetrate Masaya and León, and no progress was reported in the Southern front. By July 10, Matagalpa was also liberated. Desperate, Somoza attempted to internationalize the conflict by having his planes strafe several towns in Costa Rican territory on July 11. On July 13, he secretly flew to Guatemala for consultation with CONDECA's high ranking officials. Promising his officers that he was not going to give up, he pointed to the acquisition of an undisclosed number of T-28 planes, which, he claimed, could facilitate a vigorous counter-offensive.[42] Actually, he and his Guard had already lost the war to the people of Nicaragua. The U.S. government, which had acted as the main impediment to a decisive Sandinist victory on the one hand, and Latin American solidarity on the other, helped determine the timing of the final departure of the "last Marine" from Nicaragua.

The Guard began to dissolve. Most of its officers fled to neighboring countries, particularly Honduras. Entire contingents of Guard units also escaped, but some 7,000 surrendered to the victorious FSLN forces. The Revolutionary Junta was proclaimed in Managua, on July 19, 1979.

Conclusion: Nicaraguan Vs. Cuban Experience

Taking the insurrectionary stage that preceded the Cuban Revolution as a reference point, it becomes clear that the Nicaraguan War of Liberation of June-July, 1979 was an original revolutionary model. By the time the provisional Junta assumed power in Nicaragua, the process of organizing the popular classes, through political mobilization, had reached a certain degree of maturity. In addition, since the revolutionary situation was more widespread in Nicaragua than in Cuba, the transfer of power in the former was also more extensive than in the latter.[43] We have to recall that in Cuba individual leadership in the person of Fidel Castro was the model. Moreover, most of the time prior to the meeting at Los Altos de Mompié on May 5, 1958, distinct and somewhat opposed leaderships advocated different strategies (rural guerrilla warfare, or urban insurgency, or direct action). In Nicaragua, however, collective leadership had been maintained even during the most difficult times, and no real split ever occurred. Indeed, internal controversy had matured into interdependence (the division of revolutionary labor).

Another factor which differentiates the Cuban experience from that of Nicaragua is the issue of "military" vs. "political." The Cuban experience was more military, with the struggle for political power following the military victory. Initially, Castro was not himself a member of the new state apparatus. At first, he let others run the country formally. In Nicaragua, however, there was a more integral approach in which politics and arms complemented each other. With military victory, political power was also decided in Nicaragua.

The extensiveness of the armed struggle, both geographically and demographically, was also more significant in Nicaragua than in Cuba. This difference was largely determined by two sets of conditions:

1. The brutality of the regime. Somoza's genocidal response to the September insurrection precipitated his own downfall by alienating entire sectors of the population.
2. The control that the Somoza regime had assumed over most of the economy. Regardless of the devastation that would follow, clearly only the general mobilization of the people could have positive results.

A final major difference between the Cuban and Nicaraguan experiences concerns the attitude and behavior of the U.S. government. In the case of Cuba, though certainly not friendly to the popular cause, Washington generally let events unfold according to their own dynamics. Though this also happened for a short while in Nicaragua, the Carter Administration late in 1977 quickly changed its tack when it began to realize that it had underestimated the strength and popular appeal of the FSLN. Worried about the spectre of a "second Cuba," it actively sought to block a popular victory. In doing so, it prolonged the struggle and, ironically, contributed unwittingly to the political mobilization of the Nicaraguan people.

In sum, the differences between the Cuban and Nicaraguan revolutions in their insurrectionary stages were a matter of kind rather than of degree. Whereas the more classical techniques of guerrilla warfare had been employed in Cuba, a new revolutionary model of popular insurrection emerged from the Nicaraguan experience. Of necessity, the character of the latter shaped the revolutionary outcome more clearly than had that of the former.

Notes

[1] Ronald H. Chilcote and Joel C. Edelstein, eds., *Latin America: the Struggle with Dependency and Beyond* (New York: John Wiley and Sons, 1974), p. 81

[2] Jorge I. Domínguez, *Cuba; Order and Revolution* (Cambridge: Harvard University Press, 1978), p. 132. Also Vania Bambirra, *La Revolucíon Cubana. Una Reinterpretación* 2 Ed. (México: Nuestro Tiempo, 1974).

[3] Thus it has been possible to carry out two major tasks of social reconstruction in Nicaragua, in the first year, which were possible in Cuba only during the second and third years of the revolution: (1) the Nationl Literacy Crusade, and (2) the creation of the armed forces of the Revolution.

[4] Fidel Castro wrote to Celia Sánchez, August 11, 1957, the following: "All weapons and ammunitions obtained from now on as well as any resources available must be sent to the Sierra." In Carlos Franqui, *Diario de la Revolución Cubana* (Barcelona: R. Torres, 1976), p. 300.

[5] Ernesto Ché Guevara, *Escritos y Discursos* (La Habana: Editorial de Ciencias Sociales, 1977), Vol. 2, p. 187

[6] Robert Taber, *M-26, Biography of a Revolution* (Cambridge: Cambridge University Press, 1961), p. 245.

[7] Ramón Bonachea and Marta San Martín, *The Cuban Insurrection, 1952-1959* (New Brunswick, N.J.: Transaction Books, 1974), p. 277.

[8] Guevara, *Escritos*, pp. 200-1

[9] Bonachea and San Martín argue strongly that Castro was responsible for such a failure; whereas Taber suggests that he opposed the strike because he had little faith in Havana, though he was persuaded by the National Direction of the M-26-7. Bonachea and San Martin, *The Cuban*, p. 214; and Taber, *M-26, Biography*, p. 218.

[10] Carlos Franquí, Diario, p. 433.

[11] Ibid, p. 667.

[12] Richard Millet, *Guardians of the Dynasty* (Maryknoll, N.Y.: Orbis Books, 1977).

[13] Commando Juan José Quezada, *Frente Sandinista: Diciembre Victorioso* (México: Editorial Diógenes, 1976), p. 102

[14] Doris Tijerino, *Inside the Nicaraguan Revolution* (as told to Margaret Randall) (Vancouver: New Star, 1978), p. 148; and Philip Wheaton and Yvonne Dilling, *Nicaragua: A People's Revolution* (Washington, D.C.: Ecumenical Program for Interamerican Communication and Action, 1980), p. 10.

[15] Julio Buitrago, Leonel Rugama Casimiro Sotelo, David Tejada, Oscar Turcios, Ricardo Morales, Juan J. Quezada, Jonathan González , to name a few.

[16] Tijerino, *Inside*, p. 152. For first-hand accounts of the events, see Lázslo Pataky, *Llegaron los que no estaban invitados. . .La sombra de Sandino* (Managua: Pereira, S.A., 1975); and Miguel Obando Bravo, *Golpe Sandinista* (Managua: Unión, 1975).

[17] Comando Juan José Quezada, *Frente Sandinista, p. 106.*

[18] Superficial viewpoints on this were offered by: Beldon Bell, ed., *Nicaragua: An Ally Under Siege* (Washington, D.C.: Council on American Affairs, 1978), o. 58; and Neale J. Pearson, "Nicaragua in Crisis," *Current History* (February, 1979), p. 80. A much better understanding of the disagreement was given by Alejandro Bendaña, "Crisis in Nicaragua," NACLA's *Report on the Americas XII*, No. 6 (Nov., 1978); and Wheaton and Dilling, *Nicaragua: A People's Revolution*, pp. 10-11.

[19] Julio López, Orlando Núñez, Carlos Fernando Chamorro, and Pascual Serres, *La Caída del Somocismo y la Lucha Sandinista en Nicaragua* (San José, Rica: EDUCA, 1979.

[20] A creation of the Inter-American Defense Board, a key factor of the U.S. counter insurgency program in Latin America, formed by the U.S. in the early 1960s.

[21] Belden Bell, *Nicaragua*, pp. 87 and 102.

[22] *La Prensa*, Feb. 7, 1978

[23] *La Prensa*, Feb. 9, 1978.

[24] *La Prensa*, Feb. 11, 1978.

[25] López et al., *La Caída del Somocismo*, p. 179.

[26] Manuel Eugarrios, *Dos...Uno...Cero Comandante*, 3rd Ed. (San José, Costa Rica: Lehmann, 1979); and Gabriel García Márquez, "El Golpe Sandinista: Crónica del Asalto a la 'Casa de los Chanchos.'" *Alternativa)* Bogotá, September, 1978), pp. 4-11.

[27] Wheaton and Dilling, *Nicaragua: A People's Revolution*, p. 33.

[28] López et al., *La Caída del Somocismo*, p. 183.

[29] Inter-American Commission on Human Rights, *Report on the Situation of Human Rights in Nicaragua* (Washington, D.C.: OAS, 1978).

[30] Mistakenly the London-based Latin American Bureau reported that The Twelve suggested the plebiscite. *Nicaragua: Dictatorship and Revolution* (London, 1979), p. 26. This was also substantiated by Fernando Cardenal, S.J., interviewed by the author, Nov. 23, 1980.

[31] López et al., *La Caída del Somocismo*, pp. 257-8.

[32] Charles Tilly, *From Mobilization to Revolution* (Reading, Mass.: Addison-Wesley, 1978) p. 191.

[33] Ibid.

[34] Tilly, *From Mobilization*, p. 200.

[35] Latin American Bureau, *Nicaragua*, p. 26.

[36] Wheaton and Dilling, *Nicaragua*, p. 59.

[37] Comandante Carlos Núñez Téllez, *Un Pueblo en Armas* (Managua: Secretaría Nacional de Propaganda y Educación Política del FSLN, 1980), p. 10.

[38] Ibid., Chapter IV.

[39] Ibid., p. 39.

[40] Ibid., p. 53.

[41] William P. Yarborough, "Nicaragua's Guardia Nacional: Solution or Part of the Problem," in Bell, ed., *Nicaragua*, p. 96.

[42] Viktor Morales Henríquez , *Los Ultimos Momentos de la Dictadura Somocista* (Managua: Unión, 1979), p. 48.

[43] Tilly, *From Mobilization*, p. 212, argues that "the more extensive the revolutionary situation, the greater the likelihood of an extensive transfer of power."

Chapter 2

The Ideology
of the Insurrection

HARRY E. VANDEN

> . . . you can fool everyone once, but you can't fool all the people forever.

Augusto C. Sandino

> We could say that we did not invent the fundamental elements of our liberation ourselves. The vanguard gathered these ideas from Sandino, from our own people, and this is what enabled us to lead the people toward their liberty. We found political, military, ideological, and moral elements in our people, in our own history . . . .

Humberto Ortega Saavedra
La revolución a traves de nuestra dirección nacional, p. 9

The ideas that inspired the revolution in Nicaragua did not emerge full blown in the politically charged atmosphere that characterized Latin America after the Cuban Revolution. Rather, these beliefs had their roots in the national past, in the history of a nation that strove to free itself from foreign domination and internal despotism. Sandinism (*Sandinismo*) became the repository of national consciousness. It represented the culmination of a long process that finally allowed the Nicaraguan people to gain an understanding of their own history. It became the ideological vehicle through which the national past was recaptured by the Nicaraguan masses.[1]

Before Sandinismo—and Sandino—Nicaragua was a little like Gabriel García Márquez's tragic town of Macondo.[2] It was a place where the people could not comprehend their present reality because they had lost their sense of history. Most of the country's leaders did not realize that the nation's development was not the same as the aggrandizement of personal

---

Sections of this chapter were written in very close consultation with Fred Murphy and reflect the wisdom of his research and field experience, though not necessarily his political views. (Also see footnote 1 at the end of this chapter.)

interest, or that cooperating with an expanding imperial presence would ultimately compromise national dignity and the nation itself. Even many who fought for the Liberal cause were like Colonel Aureliano Buendía in *One Hundred Years of Solitude*—they became mired in the struggle itself and lost sight of what they were fighting for. As García Márquez seems to affirm in his novel, "a consciousness of history is a necessary precondition for a society's survival and autonomous development."[3] However, Nicaraguans gained such a consciousness only through better than fifty years of Sandinista struggle. And even during the struggle, the reactionary forces "always denied [the] people the knowledge of their own history."[4]

The beginning of a modern national consciousness that included the Indian and mestizo masses emerged only toward the end of the nineteenth century in Nicaragua. This was more than a generation after the pro-slavery adventurer William Walker carried out the first in a long series of U.S. interventions in national affairs. Only then could a few intellectuals begin to look toward their distant indigenous past to rediscover their nation's historic identity and thus transcend the narrow Hispanicism that had continually constrained national politics, thought, and literature.

Even the great Nicaraguan poet Rubén Darío had to break with the stultifying forms of continental Spanish literature before he could discover truly Nicaraguan and Latin American literary forms, before he could develop "Modernism." As he said in *Prosas profanas* (1896), "If there is poetry in our [Latin] America, it is to be found in the old things: in Palenké and Utatlán, in the legendary Indian and refined Inca; in the great Montezuma on his throne of gold."[5] With the development of modernism, America was rediscovered.

Darío thus demonstrated how the most remote seeds of the struggle for national liberation and the development of a modern national consciousness resided in the indigenous struggle to resist Spanish colonization. "Our people"—Tomás Borge writes—"have tenaciously sought to recover their cultural identity and have fought for their right to be the authors of their own historical process, which has already been interrupted and truncated by imperialism innumerable times."[6] This struggle to create a national historic consciousness and repel foreign intrusion dated from early colonial times when indigenous leaders like the cacique Diriangén fought to repel the Spanish invaders.[7] Darío's poetic sensibility enabled him to see the continuity of the struggle more clearly than most Nicaraguan politicians of his day.[8] In his famous "Ode to Roosevelt" (1904), Darío underlined the glories of "Our America, which has had poets since the ancient times of Netzahualcoyotl," but like Bolívar in his "Jamaican letter" he noted the growing power of the United States, which (as manifest in Roosevelt) he saw as "the future invader of our native Indian America."[9]

The modernist poets who followed Darío also contributed to the growth of a historic identity in Nicaragua and were, with Darío, the founders of Nicaraguan literature.[10] They too were affected by the socio-political situation of Nicaragua, and were among the first to rediscover an awareness of Nicaragua's popular history. In so doing they began to disseminate the ideas that, as they found fertile ground in a people long denied an awareness of their place in history, were to contribute to the growing nationalist awareness that was to become manifest in the struggle of Augusto C. Sandino and his Army to Defend National Sovereignty.

Some of Nicaragua's Liberal politicians also began to realize that the country's political structures were inadequate. Although the Liberal reform movement did not develop in Nicaragua until the late nineteenth century, it carried a vision of society similar to that of other reform movements in Mexico (under Benito Juárez) and elsewhere in Latin America.

José Santos Zelaya's Liberal Revolution of 1893 marked the beginning of the modern Liberal movement in Nicaragua. Although constrained by bourgeois Liberalism, he introduced some progressive ideas and began to challenge the traditional oligarchy and the power of the Catholic Church. His successful drive to recover the Atlantic Coast from British colonialism also stimulated the growth of a national consciousness. Supported by elements of the national bourgeoisie, Zelaya introduced reforms that soon alarmed the Conservative forces and threatened the interests of U.S. capital (which was antagonistic to the growth of a vigorous independent national capitalist class in Nicaragua). As Zelaya faced increasing internal and external pressure, his regime degenerated into a dictatorship. In 1909, Washington forced him to resign before he could implement his plans to modernize Nicaragua.

The national bourgeoisie did not achieve the changes necessary to develop a modern nationalist capitalist system. Using various pretexts, the U.S. Marines intervened in 1909 to reinstate Conservative rule and ensure the dominant position of U.S. capital. As U.S. intervention increased over the next years (the Marines were again landed in 1912 to prop up the puppet regime of Adolfo Díaz, and did not leave until 1925), anti-interventionist sentiment grew among the Nicaraguan people. This tended to radicalize many supporters of the Liberal movement, and even prompted a few Conservatives to join the many armed uprisings against U.S.-installed governments.[11]

With the outbreak of a new Liberal uprising against a Conservative coup in 1925 and the U.S.-inspired reinstallation of Adolfo Díaz as president, the struggle began to take on clear nationalist and anti-imperialist overtones. The Marines once again intervened. It was at this point that Augusto C. Sandino returned from Mexico and joined the now strongly nationalist Liberal struggle. Although Sandino (a mechanic) encountered open hostility from the upper-class head of the Liberal Army, José M. Moncada, he was able to arm and organize his own Liberal band and participate in the increasingly successful Liberal offensive. The Liberal struggle was meeting with enthusiastic support from the masses, who were participating in growing numbers. Just as the Liberal forces were in sight of a clear military victory, the U.S. arranged a compromise solution that was accepted by Moncada and eventually supported by all the Liberal Generals, save one—Sandino.

None of the bourgeois leaders supported Sandino. But the peasants, miners, artisans, workers and Indians who had fought with him followed him to the Segovias,a remote mountainous region in the north. Their armament had been augmented a few months earlier,when a group of prostitutes in the Atlantic coast town of Puerto Cabezas helped them recover fifty rifles that the U.S. Marines had confiscated from other Liberal forces.

From its inception, Sandino's struggle inspired and was supported by the lower classes in Nicaragua. In contrast to the bourgeois politicians, even the humble prostitutes in Puerto Cabezas realized that the country could only be freed by the force of arms, and not by self-serving compromises with the forces of imperialism. Sandino and his Army to Defend National Sovereignty were forced to rely on little more than their own ingenuity and the support of Nicaragua's lower classes. This was to become a popular national struggle par excellence.

Like the members of the toiling masses who joined the struggle, Sandino brought the wisdom of his previous life experience. His humble birth (he was the son of a *mestiza* servant girl) and early life in rural Nicaragua inseparably linked him to the peasants and Indians in the countryside; his labor as a mechanic and worker in a variety of foreign and domestic corporations united him with the interests of the proletariat of Latin America and the rest of the world. While working for the U.S.-owned Huasteca Petroleum Company in Tampico, Mexico, he was affected by the nationalist radicalism of the Mexican revolution and soon "began to identify himself with a broad nationality embracing all Americans of Iberian and Indian descent."[12]

During the years he stayed in Mexico, Sandino witnessed first-hand the militant oil workers' struggles in Tampico. He was exposed to the radical notions of the Industrial Workers of the World (IWW), to militant anarchism, and to Marxist internationalism. Many of these ideas—along with his ardent Nicaraguan and Latin American nationalism—would be manifest in his later thought and writing. In one of his first manifestos ("Manifiesto Político," July 1, 1927), Sandino wrote that he was Nicaraguan and proud to be of Indian parentage (which, he said, perhaps explained the mystery of his patriotism). Further:

> The tie of nationality gives me the the right to take responsibility for my actions regarding Nicaragua, and therefore, Central America and the entire continent that speaks our tongue...I am a worker from the city, an artisan as they say in my country. But my ideal is to be found on the broad horizon of interna-

tionalism, in the right to be free and demand justice . . . . That I am a plebian, the oligarchs (that is, the swamp rats) will say. No matter— my greatest honor is to arise from among the oppressed who are the soul and nerve of the race, from those of us who have been left behind to live at the mercy of the shameless assassins who helped to inspire the crime of high treason: the Conservatives of Nicaragua. . . .[13]

Although a Nicaraguan above all, Sandino realized that Nicaragua's struggle was part of a larger movement: "At the present historical moment our struggle is national and racial; it will become international as the colonial and semi-colonial peoples unite with the peoples of the imperialistic nations."[14] Without being a Marxist, Sandino enjoyed an internationalist vision of a revolutionary nationalism that was linked to other revolutionary movements throughout the world: "It would not be strange for me and my army to find ourselves in any country of Latin America where the murderous invader had set his sights on conquest."[15]

What had begun as the outgrowth of a liberal uprising was being transformed into a revolutionary anti-imperialist struggle by the most exploited classes in the country: "Only the workers and peasants will go all the way; only their organized forces will bring about the triumph."[16]

Sandino's growing army of miners, Indians, peasants, artisans and workers finally forced out the Marines. Their political work and the increasing sophistication and tenacity of their popular guerrilla war had gained the support of the Nicaraguan masses, growing numbers of Latin Americans, a few informed North Americans and many Latin American intellectuals.[17] The ferocity of the conflict with the Marines continually forced Sandino and his followers to upgrade their military tactics and strengthen their ties with the rural masses who supported their struggle.

But not even the revolutionary government of Mexico would offer Sandino and his followers any assistance.[18] They were thus forced to become more and more self-reliant and to learn how to make optimum use of their only abundant resource—the Nicaraguan people. Rifles from the Spanish— American War, war matériel captured from the invaders, bombs made from the sardine cans the Marines discarded, and a sea of machetes wielded by ever more determined *campesinos*–such were the armaments used to confront machine guns and dive bombers.[19]

This was one of the first modern examples of what a guerrilla army with mass popular support could do against a technologically superior invader, even when the latter was supported by local Quislings and the mercenary military forces at their disposal. Mobile guerrilla bands as the components of an egalitarian people's army, political as well as military organization, integrated political and military actions, close ties to the peasants, and, most important, popular support and involvement—such were the lessons to be learned from Sandino's people's war against

GOSHEN COLLEGE LIBRARY
GOSHEN, INDIANA

imperialism.[20] These lessons were not forgotten by the leadership of the FSLN: "In the study of Sandinism, in which our Commander Carlos Fonseca was teacher and example, we found the important elements to achieve our triumph."[21]

Nor did others miss the importance of the nature of Sandino's struggle—Ché Guevara "discerned the reasons for Sandino's success in resisting the Marines: the inspirational quality of his leadership and his guerrilla tactics."[22] Colonel Alberto Bayo, the Spanish Republican guerrilla fighter who later trained Castro's original force in Mexico, was also much impressed by the military tactics Sandino's army employed.[23]

Tragically, although Sandino's political support had enabled him to achieve his primary objective, the departure of all foreign troops, he disbanded his army before he could achieve the far-reaching political and economic change he was planning at the time of his murder in 1934. At the height of his power (late in 1932), he had written that "Our Army is preparing to take the reins of national power to proceed with the organization of large cooperatives of Nicaraguan workers and peasants, who will exploit our own natural resources for the benefit of the Nicaraguan family in general."[24] He began to set up agricultural cooperatives in the Segovias, and seemed to favor the type of communal organization that his Indian ancestors had used centuries before.[25] He had also become fully cognizant of how little the traditional parties served the interests of the Nicaraguan people and, at the time of his death, he was planning to start a national political movement. After his treacherous death at the hands of Somoza's National Guard (1934), the cooperatives were attacked and most of Sandino's followers were soon slaughtered by the U.S.-trained National Guard. Some Sandinist columns fought on for a few more years in remote areas, but they too were eventually forced to abandon systematic armed resistance. Nonetheless, the spirit of Sandino and the example of his army lived on in the popular mind, nourished by eyewitness accounts and first-hand stories from Sandinist survivors.

By exploiting his close ties to Washington and his position as head of the National Guard, Anastasio Somoza García soon emerged as the most powerful political figure in the country. He realized that Sandino and his Army to Defend National Sovereignty represented the greatest threat to the reestablishment of rule by a U.S.-backed elite. No doubt he also sensed that Sandino was the symbol of popular struggle and the key to the rediscovery of their true history by the people. Thus the dictator was not content to have ordered the execution of the popular leader.[26] He attempted to distort the popular memory of Sandino and his followers by having a slanderous anti-Sandino book published under his name.[27] Somoza's efforts achieved some success, in that it was soon very difficult for the masses of Nicaraguans to obtain any favorable written accounts of the Sandinist struggle within the country.

After Somoza took direct control of the government in 1936, he instituted an increasingly repressive family dictatorship that—mostly because of its close ties to the U.S.—would endure until militarily defeated by the FSLN in 1979. However, despite bloody repression and the intense vilification of Sandino and his followers, popular struggle continued through the 1930s, 1940s, and 1950s, though clearly at a relatively low level. This period of struggle included military actions by both old Sandinistas and younger patriots such as the "Generation of 44".[28]

By the 1940s, the full force of the Somoza dictatorship was being felt. Somoza had proven to be one of the U.S.'s best "good neighbors," and had been lavishly received by F.D.R. in Washington. By the 1950s, Nicaragua was a fully dependent producer of primary goods (mostly coffee and cotton), and an integral part of the U.S. system of political and economic control in the Western Hemisphere. Sandino's anti-imperialist popular struggle seemed to have been for naught. The guerrilla hero and the popular revolutionary struggle seemed to be slowly disappearing from the popular mind. There were occasional armed actions or *putsch* attempts by old Sandinists and other Nicaraguans who could no longer countenance the heavy-handed political and economic manipulation that characterized the Somozas and their friends. Students and workers (as in 1944) occasionally demonstrated against the regime, but lacked any clear ideological perspective in which to place their struggle. Opposition to the dictatorship came to be symbolized by the Conservative Party. Even the Nicaraguan Socialist Party (founded as a pro-Moscow Communist Party in 1944) often collaborated with traditional bourgeois politicians and Somoza-controlled unions, at the workers' expense. Somoza had taken over the Liberal Party and even went so far as to make pacts (1948 and 1950) with the Conservative Party in an attempt to co-opt the only major focal point of opposition to his regime. Without even the militant Liberalism that had initiated Sandino in his struggle, it was difficult for the diffuse opposition forces to gain the ideological perspective necessary to again mobilize the masses against the forces of imperialism.

A poet once again helped the people take charge of their future. Rigoberto López Pérez was one of the Nicaraguan intellectuals who directly felt the far-reaching cultural implications of a dependent dictatorship that was subservient to U.S. imperialism. He, like the Cuban poet José Martí, felt compelled to exchange pen for pistol to liberate his country. In 1956, the young poet assassinated Somoza. In so doing, he not only avenged Sandino, but spurred a much-needed reexamination of national conscience that would increasingly challenge the status quo.

> Rigoberto López Pérez's action and the different armed attacks and popular uprisings that the Nicaraguan people unleashed [from 1956 to 1960], in great part reflect the gradual loss of Conservative political control over the popular masses. Bringing Somoza to justice and the subsequent series of armed

> movements were done outside of the tutelage of the bourgeois
> opposition, and come to be the first attempts *to reintegrate the
> revolutionary Sandinist movement;* they represent an important
> step in the revolutionary war begun by Sandino.[29]

Little by little, the spirit of Sandino's struggle was once again being felt across the land. A new wave of guerrilla activities broke out in the countryside; one of the more famous of these was even led by Ramón Raudales, a veteran of Sandino's Army. The university students also began to show a new militancy and, for the first time, a small group began to study Marxist theory.[30]

By the late 1950s, sectors of the Nicaraguan people were beginning to recover their popular history through the continuation of Sandino's struggle. But now historic conditions had changed substantially from the time of the first Sandinista struggle. Western-style bourgeois democracy was increasingly being called into question in the Third World. The ardent Mexican nationalism that had so inspired Sandino was in large part discredited among Latin American intellectuals because of the failure of the subsequent Mexican regimes to implement the economic and social transformations promised by the Mexican Revolution.

In China and Vietnam, meanwhile, national liberation struggles had grown into socialist revolutions. Cuba was soon to take this road as well. The prestige enjoyed by the Chinese and Vietnamese Communist Parties[31] under Mao Zedong and Ho Chi Minh prompted many other leaders of national liberation struggles, such as the FLN in Algeria, to try to apply Marxist ideas to their own countries.

Leaders of the anticolonial upsurge that swept Africa in the 1950s were likewise openly suspicious of capitalist democracy and called for the development of new forms of "African Socialism."[32] Henceforth, Third World nationalist movements would increasingly turn to socialism and Marxism to explain their realities and nourish their revolutionary movements. Nicaragua would be no exception.

In Latin America, the development of Marxism before the advent of the Cuban Revolution did not facilitate the application of the ideology to national conditions. José Carlos Mariátegui (Peru, 1894-1930) was one of the few who attempted creatively to apply Marxism to Latin American reality. His efforts were met with the most caustic criticism from the Communist International and many Latin American Communists.[33] After this, the type of Marxism that was espoused by the Communist Parties in Latin America tended to be dogmatic, sectarian, and generally not well suited to Latin American conditions. The development of Nicaraguan Communism was no different. The Nicaraguan Socialist Party was founded in 1944 and maintained the closest of ties to the Soviet Union. Like most Latin American Communist Parties prior to the 1960s, its ideology was modeled after that of the Stalinist bureaucracy in the Soviet Union. It was thus ill-equipped to creatively fuse Marxism with the national reality of Nicaragua. Nonetheless, the Party was virtually the only institution in the country where Marxist ideas were taken seriously. As such, it attracted the attention of emerging young student radicals like Carlos Fonseca Amador and Tomás Borge.

The PSN's conception of Marxism soon, however, proved inadequate for the tasks the young militants were planning. The party had been founded to help support Somoza during World War II and had sporadically participated in elections during the dictatorship, sometimes in alliance with the Conservative Party.[34] The PSN dismissed Sandino as a petty-bourgeois nationalist and, like other traditional Communist Parties in Latin America during the 1950s and early 1960s, was unwilling to engage in revolutionary activity. It claimed that the objective economic conditions did not yet allow for revolutionary class struggle.[35] In contrast, the example of the Cuban revolution had already helped to inspire some of the previously mentioned guerrilla activity in the late 1950s. As the Cuban revolutionaries responded to U.S. pressures and threats by deepening the social transformations on the island and openly adopting Marxist-Leninist ideas, their example became increasingly attractive to the young militants in Nicaragua. In July 1961, Carlos Fonseca, Tomás Borge, and Silvio Mayorga founded a new revolutionary organization—the Sandinist Front of National Liberation (El Frente Sandinista de Liberación Nacional [FSLN]). Like many young Latin American revolutionaries, they modeled their organization on Fidel Castro's 26th July Movement and believed that guerrilla warfare—as outlined by Ché Guevara[36]—was the best method of implementing political change. Their sympathies thus moved from the Stalinist outlook of the PSN to the dynamic and revolutionary Marxism being developed by the Cuban leaders. Ché's theory of rural guerrilla warfare had borrowed from Sandino. The Sandinistas would, in turn, borrow from the Cuban example to continue Sandino's struggle: "With the victory of the Cuban Revolution, the rebellious Nicaraguan spirit recovered its brilliance. The Marxism of Lenin, Fidel, Ché, Ho Chi Minh was welcomed by the Sandinist Front of National Liberation."[37]

The new generation of Sandinistas thus began a movement that was the continuation of the popular struggle of Augusto Sandino's guerrilla army. Drawing heavily on the Cuban revolutionary experience and the writings of Ché Guevara and Fidel Castro, they began to reinterpret Sandino's original struggle in light of historic and ideological developments following his death. Even during his guerrilla war, Sandino had concluded that the Liberal and Conservative politicians were traitors and cowards and must be replaced by worker and peasant leaders.[38] By studying their own fight for national identity and liberation in light of similar struggles in Cuba, Vietnam, and elsewhere, the Sandinistas were able to build on Sandino's populist notions and begin to infuse their movement with a coherent ideology.

At the urging of Carlos Fonseca, FSLN militants began to study Sandino's writings and tactics as they prepared for their first guerrilla actions in 1963. Colonel Santos López, one of the survivors of Sandino's army, joined the FSLN and offered valuable advice on military tactics. Stimulated by the Cuban example, the Sandinistas believed that the only road to power was through armed struggle. However, like other young Fidelistas throughout Latin America, they felt that launching rural guerrilla warfare was all that was necessary to convince the popular masses (beginning with the peasantry) to take up arms and join the guerrillas. In Nicaragua, as elsewhere in the region, this was a fundamental and very costly error. The FSLN's first attempts at guerrilla warfare (Río Coco and Río Bocay, 1963) met with tragic defeat. The new Sandinistas had failed to do what their namesake had done so well—mobilize the local populace on the side of the guerrillas through well-planned political and organizational activitycoordinatedwith the armed struggle. Tomás Borge would later explain: "We committed the error of moving into the zone without first undertaking preparatory political work, without knowing the terrain, and without creating supply lines."[39] Even basic communication with the people was a problem. Many of the local inhabitants in the area of the first fronts spoke only indigenous languages like Miskito.[40]

Retiring from their guerrilla adventures in the inhospitable mountainous jungle of northern Nicaragua, most of the remaining Sandinistas began to engage in semilegal political work in urban areas, in uneasy cooperation with the Nicaraguan Socialist Party. However, a few Sandinistas such as Rigoberto Cruz (Pablo Ubeda) did remain in some rural areas to initiate important political work with the peasants.

The absurdity of the electoral farce that was developing for 1967 and the antirevolutionary political opportunism of the PSN soon convinced the FSLN that returning to armed guerrilla struggle in the countryside was the only effective means of defeating the Somoza dictatorship and returning the country to the people. Stimulated by Carlos Fonseca's leadership and the intensive study of Sandino's tactics and writings he advocated,[41] the Sandinistas gradually began to understand that more political and organizational work was necessary to ensure mass participation in the struggle against the dictatorship. However, before the vital importance of this lesson was completely clear, the second wave of FSLN guerrillas were already engaging the National Guard in combat in the region of the Darién Mountains in Matagalpa. Once again, the FSLN proved incapable of withstanding the superior military power of the National Guard. They had not yet fully assimilated the lessons to be learned from popular struggles for national liberation like those led by Sandino, Mao, Ho Chi Minh, or Castro. They had not yet learned that the people's vanguard must become one with the people so that the masses themselves can rise up to sweep away their enemies in a popular war of liberation.

Tragically, some of the FSLN's best cadres became isolated and surrounded at Pancasán in mid-1967. Although they offered heroic resistance, most were killed as the National Guard closed their trap on the guerrillas. Like the Fidelista guerrilla currents all over Latin America (Ché, for instance, was killed in Bolivia the same year) they suffered a disastrous military setback.

While this was occurring in the countryside, things were even worse in the cities. The traditional opposition forces continued to demonstrate their ineptitude. One of the most notorious examples of this happened in Managua in January of 1967. Here, the Conservative leader Fernando Agüero took advantage of a large peaceful demonstration against the dictatorship to try to carry out an ill-planned and unorganized *putsch* against Somoza. This resulted in the massacre of over 100 unarmed demonstrators and a further loss in prestige for the bourgeois politicians. In contrast, the tenacity of the resistance waged by the FSLN focused national attention on their struggle, and helped to turn a military defeat into a political victory. Beginning with the peasants and university students, the process of merging the vanguard and the mobilized masses into a unified fighting force was slowly getting underway. As Commander Henry Ruiz put it, "Pancasán reverberated in the popular conscience; its echo was felt in the bosom of the Nicaraguan people and the name Frente Sandinista began to spread to the most remote corners of the nation."[42]

The masses were beginning to stir for the first time since Sandino; the national reawakening was finally beginning. The road to retake popular control of the nation's destiny would, however, be long and bloody. There was still much to learn before the masses could throw themselves into popular war against the dictatorship.

Unlike many other guerilla movements in Latin America, the Sandinistas were able to learn from the mistakes they made in Río Bocay and Pancasán. They demonstrated a great capacity for self-criticism and were thus able to transcend their initial error of isolating themselves from the masses.[43] Through painful trial and error and through an increasingly astute study of Sandino's thought and tactics, and those of other revolutionary movements throughout the world, they were able to fashion a strategy that would eventually unleash the full power of the Nicaraguan people against the dictatorship.

In the period after Pancasán and the 1967 elections, the FSLN's increased prestige brought many new recruits, especially from among the student youth in the cities. At this time, the organization focused mainly on developing a base among the *campesinos* in the north central part of the country, in the mountains around Zinica. It was there that the urban recruits were sent. The work bore fruit and became the axis of the "prolonged people's war" concept that dominated the Sandinistas' thinking at the time. Commander Henry Ruiz subsequently explained:

> . . . in the balance sheet drawn up on Pancasán, prolonged peo-
> ple's war was mentioned . . . .That idea took shape from study-
> ing a little of the Vietnamese and the Chinese experience.
> Without leaning toward the Cuban experience (that of a guer-
> rilla movement that would generate activity toward total war),
> we involved ourselves in the urban question at the same time we
> did organizational work in the countryside."[44]

While the Zinica front was the focus of the FSLN's armed activity following Pancasán, increased attention was being paid to urban work that was necessarily clandestine. The FSLN began to establish what it called "intermediate organizations." Indeed, "intermediate organizations made up the umbilical cord to [the masses]. We had student organizations, worker organizations, neighborhood committees, Christian movements, artistic groups, and so on. . . . We led these intermediate organizations ourselves, through *compañeros* who followed the orientation of the Front."[45]

The success the Sandinistas were having in winning *campesinos* to their cause in the mountains alarmed Somoza and the US embassy. Large-scale, brutal counterinsurgency operations were launched. Peasants suspected of collaborating with the FSLN "disappeared," were tortured, hurled out of helicopters or otherwise murdered. What amounted to concentration camps were set up in Waslala and Río Blanco at the northern and southern extremities of the area where the Frente was operating. The counterrevolutionary terror became so intense that the guerrillas were forced further and further back into the mountains, and progressively separated from the inhabited areas where they had been gaining support. The "prolonged people's war" strategy that demanded a secure rural base area was reaching an impasse. The dictatorship's political and economic crisis was maturing, but it was still in a position to deal heavy military blows to the Sandinistas.

While the Sandinistas evolved their theory of mass struggle, progressive sectors within the Catholic church became more concerned with the conditions of the masses. Motivated by this concern and the growing "Liberation Theology" movement, they began to intervene actively in the process of social change. In Nicaragua, part of this activity was channelled through the Institute for Human Advancement (INPRHU). Employing the "concientization" process developed by Paulo Freire in *The Pedagogy of the Oppressed*,INPRHU began to raise the awareness of popular groups in rural and urban areas. This led to the development of mass-oriented organizations like The Federation of Rural Organizations, The Movement for the Liberation of the Women and the National Movement of Youth. Stressing literacy and popular education, critical thinking, and a problem-solving orientation, the Institute and the popular organizations that grew from it also began to mobilize segments of the masses. As this process developed (from the mid-sixties on), it helped to buttress the FSLN's awareness of the need for mass mobilization. It would contribute significantly to the organized incorporation of the masses into the armed struggle in the late 1970s. These developments also further strengthened the ties between progressive Catholic elements and the FSLN. Such ties would eventually become so strong that prominent Chruch figures like Fathers Ernesto and Fernando Cardenal and Father Miguel D'Escoto would become part of the Sandinista movement. Others, following in the footsteps of the Colombian priest Camilo Torres, not only encouraged their parishioners to join the struggle, but even took up arms themselves.[46]

Between Pancasán and late 1974, the FSLN carried on what it termed "accumulation of forces in silence." "Our work in that entire period took place through intermediate organizations, in ways that any theorist or dogmatist might have criticized. Everything from sending our militants to build latrines, teaching adults to read and write, treating the sick, or organizing festivals for the youth in order to introduce them to a process of political life, to the formation of organizations with revolutionary content."[47] The "silence" was broken in a spectacular way with the December 27, 1974, seizure of the home of a wealthy and prominent Somozaist during a gala party for the U.S. ambassador. An FSLN commando unit held more than a dozen foreign diplomats and top Somozaists for several days, finally forcing Somoza to release Sandinista political prisoners, pay a large sum of money, and broadcast and publish FSLN communiques.

Developments subsequent to December 1974 were contradictory. On the one hand, the FSLN's spectacular feat earned it further prestige and belied Somoza's repeated claims that the guerrillas had been wiped out. But the state of siege the dictatorship imposed and the repression launched against the trade unions and other expressions of urban opposition—as well as the rural terror described above—caused the mass movement to undergo an abrupt downturn after the increasing struggles that had taken place in 1973-74.

Discussions concerning strategy intensified among the Sandinistas. This was a period of reassessment throughout the Latin American left. Most of the guerrilla fronts launched during the first wave of struggle after the Cuban revolution had gone down in defeat—the MR-13 and FAR in Guatemala, the FLN-FALN in Venezuela, Ché Guevara's heroic effort in Bolivia, the struggles led by Hugo Blanco, Luís de la Puente Uceda, and Hector Bejar in Peru. The shift to urban action by the surviving guerrilla currents was focusing on military action and individual terrorism, which likewise proved unsuccessful. At the same time, the electoral victory of the Popular Unity Coalition in Chile in 1970 led many on the left to believe a "peaceful road to socialism" was possible. This usually meant working with segments of the bourgeois class in electoral action of the type rejected by the Sandinistas in 1966-67. The initial appeal of these unsuccessful approaches would, however, take some time to dissipate, even after the Allende regime and the popular upsurge it generated came to a bloody end in September 1973.

It is to the Sandinistas' great credit that they held firm against both the electoral illusions and the focus on military action that were widespread among Latin American radicals in the early and mid-1970s. While details on the internal debate in the FSLN that broke out in 1975 remain sketchy, it can be said in retrospect that all the currents that were soon to emerge as three separate tendencies were grappling with the problem of how to incorporate the masses into the struggle, without minimizing the crucial importance of the armed seizure of power and the revolutionary destruction of the dictatorship's apparatus of political repression, social oppression, and economic exploitation.

The FSLN's consciousness of the need to mobilize the masses was already apparent in Carlos Fonseca Amador's landmark essay of 1968, *Nicaragua: hora cero*. Drawing a balance sheet on the Pancasán period, Fonseca wrote that: "Organized mass work (student, peasant, worker) was paralyzed. On the one hand the quantity of cadres necessary for this work was lacking, and on the other, the importance this activity could have in the course of the development of the armed struggle was underrated." To overcome this weakness, Fonseca pointed to the need "to pay attention to the habits the capitalist parties and their hangers-on have imposed on the mass of the people. . . ." Many, he said, sympathized with the armed struggle but did not show this in action. "This leads to considering the need to properly train a broad number of individuals from among the people so that they will be capable of supporting the armed struggle. To seek the people is not enough—they must be trained to participate in the revolutionary war."[48]

The debate in the FSLN was over how best to carry out this task. The first current that took shape was the Proletarian tendency. It called for *shifting* the focus of the Frente's work from the countryside to the urban working class, with the aim of building a Leninist revolutionary party. The majority of the leadership opposed this perspective and the Front's lack of experience in handling internal discussion of sharp political differences led the majority to take administrative measures against the Proletarian tendency.[49]

Though autonomous organizationally, the *Proletarios* continued to function as a part of the FSLN and uphold its legacy, while they sought to put their own ideas into practice in the cities. Fresh work was developed not only among workers in factories but also in poor and working-class neighborhoods and among students.

Meanwhile, further disagreements arose inside the majority current of the FSLN. These centered on tactical questions such as the pace of the struggle, the possibilities for a rapid acceleration of armed action leading to insurrection, the nature of alliances with petty-bourgeois and bourgeois opposition sectors, and so on. This debate gave rise to the Prolonged People's War (GPP) and the Insurrectional (or *Tercerista*) tendencies.

The GPP felt the time was not yet ripe for the bold military moves advocated by the Insurrectionalists, and they were skeptical of the latter's efforts to forge links and tactical alliances with sectors of the traditional bourgeois opposition to the Somoza dictatorship. For the GPP, a further period of "accumulation of forces in silence" combined with small-scale rural guerrilla activity was called for. The Insurrectionalists, on the other hand, called for rapidly building a regular army and launching a military offensive against the National Guard, for which they hoped to obtain support from the bourgeois opposition and from governments such as those of Costa Rica, Panama, and Venezuela. Events subsequent to the Insurrectionalists' October 1977 offensive would show that this was not an unrealistic perspective. Likewise, the revolutionary thrust of the insurrectionist strategy clearly belies the accuracy of the Social Democratic label that some observers attached to this group.

The separation into tendencies did not mean the disintegration of the Frente. Each current pursued the struggle according to its own lights, and as the crisis of the dictatorship deepened, all achieved successes. Efforts by the leaders to reestablish unity did not cease, although they were hampered by the imprisonment of key figures such as Tomás Borge and by the National Guard's murder of Carlos Fonseca Amador in November 1976.

The three tendencies would converge around the fresh tactical and strategic questions brought to the fore by the upsurge of mass struggle that opened in late 1977. As the urban masses moved into action after Pedro Joaquín Chamorro's murder in early 1978, the trend was for all three tendencies to learn both from the masses and from each other. Some examples of this can be cited:

• After the first serious confrontation between the urban masses and the National Guard—the uprising in the Indian community of Monimbó in February of 1978—the Insurrectional tendency adjusted its policy as follows: "After the insurrection in Monimbó . . . we decided to dismantle the guerrilla column we had on the Carlos Fonseca Amador Northern Front and all the cadres that were in those columns. . . . The columns had been victorious; nonetheless, the mass movement in the cities demanded immediate leadership from the vanguard of the movement. So we decided to dismantle those guerrilla columns and send all the cadres to lead the mass struggle."[50]

• Disagreements over the question of alliances had led the Insurrectionalists to participate in the Broad Opposition Front (FAO) through their supporters in the "Group of Twelve" while the GPP and the Proletarios were concentrating on building what was to become the United People's Movement (MPU). The political capitulation of the bourgeois opposition elements in the FAO to the U.S.-sponsored "Mediation" in October 1978 quickly led the Insurrectionalists to adjust their policy and withdraw from the FAO, denouncing the imperialist maneuvers. All three tendencies then collaborated to establish the National Patriotic Front (FPN), which had the MPU as its axis. The FPN took on the character of an anti-imperialist united front, drawing in the trade unions, two of the three factions of the old PSN, student groups, and petty bourgeois formations such as the People's Social Christian and Independent Liberal Parties—all under FSLN hegemony.

• Finally, the experience of the September 1978 attempt at insurrection—which the Insurrectionalist tendency spearheaded most enthusiastically—taught the need for better organization and preparation. This paid off in June 1979.

The mid-1970s division of the FSLN reflected different approaches and partial answers to the complex problem of taking political power and smashing the dictatorship. This problem was resolved as all three tendencies brought the best of their particular experiences and approaches to the final struggle. This process was facilitated through their mature handling of unification and their willingness to learn from each other and work together even before the achievement of full unity in March 1979. The old divisions were then superseded by the historic victory of July 19, 1979. Commander Humberto Ortega summed this up:

> The leaders of the three tendencies were concerned with the overall problems of the revolution.
>
> The problem was that each one wanted to lead the process, wanted to be the one that stood out the most, but that was overcome in the course of the struggle itself and everybody realized the importance of everybody else's work. . . . The whole Sandinista movement agreed on a single policy which upheld the insurrectional nature of the struggle, called for a flexible policy on alliances and the need for a broad-based program, etc. This programmatic political and ideological foundation made it possible for us to coordinate our efforts with increasing effectiveness and pave the way for our regrouping. I think it would be more correct to say that we regrouped rather than united. The three tendencies all had a great desire to become a single FSLN once again, as shown by the enthusiasm, love and zeal with which this unity is preserved now. . . .[51]

Conclusion

In Nicaragua, the ideology of insurrection—*Sandinismo*—thus developed out of the national struggle for popular liberation. It incorporated not only the political tactics and organizational advances of Sandino, but those of other radical movements in the Third World. And if indeed the history of a people is one of the struggle to improve their lives and gain freedom and independence, then "The history of Nicaragua is a history full of struggles and heroic acts by its people, from the time of the Indians who resisted Spanish colonialism, passing through Sandino's heroic actions to the war of national liberation. . . ."[52] The ideology that unified and focused the popular struggle was that of a very flexible and nonsectarian Third World Marxism that was carefully applied to the specific conditions in Nicaragua. Although it was influenced by the ideology and tactics of other Third World nations that also had to struggle for their liberation (Vietnam and Cuba for instance), *Sandinist ideology was very much Nicaraguan and was not a copy or imitation of any other nation.* Specific tactics and strategies of the revolution (revolutionary praxis) were developed in the process of struggle as revolutionary theory tempered political and military action and was at the same time changed by it.

Strategy—like ideology—was not completely defined and detailed at the beginning. It developed dynamically: "One must have the necessary flexibility, the capacity to change paths, to accommodate the line of action to the historic circumstances that develop, but without ever losing sight of the strategic objective. This is the great lesson of the Front."[53] The developing ideology, like the revolution itself, depended on the ability of the FSLN leaders to apply the lessons of Nicaraguan and world history to the tasks at hand: "We began with Sandino's thought but we have never forgotten the thought of Marx, Lenin, Ché Guevara, [Emiliano] Zapata, or any other revolutionary who had something to offer."[54]

During and after the revolution, the FSLN showed itself to be quite willing to cooperate with a variety of groupings to achieve common objectives. As the above quotes suggest, however, they never lost sight of their objectives and—as though guided by our opening quote from Sandino—never allowed themselves to be fooled by the bourgeois elite. Thus in the months following the Sandinista victory on July 19, they quickly clarified their position when a faction of the Conservative Party formed the "Sandinist Social Democratic Party," called for fostering the development of capitalism as a "first stage" in the revolution and took up the slogan *Sandinismo sí, Comunismo no.*" Only the FSLN, a statement by the National Directorate said in response, had upheld the anti-imperialist legacy of Sandino through its struggle. The rebaptized Conservatives, on the other hand, had failed to support the popular struggle and had openly opposed the Sandinist Front throughout its history.[55]

From July 19 on, the new revolutionary government, led by the FSLN, took concrete steps in favor of the workers and the peasants, while encroaching more and more on the prerogatives of capitalists who would not contribute to the tasks of economic reconstruction and upholding national unity. As Carlos Fonseca said, "It is not a question simply of changing the men in power, but rather of changing the system, of overthrowing the exploiting classes and bringing the exploited classes to victory."[56] Responding to another bourgeois politician's attempt to usurp the FSLN's power (Alfonso Robelo, March, 1980) the Front issued a declaration entitled "Sandinism is not Democratism." The statement suggested that Robelo's move represented "the most recent effort to revise Sandino and recast him in terms of liberal bourgeois ideology, turning into an abstraction the anti-imperialist, class character of Sandinism. . . ." While all Nicaraguans could take up Sandino's legacy, "Sandinism . . . is now the expression of the interests of the workers and peasants—whose task it is to lead the patriotic sectors and never again be led by some other social force."[57] Indeed, the displacement of the old bourgeois forces by the FSLN-led workers and peasants has become a cornerstone of Sandinist ideology. In this way, the new government would put an end not only to imperialist domination and national oppression, but economic exploitation as well. Thus, "Counter to the aspirations of the bourgeoisie, once the movement is underway, the masses do not limit themselves to demanding justice and democracy, but tend to go beyond bourgeois projects. . . ."[58]

In Nicaragua, this process had actually begun under Sandino, as the popular forces on which he based his army rapidly swept the movement beyond its Liberal origins. The FSLN not only restored this revolutionary content to Sandinism, but also enriched it with the new lessons that emerged from post-World War II anti-imperialistic struggles in the Third World and those from the Cuban Revolution in particular. Indeed,

> The principal objective of the people's revolution on the continent is the seizure of power by means of the destruction of the bureaucratic-military apparatus of the State and its replacement by the people in arms in order to change the existing economic and social regime. This objective can only be achieved through armed struggle.[59]

Once the popular forces are in power, some polarization and radicalization is also natural, ". . . with the urban working class, the agricultural laborers, the peasants, the students, the most progressive middle strata, the underemployed, the unemployed, the Indians and the Negroes on one side, closely united, fighting militantly for their liberation. . . ."[60]

The ideology of the Nicaraguan Revolution is at once the recuperation of a long history of national struggle and the specific Nicaraguan manifestation of the new wave of revolution that is sweeping the Third World. As such, it shares some beliefs with sister nations like Cuba, while others are uniquely Nicaraguan. As in the past, the way in which Sandinist ideology is applied will in large part depend on evolving national conditions. Thus the specific nature of Nicaraguan social formations have, according to one Sandinist theorist, allowed certain segments of the middle class to play a much more revolutionary role than in past revolutions.[61] Likewise, the role of members of the church in the revolutionary process has allowed them (and Liberation theology) to occupy a unique position in the new society that is being constructed. Indeed, the genius of FSLN ideology has been its consistent practical application of Sandino's thought and Marxist concepts and methodology to the Nicaraguan reality.[62] It has become the means by which the Nicaraguan people have rediscovered their own popular history and—unlike the tragic inhabitants of Macondo—have taken charge of their own destiny. Thus, in Darío's land ideology and struggle have given the people hope for the future. A new nation is now being built as though a poem of its people were being written:

> El dolor ha sido reto
> y el porvenir esperanza
> construimos como escribiendo un poema
> creando, borrando, y volviendo a escribir.
> (Pain has been a challenge
> and the future a hope
> we construct as if writing a poem
> creating, erasing, and writing again.)[63]

Footnotes

[1] The author would like to thank his many friends in Nicaragua and the United States for generously providing information and documentation. He would also like to thank the National Endowment for the Humanities and all the participants in the 1980 N.E.H. Summer Seminar on "Latin American Views of Society and Culture" (directed by Bob Levine in Stony Brook, N.Y.) for stimulating him to think about the importance of the masses, their poets, writers, and revolutionary leaders in discovering their own popular history.

[2] See Gabriel García Márquez, One Hundred Years of Solitude (Cien años de soledad) (New York: Avon Books, 1971) and especially the excellent article by Anna Marie Taylor, "Cien Años de Soledad: History and the Novel," Latin American Perspectives, 2 (1975): pp. 96-112. The author wishes to thank Jesse Fernández for bringing this article to his attention.

[3] Anna Marie Taylor, Ibid., p. 110.

[4] Tomás Borge in the Preface to Humberto Ortega Saavedra, 50 años de lucha sandinista (Managua: Colección las Segovias, Ministry of Interior, [1979 or 1980]): p. 3.

[5] Rubén Darío," Prosas Profanas," Obras completas (Vol. 5, Madrid: Ediciones Castilla, 1953):763.

[6] Tomás Borge, in Humberto Ortega, 50 años, p. 2.

[7] See Jaime Wheelock, Las raices indígenas de la lucha anticolonial en Nicaragua (Mexico: Siglo XXI, 1975).

[8] We are grateful to Julio Valle-Castillo for helping us confirm this aspect of Darío's writing. See, inter alia, Rubén Darío, Textos socio-políticos (Manaqua: Ediciones de la Biblioteca Nacional, 1980), Nuestro Rubén Darío, op. cit.; Valle-Castillo's Introduction in his edited work Poetas Modernistas de Nicaragua (1880-1927) (Managua: Promoción Cultural, Banco de América, 1978); and Angel Rama, Rubén Darío y el modernismo, circunstancia socio-económica de un arte americano (Caracas: Universidad Central de Venezuela, 1970).

[9] Nuestro Rubén Darío (Managua: Ministerio de Cultura, 1980), p. 47. For an even stronger statement of Darío's "Americanist" views, see "El Triunfo de Calibán," which concludes with the following: "Miranda will always prefer Ariel . . . all the mountains of stone, gold, and bacon are not enough for my Latin soul to prostitute itself to Calibán," Textos socio-políticos, p. 33.

[10] Julio Valle-Castillo in Poetas modernistas, p. xxvii.

[11] Humberto Ortega Saavedra in La revolución a través de nuestra dirección nacional (Managua: Secretaría Nacional de Propaganda y Educación Política del FSLN, 1980), p.10. The

Nicaraguan people were involved in some thirty armed uprisings from 1906 to 1926.

[12] Neil Macaulay, *The Sandino Affair* (Chicago: Quadrangle Books, 1967), p 53.

[13] Sergio Ramírez (ed.), *El pensamiento vivo de Sandino*, 5th Ed. (San José, Costa Rica: Editorial Universitaria Centroamericana, 1979), pp. 87-88.

[14] Letter to Henri Barbusse (1928), cited in Macaulay, *The Sandino Affair*, p. 113.

[15] Sandino, as cited in José Benito Escobar, *Ideario Sandinista* (Managua: Secretaría Nacional de Propaganda y Educación [1979 or 1980]), p. 5; see also Augusto César Sandino, *Ideario Político*, selection by Carlos Fonseca Amador (2nd Ed., San José, Costa Rica: Editorial Porvenir, 1979) for the same essay. By August of 1931, Sandino notes that "It is with great pleasure that I declare that our Army awaits the coming world conflagration to begin to develop its humanitarian plan in favor of the world proletariat," in Ramírez, ed., *El pensamiento vivo de Sandino*, p. 233.

[16] Sandino, as cited in Carlos Fonseca Amador, *Sandino: guerrillero proletario* (Managua: Secretaría Nacional de Propaganda y Educación Política del FSLN [1979 or 1980], p. 5.

[17] Macaulay mentions, for instance, the support work done on Sandino's behalf by the poet Gabriela Mistral (Chile), by Joaquín García Monge (Costa Rica), and by José Carlos Maríategui (Peru). *The Sandino Affair*, p. 113.

[18] In his pamphlet, *Manifesto a los pueblos de la tierra y en particular al de Nicaragua* (Managua: Tip. La Prensa, 1933; reproduced by "Ediciones 79" in Feb. 1980) Sandino recounts his fruitless trip to Mexico to secure material assistance for his army. He ends his Manifesto by proclaiming that "during the seven years of war that we have fought to restore national autonomy in Nicaragua, we have not received any help nor have we accumulated political debts with anyone" (p. 24).

[19] See Macaulay, *The Sandino Affair*, Chapters 4, 5, and 6; and especially Gregorio Selser, *Sandino, general de hombres libres*, 2nd Ed. (San José, Costa Rica: Editorial Universitaria Centroamericana, 1979), pp. 340-41. An English translation of Selser's book is being published by Monthly Review Press (New York).

[20] Macaulay underlines the close ties Sandino's guerrilla fighters had with the local populace (p. 10) and notes that Sandino's tactics "essentially were the same as the tactics of the People's Liberation Army in China, the National Liberation Front in Algeria, the 26th of July Movement in Cuba and the Viet Minh and Viet Cong in Vietnam" (p. 10). That is, a mobile guerrilla force supported by the politically aware mobilized the masses first in an expanding series of rural areas and eventually in urban areas as well.

[21] Humberto Ortega Saavedra, *La revolucíon a través de nuestra dirección nacional*, p. 9.

[22] Macaulay, *The Sandino Affair*, p. 262.

[23] Ibid.

[24] Ramírez, *El pensamiento vivo de Sandino*, p. 254.

[25] Macaulay, *The Sandino Affair*, p. 248.

[26] Selser, *Sandino, general de hombres libres*, Chapter 12; and see also Sergio Ramírez's introduction in *El pensamiento vivo de Sandino*, especially pp. xiv and xv.

[27] Anastasio Somoza García, *El verdadero Sandino, o el cavario de las Segovias*, (Managua: Tipografía Robelo, 1936). This book is generally believed to have been ghost-written for Somoza. For a better understanding of the role of Sandino in the development of national consciousness, see Charles E. Frazier, Jr. *The Dawn of Nationalism and Its Consequences in Nicaragua* (Austin: University of Texas, Ph.D dissertation, 1958).

[28] This period of struggle is discussed in Jesús Miguel Blandón, *Entre Sandino y Fonseca Amador*. (2nd ed. [Managua?]: N.P., printed by "Impresiones y Troqueles, S.A." February 1980). The "generation of 44" refers to a younger group of militants who emerged in 1944 as a consequence of labor and student demonstrations against the dictatorship in that year.

[29] Humberto Ortega Saavedra, *50 años de lucha sandinista* (Managua: Colección las Segovias, Ministerio del Interior, 1980), p. 81.

[30] Ibid., p. 83.

[31] The convergence of Marxism and nationalism in Vietnam is now well known. The example of the people's war waged in Vietnam was also of the utmost importance for other Third World wars of national liberation. The Sandinists studied the struggle in Vietnam carefully and

were well acquainted with works such as Vo Nguyen Giap, *People's War, People's Army* (New York: Bantam, 1968).

[32] See Julius Nyerere, *Freedom and Socialism* (London: Oxford University Press, 1970); Franz Fanon, *The Wretched of the Earth* (New York: Grove Press, 1963), especially Chapter 3, "The Pitfalls of National Consciousness."

[33] We refer here to José Carlos Mariátegui's attempt to create an Indo-American Marxism. See H. Vanden, "Mariátegui: Marxismo, Comunismo, and other Bibliographic Notes." *Latin American Research Review* 14, 3(1979), pp. 61-86.

[34] Carlos Fonseca Amador, *Nicaragua: hora cero* (Managua: Secretaría Nacional de Propaganda y Educación Política del FSLN, 1980), p. 21-23.

[35] See Regis Debray, *Revolution in the Revolution* (New York: Grove Press, 1967) for a general condemnation of the unrevolutionary nature of Latin American C.P.s at this time.

[36] Ché Guevara, *Guerrilla Warfare* (London: Penguin, 1969).

[37] Carlos Fonseca Amador, *Sandino, guerillero proletario*, p. 6.

[38] Sandino, as cited by Sergio Ramírez in "Análisis Histórico—Social del Movimiento Sandinista," *Encuentro, Revista de la Universidad Centroamericana* 15, p. 12.

[39] Daniel Waksman Schinca, "Entrevista con Tomás Borge" *Combate* (Stockholm), July-Sept. 1979. (Reproduced from the Mexico City daily, *El Dia.*)

[40] Ibid.

[41] Fonseca Amador assembled pithy quotations from Sandino in a pamphlet (*Ideario político de Augusto César Sandino*) and begàn to circulate short studies of his thought and tactics (*Sandino, guerrillero proletario*).

[42] Henry Ruiz, "La Montaña era como un crisol donde se forjaban los mejores cuadros." *Nicaráuac* (Ministry of Culture, Managua) I (May-June, 1980): 10. Also Frente Sandinista, *Diciembre victorioso*, 4th Ed. (Mexico City; Editorial Diogenes, 1979), pp. 101-103.

[43] Victor Tirado López, *El pensamiento político de Carlos Fonseca Amador* (Managua: Secretaría Nacional de Propaganda y Educación del FSLN [1979 or 1980]), p. 7.

[44] Henry Ruiz, "La montaña ," *Nicaráuac* 1 (May-June 1980), 14.

[45] Waksman Schinca, *Combate*, July-Sept. 1979, p. 21.

[46] Perhaps the best known priest to join the Sandinistas and take up arms was Gaspar Gracía Laviana. Before his death in the fighting, he wrote that "my faith and Catholicism oblige me to take an active part in the FSLN's revolutionary process; this is because the liberation of an oppressed people is an integral part of the total redemption of Christ." Cited in *El evangelio en la revolución* (Managua: Instituto Histórico Centroamericano [1979]), p. 7. Information on INPRHU was made available by one of the Institute's founders, Reinaldo Antonio Téfel, now director of the revolutionary government's Nicaraguan Social Security Institute. See chapter 9 for a fuller explanation of the role of the church in the revolution.

[47] Bayardo Arce, *Las fuerzas motrices antes y después del triunfo* (Managua: Secretaría Nacional de Propaganda y Educación Política del FSLN [1980]), p. 24.

[48] Carlos Fonseca, *Nicaragua: hora cero*, pp. 33-34.

[49] Later, Tomás Borge would acknowledge that this was an error: "It involved a new phenomenon, or at least one that up till then had not taken on such magnitude. Those of us who were members of the leadership did not know how to deal with it adequately. . . . So we adopted authoritarian positions and we wanted to solve the problem by decree. We did not allow in practice—even though we said that it was allowed—for a political and organizational discussion to take place. A group of comrades was sanctioned by expulsion from the organization." Waksman Schinca interview. *Combate*, July-Sept. 1979, p. 22.

[50] Humberto Ortega Saavedra, "La Insurrección Nacional Victoriosa," *Nicaráuac* 1 (May-June 1980), p. 30.

[51] Humberto Ortega Saavedra (interviewed by Marta Harnecker), *Granma Weekly Review* (Havana: Jan. 27, 1980). English translation of interview originally published in *Bohemia* (Havana, No. 52, Dec. 28, 1979), p. 4; also in "La Insurrección Nacional Victoriosa," *Ibid.*, p. 56.

[52] [FSLN National Secretariat for Propaganda and Political Education], *La revolución a través de nuestra dirección nacional*, p. 5.

[53] Henry Ruiz, "La montaña," p. 24.

[54] Victor Tirado López, *El pensamiento politico de Carlos Fonseca Amador*, p. 6

[55] Fred Murphy, "This Revolution is for Workers and Peasants" *Intercontinental Press*, XVIII, No. 35 (Oct. 1, 1979), p. 918.

[56] Cited in Fred Murphy, "100,000 Rally to Honor FSLN Founder," *Intercontinental Press* XVII, No. 44 (Dec. 3, 1979), p. 1177.

[57] *Barricada* (Managua) Mar. 14, 1980.

[58] This quotation comes from the November 1979 issue of *Pensamiento Crítico*, which is a theoretical journal that was sponsored jointly by all three FSLN tendencies. This and several such articles are reprinted in Julio López C., et al., *La caída del somocismo y la lucha sandinista en Nicaragua* (San José, Costa Rica: EDUCA, 1979). This quotation is found on pp. 223-24.

[59] "General Declaration" of the 1967 conference of the Organization of Latin American Solidarity (OLAS). (This conference included representatives of the FSLN.) English translation reprinted in *International Socialist Review* 28 (Nov.-Dec., 1967), pp. 54-55.

[60] Ibid., p. 58.

[61] See Orlando Nuñez, "La Tercera Fuerza Social en los Movimientos de Liberación Nacional," a paper presented during the IV Central American Congress of Sociology (Managua, July 1980). The author suggests that the principal purpose of his paper is to "demonstrate the significant presence of the petite urban bourgeoisie, united to the proletariat and peasantry, during the revolutionary taking and exercising of power in the formation of a process different from that of capitalism" (p. 11).

[62] Julio Godio, "América Latina: experiencia sandinista y revolución continental" *Nueva Sociedad* (Caracas) (1980), p. 31. Specifically, Godio argues that "The historic merit of Sandinism is that it has shown that 'to act politically' requires thinking in such a way as to make the universal categories of Marxism concrete by means of the political-cultural categories of the nation."

[63] Vida Luz Meneses, "En El Nuevo Pais," *Nicaráuac*, 1 (May-June, 1980), p. 123.

Chapter 3

The United States
and the Nicaraguan Revolution

WILLIAM M. LEOGRANDE

The history of U.S. involvement in Nicaragua stretches back to the eras of gunboat and dollar diplomacy, when Washington sought to make Central America and the Caribbean safe for the United States. The interventions of that period were motivated by a desire to ensure that the emerging world of the United States would be economically and militarily unchallenged "in our own backyard."

In 1912, the Marines landed in Nicaragua, ostensibly to protect U.S. citizens and property during a period of civil strife. They remained, except for a brief interlude in 1925-26, for 21 years.[1] Before the troops departed, they created a National Guard to ensure Nicaragua's stability. No sooner had the Americans left than the Guard, under the command of Anastasio Somoza García, deposed the civilian government and inaugurated what would become a Somoza dynasty lasting for decades.

Though the dynasty was far from the civilian democracy originally envisioned by the United States, it was nevertheless stable, pro-American, and anti-Communist. Somoza's Nicaragua was an ally, and for many years, that was enough to guarantee the friendship of the United States.

Somoza's Nicaragua was one of the first and most logical targets of the Carter Administration's efforts to promote human rights abroad. The 1972 earthquake that destroyed the capital city of Managua also stimulated opposition to Somoza's economic and political empire. Worsening economic conditions alienated not only the lower classes but even the middle and upper classes who had traditionally been at least the passive accomplices of the dynasty. Somoza responded to the growing opposition with political repression. The reign of terror visited upon Nicaragua by the National Guard in 1975 and 1976 attracted substantial international criticism and made Somoza the chief nemesis of the human rights advocates in the U.S. Congress.

The long history of Somoza's ties to the United States and his willingness to cooperate with U.S. policy objectives in the hemisphere suggested that Nicaragua might prove especially malleable to U.S. influence. In Nicaragua, the Carter Administration sought a quick success on human rights that would defuse conservative skepticism over the feasibility of such an idealistic policy.

In 1977, there appeared to be few countervailing forces to undermine a strong human rights stance toward Nicaragua. Somoza's repression had apparently eliminated the Sandinista National Liberation Front (FSLN)—a small group of radical guerrillas who had made little significant political progress since their founding in 1962. Thus there seemed to be no clear and present threat to Nicaragua's internal security. On the economic front, the Somoza family had so successfully monopolized the most profitable sectors of the national economy that U.S. businessmen could find few investment opportunities. Thus there were no powerful voices from the private sector in the U.S. that would rise to Somoza's defense over human rights. On balance, it appeared in 1977 that even the "worst-case" outcome of pressuring Somoza on human rights would entail no serious costs. Alienating Somoza would pose a threat to neither U.S. national security nor economic interests.

This assessment proved faulty on a number of counts. The FSLN had been driven deeper underground by the repressive wave of 1975-76, but it had not been eliminated. It was still active enough to provide an organizational outlet for the growing popular revulsion toward Somoza's rule. And though Somoza had few friends in the U.S. private sector, he had several powerful ones in the Congress of the United States. As instability gave way to insurrection in Nicaragua, the Carter Administration was caught in Hobson's choice of standing by its commitment to human rights or subordinating humanitarian concerns to the traditional ones of national security. While it wrestled with this dilemma, it was also buffeted by powerful Congressional factions on both sides of the issue. The result was a paralysis of policy during the critical months of 1978, and an eventual decision to salvage Somoza long after that became an impossibility.

Shortly after President Carter's inauguration, Nicaragua's Catholic bishops, led by Archbishop Obando y Bravo, issued a pastoral letter condemning the reign of terror which the National Guard had been conducting in the countryside for some two years. The United States Ambassador to Nicaragua, James Theberge, acknowledged the accuracy of the allegations, but Washington was unwilling to endorse the bishops' criticism without "further study."[2] In Congress, the advocates of human rights were less reticent to speak out. Representative Edward Koch (D-NY) reacted to the pastoral letter by calling upon the newly installed Secretary of State, Cyrus Vance, to suspend U.S. economic aid to Nicaragua pending an improvement in human rights.[3] The Administration made no immediate policy response.

In June, Koch led an unsuccessful fight to delete economic and military aid to Nicaragua from the foreign assistance appropriations bill. The Administration, however, then joined in the battle by announcing that it would withhold the military credits appropriated for Nicaragua in both 1977 and 1978, and that it would suspend the disbursing of $12 million in economic aid until Somoza improved his human rights record.[4]

With his acute sensitivity to political winds in the United States, it did not take Somoza long to receive these signals that the Carter Administration was serious about its pledge to promote human rights. In September, he sought to improve his image by lifting the state of siege which had been in force for nearly three years—since the FSLN had managed to kidnap a Christmas party full of Nicaraguan luminaries in December 1974. Washington responded to the end of the state of siege by signing a $2.5 million military aid agreement, though full implementation of the existing economic agreements were still held up to see if Somoza had truly turned over a new leaf.[5]

Though the economic and military effect of holding up aid to Nicaragua was insignificant, the symbolic impact was immense. For Nicaragua's moderates, Somoza's power had always seemed unassailable because he had the power of the United States behind him. Somoza was a clever enough politician to actively foster this perception. The Carter Administration's criticism of Somoza galvanized the moderates into active opposition by suggesting that Somoza's ultimate base of power was no longer secure.

In October, the FSLN re-emerged on the national scene by launching a series of small but coordinated attacks on National Guard garrisons around the nation. Los Doce, a group of 12 prominent Nicaraguan intellectuals, endorsed the FSLN action and forged the first bridge between Somoza's radical and moderate opponents. This crisis marked the beginning of a new stage in the struggle against Somoza, and it is notable that the United States stood aloof from it. Washington announced neither support for Somoza nor support for a moderate initiative urging negotiations between Somoza and his opponents.[6]

On January 10, 1978, Pedro Joaquín Chamorro, the editor of La Prensa and leader of the moderate opposition, was assassinated in Managua. His murder detonated two weeks of spontaneous rioting in the capital, followed by a general strike organized by the business community. Somoza's National Guard tried to restore order with their usual brutality, and the U.S. responded by once again freezing military assistance.[7]

The violence surrounding Chamorro's assassination was the first clear signal that Somoza's regime was in serious trouble. As in October, the U.S. adopted an essentially neutral positon. Washington urged Somoza to enter into a dialogue with his opponents, as the moderate opposition had suggested in October. But neither Somoza nor the opposition were in any mood for compromise. During the next eight months, Nicaraguan politics underwent a fundamental realignment. The moderate opposition waited in vain for the United States to help them wrest power from Somoza. The

FSLN used the time to organize the rural villages and urban barrios.

In Washington, this crucial shift of the political initiative from moderates to radicals went unnoticed. In fact, the relative calm that followed the political violence of January and February was interpreted as a return to normalcy. Somoza, it appeared, had restored Nicaragua's political equilibrium. Chamorro's assassination had laid bare the fragility of Somoza's control, and the specter of political turmoil in Nicaragua threw the Carter Administration's human rights policy there into question. Within the Administration itself, traditionalists argued forcefully that the United States could ill afford to further undermine Somoza's position by continuing its human rights criticism. The issue of national security, which had seemed so peripheral in 1977, now loomed large.[8]

Within the U.S. Congress, Somoza's supporters also went over to the offensive. In May, Representative Charles Wilson (D-Texas) promised to use his post on the Appropriations Committee to hold the whole Foreign Assistance Bill hostage unless the Administration relaxed its aid embargo on Nicaragua. The Administration gave in by releasing the $12 million economic aid package that had been held up for nearly a year, although the ban on military aid continued. The transparent rationale given for this about-face was that Somoza had lifted the three-year state of siege nine months earlier.[9]

On August 1, over the objections of some of his own key advisors on Latin America, President Carter sent Somoza a letter congratulating him on his improved human rights record.[10] This was arguably the worst policy error made by the United States during the entire Nicaraguan crisis. Since Somoza's human rights practices had not changed in any significant way over the preceding months, both Somoza and his opponents interpreted the letter as an endorsement of Somoza's rule. The effect was to stiffen Somoza's resistance to any sort of compromise with the opposition, and to convince his moderate opponents that the United States would not help them after all. They turned, almost immediately, to a united front with the radical oppositon as their only practical alternative.

In the United States, policymakers were deeply divided over how to proceed in Nicaragua. One camp argued for greater pressure to force Somoza's resignation because of his abysmal human rights record and because his departure was the only way to engineer a moderate succession. Others argued that the human rights policy was largely responsible for Somoza's difficulties and that the United States ought to reassert support for him, both because he was a loyal ally and because he constituted the most reliable bulwark against the FSLN.[11]

On August 22, the FSLN seized the National Palace, taking some 1,500 captives—including virtually the entire Congress. Their audacity captured the popular imagination; as they drove to the airport with fifty-nine newly released political prisoners, thousands of Nicaraguans turned out to cheer their triumph. The following month, the FSLN launched small-scale attacks on National Guard garrisons in several cities as they had done the previous October. But this time, the populace rose up in support of them and five of the nation's cities fell under FSLN control. The National Guard was able to retake them only after three weeks of battle during which it bombed and shelled the cities into rubble. In its "mopping-up" operations, the Guard systematically massacred as many young men as it could lay its hands on.[12]

During the insurrection, the United States repeatedly called upon Somoza to "discipline and control" his troops, but to no avail. The stories of National Guard atrocities were so horrific that the United States was finally moved to demand an OAS investigation, though Washington took no unilateral sanctions against Somoza. Though Washington was unwilling to call for Somoza's resignation, it did ask that all parties to the war make "appropriate concessions and sacrifices" to end the bloodshed, and "engage in discussions for a peaceful and democratic solution."[13] This was to become the formula for resolving the conflict which the United States would pursue through three months of mediation under the auspices of the Organization of American States.

The most important effect of the September insurrection on U.S. policy was to convince officials in Washington that Somoza would never be able to restore political stability. This, combined with the popular support demonstrated by the FSLN, prompted Washington to begin the search for a way to transfer power from Somoza to his moderate opponents while leaving the FSLN politically isolated. From this point onward, the clear goal of U.S. policy was to prevent the formation of a post-Somoza government in which the FSLN would have any significant political influence.

The battles in Nicaragua set off a storm of Congressional protest over the Carter Administration's policy. In early September, Senator Frank Church (D-ID), Chairman of the Senate Foreign Relations Committee, called upon Carter to cut off all aid to Nicaragua.[14] The potent pro-Somoza "Nicaragua Lobby," headed by Representatives Wilson and John Murphy (D-NY), quickly responded with a letter to Carter signed by seventy-eight Congressmen, including majority leader Jim Wright (D-TX), demanding that the Administration come to Somoza's aid.[15] Not to be outdone, human rights advocates Representatives Donald Fraser (D-MN) and Tom Harkin (D-IO) reiterated Church's position in a letter to Secretary Vance, which eighty-six members of Congress signed.[16]

Whether or not by design, the Carter Administration tried to craft a policy between these two poles. U.S. Ambassador to Panama William Jordan was sent on a mission through Central America to build support within the OAS for some sort of compromise settlement. At Washington's initiative, the OAS met in late September and authorized the United States, Guatemala, and the Dominican Republic to undertake a mediation effort. Jordan secured Somoza's acquiescence to the mediation, and that of the

Broad Opposition Front (Frente Amplio Opositor—an umbrella group of Somoza's moderate opponents), but the FSLN, which was waging the war against Somoza, was not even consulted.[17]

Washington's central objective in the mediation was to devise a formula for peaceful transition to a new government of moderates that would either exclude the FSLN or restrict it to minimal participation. Specifically, the head of the U.S. mediation team, William Bowdler, proposed an "interim government" to be composed of the FAO and Somoza's National Liberal Party. This government would prepare elections for 1981, while the National Guard continued to safeguard internal security. To secure the FAO's agreement, Bowdler promised a well-spring of economic aid to a new government, and threatened full U.S. support for Somoza if the FAO balked. To get Somoza on board, Bowdler threatened an all-out U.S. effort to remove him if he refused to cooperate.[18]

The mediation was an abject failure. By forcing the FAO to even consider retaining the hated National Guard, the United States fractured the moderate opposition. The more progressive groups began leaving the FAO in October, and defections continued until the mediation's final collapse. The very groups that the U.S. hoped to rely upon to keep the FSLN out of power were thoroughly delegitimized by the mediation into which their erstwhile allies in Washington had forced them. When, in January, Somoza finally rejected the mediator's last proposal for an internationally supervised plebiscite, the moderate opposition was so fragmented and demoralized that it could play no more than a subsidiary role in the political battles to follow.

Somoza, on the other hand, had managed the mediation with consumate skill. For nearly three months, the United States had tried to cajole him into making meaningful concessions while publicly repeating over and over that it did not seek his resignation. Sensing that Washington could not bring itself to oust him, he had held firm in his demands in spite of Washington warning that his obstinacy would "affect the whole gamut of relations with the United States."[19] But when the mediation finally collapsed, U.S. retaliation was largely symbolic. Instead of breaking relations or calling for Somoza's resignation, the Carter Administration did no more than recall a few dozen U.S. officials.[20]

This minimal response was due partly to Congressional pressure, and partly to a growing belief in Washington that Somoza might survive after all. Representative Murphy, as Chairman of the House Merchant Marine and Fisheries Committee, threatened to hold the implementation legislation for the Panama Canal treaties hostage if Carter took strong measures against Somoza.[21] But more significantly, Somoza seemed to be stronger in early 1979 than he had been in over a year. His moderate opponents were demoralized and in disarray after the mediation; the FSLN was relatively silent; and the National Guard had been rearmed and reinforced. Intelligence analysts in Washington were confidently predicting that the Guard would militarily defeat any offensive the FSLN could launch.[22] It looked to some as if Somoza offered the best chance of keeping the radicals from power after all. In May, the United States supported Nicaragua's application for a $66 million loan from the International Monetary Fund.[23]

When the FSLN launched its "final offensive" against Somoza in early June, any illusions concerning the viability of the Somoza regime quickly melted away. Within days, the FSLN gained control of every major city outside the capital. Washington responded by trying to revive the mediation. Special Ambassador William Bowdler toured Latin America in search of some multilateral formula for Nicaragua, but found many of Washington's closest allies in Central America and the Andean Pact supporting the FSLN.[24]

At the initiative of the U.S., another special OAS meeting was convened to discuss the Nicaraguan crisis. Secretary of State Cyrus Vance outlined the U.S. position, beginning with Washington's first public call for Somoza's resignation. Other elements of the U.S. plan called for an embargo on arms transfers to all sides, a ceasefire, an OAS peacekeeping force to enforce a ceasefire, and a "broadly based government of national reconciliation." To Washington, a "broadly based" government still meant a government which would include Somoza's cronies and would retain the National Guard. In essence, this formula was no different from the formula advanced under the first mediation.[25]

The reaction to Vance's proposals may well have marked the nadir of U.S. influence in the OAS. Only Somoza favored the U.S. package. The call for a peacekeeping force was widely condemned as a transparent effort to justify intervention against the FSLN, which it was. The feeble efforts of the U.S. delegation to raise the specter of Cuban involvement as justification for the peacekeeping force convinced no one, since at least half a dozen other Latin American states were providing more aid to the FSLN than the Cubans were. The mendacity of Washington's purported neutrality was starkly revealed when the U.S. representatives sought, unsuccessfully, to prevent Miguel d'Escoto, Foreign Minister of the Provisional Government of National Reconstruction of Nicaragua, from addressing the OAS meeting.[26]

The U.S. position at the OAS was based upon a thorough misreading of political realities both within the OAS and, more important, within Nicaragua. With the FSLN on the verge of military victory, the idea that it would agree to a transitional government that preserved the National Guard was utterly fantastic. One explanation for the lack of realism behind U.S. policy during these weeks lies in the interplay of bureaucratic politics within the Carter Administration. When the FSLN's final offensive began, the exploding crisis in Nicaragua came immediately under the authority of the White House Special Coordinating Committee for crisis management.

This committee, the lineal descendant of the old "40 Committee", was composed of senior foreign policy officials: Deputy Secretary of State Warren Christopher, Defense Secretary Harold Brown, CIA Director Stansfield Turner, and National Security Advisor Zbigniew Brzezinski. This group took over the management of U.S. policy from the State Department's Task Force on Nicaragua i.e., from the Latin American specialists. Under Brzezinski's chairmanship, the Committee pointedly ignored the recommendations of the State Department's specialists, who warned that the peacekeeping proposal would meet with widespread derision within the OAS.[27]

From Washington's perspective, the only positive outcome of the OAS meeting was the passage of the final resolution calling upon member states to "facilitate an enduring and peaceful solution of the Nicaraguan problem".[28] U.S. policymakers took this as a sufficient mandate to try once again to fashion a mediated settlement. At the end of June, the U.S. devised a new, five-step secret plan for settling the Nicaraguan crisis. Somoza would resign in favor of a constitutional successor. This successor would appoint a council of prominent non-Somocista Nicaraguans and then resign, turning the government over to the council. The council would then mediate between Somoza's forces and the opposition to create an interim government composed of both. Finally, this new government would prepare elections for 1981.[29]

Despite the convoluted game of governmental musical chairs outlined in this scheme, it was not significantly different from previous U.S. formulas. It still envisioned an interim government including Somocistas (though without Somoza) and it would still have left the National Guard intact. While the FSLN's strength was now obviously too great to completely freeze it out of any post-Somoza government, the goal of U.S. policy was still to minimize the FSLN's influence. Inexplicably, U.S. policymakers themselves did not seem to recognize the old wine they had rebottled in this new package. With the FSLN only weeks away from a full military victory, U.S. policymakers honestly thought they had hit upon a workable alternative for Nicaragua's future. They could hardly have been more mistaken.

Within a week, Washington's new plan had to be abandoned because nobody accepted it. Somoza, his resolve stiffened by his U.S. Congressional friends, rejected it and promised to fight until the end. The opposition Government of National Reconstruction (GRN) rejected the plan outright, arguing that it already *was* a broad-based government. And Washington could find no prominent Nicaraguans who would be willing to serve on the sort of governing council Washington sought to construct; they were all supporting the GRN.[30]

The final U.S. effort to influence the outcome of the Nicaraguan insurrection began during the second week of July, less than two weeks before the collapse of Somoza's dynasty. The universal rejection of Washington's five-point plan finally convinced U.S. officials that the GRN could no longer be ignored. Bowdler made contact with the GRN in Costa Rica, and outlined the latest U.S. proposal. Demoralized by the FSLN's military victories and the OAS call for his departure, Somoza promised he would resign whenever the U.S. told him to. In exchange for Somoza's resignation, Bowdler asked for the addition of two more moderates to the five-member Junta of the GRN, and a guarantee of the continued existence of Somoza's National Liberal Party and the National Guard.[31]

The Junta flatly rejected this proposal. It could hardly have done otherwise. Since the FSLN was on the brink of militarily defeating the National Guard, it was clear that a post-Somoza government would be formed only at the sufferance of the Sandinistas. The FSLN had appointed the GRN Junta and therefore recognized its authority, but if the Junta had acceded to U.S. demands and bargained away the Sandinista victory, it would have quickly ceased being the provisional government. The Junta refused to do more than guarantee the lives of Somocistas and Guardsmen. As the FSLN moved closer to military victory, the United States was finally moved to accept this minimal concession.[32] On July 17, 1979, Somoza went into exile in Miami; two days later, the GRN entered Managua.

In the wake of Somoza's defeat, U.S. policy toward Nicaragua shifted nearly 180 degrees, from an attitude of outright hostility toward the FSLN to an attitude of cautious cordiality towards the new revolutionary government. The change was no less stark for having been forced by circumstances, since it carried the implication that even radical social and political change in Nicaragua did not necessarily endanger the vital interests of the United States.

Nevertheless, considerable tension born of mistrust lay below the surface of this peculiar friendship. The long history of U.S. support for Somoza could not be wholly forgiven or forgotten by Nicaragua's new leaders, nor could they shake the fear and suspicion that Washington might yet concoct a counterrevolutionary scheme to rob them of their victory. In Washington, policymakers could not ignore the Marxist origins of many Sandinista leaders, even though Somoza's defeat had been engineered by a politically heterogenous multiclass coalition. There was always the possibility that the guerrillas, having won power, would shed their moderate garb, dump their middle-class allies, and steer the revolution sharply to the left, down the road of Cuban-style Marxism-Leninism.

Yet the interests of both Nicaragua and the United States lay in maintaining cordial relations. Nicaragua was in desperate need of foreign assistance to help rebuild an economy shattered by the insurrection. The United States had pledged to help in the recovery effort as part of the arrangement for Somoza's departure, but the maintenance of cordial relations was obviously a necessary condition for the fulfillment of that promise. Moreover, other international assistance—from Latin America, Western

Europe, and the international financial institutions—would tend to follow the lead of the United States. A deterioration of U.S.-Nicaraguan relations would therefore have economic ramifications far beyond the aid dollars from Washington alone.

For the United States, maintaining cordial relations with Nicaragua was a means of salvaging something from the failure to keep the FSLN out of power. Though, from Washington's perspective, the insurrection had been "lost," perhaps Nicaragua itself need not be. Policymakers in the United States set out, quite consciously, to avoid repeating the errors of 1959-1960, when U.S. hostility drove the Cuban revolution to the left and into the arms of the Soviet Union.

A cordial relationship with Nicaragua was also the linchpin of a newly emerging U.S. policy for the Central American region as a whole. Articulated in the fall of 1979, this policy acknowledged that the oligarchic social structures and authoritarian political systems of the region (i.e., in El Salvador, Guatemala, and Honduras) were anachronistic. Recognizing the inevitability of change, the United States declared itself in favor of fundamental reform brought about by peaceful, evolutionary means. [33] As in the Alliance for Progress, reform was advanced as the best antidote to revolution. For this policy to be credible, it required that the United States maintain good relations with Nicaragua, thus proving that even radical changes were tolerable to U.S. interests. The policy also required Nicaraguan restraint towards the growing political violence in El Salvador, restraint that would be unlikely in the context of U.S.-Nicaraguan hostility.

With much at stake on both sides, U.S. and Nicaraguan officials made major efforts to stay on good terms. During the first year and a half after the triumph of the Revolution, none of the worst fears of either side materialized. Nicaragua's new government held to its promised path of pluralism; the private sector was not abolished, an independent press was allowed to operate, and Somoza's henchmen were treated with more due process than they had ever shown their adversaries. For its part, the United States offered neither aid nor comfort to the Somocista exiles plotting a return to power from Honduras.

Yet serious tensions remained. Nicaragua adopted a nonaligned foreign policy, adhering closely to the positions set by the 1979 Nonaligned Summit in Havana. This brought Nicaraguan foreign policy into conflict with the U.S. on a wide variety of issues ranging from Cambodia to Afghanistan to the Middle East.[34] Where differences were sharp, Nicaraguan spokesmen showed no hesitance to denounce "U.S. imperialism" in the strongest terms. While the Carter Administration generally reacted to such blasts with equanimity, conservatives in the Congress tended to be less charitable.

An equally irritating issue for the United States was Nicaragua's close relationship with Cuba. Within a week after the triumph of the revolution, senior Nicaraguan officials traveled to Havana, where they were hailed as the guests of honor at Cuba's annual 26th of July celebration. The guerrilla leaders of the FSLN remembered that it was Cuba that had been their longest and most reliable friend in the struggle against Somoza. Nicaragua's relationship with Cuba blossomed quickly as Cuba sent several thousand teachers, hundreds of medical experts, and scores of technical advisors (including some military personnel) to help in Nicaragua's reconstruction.[35] The Cubans made Washington exceedingly nervous, as Cubans invariably seem to do.

But the most serious source of strain between the United States and Nicaragua during the first year and a half of the Revolution was the issue of U.S. economic aid. In the immediate aftermath of the insurrection, the U.S. provided $10-15 million in emergency relief to help feed and house the thousands of refugees produced by the war. This was followed in September 1979 by $8.5 million in economic reconstruction assistance reprogramming for 1979.[36]

Though the amount involved was relatively small, the reprogramming became the first occasion for debate within the United States over what our policy toward the new Nicaragua ought to be. The Administration submitted the aid request to Congress on August 1, hoping for quick approval before the summer Congressional recess, but Representative Clarence Long (D-MD) insisted upon holding hearings before his subcommittee on Foreign Operations. Thus consideration of the reprogramming was delayed until after the recess. In the ensuing weeks, a number of Nicaraguan officials complained publicly about the slow pace of the promised U.S. aid effort.

When Congress reconvened, the conservative oppositon to aiding Nicaragua was well organized. On September 6, Rep. Robert Baumann (R-MD) proposed an amendment to the Foreign Assistance Act which would have banned all aid to Nicaragua without the explicit prior approval of Congress. The motion narrowly failed 221-189.[37] In response, the Administration marshaled its resources for the reprogramming hearings. U.S. Ambassador to Nicaragua Lawrence Pezzullo, Assistant Secretary of State Viron Vaky, and Deputy Secretary Warren Christopher all travelled to Capitol Hill to testify in support of the aid. All insisted that it was essential to maintaining friendly relations with Nicaragua and to reenforce moderate elements within the new government. The reprogramming was approved, but this battle was merely the prelude.

On the drawing boards of the Carter Administration was an $80 million supplemental aid request for FY80, $75 million of which was targeted for Nicaragua. Though the proposal was ready in August, it was not sent to Congress until November 9.[38] The delay was due partly to the difficulty the Administration encountered on the August reprogramming request, and partly to debates within the Administration over whether to resume military aid to El Salvador, Guatemala, and Honduras.[39] By submitting a request that included both economic aid for Nicaragua and renewed military aid for rightist governments in the region, the Administration hoped to disarm both its conservative and liberal critics.

The final reason for the delay was purely political. With the presidential campaign underway, the Administration wanted to minimize its political vulnerability by delaying the proposal for a few months until it was sure the FSLN was not going to immediately move the revolution to the left. The events of August, September, and October were encouraging: there was no bloodbath; La Prensa resumed publication; and the FSLN continued to pursue the coalitional brand of politics that had won the revolution.

The aid package that went to Congress on November 9 included a $70 million loan on concessionary terms to help cover Nicaragua's balance of payments deficit, $5 million in technical assistance for Nicaragua and $5 million in military aid for El Salvador, Honduras, and the Carribbean. Hearings were held in December, but the package did not reach the floor of either chamber until January 1980.[40]

The authorization bill passed the Senate with only minor amendments, the most important of which required that 60 percent of the money be used to assist the Nicaraguan private sector. Though the Nicaraguans were annoyed by this restriction, it had little practical significance because most of the private sector's capital was already coming from government loans. The authorization battle in the House was much harder fought. Conservatives succeeded in attaching sixteen conditions to the bill restricting how the money could be used and adding to the circumstances under which it would be terminated. In addition to the Senate's requirement that 60 percent of the funds go to the private sector, the House specified that only U.S. goods could be purchased with the aid, that none of the money could be used for educational projects in which Cuban advisors or teachers were involved (e.g., the literacy crusade), and that 1 percent of the funds had to be used to inform the people of Nicaragua of the U.S. aid program.

Aid would be terminated if Nicaragua engaged in a consistent pattern of gross human rights violations, aided or abetted acts of violence in another country, allowed Cuban or Soviet combat troops to be stationed on its territory, violated the right of unions to organize and operate, or violated the rights of free speech and press. A number of even more restrictive amendments were defeated.[41]

On February 27, after four days of debate, the authorization bill passed the House, by only five votes, 202-197. The most persuasive lobbyists in its favor were members of the Nicaraguan private sector who argued that without U.S. aid their economic and political position in Nicaragua would be untenable.

The Nicaraguan aid package was then added to the Foreign Assistance Act of 1980, but that bill was aborted when the Senate "closed the budget window" less than a week later, halting all appropriations pending further budget resolutions by the Congress. For two and a half months, the entire process lay dead in the water; no further effort was made to bring the Senate and House versions of the authorization bill into conformity with one another, and no further action was taken on the appropriation. Most observers, including the Nicaraguan government, assumed the aid package was dead.

During those two months, several political developments made eventual passage of the Nicaraguan aid package even more unlikely. In mid-March, a delegation of Nicaraguans travelled to the USSR and Eastern Europe in search of economic aid and came away with nearly $100 million worth. In April, Violeta Chamorro and Alfonso Robelo, the two moderates, resigned from the governing junta. Though this political crisis was eventually settled by the appointment of two new moderates, Robelo's political attacks on the FSLN echoed many of the arguments advanced in the U.S. by conservative opponents of aid to Nicaragua. Finally, in May, Nicaragua acknowledged it was hosting a small contingent of Cuban military advisors.

Despite these events, the Carter Administration was not prepared to abandon the aid package. On May 19, the Senate adopted the House version of the authorization bill because the House leadership felt it could not muster the votes needed to send the bill to conference. In June, the appropriation bill was passed with the Nicaraguan aid intact when the House leadership defeated one final conservative effort to delete half the appropriation for Nicaragua.[42]

But the odyssey of the aid package was not yet over. Before the funds could be disbursed, the President was required to certify that Nicaragua was not exporting revolution to its neighbors. Three months were consumed by this process as aid opponents within the Administration itself sought to delay certification until after the November election. In September, certification was made, and the aid to Nicaragua began to flow—over a year after the aid proposal had first been drafted.[43]

The Carter Administration's policy toward the Nicaraguan revolution was more than a little schizophrenic. The strategy of containing the insurrection to keep the FSLN out of power was a dismal failure, largely because of the Administration's inability to realistically assess the balance of political forces in Nicaragua and the depth of popular animosity toward Somoza. In the critical months between January 1978 and July 1979, none of the initiatives taken by the U.S. succeeded.

Yet in the year and a half after July 19, 1979, the Administration managed to chart out a policy that was both realistic and successful, as far as it went. Once the insurrection was over and the FSLN was firmly lodged in power, Washington sought to avoid a deterioration of relations and to preserve a set of circumstances both internationally and within Nicaragua that would allow pluralism to persist. Though the Carter Administration was not as adept as it might have been in handling the $75 million aid package, the domestic political opposition to the aid was considerable. As Jimmy Carter left the presidency, U.S.-Nicaraguan relations were normal, if not friendly, and the radicalization of the revolution which Carter sought to avert had not yet happened.

Notes

[1] For the best history of U.S.-Nicaraguan relations, see Richard Millet, *Guardians of the Dynasty* (Maryknoll, N.Y.: Orbis, 1977).

[2] *New York Times*, Mar. 4, 1977.

[3] *Washington Post*, Mar. 4, 1977.

[4] *New York Times*, June 24, 1977.

[5] Ibid., Oct. 30, 1977.

[6] Ibid.

[7] For a more extended discussion of domestic political developments in Nicaragua after Chamorro's assassination, see William M. LeoGrande, "The Revolution in Nicaragua," *Foreign Affairs*, fall, 1979, 28-50; and *Nicaragua: A People's Revolution* (Washington, D.C.: EPICA, 1980).

[8] *Washington Post*, May 16, 1978.

[9] Ibid.

[10] Ibid., Aug. 1, 1978.

[11] Ibid., Aug. 29, 1978.

[12] For accounts of the September insurrection, see the *New York Times, Washington Post,* and *Wall Street Journal,* September 9-30, 1978.

[13] *Washington Post*, September 21, 1978; *Wall Street Journal*, Sept. 12, 1978.

[14] *Christian Science Monitor*, Sept. 19, 1978.

[15] *Washington Post*, Sept. 24, 1978.

[16] Ibid., Oct. 15, 1978.

[17] *Nicaragua: A People's Revolution*, pp. 46ff.

[18] *Washington Post*, Nov. 14, 1978.

[19] *New York Times*, Dec. 28, 1978.

[20] *Washington Post*, Jan. 31, and Feb. 22, 1979.

[21] *New York Times*, Jan. 24, 1979; *Washington Post*, Dec. 7. 1978.

[22] *Washington Post*, June 13, 1979.

[23] *International Bulletin*, May 21, 1979.

[24] Ibid.

[25] "Statement by Secretary of State Cyrus Vance at the OAS Meeting of Foreign Ministers," June 21, 1979 (Washington, D.C: Department of State).

[26] *Washington Post*, June 23, 1979.

[27] Ibid., June 26, 1979: *New York Times*, June 22 and 23, 1979.

[28] Ibid., June 24, 1979: *Nicaragua: A People's Revolution*, pp. 61-63.

[29] *Washington Post*, June 28, 1979.

[30] Ibid., July 2, 1979.

[31] Ibid., July 6 and July 7, 1979.

[32] *New York Times*, July 16, 1979.

[33] For a full explication of this policy, see "Statement by Assistant Secretary of State Viron P. Vaky before the Subcommittee on Inter-American Affairs, U.S. House of Representatives," (Washington, D.C.: Department of State), Sept. 11, 1979.

[34] *Nicaragua: A People's Revolution*, pp. 96-99.

[35] Both Nicaraguan and U.S. sources confirm the nature of Cuban aid to Nicaragua.

[36] "Statement by Deputy Secretary of State Warren Christopher before the Subcommittee on Foreign Operations, U.S. House of Representatives, Sept. 11, 1979," (Washington, D.C.: Department of State).

[37] *Congressional Record*, Sept. 6, 1979, H7378-7387.

[38] *Hearings Before the Committee on Foreign Relations*, U.S. Senate, December 6 and 7, 1979.

[39] *Washington Post*, Aug. 2, 1979.

[40] *Hearings*, op. cit.

[41] *Congressional Record*, Feb. 27, 1980, H2009-H2020.

[42] *Washington Post*, May 20, 1980.

[43] *New York Times*, Sept. 13, 1980.

PART III
INITIAL IMPRESSIONS

In an emotional sense, an authentic revolution is a bit like a hurricane. The first phase, the insurrection, mounts in intensity to its successful climax. With the victory comes a tremendous euphoria and a sense of well-being—the calm, if you will, of the eye of the hurricane. Inevitably, this mood soon gives way to growing tension and a renewed sense of struggle as the revolutionaries embark on the tremendous task of implementing their redistributive social and economic policies while, at the same time, guarding against counterrevolution. The purpose of the single chapter in this part is simply to convey the sensations—sights, sounds, emotions—of a very special historical moment, the period immediately after the rebel victory.

Chapter 4

Images of the
Nicaraguan Revolution

THOMAS W. WALKER

The overthrow of the Somoza dictatorship and the victory of the Sandinist Front of National Liberation (FSLN) on July 19 was probably the most significant political event to have occurred in Latin America in at least twenty years. It dramatically demonstrated once again the simple fact that no military establishment—no matter how well trained and equipped—can stand up indefinitely against a determined guerrilla operation backed by a united civilian population. Further, it marked the coming to power of the first social revolutionary government in Latin America since the ascent of Fidel Castro in Cuba on January 1, 1959.

For these reasons, when I heard the news, I decided I had to travel to Nicaragua. Within a day I was on my way to Tegucigalpa, Honduras (commercial air service to Nicaragua had been discontinued). There, on Saturday, the 21st, I looked into ways of getting to Managua. What I found was not heartening. The Nicaraguan embassy was still in a state of interregnum—so I could not get a visa. Further, though there was some possibility I could catch a ride to Managua on a Red Cross mercy flight, I would have had to have waited at least until Monday to do so. Impatient to arrive as quickly as possible, I finally decided to travel to the border by land, to cross without a visa, and to make my way to Managua by whatever means possible. The following are my impressions as recorded during the ensuing five days:

July 22. The ride from Tegucigalpa to the border at El Paraiso-Las Manos takes three hours. We stop for breakfast at a hotel near the border. The parking lot is loaded with luxury cars bearing Nicaraguan license plates. The hotel, however, is not particularly crowded. Somocistas fleeing Nicaragua apparently took out several cars apiece and then left some of them in storage before heading further north into exile. At the border itself, on the Honduran side, there are a number of large logging trucks. The Somoza regime—in return for a cut of the action—had been allowing foreign firms to indiscriminately rape the pine forests of northern Nicaragua.

At the border I ask various people milling around on the Honduran side whether and how one can get to Managua. No one seems to be sure. Holdout National Guard troops apparently slaughtered a number of people near Sébaco yesterday. They are still being "mopped up." The road south of Estelí may not yet be open.

I learn that the Honduran authorities are not letting people who have entered Nicaragua return to Honduras. Therefore, I get special permission from the Hondurans to cross the border to talk with the FSLN before formally passing Honduran customs. Ahead, the red and black Sandinista flag waves from the Nicaraguan customs building. FSLN guerrillas are shaking hands and being hugged and congratulated by returning Nicaraguans. There are several FSLN checkpoints in the hundred yards of dirt road I have to walk before I arrive at the Nicaraguan customs office. When I enter that building, I talk with the FSLN commander who is dressed in battle fatigues and has hand grenades strapped to his chest, explain who I am, and ask if I may have permission to travel to Managua. "Yes, of course." He responds. "This is now a free land." I ask if the road is open to Managua. He does not know. But at least I can get to Estelí today.

I decide to start my trip to Managua—even if I have to spend the night in bombed-out Estelí. After passing through Honduran customs I return to Nicaraguan territory. A woman guerrilla fighter records my vital statistics, and then a male *comandante* stamps my passport, writes "FSLN" across the stamp, and adds the codeword "Plomo" below. I ask where I can get transportation and am directed by the FSLN to a truck with grip ropes tied between the racks. I ask the driver's aide what they are charging and am told, "Nothing, this is a new Nicaragua." There is an FSLN flag on the rear-view mirror of the driver's door. The driver has an FSLN bandana. Everyone is in a holiday mood. There is a tremendous spirit of cooperation. I ask one "compa" (an FSLN term of address short for *compañero*) if I can take photos of them. "Of course." They pose.

Off we go in the back of the truck. The wind blows in our faces. Immense excitement, joy! Most of the people on the truck are returning to homes in Ocotal, Condega, and Estelí. Their joy is mixed with anxiety about homes and loved ones. Estelí has been bombed into rubble. One middle-aged worker is going to Condega to look for a son (FSLN) from whom he had not heard in over a month. The people bring with them simple tables, beds, and other furniture which they had taken to Honduras as refugees.

Most of the houses along the roadside display either white or red and black flags. We speed past burned-out trucks, buses, jeeps and cars and slow down to cross partially-filled trenches across the road. There are several FSLN checkpoints.

We arrive at Ocotal and pass a former Guard outpost with "compas" sitting in front. The people burst into cheers when they see the red and black flag flying above it. "Fogatas," or tire fires, smolder in the streets. Normally built by townsfolk to illuminate attacking guardsmen, these were probably lit last night in celebration. FSLN troops and civilians mill about in a festive mood. There are many well-armed and apparently battle-hardened female "compas." I see my first *adoquín* barricades (*adoquines* are concrete paving blocks made, ironically, in a Somoza-owned factory). The city is not badly damaged.

We leave for Estelí. Again there are various FSLN checkpoints. At one, in Condega, a female "compa" finds some problem with the way my passport was stamped in Las Manos. I stay to explain while my truck goes on. Eventually, Comandante "Douglas" accepts my story and makes a small notation in my passport. The female "compa" will arrange my transportation. The ground is littered with a variety of cartridge cases. There are sandbagged bunkers nearby. I take pictures of the "compas." They obviously enjoy posing. I catch a ride south with a heavily-loaded microbus. There are many FSLN scarves among the occupants. Again, a holiday spirit.

We arrive at Estelí. Most buildings are bombed-out shells. There is the smell of rotten flesh in some sectors and everywhere the acrid odor of burnt buildings, rubber, plastic. The "compas" direct me to the Comando Central where I must apply for a safe-conduct pass to travel to Managua. I am given a lift in the back of a Datsun pickup driven by "compas." We wind past barricades and partially-filled trenches.

At the comando there is a lengthy debate between "compa" officers as to whether anyone should be given a pass. Renegade Guardsmen ("perros," or "dogs," as they call them) are still in the area. Seeing my camera and perhaps thinking that I am a reporter, a high-ranking "compa" insists that I be given a pass. It is written laboriously on an old typewriter. Although care is taken to include the correct sequence of special revolutionary passwords, the date, place and stamp are omitted. Several other people get passes. Most do not.

The next step is to get transportation. I team up with a Managua-bound couple whom I had befriended by giving toilet paper to the woman who is suffering from a bad case of the "runs." We walk to the main highway and get a ride in the back of another Datsun truck. A ten-year-old boy whom the couple had been helping accompanies us. Shortly after we get started, it begins to rain and we stop at a peasant house for shelter. We converse with the inhabitants, who are worried about renegade Guardsmen who, as they run north for the border, have been preying on peasants.

We are off again. There is the smell of rotting flesh—often near the wrecked vehicles or trenches. The man comments on the distinctive odor of rotting human flesh. Smells the same to me as any rotting creature.

We pass various checkpoints. The "compas" are vigilant and heavily armed but, at the same time, friendly and jubilant. At one point I take a photo of a group with a tripod 30-calibre machine gun. Then, with my camera they take a photo of me holding the gun with "compas" at either side. Apparently they had done this with locals several times before. They obviously get a kick out of it. So do I.

Eventually, we arrive at a checkpoint where cars going north are being held up. "The road is not yet safe." The piece we had just come through! The truck speeds on to Managua, an hour away. We pass through flat land where some mechanized planting is taking place.

The boy with us says he wants to go directly to his home in the "Las Américas" neighborhood. The woman explains, when we stop to buy onions and he is out of earshot, that she has been trying to persuade him to go first to an aunt's house in another part of town. Las Américas was devastated by Somoza's airforce. Many of its residents were slaughtered. The boy brags about his part in some of the earlier fighting. He is full of joy—unaware of what may await him.

We enter Managua through the industrial zone. Most factories lie in ruins—practically all destroyed by Somoza as revenge for the businessmen's strikes. Again, the sharp odor of burned machinery, rubber, chemicals, and so on. We pass the ruins of the opposition newspaper, la Prensa. Another of Somoza's revenges, this was done by tank and rocket fire at close range rather than by air attacks as with the other buildings. On the front wall of the la Prensa ruins is scribbled "Pedro Joaquín Chamorro is present."

The truck leaves us at the Somoza Stadium. The word "Somoza" is now gone. So, too, the statue of Somoza García mounted on a horse. "Compas" standing duty on the other side of the street accept some bananas from the couple and joke about the statue of the "two horses," which had been dragged by jubilant crowds through the streets of Managua. The "compas" at the checkpoint arranged rides for each of us with passing vehicles to our destinations. (The FSLN is coordinating this type of car-pooling throughout the country.) I get a ride in the cab of a bus-truck.

The night is dark. The truck politely dims its lights as it passes check-points. However, at one point, because of the dimmed lights, we almost run over a machine-gun toting "compa." The truck comes to a halt twenty yards further on and backs up to receive a mild warning. The driver comments later that the National Guard would have opened fire on us for such an infraction.

Due to an error in the directions I give them, the people in the truck leave me about a kilometer beyond where I should have gotten off. It is pitch dark as I walk down the road. I hear voices. Four men approach me. "Can we help you?" What choice do I have? "Yes." I explain. "Don't worry," they say, "This is a New Nicaragua. We'll take you there." At the next checkpoint, "compas" insist on halting a ride for me. An engineer who studied in Ohio takes me to my planned destination, an upper-middle-class home in the outskirts of Managua. Several young professionals, including my would-be host, are sitting around a table partaking sparingly of the last available bottle of whiskey. (Liquor is a scarce commodity and drinking is now frowned upon.) I am welcomed and my suitcases taken into the house, but soon one of the other men suggests that it would be best for me to stay in his home. His neighborhood still has water whereas this one does not. It is embarrassingly obvious that I need a bath.

July 23: I go with my host to an office where people planning the new Social Security laws are already at work. The project they decide to tackle first is the distribution of international food aid. One young woman expresses her opinion that the revolutionary Civil Defense Committees (CDCs) should be involved as much as possible at the grass-roots level. Another young professional suggests that existing church relief organizations be employed to distribute supplies nationally and regionally.

My host's driver takes me on a tour around the city. First we go to the entrance of Somoza's "Bunker." Jubilant "compas" on foot and in command cars are here to see the headquarters of their former enemy. Many are from the southern front, fresh from bloody trench combat around the city of Rivas.

Apparently moans and cries have been heard coming from underground vents around the "Bunker." Approximately forty prisoners were discovered yesterday in underground cells. There is fear that many still may be trapped. The main entrance to the dungeons has not yet been found.

We drive through poor neighborhoods. The barricades are being dismantled and the paving blocks laid down once again by volunteer committees. (There is the sound of automatic gunfire as I write this. My host has paving blocks stacked in his house behind the windows for protection.) We arrive at one barricade where digging is going on. I ask what is happening and am told that a mass grave of eighteen to twenty young people killed by the Guard is being dug up. Again, the smell of rotting flesh. A lone brownish-green finger protrudes through the earth and a large white carrion worm twists in the sandy soil. Workers now place paving blocks over the cap of soil covering the bodies, "so the dogs won't eat them." The final disinterment will not take place until tomorrow when equipment for identification will be available. An unexploded U.S.-made rocket lies half-buried nearby with a warning sign beside it and a circle of marker rocks around it.

Further on in a median strip we see a blue helmet and a boot hanging from a sign which reads "Here is a mercenary dog." Could this be the grave of one of the Guatemalan or Salvadorian troops who were reported to have been helping Somoza? Whoever it is, it is the loneliest and most unloved grave I have ever seen.

There are other graves beside the roadside with simple crosses and lettering and fresh flowers. *Los muchachos,* the nameless youth of Nicaragua, the country's "unknown soldiers." In the gutters everywhere there are car-

tridge cases from FAL, M-1, M-16, Uzi and Galil automatic weapons—
spent in great numbers like the lives of the fallen *muchachos*.

In a garbage dump in a poor neighborhood, we find the torso of the
statue of Luís Somoza. Scrawled across it in spray paint are the words "the
dead pigs." We find part of the horse from the statue of Somoza García next
to a garbage dump in another neighborhood. One bronze testicle has been
hacked off.

The driver takes me to the home of some friends. They show me the
schrapnel-pocked room where a National Guard rocket exploded killing
two of their sons, aged 10 and 13. The neighbor wants me to see the tail-fins
of these U.S.-made rockets. I am ushered into the back yard where I view
the grave. (The Guard would not let the dead be buried in cemeteries.) I am
shown photos of the boys. One reminds me of one of my sons. I cannot find
words. I hug them. They pose for a photo with the snapshot of their boys
and a Sandinista flag.

Someone else invites me into another house to see another patio grave.
A young man of 21, shot by Somoza's paramilitary forces. The mother
rages about the Guard, then cries and becomes incoherent. I try to console
her. Again the words fail me, I feel so clumsy, so ashamed of my government.

We come across yet another rustic grave. This time, in a field. There
are two crossed sticks with a Sandinista bandana flying from the top. There
is no identifying inscription, but the people nearby point to where the
young man had lived. The Guard had machine-gunned him as he ran and
then given him the *coup de grace* at short range. Three shots in the side of
the head. "Blew his ear away," comments a neighbor graphically.

In another place there is a big FSLN flag stretched in front of a picket
fence. A neatly inscribed cross is in front of it. The young man was killed
five days ago while buying a snowcone with two buddies at an ice cream
shop. The Guard had sprayed the three with an Israeli assault gun. The
father stands in front of the flag as I take the picture.

Another grave, this time in front of an auto mechanic's shop. Sprays of
flowers and mimosa leaves protrude from the soft earth. The victim was the
wife of the mechanic, who talks to me without expression as he works on a
cracked motor.

We are invited here and there. I look like a newspaper man, with my
camera. They want me to know. They want it recorded. They ask where I
am from. I tell them and feel ashamed.

There is often the sound of gunfire. Everyone is nervous. At one point I
hear the rattle of many automatic weapons nearby. "Don't worry. The
'compas' are firing salvos at a burial." There are checkpoints everywhere.
Renegade Guardsmen are still being mopped up. As we return this evening
to the house where I am staying 14 kilometers out of town, the "compas"
are out in force in one sector. We are stopped by one group, checked and

told to drive very slowly past the rest—Guardsmen had sped by firing a short while before. Always the question: "Why do they keep on killing?"

July 24. Bands of simple thieves are still operating in urban and rural areas alike. Many are heavily armed with automatic weapons abandoned by the Guard. Last night there was an intruder in the back patio of the house where I am staying. Not wanting to get shot by mistake by my host, I lay quietly in bed for about an hour after the first sounds until my host came downstairs and asked me to join him, pistol in hand, to patrol the inside of the house. The intruder(s) had apparently left.

Renegade Guard sniper and sapper units are still causing problems. Last night there was a firefight in the elite Las Palmas neighborhood. Five "guarditas," as the "compas" like to call them condescendingly, were killed. As one "compa" commented philosophically, "I guess they simply want to die."

Some people are showing signs of considerable stress. This morning I telephone to check on the sister of a Nicaraguan friend I had visited with in Honduras. She is obviously distraught. Yesterday, a spent round from one of the funeral salvos had struck her daughter's foot. Two weeks previously, her brother, my friend, had been shot in the neck by an intruder. And, now, the firefight last night in la Palmas (her neighborhood).

People are worried about the economic situation. Nicaraguan industry and commerce are in ruins. Somoza and his associates personally looted the national treasury and banking system before leaving. There is nothing with which to pay anyone and little to buy if a person had money. People hope that international relief will come soon. But, when will the U.S. and other countries normalize relations?

I talk with three of the *grandes dames* of the elite Chamorro family. They are worried about the future. Will the revolution go farther left? They are impressed nevertheless by the discipline and integrity of the FSLN troops. One mentions the fact that when she recently visited a coastal town where there had been a seafood processing industry she noticed freezers and other equipment sitting in the streets in front of the townspeople's homes. Upon inquiry, she was told that these were items that had been looted from a Somocista plant. The townsfolk had removed them from their homes voluntarily when FSLN leaders explained that the plant was now national property and that their livelihood would depend on getting it back in working order. An FSLN truck was to come by soon and collect the looted equipment.

The Chamorro ladies also comment that so far there has been little spirit of vengeance in the post-Somoza period. For instance, a guerrilla mass for a fallen "compa" held yesterday in one of the city's main churches had been very orderly. A tone of forgiveness had been struck when the mother of the deceased called on those gathered to be compassionate in victory.

The Catholic Church is playing a major role in this revolution. One of the prominent figures in the FSLN is the rebel priest, Father Ernesto Cardenal, who now serves as Minister of Culture. Father Miguel d'Escoto, a Maryknoll priest, is the Minister of Foreign Relations. I notice that many of the guerrillas from all three FSLN factions wear Catholic medallions or crosses.

There is much talk about the popular organizations, Civil Defense Committees (CDCs) and the Popular Militia. The CDCs are grass-root revolutionary organizations which were formed in towns and neighborhoods during the war to root out Somoza spys. They now work to maintain order and to help in reconstruction and relief activities. The popular militias, formed to combat Somoza, worry the privileged sectors, who would like to see them disarmed. The latter say they are not disciplined. However, all of the "compas" I have seen—regular FSLN or militia—seem remarkably disciplined, conscientious and well-motivated.

At the Intercontinental Hotel, journalists from all over the world converse and lounge in comfort. Some interview armed "compas." Magazines for sale date from June 4, June 7, and so on. *Soldier of Fortune* has a prominent position in the magazine rack.

I talk with one "compa" near the Bunker. He tells me he fought in the south with the Benjamín Zeledon Batallion. He carries a captured Israeli Galil assault gun. The ammunition is similar to that of the M-16, the bullet about the same size. He comments that the FSLN used Belgian FAL automatic weapons more than anything else. The cartridge of the FAL is similar to that of the traditional M-1, long and with a large bullet. The Guard, he says, learned to fear the sound of the FAL.

At night I watch television. The only station on the air so far is operated by the FSLN. The technical quality of the programming is very amateurish, but the content is extremely interesting. This evening there is a long rerun of the swearing-in ceremonies and the celebration and speeches at the National Palace. The Junta, the Cabinet, and the FSLN political and military leadership are introduced to the huge crowd. The most prolonged applause is for Edén Pastora, the hero of the Palace assault of August 1978.

July 25. The U.S. recognized the Junta yesterday. A wise move. Failure to bolster the economy or any attempt to pressure the current moderate government in a rightward direction would undoubtedly trigger a *coup* to the left—an outcome that the politicians and planners in Washington would like to avoid.

Before breakfast, I tune in to Radio Sandino. Programming consists of a mix of incredibly beautiful Nicaraguan revolutionary music, personal messages (X, who fought on the Southern Front, wishes to inform his family in Y town that he is alive and well and will return home soon), and revolutionary bulletins. Among the last is a request by the Minister of Culture that troops occupying confiscated Somocista residences protect the paintings, precolumbian statuary and other objects of art housed in such buildings in order that they may be collected later for a future national museum. There is also an announcement that anyone caught in the act of looting and committing common crimes will receive stiff penalties and that snipers and other perpetuators of the continuing anti-revolutionary violence will immediately face the firing squad ("pasar por las armas.")

I spend most of the day with a friend, Carlos Chamorro Coronel, a radio-newspaper journalist. In the morning he drives me around the city visiting hotels and offices, hoping to introduce me to prominent figures in the government. Given the fact that they have much more important things to do than to talk to me, I am almost relieved that we run into only one such person, Father Ernesto Cardenal. The rebel priest recognizes my name from my writings about Nicaragua and the FSLN. He gives me a warm greeting, I learn later that there was an attempt on his life just the night before.

We have lunch at Carlos's brother's house. Beforehand we have several drinks—something very unusual in Nicaragua now. A Chilean-born brother-in-law joins us. He wears a small red and black star on his cap, an indication that he is an officer in the FSLN. Later that day I see him in full uniform, armed with an automatic weapon.

There are nine brothers and sisters in this branch of the Chamorro family (distantly related to Pedro Joaquín Chamorro). Some were actively involved in the FSLN and will have important positions in the new government and society. Others of a less revolutionary stripe have already fled Nicaragua to live in exile in Miami and elsewhere. This is a time of hard decisions for the former aristocracy.

At lunch one of the women gives me a Sandinista bandana which she claims was one of a thousand found in Somoza's Bunker. Apparently Somoza's troops kept a supply handy to put on the bodies of the civilians they executed in order to demonstrate that their victims were combatants. As we enjoy our coffee after the meal, one of the Chamorro children plays war in the lovely patio out back. He wears a U.S.-made National Guard helmet taken as a trophy after the surrender on July 19th.

Later Carlos and I go to the home of another well-to-do family. The wife, the mother of a large brood of children, is a lovely woman who is deeply involved in progressive church activities. She is the self-appointed surrogate mother of several Maryknoll nuns who work in the poor neighborhoods of Managua. But the Revolution poses hard questions and dilemmas for her family, too. As we sit in their beautiful home sipping fruit juice served to us by a maid, a young man asks me with great intensity what I, as a political scientist, think the revolution will mean for their class. It is not an easy question, but there is no use mincing words. The power, I respond, is obviously now in the hands of the common people. It is they who have the guns. If the middle and upper class are to salvage anything from the situation, they must help make the revolution. Inevitably this will mean personal sacrifice.

Still later we visit a poor neighborhood which now bears the name "Barrio Sandino" (formerly "Open Tres"). The people there are very happy and friendly. I take photos of the FSLN Comando. I am given an FSLN bandana. Unlike the phony one from Somoza's Bunker with its carefully sewn hems and exact matching of threads, this one was obviously put together quickly on a home sewing machine.

While at Barrio Sandino, I witness the arrival of a huge truck loaded with corn, rice, oats, and so on from the U.S. I am impressed at the speed with which relief aid has reached the needy. Had Somoza still been in power, this food would probably have been stolen and sold by the National Guard as it was after the 1972 earthquake.

This evening I watch TV coverage of an important government press conference. The topics addressed range from the nationalization of the country's banking system and the repayment of the Nicaraguan foreign debt to the future of foreign investment, the character of agrarian reform, and the new government's current status in the world community. Government officials are open and frank in responding to questions: Given the chaotic state in which Somoza left the Nicaraguan banking system, the new government had no choice but to nationalize. Foreign debt will be respected except for $5 million dollars owed Israel and Argentina for the purchase of arms and ammunition by the Somoza government during the last year. Foreign investment will be regulated in the interest of the nation. Agrarian reform "for a considerable period of time" will work exclusively with lands formerly owned by Somoza and his associates. Nicaragua seeks amicable relations with all nations and is rapidly receiving formal recognition from most countries.

July 26. Today I return to Honduras. Carlos Chamorro takes me to the bus-stop. I get on a crowded bus for Estelí and stand in the isle most of the way. Periodically "compas" at checkpoints ask all men to get out and be examined. They are trying to stop renegade Guardsmen fleeing north. At the first checkpoint a young man from our bus is detained—he is wearing Guard boots. At another, we men are asked to face a low wall as we are examined from behind. In front of us a shabby group of National Guard prisoners stare blankly at us through the bars in the windows of a school now serving as a jail. I am tempted to take a photo, but then, feeling sorry for them, I decide not to. One Guardsman sees a familiar face in our group and begs that individual to carry word of his whereabouts to his family. Further on, at another checkpoint, a group of "compas" brag that they just caught a "dog" going north.

One wonders what will happen to these people. So far there has been only one execution, that of the infamous "Macho Negro," a man himself responsible for many summary executions. The FSLN has exhibited amazing compassion in its hour of victory—even though many feel that some Guardsmen richly deserve the firing squad or worse.

From Estelí onward I travel by "ride" (free lifts). My first "ride" is a Toyota going to Condega. The truckbed is crammed with people returning to their homes in the north. One is a "compa" with a schrapnel wound in his hand. A Catholic medallion hangs from his neck. He says he fought in Matagalpa, Estelí, and, later, on the Southern Front. He is rubber-legged and obviously very tired. After a while, the driver's aide offers him a seat in the cab.

Two more "compas" get on, one in the cab and one in the truckbed. The latter says he fought with the Benjamín Zeledón battalion on the Southern Front. He took part in the bloody battle for Rivas. "We lost many compas," he comments without expression.

There is a foul smell of rotting flesh. I ask what it was. Someone comments nonchalantly, "A Guardsman—killed three days ago." It seems the Nicaraguans are in no hurry to bury dead Guardsmen. "He is growing a nice paunch," he adds with a laugh.

We arrive at Condega. I sit under the intense midday sun at a crossroad waiting for another ride. Two girls in their late teens join me. They too need a ride to Las Manos. They tell me they graduated from high school a year ago in the midst of the war. Their family farm served as a base for more than 200 FSLN troops. The girls themselves had helped in procuring foodstuffs and preparing meals for the troops.

Some "compas" in a Datsun pick us up and we head north again toward the border. The girls continue talking about the war. Everyone, they say, lost family members. "But, that doesn't matter," adds one. "The Revolution triumphed. I feel as if I was just born—like a little baby with a whole life ahead of me." The "compas" let us off at another checkpoint. Other "compas" stop a jeep and ask the driver if he can take us. "Of course," comes the habitual answer, and we hop in the back.

Soon we are at Las Manos. I enter the customs office and am passed through. A female "compa" labors with the obviously unfamiliar keys of an old manual typewriter to record my vital statistics. Is my surname Woodley? (In Spanish the surname is the middle name.) "No, Walker." The passport is stamped and I walk the 100 yards to the Honduran border. I feel sad to leave. What a magnificent, proud people!

PART IV

POWER AND INTERESTS IN THE NEW NICARAGUA

Authentic revolution implies a significant restructuring of the social configuration of political power. A government responding to the organized demands and interests of the formerly dispossessed majority replaces one based in the support of a privileged and influential minority. In Nicaragua, the foundations for a massive reordering of power relationships were laid even before the Liberation. As the chapters in this part demonstrate, Church groups, the women's movement, and the FSLN all worked with considerable effectiveness in promoting mass mobilization against the dictatorship.

After the Liberation, these "mass" or "popular organizations" reconstituted themselves as explicitly Sandinist groupings. The common people of Nicaragua—mobilized by the hundreds of thousands into these organizations—together with the new politically and socially conscious Sandinist army, police, and militia served to guarantee the direction of the Revolution. The political parties and interest organizations representing the old privileged minority were now greatly diminished, if not totally eclipsed in political power.

Significantly, however, the revolutionaries also showed a very real interest in encouraging some degree of pluralism in the political system. While the FSLN Directorate, based in the mass organizations and the new revolutionary military institutions, would set the direction of the government, a remarkable effort would also be made to preserve relative freedom of expression and real input from groups which were not explicitly Sandinist. The chapters on the Church and the mass media illustrate not only this concern with pluralism but also the practical dilemmas and contradictions which arose from it.

Chapter 5

The Sandinist
Mass Organizations

LUIS SERRA

The purpose of this chapter is to describe the functions of the mass organizations (OMs) and to analyse their articulation with other elements of power. We will attempt objectively to present not only the principal successes of these organizations in their first year, but also related problems and limitations and the solutions that were being implemented to overcome them. When we speak of the mass organizations we refer to the Sandinist Defense Committees (CDS), The Sandinist Workers' Central (CST), The Association of Rural Workers (ATC), The Luisa Amada Espinosa Association of Nicaraguan Women (AMNLAE), The July 19th Sandinist Youth (JS-19), and The Sandinist Children's Association (ANS).

The General Characteristics of the Mass Organizations

The OMs were autonomous institutions which drew together diverse social sectors in order to defend and deepen the process of revolutionary transformation and to channel their demands to the government. They were conceived as basic pillars of popular revolutionary power, the centerpieces of Sandinist democracy. Through them, the people had the power to express their aspirations, to learn about and discuss government programs, to contribute to the solution of immediate problems, to elect their representatives and defend the advances made since the Liberation.

The mass organizations were described as "the form in which the elements of one social sector come together to defend their interests."[1] Comandante Carlos Nuñez Tellez, then codirector of the FSLN's Secretariat of Mass Organizations, once said that these groupings "are guided by two basic principles. In the first place, . . . they should guard and work to fortify the political goals of the Revolution, and in the second place, [they should] be true instruments for the expression, channeling, and reception of the most urgent demands of the masses."[2]

These organizations were independent of the government on the organizational and financial, as well as political planes. Membership was open to any person of the social sector which a given organization represented. For instance, any woman could join AMNLAE; any peasant, the ATC; and any resident, his local CDS block organization. Although all OMs recognized the FSLN as their legitimate vanguard, it would have been a mistake to have seen them as simple appendages of the Front. The relationship was dialectic. As CST Secretary General Iván García put it, "To follow the direction of the FSLN does not mean that the Front imposes its ideas on the workers in an authoritarian way. To the contrary, the FSLN enriches its political understanding and consolidates its position as vanguard by coming to understand the interests of workers."[3]

Sandinist Popular Democracy

The mass organizations were key elements of the new political system. Unlike the "developed" capitalist countries which traditionally defined "democracy" as a game of various political parties and periodic elections, the Sandinistas saw democracy as "the intervention of the masses in all aspects of social life."[4] The OMs were formed precisely to assure an effective participation of the people in all matters that affected them, be they in the neighborhood, the workplace, or the school. The mass organizations became real schools of democracy with all the attempts and failures that accompany the early learning process. The leaders of the Revolution knew that democracy could not be created by decree, certainly not in a country steeped in a long tradition of corrupt dictatorship. It would have to be developed by practice and through reflection on that experience. Such was the task that the OMs faced.

Soon after the Liberation, the opposition parties, which represented the class interests of a privileged minority of the population, began clamoring for general elections. Though they would have had no chance of winning an election in their own right, they undoubtedly sensed that the immediate calling of elections might have caused the Revolution to degenerate into a sort of directionless populism (a la Mexico in the 1920s and 1930s and Bolivia in the 1950s) which they would have had a greater chance to manipulate. At any rate, the response of the FSLN and the Government of National Reconstruction was that elections would take place, but not until 1985, since it was much more urgent to reconstruct the country and to begin to educate and improve the standard of living of the people.[5]

In fact, the Sandinist Revolution was making giant steps toward establishing the solid basis of an original form of democracy appropriate to Nicaragua's historic circumstances. In the mass organizations, the people were developing their capacity to govern themselves through their own elected representatives. The legitimacy and democratic character of the OMs was underscored by the country's Catholic hierarchy when it noted that "the conscious and active participation of the Nicaraguan majority in the revolutionary process that we are living appears to us [to be] very necessary; it should emerge through the organisms of direct popular democracy that now exist and are being created."[6]

The Objectives of the Mass Organizations

The mass organizations had various general objectives. Among these were (1) to promote the active, conscious, and organized participation of diverse social sectors in the solution of collective problems; (2) to defend the Revolution; (3) to express popular demands and desires and to be a forum for information about, and discussion of, the directions of the government and the FSLN; (4) to elevate the standard of living of the people in the educational, cultural, and political, as well as the material, senses; (5) to unify forces in erradicating the unjust social, economic, and ideological structures inherited from *Somocismo;* (6) to support the process of economic reactivation; and (7) to help forge the New Sandinist Man. Some of these objectives deserve closer examination:

The felt need to defend the Revolution was by no means a matter of frivolous paranoia. The new system had clear and dangerous enemies. In the first place, since this was a real social revolution aimed at improving the standard of living of the impoverished majority, significant sacrifices were being asked of the former middle and upper classes. Inevitably, these groups, totaling less than 20 percent of the population, resented the Revolution and increasingly came to engage in counterrevolutionary activities. Then, too, the Sandinistas were worried about the continuing and somewhat mysterious presence of large encampments of exiled National Guard troops in Honduras. Finally, the revolutionaries were aware that their new system was by no means popular in some circles in the United States. It was no secret that, although the Carter Administration had attempted to maintain formally correct and ostensibly friendly relations with the new government, there was a strong countervailing feeling in the CIA, the Pentagon and the National Security Council that the Sandinist Revolution was an unacceptable and dangerous extension of Soviet-Cuban influence into Central America. In January of 1980, an article by former CIA agent, Philip Agee, titled "The Plan of the CIA in Nicaragua" had appeared in translation in the conservative daily, *La Prensa.* In that essay, drawing on the past behavior of the CIA in other Latin American and third world countries, Agee speculated in detail on the various destabilizing and counterrevolutionary activities in which he felt the CIA would probably engage in Nicaragua.[7]

Whoever was responsible, there certainly *were* a variety of counterrevolutionary activities in Nicaragua in 1980. These included armed attacks by units of the former National Guard and the right-wing "Democratic Armed Forces;" at least two major plots to kill the leaders of the FSLN; an international propaganda campaign apparently aimed at demonstrating that the Government of National Reconstruction was totalitarian, atheistic, and a puppet of Cuban and Soviet communism;[8] and considerable footdragging by some elements of the private sector in regard to the government's program to reactivate the economy.

Under these circumstances, it was not surprising that the mass organizations would be asked to defend the Revolution. They did so not only by guarding against counter-revolutionary activity but also by disseminating information aimed at quieting false rumors, and by actively supporting the government's programs for economic recovery.

A second very important purpose of the mass organizations was to help in improving the standard of living of the people. Given the government's pressing financial problems, the voluntary participation of the OMs in the Revolution's social programs was of crucial importance. The OMs helped enforce price controls on basic necessities; they cooperated in the establishment of basic supplies centers (CAP); they were involved in nutritional, hygiene, and health projects; they helped to promote mass participation in sport through the creation of Voluntary Sports Committees; they cooperated with the Ministry of Culture in stimulating national and popular cultural and artistic activities; they provided crucial assistance in the National Literacy Crusade of 1980; and they participated in public programs aimed at controlling such hangovers of the old regime as alcoholism, drug addiction, prostitution, delinquency, caudillismo, and corruption. An important target of the mass organizations was "bureaucratism" in the form of unnecessary positions, delays in paperwork, unresponsiveness, administrative irresponsibility, and the abuse of public office.[9] At the same time, the OMs were concerned with creating a "New Man" steeped in Sandinist and Christian values: solidarity, fraternity, altruism, humility, and an unconditional committment to work to improve the condition of the oppressed.[10]

Yet another important purpose of the mass organizations was to facilitate effective popular political participation. The ways in which this was being accomplished were numerous and diverse. In the first place, the political weight of the OMs was demonstrated by their representation in the national legislative body, The Council of State, created in May 1980. Designed by the FSLN to promote national unity among the diverse sectors who claimed to be committed to National reconstruction, the Council provided functional representation for 29 different organizations. Of these, 5 mass organizations were allotted 17 out of the total 47 seats: 9 for the CDS's, 3 for the ATC, 3 for the CST, 1 for the AMNLAE and 1 for the JS-19. In this way, the demands of the people could reach the new national legislative body, and vice versa: bills being considered by the Council could be taken by the OMs to the people to be discussed.

Another way of encouraging popular participation through the OMs was the creation of Programatic Coordinating Commissions (CPCs). These commissions, which existed at the national as well as departmental levels, included representatives of the mass organizations as well as functionaries of the various ministries of the government. There were commissions dealing with finance; agricultural production; the state sector; industrial production; basic foods, consumption and prices; foreign trade; infrastructure and projects; the work force and wages; education and culture; planning and information; and so on. In this way, then, the OMs were being involved in the day-to-day planning of public policy.

In the immediate postwar period, the OMs also helped in the creation of municipal and departmental *juntas*, or governments. Together with the FSLN, they assisted in the selection of candidates from among the leading figures in the local struggle against the dictatorship. Government officials were then elected by the citizenry in public assemblies, where the vote was by show of hands. In most cases, the new local governments held office for a trial period until the National Governing Junta came to preside over a formal election and swearing-in. But the function of the OMs did not stop at that point, for, as Comandante Daniel Ortega remarked at one such occasion, ". . . after the election, you should be vigilant that your representatives fulfill their functions in an honorable and efficient manner, you should make necessary suggestions and constructive criticism, and you should cooperate with the Junta in the solution of community problems."[11]

Though mentioned above, the participation of the mass organizations in the 1980 Literacy Crusade deserves a more detailed treatment at this juncture. Without the enthusiastic cooperation of the OMs, especially the Sandinist Youth, the Literacy Crusade could never have succeeded. The OMs participated in all the activities of the Crusade: the initial census, the training and equipping of volunteers, publicity, logistical support (clothing, food, transportation and communications), and the personal protection of the *brigadistas*. Institutionally, the OMs were part of the Crusade's national, departmental, and municipal commissions.[12] Without doubt, the Literacy Crusade was a difficult challenge for the mass organizations, but through it they proved their mettle. The Crusade was an experience which helped the OMs develop leadership and overcome organizational weaknesses.

Finally, the OMs also provided informal channels of political participation. The most important of these were mass meetings, of a type and frequency never before seen in Nicaragua, where the people expressed their opinions directly by means of banners, posters, and songs. These demonstrations focused on themes such as the quite offensive strings attached to U.S. aid; CIA activities in Nicaragua; the need to punish individuals who were attacking literacy volunteers; agricultural workers's demands that no confiscated lands be returned to big landowners; and a concern with controlling the demagoguery of opposition leader Alfonso Robelo. In addition, the OMs also organized various open town meetings to discuss local issues, disseminate information, and receive feedback on the activities of OM representatives in the Council of State.

Organizational Principals and Structure
The mass organizations gave access without regard to politics, religion, race, and so on, to all persons belonging to the social group that the given organizations specifically represented. The same person could belong to various OMs, although that generally did not take place for reason of time and workload. Freedom of entry, however, did not imply that disruptive or personally ambitious elements were tolerated indefinitely. Many such individuals did join the OMs in the early days—in many cases causing these organizations to commit excesses and abuses of power. Thanks in part to the criticism leveled at these abuses by all three major newspapers, and the internal practice of self-criticism, trouble-making individuals were gradually weeded out and there was a progressive improvement in OM behavior.

The mass organizations attempted to maintain three basic avenues of open communication: (1) *From bottom to top.* The desires, criticisms and suggestions at the grass roots (base) level were communicated upward to the top directorate of the OMs, the FSLN, and the government. (2) *From top to bottom.* The proposals and directives of the leadership were presented to, and discussed by the base. (3) *Lateral.* The individual OMs attempted to maintain coordination among themselves in order to avoid unnecessary duplication of effort and to maximize joint action.

The basic principles underlying the functioning of these democratic organizations were the following: (1) *Democratic-Centralism.* Though issues were freely discussed and decisions were based on majority opinion, the administration and execution of policy, once arrived at, was centralized. It was felt that decisions, once made in this manner, should be carried out with discipline.[13] (2) *Collective leadership.* This original contribution of the Sandinist Revolution was visible not only in the government and the Directorate of the FSLN but also in the OMs. Collective decision-making not only prevented the concentration of personal power but also enriched decisions with wide support and forced the suppression of individualistic concepts of work. Though decisions were made by the majority, responsibility for execution was unipersonal. (3) *Representativeness.* OM representatives, elected by the "grass roots," were obliged periodically to give an account of their work, and could be recalled at any point by the membership. Though some representatives received per diem allowances, their positions were largely without remuneration. (4) *Criticism and self-criticism.* Constant mutual and self-evaluation was promoted in order to correct problems at an early stage. Criticism, however, was expected to be constructive—an honest and open type which would analyse problems and propose concrete solutions. (5) *Division of labor.* Work was divided according to categories and assigned to the individuals with the most appropriate skills. (6) *Planning of labor.* Emphasis was placed on careful planning. Objectives were determined, resources were carefully allocated, and tasks were given priorities and coherently planned within a time schedule and in accordance with the current political reality.

Though there were differences between the mass organizations and periodic changes were taking place, all the OMs exhibited certain structural similarities. In the first place, they were organized territorially at four levels. At the *base*, cells were set up by block (CDS), place of work (CST), schools (JS-19 and ANS), or by hacienda and rural district (ATC). Above this level came the *municipal, departmental* and *national* organizations, reflecting the longstanding administrative division of the country into 103 municipalities (somewhat like counties in the U.S.) and fourteen departments (vaguely analogous to states). At each level, there was an executive committee, headed by a secretary general, and composed of various commissions and secretariats concerned with tasks such as organization; publicity and political education; and finance. Other organisms common to the OMs were the councils. At the base, these were usually called "assemblies" and were composed of all members. The municipal, departmental, and national councils were composed of the executive committees of the organizations at the level directly below them. These councils met every two or three months to decide on general policies for each OM.

Achievements

Some assessments of the mass organizations were negative because they compared the real situation with an ideal model, that which *ought* to have been. However, when we evaluate the OM's from a realistic perspective—that is, compare them with the situation which existed prior to the Sandinist triumph—we are overwhelmed by the achievements attained in their first year of life.

The rapid growth of the OMs was particularly remarkable. During the Somoza dictatorship, all attempts to organize the people were suppressed as threats to the existing power structure. The mass organizations were born in the heat of the War of Liberation as a political and military prerequisite to the defeat of that terrorist regime. After the victory, with the support of new and unprecedented freedom that the Revolution provided, the OMs expanded at a dizzying pace to all departments and municipalities. By October 1980, they had a total estimated membership of around 260,000 persons.

More important than numbers, however, is the fact that the voluntary cooperation of the OMs made it possible for a financially-beleaguered revolutionary government to attain a number of major achievements at very little monetary cost to itself. The OMs played an important role in each of the following: (1) *The Literacy Crusade.* Illiteracy was reduced in six months from over 50 percent to less than 13 percent and Sandinist Popular Education Collectives (CEP) were set up to provide followup support for the newly-literate. (2) *The real income of the masses* was raised through the enforcement of price and rent controls and the establishment of basic staples centers and Production Collectives. (3) *In health,* there was a new oral rehydration program for children, a massive vaccination campaign against polio and measles, and the creation of people's pharmacies. (4) *Popular Militias* were organized throughout the country and in practically all work places. (5) *Political training* schools, study centers, and seminars were organized. (6) *Voluntary labor* was utilized for harvesting, neighborhood repair and improvement, and the installation of local infrastructure such as systems of potable water. (7) *Many festivals*, and cultural and artistic activities were developed. (8) *Personal and material* assistance was given to flood victims. (9) *Successful campaigns to conserve sugar* and other products took place. (10) *The 1980 Plan for Economic Reactivation* not only was implemented but, as of October, appeared likely to come within a few percentage points of achieving its production goals for that year.

Problems

It would be wrong to project an idyllic image of the mass organizations since ". . . true revolutions . . . and Nicaragua's is one of them, are full of contradictions. They draw their sustenance from them, they live on them."[14] It would be strange if a people, accustomed to exploitation and marginalization dating to the Spanish Conquest, could develop a political system of full democratic participation in one short year. As the leaders of the FSLN noted on many occasions, the 19th of July 1979, was only *one* victorious battle in the ongoing war for the liberation of the Nicaraguan people. How could the enormous weight of behavior, attitudes, and values nourished by the old social system be thrown off overnight? How could corruption, alcoholism, apathy, egoism, individual lust for power and riches, *machismo*, violence, and authoritarianism be erradicated? If the experience of other countries in transition to socialism teaches anything, it is that old ideological legacies have much more weight than revolutionary theory supposes.

Obviously these legacies did not emerge and reproduce themselves in isolation from an infrastructure. They were fed by a capitalist mode of production which, although restricted and controlled by the new government of Nicaragua, played an important role in the development of productive forces in the 1980 Plan for Economic Reactivation. Herein lay the roots of the contradictions that fed the Revolution.

The problems confronting the mass organizations could be classified into four categories: (1) those that were inherent in the development of these organizations; (2) others flowing out of the legacy of *Somocismo;* (3) those which derived from the newness of the Sandinist state; and (4) those created by the counterrevolution.

Problems Inherent in OM Development

The way in which the mass organizations developed created three problems. First, their rapid expansion resulted in some lack of coordination and control. In the words of Patricia Orozco, the General Secretary of the CDSs, "There is no relationship between number and quality of members."[15] There was also "a lack of politically trained leadership" due to the death of many militants during the war, the enormous demand for trained personnel in government, and the explosive expansion of the OMs.[16] Finally, there was a lack of understanding at the grass-roots level about the nature and importance of participation in the mass organizations due to general educational and political backwardness; the lack of information, rumor-mongering by counterrevolutionaries, and errors committed by some novice or opportunistic leaders.

Limitations Deriving from Inherited Structures
Problems also flowed out of inherited ideological characteristics that had been systematically transmitted by the educational system, the mass media, the family, and certain traditional sectors of the Church. This was an ideology that preached that the people were simple objects of history. Comandante Tomás Borge spoke out strongly against the danger of continuing to view the masses as passive "objects" to be educated and molded:

> We ought to uproot all vestiges of paternalism, of elitism. We ought to understand that while it is necessary to lead the masses, we must also learn from [them]; have sufficient humility to understand that the people are full of wisdom . . . to learn from the masses in order to educate the masses, this ought to be the guide for our organizations.[17]

Inherited economic structures also caused problems. Inevitably the revolutionary triumph and the formation of mass organizations stimulated material expectations on the part of the people which could not be satisfied immediately due to the postwar economic crisis. The grim economic situation of the country was a product not only of the destruction caused by the war and of four decades of systematic looting by Somocistas, but also it had its roots in a system of agroexport which was dependent on an international economic order designed to benefit imperialist powers. This material basis placed limits on the development of the type of cooperative, disinterested, and fraternal "New Man" needed for the ideal functioning of OMs. The key issue was how, under these circumstances, the Revolution could assure the satisfaction of the basic needs of the majority in order that life would be something other than a daily and unequal struggle for physical survival.

Limitations Related to the New State
The mass organizations also had a difficult task in showing, on the one hand, that the new state was not a traditional single-class instrument of exploitation while, on the other, maintaining their autonomy from the state and energetically expressing popular demands.[18] Often the OMs adopted the passive position of not pressuring the state due to the fact that they were confused as to their role and the nature of the new state. Yet while the

revolutionary state was different from that of the Somozas, it was not a socialist (workers' and peasants') state but rather the product of a class alliance under the hegemony of the working classes represented by their vanguard, the FSLN. The idea that the OMs should maintain their autonomy from, and energetically make demands of the state was expressed in an editorial in *Barricada:*

> The passivity which, to this moment, has quieted some mass organizations should be broken and [the OMs] should struggle to maintain their class independence from the state, as such, their behavior should manifest itself in concrete actions that tend to transform and strengthen the state, without passively waiting for all of the decrees, . . . advances, and transformations to fall from heaven. It is as important to maintain the political independence of the working classes and the masses from the bourgeoisie as it is to defend it with respect to the state.[19]

On the other side of the coin, some state agencies and administrators tended to view the OMs as simple appendages of the government, as instruments for their plans or "fire extinguishers" for problems they, themselves, had created. The problem of "bureaucratism" we mentioned earlier was real, as was the intense campaign which was being carried out to erradicate it. But the task was not an easy one since "bureaucratism" had originated

> . . . in the specialization of tasks and . . . [the fact that] those who could perform those tasks were few [in number]. Technocracy is produced in unequal societies where few people can participate in wealth, culture and higher education. Bureaucracy will end when . . . the workers have the capacity to undertake any political and economic task. . . .[20]

If that analysis was correct, the elimination of the causes of bureaucratism was not likely soon to take place in the Nicaraguan Revolution. But what *was* important was the consciousness that had developed concerning the problem and the firm decision to combat it. The Nicaraguan Revolution possessed the strength to accomplish incredible things.

Problems Posed by the Counterrevolution
The mass organizations were a permanent target of groups opposing the Sandinist democratic process. The tactics employed were infiltration, threats, assassination of leaders, and slander. Accusations ran the gamut from claims that the OMs were serving as FSLN spys to a depiction of them as totalitarian organizations at the service of atheistic communism, inquisitorial and antifamily Marxism. All this was accompanied by constant criticism, especially in *la Prensa*, of their activities and legality. While it is undeniable that there were abuses and errors committed by all of the OMs, for the reasons mentioned above, at heart, the reactionaries were not ques-

tioning the imperfect functioning of these organizations but rather their very *existence*. The privileged sectors resented the growing organization, increased awareness, and combativeness of workers and peasants as an inadmissable subversion of their traditional political, economic and ideological authority over those "inferior classes."[21]

The Individual Characteristics of the Major Mass Organizations

Having discussed the general characteristics of the mass organizations, we can now examine the individual nature of some of these major groupings. As we noted earlier, OMs consisted of the Sandinist Defense Committees (CDS), The July 19 Sandinist Youth (JS-19), The Sandinist Children's Association (ANS), the Luisa Amada Espinosa National Association of Women (AMNLAE), The Sandinist Workers' Central (CST), and the Rural Workers' Association (ATC). For reasons of space, and since they are discussed in detail in the chapters in this volume dealing with the working class and women, we will omit an examination of the CST and AMNLAE and concentrate instead on the other four mass organizations.

The Sandinist Defense Committees (CDS)

The most important of the mass organizations, the Sandinist Defense Committees, had their roots in an organizational effort which actually took place during the War of Liberation. In the eighteen -month period from January 1978 to July 1979, the FSLN, the national woman's organization (then, AMPRONAC) and various Church groups worked to organize the citizens of local neighborhoods into Civil Defense Committees (CDCs). The latter contributed immeasurably to the success of the revolutionary struggle by providing "safe houses," clinics, places for the storage of arms, clandestine printing facilities, meeting and training areas, and a variety of other forms of support. Indeed, the role played by the CDCs was one of the most remarkable and unique characteristics of the Nicaraguan Revolution.[22]

After the Liberation, the CDCs metamorphosed into Sandinist Defense Committees (CDSs), which expanded rapidly throughout the country and began tackling urgent problems such as the distribution of relief food supplies, the reconstruction of housing, the reestablishment of public services, and maintainance of vigilance against Somocistas. The CDSs cooperated with the government in attempting to do away with various forms of exploitation suffered by the inhabitants of working-class neighborhoods: the poor distribution and high price of basic products, poor housing conditions and high rents, and the scarcity of services (transportation, water, electrical, medical, educational).

Defined as the "primary and elemental connection between our people and the Revolution,"[23] the CDSs were organized by block, rural area, or village. In the cities, each fifteen to twenty CDSs formed a neighborhood committee. Above these were zonal and municipal committees. Organization in the rural areas depended on demography and other factors. In all cases, however, any person over 14 years of age could join. The CDSs held weekly meetings in which they discussed various themes relating to the Revolution and evaluated the projects they had undertaken and planned future activities.

The two broad purposes of the CDSs were to unify the people behind the Revolution and its vanguard and to create structures capable of responding to the tasks faced by the Revolution. More specific objectives included controlling speculation, hoarding, and the maximum pricing of basic products; promoting voluntary labor to repair streets, schools, and so on; eradicating delinquency, prostitution, and other vices; enforcing rent controls and identifying abandoned housing; training members in first aid and preventive medical skills; establishing people's drugstores and clinics; conserving water, electricity, and so forth; forming Voluntary Sports Committees; reconstructing housing; overseeing the functioning of public services; promoting the Post-Literacy Campaign and the creation of "work-schools" and popular libraries; conducting censuses; promoting small-businessmen's associations; beautifying neighborhoods and planting trees; purging Somocista, opportunist, or delinquent politicians from the CDS; and gathering evidence for the special tribunals which were trying individuals accused of committing crimes against the people under the Somoza regime.

As with any human organization, the CDSs were prone to problems and limitations as well as successes. Some of the most common criticism leveled against them concerned abuses of power; *caudillismo* and personalism; a lack of coordination, both internal and with other organisms; a lack of fluid communication between the grass roots and the top leadership; insufficient base participation in the setting of tasks; the passivity of some CDSs; and the continuing presence within these organisms of some "last-minute Sandinists" (opportunists). On the other hand, however, most of the objectives originally set by the CDSs were at least partially fulfilled. On the positive side there was the creation of some 15,000 CDS organizations in all departments of the country; very successful vaccination campaigns; the reconstruction of many homes, streets, and sewage systems; the distribution of emergency foods; the enforcement of price control; the Literacy and Post-Literacy Crusades; the formation of production collectives; and neighborhood cleanup and sanitation campaigns.

The Association of Rural Workers (ATC)

The Nicaraguan peasant has a rich revolutionary tradition which includes participation in both the War of the Comuneros (a valiant but unsuccessful peasant uprising in 1881 against the massive dispossession of peasants by the coffee producers) and Augusto César Sandino's patriotic guerrilla effort against Yankee occupiers and their local allies from 1927 to 1933. But the immediate antecedents of the ATC flowed out of the work of the Celebrators of the Word Movement organized in the late 1960s in rural areas by progressive elements of the Catholic Church.[24] Later, in 1976, Rural Workers' Committees were set up to protest the miserable condition of rural poor and the FSLN organized the peasants to join workers and students in the guerrilla struggle.[25] In March of 1978, the ATC was founded by representatives of four departments. As the struggle grew, military training schools for ATC members were created. Peasant homes were used for refuge, the storage of arms, and supply depots for the guerrilla army.

After the Sandinist victory, the objectives of the ATC changed. As Edgardo García, ATC Secretary General, put it, "It is not now a matter of organizing rural workers for the armed struggle . . . now we confront a much more complex task: to transform the society we inherited from Somocismo."[26] Toward the end of December 1979, a formal National Constitutional Assembly of the ATC took place. At that point, 250 delegates from the 14 departments approved a set of Statutes and a declaration of principles and elected a National Executive Committee. The major objectives of the ATC were to defend and deepen the agrarian reform; to organize small holders into cooperatives; to organize rural workers on private and state farms for participation in the administration of those entities; to elevate the peasants' standard of living and political consciousness; to promote Reactivation Assemblies, Committment Assemblies, Permanent Committees, and Collective Work Conventions;[27] to create rural supplies centers; to develop year-round employment for seasonal workers; to reform the labor code; to unite with urban workers in the National Intersyndical Commission; to take over all Somocista-owned lands; and to make sure that no land be left fallow.

Like the other mass organizations, the ATC has experienced problems and contradictions as well as successes. On the positive side, as is shown in Chaper 12 (on the agrarian reform program) the government in the first year supported rural workers through the ATC in a variety of ways. In addition, the ATC attained a number of successes in its own right, including (1) the formation of 3,081 chapters with 108,177 affiliates as of July 1980; (2) institutional integration into the National Intersyndical Commission; (3) the nearly total fulfillment of the objectives they were asked to achieve by the government; (4) the creation of a National Committee of small and medium producers;[28] (5) setting up ten schools of political capacitation, permanent seminars, and study circles; and (6) involvement in a plan for the development of "appropriate technology" (Estelí). The great dispersion of peasants and the exploitation and marginalization they had suffered for centuries were major obstacles to the work of an economically strapped ATC. In addition, among some peasant groups, the influence of certain reactionary religious elements was considerable. The deeply religious yet uneducated peasantry was a fertile ground for the spreading of rumors about the coming of "atheistic communism." Nevertheless, in general, the communal solidarity, cooperativeness, humility, and frankness that characterized the peasantry placed it much closer to the values of the New Sandinist Man than were the urban sectors.

The July 19th Sandinist Youth

It was Nicaragua's youth who succeeded in gestating, developing, and consolidating the revolutionary vanguard. Youth organizations were the most dynamic source of support for the FSLN both before and after the Liberation. If we look back in history, we find that first there was the Nicaraguan Patriotic Youth; then, the Revolutionary Student Front; and later, the Nicaraguan Revolutionary Youth, the Sandinist Revolutionary Youth, and other high-school and university student movements. Especially after the Monimbó uprising of February 1978 and the first general insurrection the following September, large groups of young people spontaneously joined the struggle against the dictatorship. Their strength and defiance in the face of institutionalized injustice converted them into the backbone of the guerrilla army. "For that reason . . . [Nicaraguan youth in general] were persecuted with fury, jailed, tortured, and murdered. For the youth there was no alternative but to fight or die."[29]

After the victory, the Sandinist Youth did not grow as quickly as some of the other mass organizations. This perhaps was due to the overly careful selection of members and a scarcity of leaders (many capable young people had sacrificed their lives and others had been assigned to other tasks). Whatever the reason, the JS-19 had only 4,000 members late in 1979. The National Literacy Crusade, however, served to reverse this condition by stimulating the organizational activity of Sandinist Youth and educating its members: "The Sandinist Youth finds in the Popular Literacy Army (EPA) a natural source of rank and file members."[30] While the insurrectional war had drawn together some 15,000 young people, the EPA now united more than 70,000 in the fight against illiteracy. In addition to teaching most former illiterates how to read and write, the Crusade afforded the student-volunteers the opportunity to come to know the harsh reality of peasant life, to learn to till the earth, to investigate the culture and history of the Nicaraguan people and, at the same time, to develop their sense of responsibility and discipline.[31]

The Sandinist Youth organizations within the Literacy Crusade corresponded to the structure of the EPA with its basic "squadrons" of 30 volunteers, its "columns" composed of 4 squadrons, its "brigades" made up of all squadrons within a given municipality, and finally the 6 "fronts" into which the country was divided, as during the War of Liberation. The heads of the squadrons, columns, brigades and fronts were members of the JS-19. Together with the representatives of the other mass organizations and of the ministries, JS-19 representatives also participated in the national, departmental, and municipal commissions which served as the maximum authorities in the Crusade.[32]

In July 1980, the JS-19 held its First National Assembly of Commitment. On that occasion, it was decided that the Sandinist Youth would work to strengthen the organization and discipline of the EPA; select 500 new members for the JS-19; participate actively in the economic tasks of the Revolution; and launch a general offensive against remaining vestiges of illiteracy. In October, the Sandinist Youth held their first National Congress and approved Provisional Statutes.[33] In the latter the JS-19 was defined as

> . . . a massive political organization which aspires to include in its ranks all young people who want to participate in an organized and disciplined manner in the National Reconstruction, under the direction of the FSLN. (Art. 1)

> The purposes of the Sandinista Youth are: (a) to contribute to the integral revolutionary education of young people and children, (b) to promote and lead the incorporation of the young masses into the fundamental tasks of the Revolution, (c) to be a permanent aid to the FSLN in its revolutionary political work." (Art. 2)

Two categories of membership were created: affiliate and militant. To be promoted to militant, the affiliate was required to complete six months in the organization and "be outstanding in the fulfillment of duties." (Art. 6) Among such duties were "To be an exemplary youth. To maintain a humble and fraternal attitude. To maintain an attitude of criticism and self-criticism in order to identify and overcome errors. . . ." (Art. 10)

The JS-19 had various specific goals. There were committments to support the development of a new educational system (work-schools); to struggle against the inherited vices of youth (drugs, alcohol, and so on); to support the Sandinist Children's Association; to promote national and popular artistic and cultural groups; to stimulate the active involvement of young people believing in the Revolution; and to attempt to unify the university student movement.

Perhaps no other social sector had experienced such a rapid and profound change in its way of thinking as these Nicaraguan youth who participated in the National Literacy Crusade and were later admitted to the JS-19. As Commander Humberto Ortega pointed out at the ceremonies celebrating the victory over illiteracy:

> With this campaign, the anti-imperialist spirit, the class-conscious spirit, and the popular spirit of this Revolution have been fortified because [the youth] have become aware of the terrible nature of all exploitative and oppressive regimes [as inflicted on] our poor Latin American peoples."[34]

The Luis Alfonso Velásquez Sandinist Children's Association

The children of the working classes were the ultimate and most vulnerable victims of the exploitative system of Somocismo. The economic conditions of their families obliged the children to work or beg at an early age, thus cutting short possibilities for study and personal development. Like their hero Luis Alfonso Velásquez, who died in the struggle against the Somoza dictatorship, these children matured rapidly and many actually participated in various aspects of the armed insurrection. After the victory, the leaders of the Sandinist Children's Association (ANS) declared that:

> Children are thinking beings and ought to be treated as such; they ought to know their reality, the problems that confront the process . . . in order that they draw their own conclusions and not have to adhere by force to the conclusions of adults . . . children have to be made to understand the importance that they have in society and the support that they should give to it.[35]

Dependent on the Sandinist Youth, ANS was a mass organization. It was designed to help build children politically, culturally, and in sports; to develop human and revolutionary values; to encourage brotherhood with all the children of the world; and to build respect for elders, reverence for the memory of the fallen heroes of the Revolution, and humility and honesty.[36]

The ANS was comprised of three types of groups by age: "mascots" from 4 to 6 years, "Carlitos"[37] from 7 to 10; and "pioneers" from 11 to 14. Within each category, children organized each school or street into "fists" (5 individuals), brigades (15) and "collectives," (75). In both the schools and neighborhoods there were adults in charge, generally a teacher in addition to a member of the Sandinist Youth. Parental permission was required of all potential members.

As of late 1980, the Sandinist Children's Association had made several achievements. ANS had set up organizations in all fourteen departments. In addition, during the Literacy Crusade, ANS and the Ministry of Education cooperated in a joint effort called "Operation Quincho Barrilete." Named after another beloved child-martyr, this program was aimed at very poor children, many of whom were street vendors. At midday they were offered an educational program which included sports, artistic activities, classes, recreation, food and medical assistance. This was a clear example of the priority attention the Revolution assigned the most marginal groups in society. At the same time, in the schools, all the children at the primary level were involved in a "Literacy Rear-Guard Plan" which was designed to promote recreational, artistic, and sports activities.

Conclusions
The mass organizations had become the principal channels and the practical

schools of an original democratic system created, through trial and error, by the Sandinist Revolution. For those who liked to identify "democracy" with the political system operating in "developed" capitalist countries, the Nicaraguan Revolution was not "democratic." But for those who understood that democracy can be institutionalized in various ways according to the historic circumstances of each country, the political system which had been developed in Revolutionary Nicaragua represented an original and valuable form of democracy.

At the heart of the debate were two antagonistic positions. At one extreme were those who felt that a democratic regime could exist only when various political parties competed in free and periodic elections even though the economy of the country might remain under the control of a small group of people. In such a regime, the participation of the people would be restricted to the "political" sphere while businesses, the mass media, banks, big landholdings, and other means of production would remain outside of the public decision-making process. Combating that position were people who maintained that popular participation ought to take place in the social, cultural and economic *as well as* political spheres. For this group, the mere existence of a variety of parties and periodic elections was often little more than a system in which the people participated only occasionally and imperfectly in decision-making regarding public issues that concerned them profoundly. This group argued that only through permanent education and organization of all sectors of a society could effective popular participation be guaranteed. First, however, the necessities basic to the human survival of the people had to be attained. This position did not exclude multipartism and free, periodic elections, but it sought to complement and enrich them in order that there be an integral form of democracy, a democracy that embraced all aspects of social life.

This second position was the one held by most of the Nicaraguan people as well as the leaders of the Sandinist Revolution. In their first year of life, the mass organizations had played an extremely important role in the huge task of constructing, for the first time in Nicaraguan history, a system of integral democracy. The challenge which they faced was difficult and complex. On the one hand, they had to deal with the legacy of a corrupt, repressive, and bankrupt social system while, on the other, they faced constant harassment from internal and external counterrevolutionary groups. But if the challenge was enormous, the volcanic power of the Nicaraguan people, which had proved capable of rekindling the torch of hope and justice in Latin America, was greater still.

Notes

[1] Unión Nacional de Empleados, "Sobre las Organizaciones de Masa" (Managua: UNE, 1980).

[2] Carlos Nuñes Tellez, *El Papel de las Organizaciones de Masas en el Proceso Revolucionario* (Managua: SENAPEP, 1980) p. 20.

[3] Iván García, "Papel de los Trabajadores en el Plan 80," (Managua; Central Sandinista de Trabajadores, 1980, a mimeographed speech).

[4] FSLN, "Declaración del FSLN Sobre la Democracia," *Barricada,* Aug. 24, 1980.

[5] Ibid.

[6] Episcopado Nicaragüense, *Carta Pastoral del Episcopado Nicaragüense: Compromiso Cristiano para una Nicaragua Nueva* (Managua: Unión, 1979), pp. 7 and 8.

[7] Philip Agee, "El Plan de la CIA en Nicaragua," *La Prensa* (Jan. 2, 1980), pp. 1, 7.

[8] An excellent example of the slanted coverage that Nicaragua received is the ninety-minute NBC "White Paper" titled "The Castro Connection," aired on September 3, 1980.

[9] "Burocracia o Administración Sandinista," *Poder Sandinista,* 14 (1980) p. 3.

[10] Carlos Fonseca, Ricardo Morales, Oscar Turcios, *Que es un sandinista?* (Managua: SENAPEP, 1980). Concerning the confluence of Christian and Sandinist values, see: "Un paso más en la formación del Hombre Nuevo," *Nuevo Diario,* Aug. 26, 1980.

[11] From a speech by Daniel Ortega in Chinandega in February 1980.

[12] Cruzada Nacional de Alfabetización, *La Alfabetización en Marcha* (Managua: Ministerio de Educación, 1980).

[13] Carlos Nuñez Tellez, *Los Métodos de Planificación y la División del Trabajo de Masas* (Managua: SENAPEP, 1980) and "Estructura Organizativa del FSLN después del Triunfo de la Revolución Popular Sandinista," a pamphlet of the Ejército Popular Sandinista, 1980.

[14] Jorge G. Casteñeda, *Nicaragua: Contradicciones en la Revolución* (México: Tiempo Extra, 1980), p. 15.

[15] *Barricada,* Dec. 31, 1979, p. 13.

[16] Ibid.

[17] Tomás Borge, *Aprender de las Masas para educar a las Masas* (Managua: Ministerio del Interior, 1980), p. 15.

[18] Carlos Nuñez Tellez, *El Papel de las Organizaciones de Masas,* p. 16.

[19] Editorial, *Barricada,* Jan 2, 1980.

[20] "Nueva Administración: Autoritarianismo o Democracia," *Poder Sandinista,* 13 (1980), p. 7.

[21] Sergio Ramírez, "Sandinismo, Hegemonia y Revolución," a speech published in *Barricada,* July 8, 1980.

[22] *Nicaragua: Reforma o Revolución;* Vol. III, "La Coyuntura Política y la Insurreción Popular" (Managua: Instituto Histórico Centroamericano, 1978) pp. 94-6.

[23] "Linea Organizativa de los Comités de Defensa Sandinista" (Managua: CDS, 1980), a pamphlet.

[24] See Chapter 9 in this volume, on the role of the Church, for greater detail concerning this aspect of Church involvement.

[25] Edgardo García, "Informe Central," in *Asamblea Nacional Constitutiva de la A.T.C., Memorias* (Managua; SENAPEP, 1980), pp. 14-21

[26] Ibid., p. 19.

[27] The Reactivation Assemblies (*Asambleas de Reactivación Económica*) were meetings of workers and state administrators in which information was exchanged on the state of production. In Commitment Assemblies (*Asambleas de Compromiso*), workers, owners, and representatives of the state established mutual commitments to achieve additional goals through voluntary labor. The Permanent Production Committees, composed of the same participants, were in charge of controlling and evaluating production. The Collective Conventions (*Los Convenios Colectivos*) set work and utilization rules between workers and private owners as previously authorized by the Ministry of Labor.

[28] This was a critical success since the big landholders had wanted to absorb the small- and medium-sized producers into their associations, which were constantly questioning the programs of the government in behalf of the poorer sectors.

[29] Juventud Sandinista, "Plataforma General de la Juventud Sandinista" (Managua: JS-19, 1980), a pamphlet.

[30] *Primer Congreso de la Alfabetización: Documentos* (Managua: Ministerio de Educación, 1980), p. 54.

[31] Fernando Cardenal, "La Alfabetización: Un Proyecto Político"; and Bayardo Arce Castaño, "Significado de la Cruzada en la Revolución Popular Sandinista," *Documentos para Tallares* (Managua: Ministerio de Educación, 1980).

[32] Juan B. Arrién, *Revolución y Proyecto Educativo* (Managua: Ministerio de Educación, 1980), pp. 110-131.

[33] "Estatutos Provisionales de la Juventud Sandinista 19 de Julio" (Managua: Juventud Sandinista, October 1980), pamphlet.

[34] Humberto Ortega, "Discurso Prununciado ante la Plaza de la Revolución, el 23 de Agosto de 1980," *Barricada*, 1980.

[35] Dirigentes de la Asociación de Niños Sandinistas, Entrevistas en *Poder Sandinista*, 8 (1979), p. 5.

[36] "Declaración de Principios de la Asociación de Ninos Sandinistas, Luis Alfonso Velásquez Flores" y "Objectivos de la ANS" (Managua: Asociación de Ninos Sandinistas, 1980), pamphlets.

[37] "Carlitos," affectionate diminutive, after Carlos Fonseca Amador, a martyred founder of the FSLN.

Chapter 6

The Role
of the Revolutionary
Armed Forces

STEPHEN M. GORMAN

One of the major accomplishments of the revolutionary government in Nicaragua during its first year was the creation of an entirely new military establishment completely dedicated to the political-economic programs of the Sandinista Front. The revolutionary armed forces that were organized into a regular army immediately after the fall of Somoza succeeded in consolidating the hegemony of the Sandinista Front as the vanguard of the revolutionary process, and helped deter foreign intervention. In this chapter we will examine the evolution, organization, and revolutionary roles of the Sandinista Popular Army (EPS) and, to a lesser extent, the Sandinista Police (PS) and Sandinista Popular Militias (MPSs). It will be suggested that the ability of the revolutionary leadership to forge an effective military establishment committed to the defense of the popular classes was made possible by three interrelated factors: the length of the revolutionary struggle which raised the political consciousness of rebel forces, the collectivist nature of political-military leadership that characterized the Sandinista Front, and the decisive participation of the popular classes in the final offensive against the Somoza regime.

Evolution of the Sandinista Armed Forces
The Sandinista Front was formed in 1961 from a number of smaller resistance movements, and remained extremely limited in its activities during its early years. Two insurrectionary models guided the Sandinista Front during the formative years between 1961-1967: the rebellion of Augusto César Sandino (1927-1933), and the more recent Cuban Revolution.

The defeat of Ernesto "Ché" Guevara's guerrilla band in Bolivia in 1967 by U.S.-trained counterinsurgency troops was especially significant for the Sandinista Front. It demonstrated that neither the example of Sandino nor the Cuban Revolution would be easily reproducible in view of the increasing efficiency of counterinsurgency forces in isolating and destroying incipient guerrilla uprisings in the countryside. Sandino had created a fairly large, highly mobile army drawn overwhelmingly from the peasantry and rural proletariat which operated over a large expanse of backland. After early attempts to take and hold fortified towns, Sandino restricted his activities to hit-and-run tactics and to establishing a loose "control" over remote areas of the countryside. These areas were protected by an elastic defense which permitted attacking forces to penetrate rebel districts but prevented the enemy from destroying rebel forces or holding territory.[1] The Sandinista Front had intended to repeat Sandino's rebellion to achieve the objectives outlined in the foco theory that grew out of the Cuban experience. Specifically, the FSLN intended to (1) drain the central government's strength through a protracted war of attrition, (2) achieve national recognition as the political-military vanguard of the anti-imperialist, anti-Somocista struggle, and (3) precipitate the internal decomposition of the dictatorship.

The essential weakness of both models, which was exposed by Ché Guevara's defeat in Bolivia, was their predilection to concentrate military operations exclusively in the countryside, where the central government could contain and destroy rebel forces with minimal impact on the rest of the country. The FSLN responded by adjusting its strategy to the concrete realities of Nicaragua after 1967. This included increasing attention to urban organization which could complement and support continued guerrilla operations in the countryside. (The FSLN had actually begun urban organizational activities as early as 1963, but only on a limited scale.) By the early 1970s, the FSLN had created an extensive network of clandestine organizations in the leading cities, increased its recruitment from universities and unions, and established training centers close to urban areas where students and workers received basic military instruction.[2] From that point forward, the Sandinista Front (working through different factions at times) followed a dual strategy of guerrilla warfare in the countryside aimed at the gradual accumulation of revolutionary forces, and the preparation of the urban masses for an eventual popular insurrection. As James Petras observed immediately after the Sandinista victory in 1979, this proved to be one of the keys to the overthrow of Somoza, since "Both the guerrilla movement and the mass urban insurrectionary organizations were necessary for the maintenance of each other's struggle."[3] Significantly, however, control and direction of the armed resistance to the dictatorship remained with the guerrilla leaders in the countryside.

Between 1970 and 1974, the FSLN conducted numerous commando operations along side its organizational activities in the cities, culminating in the December 1974 raid on a party given in honor of the U.S. ambassador to Nicaragua, Turner Shelton. The objectives of these operations were threefold: to increase the FSLN's political visibility, demonstrate to the masses the vulnerability of the dictatorship, and obtain ransoms and the release of political prisoners. The December raid was especially successful in all three respects. But it also provoked a major counter-offensive by the National Guard (GN) over the next three years that severely damaged the armed resistance in the country. Urban cells were infiltrated and destroyed, and large areas of the provinces were turned into free-fire zones.[4]

From January 1975 through September 1977, the FSLN was thrown completely on the defensive. The apparent success of the *guardia* in repressing the resistance led to a factionalization of the FSLN over political-military strategy and three rival "tendencies" arose within the Sandinista Front stressing different revolutionary lines.[5] The tendency that followed the original FSLN strategy most closely was the Prolonged Popular War (GPP) faction. The GPP remained committed to rural guerrilla warfare patterned after the Cuban Revolution designed to involve the enemy in a war of attrition. Its leaders perceived the revolution as a struggle for the accumulation of forces (e.g., experience, organization, weapons, numbers, and so on) in which guerrilla activities were preferable to premature mass insurrectionary tactics. A popular insurrection was considered appropriate only when the correct "insurrectionary moment" had been achieved through guerrilla warfare.

A second faction, the Proletarian tendency (TP), proposed to concentrate on the organization of the urban working class as the most direct and effective strategy for preparing the ground for a future mass-based insurrection. The TP argued that the capitalist development of Nicaragua had turned the proletariat into the most revolutionary class. As Jaime Wheelock explained, the Proletarian tendency was concerned that the Sandinista Front become   "more than simply a guerrilla force or an organization of more or less radicalized university students, but the vanguard organization of the working class. . . ."[6] Like the prolonged popular war tendency, however, the TP understood the revolutionary process as a prolonged struggle in which the masses (in this case the urban proletariat) would have to be carefully prepared both politically and militarily for the final offensive at the correct "insurrectionary moment."

In complete contrast to the GPP and TP factions, the *Terceristas* (Third Force) called for the immediate initiation of urban insurrectionary activity in cooperation with all opposition parties (including the progressive bourgeoisie). This revolutionary line was bitterly attacked by the other two Sandinista tendencies because, in their view, it threatened to draw the armed resistance into a premature frontal assault on the dictatorship. This opposition within the Sandinista Front notwithstanding, the Terceristas proceeded to organize FSLN-led popular insurrections in a number of cities for October 1977. The scale of these uprisings drew almost the entire Sandinista Front into action against the GN, and effectively exploded the myth that the dictatorship had successfully contained and systematically destroyed the armed resistance in the country. The participation of the masses in the October rebellion illustrated the growing revolutionary potential of the country, and allowed the FSLN to retake the initiative against the *guardia*. It also demonstrated that the three FSLN tendencies were, in effect, complementary and therefore opened the way to the reunification of the Front.

The next major FSLN offensive came in August 1978 with the seizure of the National Palace, which succeeded in gaining the release of prisoners, the payment of a ransom, and the broadcasting of political communiques. The following month, the action also helped detonate a popular insurrection which was joined by Sandinista guerrillas who felt obliged to defend the population against the military reprisals of the GN. Thereafter, the Sandinista Front was confronted with the dilemma that while it was still not strong enough to engage the GN in a frontal assault, its limited armed actions in builtup areas increasingly sparked popular resistance to the dictatorship with the result that FSLN guerrillas were then forced to defend such areas.[7] This tended to draw guerrillas into fixed-location warfare at times and in places other than of their own choosing. But it also permitted the FSLN leadership to appreciate that the correct insurrectionary moment was near. The most important prerequisite to initiating the final offensive against the Somoza regime then became the reunification of the FSLN.

The three tendencies agreed in principle to the reunification of the Sandinista Front in June 1978. Negotiations took place during late 1978 and early 1979, and complete reunification was achieved by March 1979 (although it had been announced as early as December 1978 by Tomás Borge). By this time, the Sandinista armed forces had acquired, if only superficially, many of the attributes of a regular army. In subsequent operations, some ground forces received air cover from the fledgling Sandinista air force, and attacking guerrilla columns began to employ artillery against fortified GN locations. Finally, a unified central command coordinated actions on three fronts, while each front, in turn, contained its own general staff.

The final offensive began on May 20, 1979. Up to this point, the strength of the Sandinista Front had been estimated at no more than 1,200 guerrillas, and the largest military operation had involved a column of only 200 guerrillas (the April 7-14 occupation of Estelí). But in May the FSLN launched three simultaneous actions: attacking Jinotega in the north with a column of 350 guerrillas, entering important districts of Managua with a column of 200 guerrillas, and invading Nicaragua from Costa Rica with a column of 300 guerrillas. On June 4, the FSLN called a general strike as fighting in the north shifted to Chinandega, León and Matagalpa. On June 8, the Battle for Managua began in earnest as 300 popular militias were joined by Sandinista guerrillas. These actions led to an upward revision of estimated FSLN strength to 5,000.[8] But in effect the number of veteran Sandinista guerrillas probably never exceeded 2,000, the remainder being composed of popular militias more or less under Sandinista control, a detachment of foreign volunteers drawn from throughout Latin America, and partially trained Sandinista reserves called into action from the universities and factories. Finally, there were numerous individuals who spontaneously took up arms against the *guardia.*

By late June, the FSLN had captured León, Masaya, and at least fifteen other important cities. Somoza's indiscriminate bombing finally forced the FSLN and popular militias to retreat on June 27 from Managua to Masaya, which had been turned into a Sandinista training camp for recruits. But on July 5, the Sandinista southern front captured Jinotepe, setting the stage for a three pronged assault on Managua from the north, southwest and east. Unable to obtain foreign military intervention to rescue his regime, Somoza abandoned the country on July 17. On July 19 Sandinista forces entered the city.[9]

The tenacity with which the GN defended the Somoza regime, the scale of the conflict, and the sophistication of the FSLN military organization all combined to produce a revolutionary army that succeeded easily in filling the power vacuum left by the collapse of the *guardia.* This was important because it allowed the FSLN leadership to consolidate political power quickly and impose national order. This latter point was extremely significant, since an inability to maintain order after the fall of Somoza could easily have been used by the United States to conjure up an image of social disintegration in Nicaragua in order to justify military intervention. Moreover, the size, discipline, and fighting experience of the Sandinista armed forces, together with their obvious popularity with the people, served as persuasive deterrents to external intervention.

Organization and Composition of the Armed Forces

Table 6.1 illustrates the institutional relationships that were established between the army, police and militias after July 1979. At the top of the command structure was the Sandinista National Directorate (*Dirección Nacional Conjunta* [DNC]), which had come into existence with the reunification of the FSLN. The DNC was composed of the three ranking members from each of the three tendencies, all of whom held the rank of Commander of the Revolution. The DNC exercised ultimate authority over the military and police forces. That authority went unchallenged by either the five-member Government of National Reconstruction or the forty-seven-member Council of State (which did not come into existence until May 1980) during the first year of the new government. The disappearance of the Patriotic Front and the United Peoples Movement (MPU) shortly after the triumph of the revolution, also served to tighten the DNCs exclusive control of the armed forces.

The actual organization of the new armed forces was worked out by three members of the Sandinista National Directorate who formed a subcommittee on the military immediately after the fall of Somoza . These three individuals subsequently assumed the most important positions within the armed forces. Tomás Borge became Minister of Interior with

TABLE 6.1

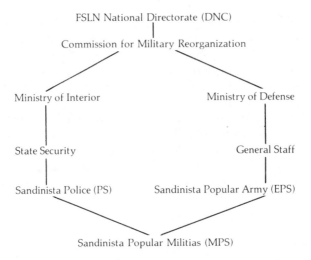

FSLN National Directorate (DNC)

Commission for Military Reorganization

Ministry of Interior   Ministry of Defense

State Security   General Staff

Sandinista Police (PS)   Sandinista Popular Army (EPS)

Sandinista Popular Militias (MPS)

control over the Sandinista Police and the State Security Forces. Under Somoza, police activities were performed by the National Guard, meaning that the Ministry of the Interior created after the revolution represented a new power structure in Nicaraguan politics. Humberto Ortega Saavedra became Commander-in-Chief of the EPS and, in January 1980, also Minister of Defense. (The position of Minister of Defense had originally been given to a former dissident colonel in Somoza's National Guard, Bernardino Larios. But Larios appears to have been little more than a figurehead intended to ease conservative fears during a period of military transition.) The third member of the DNC subcommittee on military organization, Luis Carrión, became Vice-Minister of Defense and second-in-command of the Sandinista Popular Army.

Although Table 6.1 depicts an institutional separation of police and military responsibilities, in practice the ministries of Interior and Defense were closely interrelated. The head of each ministry sat on the DNC which allowed for a constant exchange of information and coordination of activities. In addition, at the base of the organizational structure police and soldiers frequently participated in joint operations in efforts to control "counterrevolutionary" activities. Even at the level of the EPS General Staff, there existed a direct linkage with the Ministry of Interior. For example, the eleven-member General Staff appointed in July 1979 included two ranking Sandinista officials from the Ministry of Interior: Edén Pastora, Vice-Minister of Interior; and Hugo Torres, Chief of State Security. The linkages between the ministries of Defense and Interior and the concentration of key offices among a handful of Sandinista veterans served to consolidate the DNC's authority over the armed forces.

The precise responsibilities of the General Staff, whose size was subsequently increased to include two women *comandantes,* were not entirely clear during the first year. The EPS copied the Cuban example of establishing regional general staffs capable of directing military operations in different areas of the country in the event that an enemy cut communications with the central command or destroyed the national General Staff. Had a national emergency required a central command to coordinate an overall military response during the first year, that responsibility would likely have been performed by the DNC as much as by the official General Staff itself. The primary responsibilities of the General Staff were concerned with organizational and operational questions, especially (1) the standardization of weapons, (2) the elaboration of a formal system of military ranks, and (3) the imposition of a level of discipline consistent with the requirements of a regular army.

The standardization of weapons was a central concern for both the EPS and the police. When questioned on plans to standardize weapons in the EPS in November 1979, Luis Carrión responded that

> The arms market is a difficult one. We are seeking favorable conditions in Europe, the Arab countries, and in the United States. Without doubt, the diversity of arms which we are using at this moment is going to create problems; further on we will have to think about standardizing them which will mean discarding some. But our principle problem at this point in time is to acquire weapons of whatever type and from whatever source.[10]

Within the Sandinista Police, the use of strictly combat weapons was not discontinued until May 1980 when police were limited to weapons more consistent with law enforcement activities.[11] The diversity of weapons used by the armed forces created obvious problems in formalizing training programs and setting up an efficient supply system, but the overall amount of armaments and munitions in the possession of EPS appears to have been quite adequate during the first year of the new army.

The absence of a formal system of ranks also caused complications for the professionalization of the EPS during the first year. Below the three highest ranks recognized by the EPS (*Comandante de la Revolución, Comandante Guerrilla* and *Comandante*), all that existed were the semi-official "ranks" of *primero responsable, segundo responsable,* and so on (first in charge, second in charge, etc.). These ranks were routinely applied to anyone in position of responsibility regardless of the size or function of the detachment commanded, or the permanency of the command in question. By early 1980, however, the EPS announced a system of ranks (modeled somewhat after the Cuban army) to go into effect on the first anniversary of the revolution.

Obviously the most fundamental factor affecting the professionalization of the army was discipline, which in turn was conditioned by the composition of the troops. The Program of Government issued by the FSLN just before the fall of Somoza specified that the new army would be

> . . . formed from the combatants of the FSLN; soldiers and officers [of the GN] that have demonstrated honest and patriotic conduct in the face of the corruption, repression and treason of the Dictatorship and those that fought for the overthrow of the Somocista regime; from all sectors of the Nation that engaged in combat for liberation and desire to join the new Army; and from able citizens who offer themselves for military service.[12]

The army that took shape after July closely resembled the one outlined in this document, but its heterogeneity made the imposition of a uniform standard of discipline difficult.

For example, although the DNC outlawed capital punishment after assuming power, some Sandinista units in the countryside (composed of peasants or under the command of radicals) carried out summary executions and unlawful confiscations which were then concealed from the central authorities. When these abuses were discovered, a thorough purge was carried out within the EPS.[13] Other groups which had fought for the overthrow of the dictatorship, such as the *Milpas* (Anti-Somoza Popular Militas, under the control of the Trotskyist Workers Front), proved too extremist to be incorporated into the EPS, and were therefore pressured (not always successfully) to disband. But by far the most serious obstacles to the professionalization of the new army were (1) a high rate of illiteracy, and (2) a low level of political indoctrination among non-FSLN troops.

A census within the EPS in late 1979 showed an illiteracy rate of approximately 45 percent. To correct this problem, literate troops were assigned to provide ongoing instruction in educational basics to illiterate troops. To contend with the lack of adequate political orientation among some of the recruits, on the other hand, political-cultural sections were established at all levels and in all regional commands to provide continuing political indoctrination, as well as instruction in basic personal hygiene which was found to be deficient among recruits from the lowest social classes.[14] Political training was considered to be on a par with military training. As one officer connected with the General Staff explained, troops needed to fully understand whose interests they were protecting and who the enemies of those interests were. Otherwise, EPS members would eventually fall into the same elitist, anti-popular practices as the former National Guard.[15]

The content of political-cultural training in the military stressed the evolution of the Sandinista struggle, the legitimacy of the Sandinista Front's role as the vanguard in the revolutionary process, and the preeminently popular character of the new regime. While Marxist-Leninist principles were not directly interjected into the indoctrination process, the ideological thrust was essentially socialistic (although private property was not categorically rejected). The responsibility of soldiers to set moral examples for the population, to take advantage of every opportunity to work with members of the popular classes, and to avoid developing particularistic interests that might weaken their identification with the disadvantaged were especially significant elements of political-cultural training. The ideal soldier, according to the model projected by the Sandinista leadership, was one willing to oppose any and all threats to the material and spiritual well-being of the masses. A particularly interesting facet of the training was the attention given to working with children. Accordingly, the military sponsored a variety of recreational and cultural programs aimed at bringing soldiers and children together, which had a predictable socializing impact on both groups.

The decision to indoctrinate EPS members in Sandinista ideology brought some criticisms from the bourgeoisie which called for a depoliticization of the armed forces. In response, Tomás Borge pointed out that

> . . . there is no apolitical army in the world. This is a sophism. . . . There are no apolitical armies: every one serves some determinant political purpose. In the case of Nicaragua, the EPS is a Popular and Sandinista Army. It is not by accident that we call it such.[16]

The attention to political instruction clearly strengthened DNC control of the armed forces, and also helped overcome the threat of factionalism within the army posed by its heterogeneity. Political instruction was reinforced by volunteer work projects in which EPS detachments harvested coffee, helped clean up barrios, or engaged in other activities together with civilian labor brigades.

The actual size of the EPS remained a military secret after the victory of the revolution, but by mid-1980 it probably numbered between 13,000 and 18,000. The core of the army was the FSLN guerrilla veterans, of which possibly no more than 1,300 remained in the military after the fall of Somoza. Two other components were ex-National Guard troops (especially those which had defected before the final defeat of Somoza), and members of the Sandinista-led popular militias who saw action during the final offensive (between 2,500-3,500). The remainder of the EPS was recruited mainly from among those that could prove some form of participation in the struggle against Somoza. The percentage of women in the EPS by the end of its first year was between 8-10 percent (women had represented 25 percent of FSLN combatants during the revolution).[17]

The inclusion of a small percentage of former GN members in the EPS requires some clarification as does the small percentage of women incorporated into the new army. Most (although certainly not all) of the brutality associated with the GN was committed by the 3,000 elite troops under the command of Anastasio Somoza's son. Those that were apprehended were tried before special tribunals. Other GN elements that were drawn overwhelmingly from poor social backgrounds and who merely followed orders and committed no crimes against the people were considered capable of resocialization by the FSLN. Nevertheless, by early 1980 leaders of the EPS claimed that no ex-*guardia* remained in the Sandinista Popular Army (which may have meant that their former identification with the GN had been completely overcome, since troops openly conceded the continued presence of former GN elements in the EPS).[18]

The reduction in the percentage of women in the new army resulted both from the diluting effect of heavy male enlistment after July 1979, and from the active encouragement of the EPS command for women to assume nonmilitary duties in the reconstruction of the country. In the event of foreign invasion, women were still considered suitable for combat duty, but during peactime they were considered to be better suited for administrative and technical positions. Those women that remained in the military were not fully integrated into male units, but instead were provided with separate quarters or, more frequently, an allowance for off-base housing (usually with their families).[19]

The length of military service remained "indeterminant" during the first year, although plans existed to fix minimum terms of enlistment at between two and three years. In practice, the EPS was interested in recruiting career soldiers. Basic training for recruits ranged from three to six months depending on the educational level and military experience of the individual. The Cuban government supplied an unspecified number (approximately 200-300) of military personnel to assist the Sandinista Popular Army in basic training, setting up advanced training programs, and as military advisors for regional commands. Veteran troops were used immediately after July to begin training Sandinista Popular Militias in areas of the country where the danger of counterrevolutionary activities seemed greatest. It was projected that by the end of the first year there would be over 100,000 fully trained individuals organized into MPSs throughout the country capable of rapid mobilization and integration into the EPS.

The MPSs were organized at the level of neighborhoods (usually in conjunction with the Sandinista Defense Committees), and served not only as a reserve for the army but also as extensions of the Sandinista Police. Men, women, and children were organized into separate brigades, and weapons remained in the possession of MPS leaders for distribution only when a brigade was called into service. Although the MPSs proved an effective and economical way of augmenting the strength of the EPS, plans were already in the making by late 1979 to replace the militias at some future point with mandatory military service.[20]

According to Luis Carrión, once the size of the EPS had been stabilized and its members fully trained, a draft would be instituted which would provide 30 to 40 thousand recruits a year with military training, following which they would serve for a set number of years in the reserves. To provide training for such a large number of draftees each year would require a low turnover within the regular army itself, which explains why the EPS sought career enlistees almost from the outset. To minimize the financial burden on the country of maintaining such a large military establishment, it was envisioned that the military (and especially the reserves) would increasingly assume civic responsibilities in the future that could directly increase national productivity. The regular army itself was intended to level off at roughly the same size as Somoza's National Guard, but the national defense would be made significantly stronger through the system of reserves.[21]

Another issue connected with efforts to professionalize the EPS was renumeration for officers and enlistees. A general policy established for the government as a whole set a maximum salary for any public employee of approximately 10,000 córdobas per month (or about $12,000 a year) in addition to housing and food allowances for certain categories of enlistees. It was recognized that the professionalization and stabilization of the composition of the EPS would require higher pay in the future, but during the first year the General Staff was forced to rely almost exclusively on moral incentives to attract, motivate and retain quality enlistees in the EPS.[22]

Finally, it is necessary to comment on the efforts of the Sandinista leadership to prevent even the slightest United States influence in the new Nicaraguan armed forces. Although the Sandinista Front called on the United States to supply the new regime with weapons immediately after the overthrow of Somoza, this probably indicated a desire to disarm the interventionist lobby in Washington more than it signaled a willingness to continue Nicaragua's traditional reliance on American military assistance. The request was rejected by Washington, but the United States did offer to (1) provide training programs for Nicaraguan military personnel in the United States, (2) send United States military advisors and instructors in noncombat military areas to Nicaragua, and (3) provide over $2 million in noncombat military assistance to the new government. (This third offer involved money that had been originally allocated to the Somoza government, but which had been held up after the United States applied an arms embargo to the country late in the War.)

Not only did the Sandinista leadership reject all three offers, but moved to restrict access by members of the United States military mission (attached to the United States Embassy in Managua) to Nicaraguan military personnel. After early 1980, Embassy personnel were required to obtain the prior permission of the Nicaraguan Defense Minister before either visiting Nicaraguan military installations or talking with EPS officers. The intention of such restrictions and precautions appears to have been to lessen the (albeit remote) possibility of United States political influence in the new Nicaraguan armed forces. The behavior of the Sandinista leadership in setting up the new military apparatus exhibited an awareness of the potential

political ramifications of an armed forces less than enthusiastically committed to revolutionary reform. Thus the measures to prevent virtually any
form of United States influence in the armed forces were consistent with
other policies in this field.

The Role of the Armed Forces in the Revolution

The Program of Government issued by the FSLN just before the fall of
Somoza clearly envisioned a major role for the new army in the reconstruction of Nicaraguan society:

> The national Army will maintain a permanent association with
> the civil population and participate actively in the tasks of
> reconstruction and development. To accomplish this its
> members will be organized into different technical specialties
> and professions.[23]

Although the armed forces forged close ties with the general population,
and participated whenever possible in the effort to rebuild the country, little
progress was made during the first year either to develop technical
capabilities within the military directly related to national reconstruction,
or to massively involve the EPS in public-works projects. Two explanations
can be offered for this. First, the serious educational deficiencies within the
EPS required that basic instruction preceed any large-scale program of
technical training. Second, the urgent need after the overthrow of the dictatorship to organize a national defense against internal and external threats
to the revolution forced the armed forces to concentrate primarily upon
their military role. Nevertheless, whenever possible the armed forces either
participated in, or lent direct support to, a wide range of socio-economic
projects during the first year after the Sandinista victory. We will review the
separate primary roles performed by the EPS, PS and MPSs in the following
discussion, but it should be kept in mind that all three worked in close
cooperation in a variety of activities.

The Sandinista Popular Army performed three major roles during its
first year. It defended the revolution from internal and external armed
threats, provided logistical and other forms of support for socio-economic
projects, and supplied emergency labor in critical areas of the economy.

The major sources of armed aggression against the Sandinista regime
were ex-*guardias*, the ultra-leftist *Milpas*, and right-wing guerrillas. After
the fall of Somoza, as many as 2,000 members of the defeated National
Guard escaped to Honduras, where they concentrated near the Nicaraguan
frontier. The EPS was forced to station a large proportion of its best-trained
soldiers in the northern provinces to defend against periodic incursions by
ex-*guardia* elements. The Sandinista Popular Army also attempted to
strengthen the defenses along the northern frontier by giving priority to the
organization and training of the Sandinista Popular Militias in the northern

provinces, especially Estelí. Although the EPS generally succeeded in deterring any large scale counterrevolutionary actions by ex-*guardia* units, isolated attacks by groups of Somocista soldiers crossing into Nicaragua continued throughout the first year.[24]

The ability of the revolutionary government to protect participants in important projects like the Literacy Campaign from attacks by counterrevolutionary groups was viewed as a crucial test of Sandinista strength. The EPS responded by establishing closer ties with mass-based popular organizations such as the Sandinista Defense Committees (CDSs), the Association of Rural Workers (ATC) and, of course, the MPSs. While countering the threat of remaining GN elements in the north, however, the EPS also had to contain the para-military activities of the Milpas in the leading urban centers.

The Milpas engaged in a number of "counterrevolutionary" acts, ranging from keeping workers out on strike through armed intimidation to attacks on banks to finance ultra-leftist activities. But the overall intention of the Milpas was to push the government further to the left by forcing it to quicken the tempo of reform, and not to involve the EPS in a protracted armed struggle. Accordingly, it was possible for the FLSN to pursue a dual strategy of attempting to strike a political bargain with the Workers Front that controlled the Milpas, while at the same time the EPS contained and limited the activities of the Milpas.[25]

A much more serious threat was posed by the Democratic Armed Forces (*Fuerzas Armadas Democratia*—[FAD]) which began operating in the central provinces in early 1980. The FAD was a right-wing guerrilla organization financed in large part by members of the livestock component of the agroexport bourgeoisie. Its largest armed action was the capture of San José de los Remátes in the province of Boaco in May 1980. Twenty heavily armed FAD members were able to attack the EPS command in Los Remátes and hold the town of 2,000 for over five hours. Within a week of the attack, however, State Security Forces had rounded up forty-two individuals suspected of involvement, including important members of the Livestock Federation of Nicaragua accused of financing FAD activities and providing their *fincas* as training centers.[26]

Defending the revolutionary government against these sources of armed opposition forced the EPS to concentrate most of its attention on purely military functions. According to the information officer of the EPS, the central responsibility of the army during its first year remained military preparation. But to the extent that time and resources permitted, the EPS filled other roles as well. In particular, the army remained available for the transportation of supplies and workers involved in government programs or reconstruction projects. When it was discovered that many of the volunteers in the Literacy Campaign sent into remote areas could not be adequately fed by the families they were sent to teach, it became largely the responsibility of the EPS and PS to undertake a crash program to deliver provisions to these areas. Another form of participation by the EPS in the recovery of the country after the insurrection was the use of soldiers to help harvest the first coffee crop. But because of the pressing need to concentrate on military training in the regular army, the MPSs were used more often than the EPS in civic work projects and agricultural labor.[27]

The Sandinista police frequently found themselves participating closely with the EPS in controlling counterrevolutionary groups and lending material and physical assistance to national reconstruction programs. The PS also received sufficient military training to participate in national defense since in the event of a foreign threat, as Tomás Borge explained, "the police and soldiers of the Sandinista Popular Army are going to go to the same trenches and shed the same blood."[28] But under normal conditions it was intended that the functions of the police and army would be quite distinct. According to Borge,

> The members of the State Security Forces, the Sandinista Police and the Sandinista Popular Army form part of the same family and regardless of where they go they must be coordinated. United in the same force, the only thing that has to be understood is that their functions are distinct. The police are responsible for maintaining order, protecting the people—especially children and the weak—from delinquents and from antisocial enemies. . . . The army should concentrate on constant military training in order to be ready as a vanguard force in the hour of combat to confront the armed enemies of our Revolution. . . .[29]

In practice, the PS actually did concentrate on law enforcement during the first year. Three important objectives of the PS Central Command were (1) reducing street crime, (2) controlling vice, and (3) enforcing what might be termed morality and public welfare laws.

During the last stages of the civil war, a large quantity of weapons were distributed among the population, reaching some elements that had not participated in the struggle against the GN. The breakdown of the old order, coupled with a sharp rise in the number of weapons held by private citizens, helped give rise to an increase in violent crimes after the Sandinista victory. The problem was compounded by the appearance of numerous youth gangs involved in drug traffic, armed robberies, and related activities. To contend with the problem, the police began to conduct well coordinated raids in early 1980, arresting "known delinquents" for "illicit association" (when more serious charges could not be pressed). By late May 1980, the Sandinista Police Central Command was able to announce a decline in crime rates in certain categories.[30]

In the area of vice and public welfare, the police were charged with enforcing a wide variety of laws intended to moralize society and erradicate the social legacies of the decadent Somoza dynasty. Two targets of this campaign were prostitution and alcoholism. But efforts to control prostitution and drunkenness were complicated by a number of interrelated factors. First, there was a shortage of resources with which to set up rehabilitation programs and thus enforcement of laws against prostitution, for example, could only be punative (and prostitutes were not considered criminals). Second, the enforcement of laws like those prohibiting the consumption of alcohol in the market places or the sale of intoxicants before certain hours often brought the police into conflict with members of the lowest social classes and therefore detracted somewhat from efforts to increase solidarity between the police and the people. In essence, the FSLN was forced to recognize that governments cannot legislate morality. Thus, police turned a blind eye to prostitution until June 1980, when some limited efforts were finally made to enforce laws against prostitution, but laws controlling alcohol continued to be only sporadically and unevenly enforced by the police. For instance, laws restricting the sale of beer before afternoon were universally disregarded by the public, and the police relied mostly on warnings against lower-class proprietors caught violating the law rather than arrests or citations.

While the EPS concentrated primarily on military functions, and the PS on law enforcement, the Sandinista Popular Militias filled a number of roles in the revolution. The MPSs served as a reserve for the army, and also as an extension of the police. Members of the MPSs were frequently employed to guard public installations or aid police in major operations. Those militias organized in factories were used to protect the installations and equipment from destruction by ultra-leftist elements (such as the Milpas) during labor disturbances, or from owners who might attempt to decapitalize their facilities in anticipation of expropriation. In some neighborhoods, the MPSs took over a large share of the responsibility of the Sandinista Police, while in the countryside they were assigned to protect volunteers in the Literacy Campaign from right-wing terrorist activities.

In practice, it was the MPSs during the first year that provided much of the voluntary labor for harvesting crops, building public facilities, and cleaning up the *barrios*. Manpower constraints and the need to concentrate on intensive military training severely limited the ability of the EPS to participate in the reconstruction of the economy. Indeed, given the high rate of unemployment among the general population, there was no real demand for the army to supply manpower that could be easily mobilized through the CDSs, MPSs, and other mass-based organizations. Rather, the actual purpose of occasionally providing troops from the regular army to participate in voluntary labor projects was to forge closer ties with the people.

A final role performed by the armed forces as a whole which must be touched on involved the suppression of political opposition. The FSLN promised pluralist revolution, and to a surprising extent for a group that held a decisive power advantage it observed that pledge. There was considerable, if not complete, freedom of the press during the first year of Sandinista rule, and the bourgeois opposition was permitted to organize and criticize the government after it became alarmed with the perceived direction of revolutionary reform in early 1980. But the Sandinista Front, nevertheless, showed itself willing to carry out selective repressions against specific groups it considered potentially dangerous. Accordingly, the police and State Security forces were used on a number of occasions to capture political opponents of the regime who were then held secretly in violation of the new Statute of Rights issued by the FSLN, or were convicted on vague and unsubstantiated charges.[31]

Two examples of such political repression were the arrest and illegal detention of the leaders of an ultra-leftist newspaper and the imprisonment of the popular radio commentator, Guillermo Treminio. Immediately after assuming power, the Sandinista Front closed the left-wing newspaper *El Pueblo* and arrested its editor "for encouraging too divisive a line."[32] While the paper was subsequently allowed to reappear, tensions between the FSLN and the Workers' Front that controlled the paper continued. Finally, the paper was again closed, and in May 1980 its editors and the leaders of the Workers' Front detained. These individuals were held in army facilities rather than police facilities, and no charges were filed. After about a month of "negotiations" with the FSLN leaders (including Tomás Borge), the prisoners were conditionally released apparently in return for a political agreement. The case of Treminio, on the other hand, demonstrated the limits of FSLN tolerance. A moderate who had taken a mild stand against Somoza before the revolution, Treminio was arrested in mid-1980 after refusing to stop broadcasting stories critical of government programs. He was quickly convicted by a compliant court of "association with the Somoza regime" before the revolution and sentenced to eleven months in prison.[33]

Illegal detentions also occurred throughout the country as regional commanders gave in to the temptation of dealing with critics of the regime by holding them incommunicado. However, it should be stressed that the government did not use the armed forces in a *systematic* program of repression, that those who were detained were not mistreated as had been the practice under Somoza, and that the prison terms of those few actually convicted of political crimes tended to be relatively short. Therefore, the fact that the EPS, PS, and even the MPSs were employed to limit some forms of political opposition should not overshadow the reality that the Sandinista government actually exhibited considerable restraint in view of its complete and undivided control of the military institutions of the state.

Conclusions

The Sandinista Front succeeded in consolidating and institutionalizing its control over the new armed forces during its first year in power, which in turn contributed significantly to the FSLN's control over the direction of governmental policies. Therefore, the creation and rapid development of the Sandinista Popular Army, the Sandinista Police, and the Sandinista Popular Militias stands out as one of the major political achievements of the immediate "postwar" period. Several factors facilitated the FSLN's efforts to build a new and effective military apparatus in Nicaragua. First, the length of the Sandinista Front's struggle against the Somoza dictatorship forged an experienced and politically-oriented cadre of guerrillas which was able to serve as the core of the new army. It was not necessary for the new revolutionary leaders in Nicaragua to rely, even in part, on the prerevolutionary military establishment. Equally important, the Sandinista leaders who assumed the command positions within the armed forces demonstrated early their intentions of imposing discipline and centralized authority over the military, and their willingness to purge dissident elements even from among their own ranks. This emphasis on discipline and centralized authority was complemented by a vigorous program of political-cultural indoctrination of recruits. This created a noticeably different institutional mentality within the Nicaraguan armed forces from that found in other so-called revolutionary Latin American countries. Finally, the precautions against the establishment of even a modicum of United States influence in the new armed forces helped strengthen the revolutionary orientation of the army and its loyalty to the Sandinista Front.

Notes

[1] Eduardo Crawley, *Dictators Never Die: A Portrait of Nicaragua and the Somoza Dynasty* (New York: St. Martin's Press, 1979), pp. 58-64.

[2] Eduardo Crawley, *Dictators,* pp. 148-154; and James Petras, "Whither the Nicaraguan Revolution?" *Monthly Review* 31 (October 1979): 7-9.

[3] James Petras, "Nicaraguan Revolution," p. 11.

[4] The political objectives of the December action are discussed in Jaime Wheelock, *Diciembre victorioso* (Managua: Secretaría Nacional de Propaganda y Educación Política, 1979). The repression that followed is discussed in an interview with Humberto Ortega Saavedra in "La estrategia del triúnfo," *La Prensa,* Jan. 4, 1980.

[5] The positions of all three tendencies are presented in "Sandinista Perspectives: Three Differing Views," *Latin American Perspectives* 6 (Winter 1979), pp. 114-127.

[6] Ibid., p. 122.

[7] See Gabriel García Marquez, "Sandinistas Seize the National Palace," *New Left Review,* (September 1978), pp. 79-88; and part two of "La estrategia del triúnfo," *La Prensa,* Jan. 4, 1980, p. 1.

[8] *Latin America Political Report* 13 (June 1, 1979), pp. 161-62; and *Latin American Political Report* 13 (June 8, 1979), pp. 169-170.

[9] The Battle for Managua is described in detail in Roger Mendienta Alfaro, *El último marine* (Managua, Editorial Unión, 1980).

[10] Interview with Luis Carrión, "La guerrilla se transforma en ejército regular," *Cuadernos de Marcha* 1 (Jan.-Feb. 1980), pp. 99-100.

[11] *Barricada* June 4, 1980, p. 7.

[12] *Programa de gobierno* (Managua: Junta de Gobierno de Reconstrucción Nacional, 1979), p. 4.

[13] See interview with Tomás Borge, "El poder lo tienen las classes tradicionalmente explotadas," *Cuadernos de Marcha* 1 (Jan.-Feb. 1980), p. 86.

[14] See *Barricada*, Jan. 29, 1980, p. 1.

[15] Interview with Roberto Sánchez, Director of Press and Information for the EPS, Managua, June 2, 1980.

[16] Borge, "El poder lo tienen las clases," p. 87.

[17] Estimates are based on discussions with the staff of the United States Military Attaché held at the United States Embassy, Managua, May 27, 1980; interviews with reporters from *La Prensa* in January and June 1980; and the interview with Roberto Sánchez, June 2, 1980.

[18] Roberto Sánchez stated in June 1980 that no ex-*guardias* remained in the EPS. This was contradicted in conversations with platoon leaders from El Chipote, the EPS Central Command, and by individuals connected with the United States Embassy.

[19] Interview with Roberto Sánchez.

[20] See Luis Carrión, "La guerrilla se transforma," on the role of the militias. For an example of segregation of men, women, and children in the militias, see *Barricada*, June 4, 1980, p. 7. Other information on the militias was obtained from interviews in Pochocuape, Managua, during January, May, and June 1980, and in Estelí during May 1980.

[21] Luis Carrión, "La guerrilla se transforma," pp. 98-99.

[22] See interview with Adolfo Chamorro Téfel, ex-*responsable* in charge of personnel and housing for the EPS in *Barricada*, Dec. 29, 1979, p. 7.

[23] *Programa de gobierno*, p. 4.

[24] At least seven individuals involved with the literacy campaign had been killed by the first anniversary of the revolution. The most politically disturbing act was the murder of Georgino Andrade, an area coordinator for the literacy campaign in a rural village. See *El Nuevo Diario*, May 23, 1980, p. 1.

[25] *La Prensa*, June 5, 1980, p. 1.

[26] See *El Nuevo Diario*, May 28, 1980, p. 1; and *La Prensa*, June 5, 1980, pp. 1 and 4.

[27] Interview with Roberto Sánchez.

[28] *Discurso del Comandante Tomás Borge durante la promoción policial de la escuela Carlos Agüero E. (Managua: Oficina de Divulgación y Prensa, Ministerio del Interior, Dec. 16, 1979), p. 1.*

[29] Ibid.

[30] *El Nuevo Diario*, May 28, 1980, p. 9.

[31] The Statute is reproduced in Pedro Camejo and Fred Murphy, eds., *The Nicaraguan Revolution* (New York: Pathfinder, 1979), pp. 43-55.

[32] *Latin America Political Report* 13 (July 27, 1979), p. 228.

[33] See *El Nuevo Diario*, May 28, 1980, p. 1.

Chapter 7

The Working Class
in the Nicaraguan Revolution

MARIFELI PÉREZ-STABLE

The working class in Nicaragua is small and had a limited history of struggle prior to the 1970s. Trade unions were first organized by anarcho-
syndicalists after World War I. In the early 1920s, agricultural workers at
the Cuyamel Fruit Co. and the Cukra Development organized strikes,
which were brutally repressed. A few years later, in 1932, when Augusto
César Sandino was fighting in Las Segovias, workers called a strike against
the Braggman Bluff Lumber Co. Many subsequently joined Sandino's struggle in the mountains. In 1936, rising gasoline prices sparked a popular strike
in Managua. A period of popular-front politics in the forties saw Anastasio
Somoza García presiding at May 1 celebrations. Construction workers,
probably the most militant in the Nicaraguan working class, formed their
unions in 1951. With the development of the cotton industry in the fifties,
the first rural workers' unions were organized. Two trade union confederations existed throughout the period: one was created by the dictatorship and
the other, the General Confederation of Workers-Independent (CGT-I),
was affiliated with the Socialist Party of Nicaragua (PSN).[1] In the early sixties, a third confederation, the Nicaraguan Confederation of Workers
(CTN), closely associated with Christian Democracy and some claim, the
local bourgeoisie, came into existence.[2]

In the sixties, the policies of regional integration and industrialization
of the Central American Common Market brought significant consequences
to Nicaraguan society. The modern, entrepreneurial bourgeoisie which had
emerged in the fifties with the cotton industry was strengthened. Industrial
workers grew to about 70,000, out of an economically active population of
nearly seven hundred thousand.[3] Most important, capital-intensive export-
oriented industrialization accentuated the social, political and economic
contradictions inherent to dependent capitalism and aggravated in
Nicaragua by a dynastic, military dictatorship.[4] These contradictions exploded in the seventies and helped pave the road to the revolutionary victory of July 19, 1979.[5]

The Somozas' failure to achieve a ruling consensus with the bourgeoisie
was one of the contradictions which doomed their domination of Nicaragua

in the seventies. The bourgeoisie likewise failed to secure its hegemony in the struggle against the dictatorship during the crucial eighteen-month period of 1978-79. The Sandinist Front of National Liberation (FSLN) and the Nicaraguan people defeated Somoza and destroyed the foundations of *Somocismo* on July 19. An analysis of the working class in Nicaragua necessarily draws us to a closer look at class alliances during the war against Anastasio Somoza Debayle and during the first year of the Revolution. The emergence and consolidation of popular power and the frustrated efforts by the bourgeoisie to establish its hegemony in Nicaragua are key components in understanding the role of the working class in the Nicaraguan Revolution.

Class Alliances: 1978-79.

Pedro Joaquín Chamorro's assassination in January 1978 initiated the final stage in the popular struggle against the forty-five year military dictatorship. Eighteen months later, the FSLN offensive and its mass mobilizations drove the last of the Somozas out of Nicaragua. During this period, the FSLN and the popular movement established their leadership over the struggle against *Somocismo.*

By its very nature, the Somoza dynasty sowed the seeds of a bourgeois opposition. A corrupt and repressive regime was not conducive to the institutionalization of an "impartial" and efficient capitalist state. A sector of the bourgeoisie, then, opposed Somoza while striving to reform the state to satisfy its needs for efficiency and rationality. The 1972 earthquake and the subsequent reconstruction of Managua reinforced the bourgeoisie's opposition to Somoza and its determination to save the foundations of *Somocismo.*

The earthquake became just another source of enrichment for Somoza and the National Guard. The social catastrophe was aggravated by their plunder and pillage. They monopolized the key enterprises for the reconstruction of Managua (banking, construction and insurance companies, and so on). The dictatorship moreover did not give aid to Managua's middle classes, which were left in relative misery after the earthquake. Thus, Somoza considerably weakened the state's legitimacy and paved the way for an eventual tactical unity of the bourgeois and popular opposition movements.

The dictatorship's callous response to the human misery caused by the earthquake deepened popular discontent. Initially, however, this malcontent was not channelled organizationally even though the FSLN guerrillas were becoming stronger. In December 1974, an FSLN commando took over the home of Chema Castillo, an important Somocista and was successful in freeing eighteen political prisoners and extracting five million dollars from Somoza.[6] Immediately following this bold Sandinista action, Somoza declared a state of siege which lasted three years. The brutal repression during these years slowed down the organization of the popular opposition.

Nevertheless, some progress was made in organizing popular and bourgeois opposition fronts. In 1974, the Union for Democratic Liberation (UDEL) was formed. Its initial program called for political and economic reforms that had anti-imperialist overtones. Its radical content, however, was diluted shortly thereafter. Influenced by the United States, moderate elements imposed a "Somocismo without Somoza" line in UDEL. In 1977, the "Group of Twelve" was formed by prominent business, civic, intellectual, and religious leaders. The "Twelve" launched an international campaign against the dictatorship.

At the same time, the FSLN guerrillas were being violently combatted by the National Guard. Some Sandinistas consequently began to spread out to urban areas. Two tendencies then developed within the FSLN: Prolonged Popular War (GPP) emphasizing guerrilla warfare as the fundamental step in the offensive against the dictatorship and the Proletarian Tendency (TP) underscoring the primacy of popular organization in urban areas. Towards the end of 1977, Somoza lifted the state of siege thus opening new possibilities for alliances between the opposition bourgeoisie-middle classes and the FSLN-popular movement. The Tercerista (third) Tendency emerged in this context with a program whose aim was to unite the broad opposition sectors and spark a national insurrection. The Terceristas also implemented bold, surprise attacks like those of the San Carlos garrison in October 1977 and the National Palace takeover in August 1978. They contended that these attacks would prove the vulnerability of the National Guard.[7]

When Somoza ended the state of siege in September 1977, he had apparently resolved that, on the one hand, the guerrillas could be defeated militarily and, on the other, the bourgeois opposition could be pacified with concessions that would also help recover for the state some of its badly needed legitimacy. With the restoration of civil liberties, Pedro Joaquín Chamorro unleashed a campaign in La Prensa against the crimes and corruption of the dictatorship. Three months later, Somoza's son, Anastasio Somoza Portocarrero, apparently ordered Chamorro's assassination. With his death, Somoza's strategy of winning over the bourgeois opposition suffered a serious setback. The bourgeoisie immediately promoted a national protest movement. The UDEL called a general strike, which was supported by numerous popular organizations. It was the first joint bourgeois-popular action against the dictatorship. For over two weeks, the country was paralyzed except for the popular mobilizations and the guerrilla actions.

The popular opposition achieved an important organizational takeoff through the militias, the Civil Defense Committees (CDC), and the Work Defense Committees (CDT). Even though the bourgeoisie led the movement to protest Chamorro's death, the dynamics of mass mobilizations weakened its leadership. Not only were popular organizations created and strengthened, but the Monimbó insurrection (February 1978) opened new possibilities for the popular war against Somoza and the National Guard.

Throughout 1978, two opposition fronts were organized. The Broad Opposition Front (FAO) was at first led by the Twelve. The UDEL, the FSLN, and other organizations joined the FAO. The bourgeoisie, however, rapidly gained control of the FAO and imposed the U.S.-inspired device of mediation with Somoza as the Front's principal opposition strategy. The Twelve and the FSLN withdrew in protest. The FAO subsequently became the bourgeoisie's front against Somoza and against the FSLN.

The United Popular Movement (MPU) was formed during the September general strike and insurrection following the National Palace takeover in August. The MPU constituted the popular counterpart to the FAO. It concentrated its efforts in organizing the CDCs and CDTs. By early 1979, the FAO was discredited and weakened by its participation in the abortive mediation effort with Somoza, and the MPU had surpassed the FAO through its mass mobilization and organizations.

With the establishment in February 1979 of the National Patriotic Front (FPN) linking the FSLN, MPU and other organizations and the unification in March of the three FSLN tendencies under one National Directorate, the popular movement secured its hegemony over the political and military struggle against the Somoza dictatorship. The Sandinistas announced their program for government of National Reconstruction in April. In May, the FPN and the FAO agreed to join their efforts against Somoza. By then, however, there could be little doubt that the popular opposition had gained momentum over that of the bourgeoisie. A month later, the FSLN offensive and the popular insurrections propelled the fall of *Somocismo*.

The bourgeoisie and its international allies, however, made desperate last minute efforts to dislodge the FSLN from its position of leadership. These included the United States call for an OAS peace-keeping force and demands to expand the Governing Junta of National Reconstruction to seven members and to preserve the National Guard. Their efforts were fruitless. By July 1979, the impetus toward a popular victory in Nicaragua was overpowering.

A strategy of class alliances emerged as a necessity in the struggle to overthrow Somoza. After 1972, there were two ways in which to fight the dictatorship. The bourgeoisie supported the mediation with Somoza as the means to its objective of preserving the state. The FSLN advocated armed struggle to uproot *Somocismo*. The dynamics of mass mobilization and Somoza's intransigent reaction eliminated the first road. The popular forces gained the upper hand in the struggle since Somoza was reticent in establishing a dialogue with the opposition bourgeoisie. In early 1979, once it had become evident that the mediation had failed, the strategy of armed struggle became the only real option. For the bourgeoisie, then, the alliance with the FSLN became indispensable if in some way it wished to have a voice in the new Nicaragua.

On the other hand, the policy of class alliances allowed the FSLN to reach broad sectors of the population for the final offensive and insurrection against *Somocismo*. This policy was not founded on a gentlemen's agreement or a pact of any kind with the bourgeois leadership. Humberto Ortega, Commander in Chief of the Popular Sandinista Army, later pointed this out:

> We achieved that broad policy because we inspired respect and other organizations did not . . . we were perceived as strong and therefore, an alliance with us became a necessity. . . . Other organizations became our allies even though we were a movement of armed struggle with revolutionary leadership. . . . The strategy of alliances was reached through concrete actions, not agreements. We did not sustain any agreements. We simply established the rules of the game and acted accordingly . . . these alliances were implemented through actions.[8]

Popular Power and Class Alliances: The First Year

Even though the anti-Somoza bourgeoisie failed in its attempts to preserve the state in the overthrow of Somoza, it had not given up its objective of structuring the new state to fulfill the requirements of capitalist capital accumulation. Likewise, the FSLN had not renounced its goal of a future socialist transformation of Nicaragua. To keep open the possibility of attaining the goal, the FSLN and the Government of National Reconstruction had to strive increasingly to expand state economic planning. The questions of who controlled the state and who were its primary benefactors in the reconstruction process were, therefore, at the heart of the class struggle in Nicaragua.[9]

During the first year, the Revolution established new rules of the game in its alliance with the bourgeoisie. The expropriation of Somoza and the *Somocistas* placed approximately 40 percent of the Gross Domestic Product (GDP) in the hands of the state. The banking system and foreign trade were also nationalized. The bourgeoisie, thus, controlled 60 percent of the GDP. Moreover and more importantly, 80 percent of agricultural production and 75 percent of manufacturing were privately generated. The economic weight of the bourgeoisie in the new Nicaragua was self-evident. It was equally clear that the implementation of radical economic measures would have precipitated a rupture with the bourgeoisie and its international allies that would have resulted in economic chaos. The Sandinista leadership proved to be unwilling to bring upon the Nicaraguan people the additional misery that such chaos would have entailed.

The principal area of contention during the first year was, therefore, political power. While the FSLN looked favorably upon the patriotic bourgeoisie and was disposed towards taking its opinions into consideration in policy-making, the Sandinistas were intransigent about the primacy of institutions that would consolidate popular hegemony over the state.

Popular power rested first and foremost in the Sandinista army. The new Council of State in which popular organizations had a plurality of the votes was also essential to popular democracy.[10] Likewise, the creation, expansion and consolidation of the Sandinista Workers' Confederation (CST) emerged as a key component in the political struggles in revolutionary Nicaragua.[11]

Prior to the revolutionary victory, 6 percent of the labor force was unionized in Nicaragua.[12] Until the 1970s, the Somozas' brutal repression had preempted the emergence, consolidation, and militancy of popular organizations. Although repression had by no means let up during the seventies, the social, political and economic contradictions in Nicaraguan society had exploded and stirred popular mobilizations in detriment to *Somocismo*. The FSLN strategy of institutionalizing popular power was therefore directed towards maximizing the organizational benefits of the insurrection which had toppled Somoza. The CST was in the forefront of this strategy. By July 1980, out of a total of 457 urban labor unions, 360 were affiliated with the CST. This meant that more than 200,000 urban workers belonged to Sandinista unions.[13]

The most sensitive task for the CST during 1979-80 was educating workers in their rights and duties within the new revolutionary context. Numerous labor conflicts were precipitated by demands for salary increases. The CST and the FSLN maintained that the Revolution was working towards increasing the workers' social salary (i.e. benefits they received as members of society) instead of their individual salaries. Across-the-board salary increases were considered inflationary, destabilizing, and demagogic.[14]

At the Sacos Macén factory (privately owned), for example, Humberto Ortega told workers and management: "The CST is going to defend workers' rights but it is also going to educate workers in social consciousness, not just trade-union consciousness. The owners have to realize that they must operate the factory at full capacity."[15] Although workers had gone on strike for salary increases, they had also accused management of purposefully slowing down production. A few days later, Jaime Wheelock, Minister of Agricultural Development, pointed out to a group of leaders of the CST and the Association of Rural Workers (ATC) in Masaya that the working class had to be ". . . political, persuasive but careful with respect to the patriotic bourgeoisie. It must understand that the class alliance is a way of guaranteeing the Revolution's stability and maintaining national unity."[16]

At the end of October, the 700 workers at the Plywood factory (state-owned) went out on strike, again demanding salary increases. Victor Tirado, member of the FSLN National Directorate, addressed the workers: "The old ways of struggling and claiming your rights no longer respond to the present moment."[17] Minister of Labor Virgilio Gogoy Reyes conveyed a similar point after a visit to Cuba: "Rather than demanding an individual salary increase, there is another type of policy in which workers are persuaded to demand an increase in social services that becomes in fact an increase in their real salary. . . ."[18]

The beginning of 1980 saw the most serious clashes over demands for salary increases. The first took place at the Amalia sugar mill (state-owned). The CTN led the strike and claimed that the state did not represent workers' interests.[19] The gravest incidents occurred at the Monterrosa and San Antonio sugar mills, the second being the largest in Central America and privately owned. The Workers' Front (FO), a small, ultra-left organization, led the strikes.[20] The third was related to the demand for a 100-percent salary increase for the industrial unions affiliated to the Action and Labor Union Federation (CAUS). The impossibility of satisfying that demand precipitated CAUS's break from the National   Intersyndical Commission.[21]

In February, the CST announced its program of struggle to improve working and living conditions. Its main points were (1) the implementation of minimum pay for the lowest-paid workers; (2) a revision of the wage scales and labor code; (3) improvement of workers' social salary; and (4) increasing workers' participation in factory management through Production Councils.[22] The CST also stepped up its leadership in the National Inter-Syndical   Commission with the future objective of forging a single labor confederation.[23] These steps placed the CST in a stronger position to deal with workers' demands.

The CST and the FSLN were careful to point out that workers were not to blame for these conflicts. In an interview published in *Barricada*, Carlos Núñez, FSLN National Directorate member, stated:

> We are not condemning workers' attitudes, but rather appealing to their revolutionary consciences so that they understand the situation. . . . Wages policy will be revised. . . . that is frankly their right . . . their needs will be satisfied with their participation.[24]

In an analysis of trade union organizations in the sugar industry, *Poder Sandinista* noted:

> The lack of union experience and the absence of leaders with experience in handling labor conflicts created the conditions which allowed some labor federations—CTN, FO, and CAUS—to take advantage of workers' just demands to pursue their particular organizational interests."[25]

Moreover, in at least one case, the conflict at the San Rafael del Sur cement factory, the Sandinista leadership criticized the CST local representative for giving workers dogmatic, bureaucratic responses to their demands for salary increases.[26] It is also significant that the government underplayed the role of foreign intervention in these conflicts:

> When the working class has a low level of political con-
> sciousness, naturally there is a danger that the CIA and the rest
> of our enemies will try to manipulate workers' spontaneous ac-
> tions, but they do not cause these actions and certainly, workers
> are not counter-revolutionaries.[27]

At least two other types of situations provoked labor conflicts in
Nicaragua through August 1980. One way in which the bourgeoisie opposed the Revolution was through decapitalization and a slowdown in production. Workers at El Caracol factory, for example, took over the enterprise
after it had become clear that its owners were hampering its normal functioning.[28] Two months after the takeover, El Caracol production had increased by 75 percent and total employment had been raised from 121 to
155. Basic foods sale at controlled prices at the factory saved each worker
80 córdobas a month. The trade union was active in establishing social services for the workers such as a clinic and day-care center.[29] Factory
takeovers were emerging as a powerful working-class weapon for
strengthening its hegemony over the new state.

The second was related to occupational safety. The CST promoted the
creation of health committees. These were charged with investigating
hazardous working conditions, proposing ways of dealing with safety
hazards, demanding periodic medical attention for all workers and pressuring multinational corporations to operate their enterprises by international
health standards.[30] The most significant violations of safe working conditions were found in the mining industry and in banana plantations.[31] Housing conditions in sixteen privately owned plantations in Chinandega
became the object of a Council of State intervention in August. After an in-
spection of workers' living conditions by a commission of the Council of
State, a law was passed appropriating 20 million córdobas to construct adequate housing. The step was unique in that a state-owned project was to be
built on privately owned lands.[32]

Upon their victory, the Sandinistas found an economy in shambles
which allowed only modest increases in workers' social salaries during the
Revolution's first year. Moreover, inflation and unemployment restrained
the government's possibilities for further and more rapid increases in social
salaries.[33] Nevertheless, record-breaking investments were made in education and health.[34] The National Literacy Crusade reduced illiteracy to 12
percent, the third-lowest in Latin America.[35] The urban reform law slashed
rents under 5,000 córdobas a month by as much as 50 percent.[36] The safety
of working conditions became a central demand of both the government
and the trade unions. Subsidized lunches and the sale of basic foods at controlled prices through work centers helped workers fight inflation.[37] A National Commission for Professional Education was set up to promote
workers' rights to an education.[38]

While it was evident that the Revolution had at least modestly improved the life of Nicaraguan workers, its most notable accomplishment was the working class newly acquired sense of power. This sense was the starting point for the FSLN's strategy of institutionalizing popular power. In 1979-80, the revolutionary government took the first steps towards changing the social relations of production. The State Sector (APP) was in the forefront of these transformations.[39]

Although uneven, there was some discussion of the 1980 economic plan with the mass organizations, especially the CST. The Sandinista leadership was aware that mass participation could not be achieved by decree and that it would take years to develop adequate and responsive mechanisms. It nevertheless maintained that ". . . the principle of worker participation cannot be suppressed simply because workers cannot participate in the same way as a minister . . . the problem of mass participation will be one of the fundamental challenges of the Sandinista Revolution."[40]

The establishment of Production Councils was one of the CSTs' main political objectives. It simultaneously launched a campaign against bureaucratizing workers' participation.[41] It was interesting that in at least one occasion, the adjective production qualifying the councils was put into question: "To say that the grassroot organizations are Production Councils might exclude a priori dealing with political tasks that are not directly linked to production: the various ways in which surpluses are distributed, for example."[42] Furthermore, the Sandinistas recognized working class autonomy. Speaking for the FSLN National Directorate, Carlos Nuñez stated: "Should the mass organizations draw upon their own strengths in expressing and mobilizing their demands when these are not heard, when all doors are shut without answers? We believe so."[43]

Conclusions

As the Revolution celebrated its first anniversary, the Sandinistas took further steps to augment popular hegemony over the state. On July 19, 1980, Daniel Ortega, member of both the FSLN Directorate and the Governing Junta of National Reconstruction, announced that the agrarian reform would be extended to include idle lands.[44]. On August 23, Humberto Ortega told a 200,000-strong crowd in Managua that elections would not be held until 1985. Reconstruction tasks and defense of the Revolution would be overriding until then.[45] In mid-September, Victor Tirado called the nation to make greater sacrifices. He said that there would be cuts on luxury imports and that most investments would be made in the productive areas with priority in the state sector. He added that private industry would also get a boost, and that spending levels in health and education would be maintained.[46] These measures strengthened the role of the state in the economy.

The Sandinistas also sought to establish popular political institutions to go hand-in-hand with an expanded state role in the economy. The CST, the other mass organizations and the Council of State were significant steps in the institutionalization of popular power during 1979-80. The FSLN and the CST made considerable gains in organizing the working class under their leadership. The urgency of reconstruction, Nicaragua's mixed economy, and the need to secure capital investments underscored the question of how to create expedient and responsive mechanisms for workers' participation. While the alliance with the bourgeoisie was essential for economic recovery, the Sandinistas were first and foremost committed to the workers, the peasants, and the poor of Nicaragua. Their first year in power saw healthy economic growth with modest improvements in the Nicaraguan people's standard of living.[47] The institutionalization of popular power was the only guarantee that those improvements would continue and increase in the future as popular interests became the motor force in consumption and investment decisions. Whether the Nicaraguan bourgeoisie would accept its secondary role in Sandinista pluralism for the nation's well-being or whether it would turn against the Revolution through national and international economic boycotts and (or) military actions would greatly affect the future course of the Nicaraguan Revolution.

Notes

[1] The PSN was the official communist party. In the late sixties, the party lost many young cadre to the FSLN because of its position on armed struggle. In a 1967 turnabout, however, the faction opposed to armed struggle was expelled. This faction subsequently formed the Communist Party and the Action and Labor Union Federation (CAUS), which developed a base in the industrial sector in the seventies. Once again in 1976, the PSN was divided over the question of armed struggle. This time, both factions retained the names PSN and CGT. The armed struggle group founded the Organizacion Militar del Pueblo, which coordinated its actions with the FSLN. The remaining PSN and CGT joined the FSLN and the CST's call for unity in the National Inter-Syndicate Commission.

[2] The CTN, originally MOSAN (Nicaraguan Autonomus Labor Movement), was affiliated with the Christian Democratic Confederation of Latin American Workers (CLAT). Onofre Guevara, presently an FSLN militant and formerly a member of the dissolved PSN, identified the CTN as an ally of the bourgeoisie in an interview with me in Managua, April 26, 1980. Guevara was a labor specialist for the PSN. The opinion seemed to be corraborated by Salvador Sanchez's (a CTN leader) statement to me in an interview that Alfonso Robelo had done the right thing in resigning as his interests were being overlooked by the FSLN. "Nicaragua's Revolution," *NACLA Report on the Americas*, XIV (May-June 1980); p. 25 also points out: "The CTN . . . openly supports the political positions of the opposition bourgeoisie. . . ."

[3] *Datos básicos sobre Nicaragua* (Nicaragua: Secretaría Nacional de Propaganda y Educación Política del FSLN, 1980), p. 8.

[4] See Jaime Wheelock, *Imperialismo y Dictadura* (Mexico: Siglo XXI Editores, 1978); and Julio López C., Orlando Núñez S., Carlos Fernando Chamorro Barrios, and Pascual Serres, *La caída del somocismo y la lucha sandinista en Nicaragua* (Costa Rica: Editorial Universitaria Centroamericana, 1979).

[5] After the 1972 earthquake, construction workers led a series of strikes against working longer weeks (60 hours) in the reconstruction of Managua. In 1973 and 1974, an upsurge in

strikes took place, the most significant being those in construction, textile, health, and education. In 1974, under the auspices of the FSLN-Proletarian Tendency, the Revolutionary Workers' Committees (COR), the Working People's Trade Union Movement (MSPT) and the Workers' Struggle Committees (CLT) were organized. These were more militant and politically oriented than most of the other trade unions in which an economicist orientation predominated. See Bayardo Arce, "El papel de las fuerzas motrices antes y después del triunfo," (Conference at the Universidad Centroamericana) (Nicaragua: Secretaría Nacional de Propaganda y Educación Política del FSLN, 1980).

⁶ Jaime Wheelock, *Diciembre victorioso* (Nicaragua: Secretaría Nacional de Propaganda y Educación Política del FSLN, 1980).

⁷ See Marta Harnecker, "Nicaragua: La estrategia de la victoria—entrevista con Humberto Ortega," *Bohemia*, 71 (Dec. 28, 1979), pp. 2-19 and "Crisis in Nicaragua," *NACLA Report on the Americas*, XII (November-December 1978), pp. 18-27 for analysis of the FSLN.

⁸ Marta Harnecker, *Bohemia*, p. 16.

⁹ In October 1979, James Petras argued that the FSLN had already made concessions to the bourgeoisie and its international allies which compromised popular power over the state. In February 1980, Roger Burbach refuted Petras' arguments about the FSLN's strategy of class alliances. James Petras, "Whither the Nicaraguan Revolution?" *Monthly Review* (Oct. 1979), pp. 1-22; and Roger Burbach, "Nicaragua: The Course of the Revolution," *Monthly Review* (February 1980), pp. 28-39. For a more complete argument against Petras' position see *NACLA Report on the Americas*, May-June 1980, pp. 2-35.

¹⁰ Alterations of original plans for the Council of State precipitated Alfonso Robelo's resignation from the Junta on April 22, 1980. Robelo had earlier criticized the FSLN for "politicizing" the National Literacy Crusade. The literacy manuals included a biography of Carlos Fonseca Amador and a picture identifying the nine members of the FSLN National Directorate. Originally, the Council was to have consisted of 33 seats reflecting the relative strength of the FSLN, FAO and business, civic and religious organizations prior to July, 1979. As it was actually composed, it reflected the emergence of the mass organizations after the victory. The FSLN and its organizations had 53 percent of the vote. The breakdown in trade union representation was CST (3), ATC (3), CGT-I (2), CTN (1), CUS (1). CAUS (1), and Fetsalud (1) for a total of 12 out of 47 votes.

¹¹ The FSLN's clear objective was to establish a single labor federation. Its leadership claimed that if the bourgeoisie was united in the Superior Council of Private Enterprise (COSEP), then the working class had to strive to form a united front to defend its interests. *Barricada*, March 3, 1980. The bourgeoisie was opposed to this position: "The stated intentions to create a single labor confederation . . . are difficult to reconcile with political pluralism and the Fundamental Statute." Adolfo Gilly, "El programa de los empresarios y el 'bunker' de la economía," *Cuadernos de Marcha*, I (Jan.-Feb. 1980); p. 37. The CTN also opposed the FSLN's initiative towards a single labor confederation. It accused the FSLN of being totalitarian. *NACLA Report on the Americas* May-June 1980, p. 25.

¹² *Barricada*, March 16, 1980.

¹³ The Revolution impressively accelerated the rate of unionization: during its first ten months, 32 unions were created per month. In the dictatorship's last sixteen years, the rate was 27 per year. The Ministry of Labor also sped up the process of handling labor complaints. The goal was to process them in a month, not two years, the average time before the Revolution. *Barricada*, Jan. 2, 1980. The other labor confederations in Nicaragua in 1979-80 were the following: Nicaraguan Confederation of Workers (CTN), which claimed 65,000 members; the General Confederation of Workers-Independent (CGT-I), whose major affiliate was SCAAS, the construction workers' union founded in 1951; the Action and Labor Union Federation (CAUS), with 5,000 members, mostly in textile industry; the Confederation for Trade Union Unification (CUS), affiliated with the ORIT (Inter-American Regional Organization of Workers); and the Workers' Front (FO), a Maoist split from the FSLN in the early 1970s. *NACLA Report on the Americas*, May-June 1980, p. 26. The FO was disbanded in February

1980. More than 300,000 urban and rural workers belonged to the Sandinista unions, CST and ATC. The economically active population in 1976 was nearly 700,000. *Barricada*, July 27, 1980, p. 3; and Carlos Nuñez Tellez, "El papel de las organizaciones de masas en el proceso revolucionario," speech at Gruta de Xavier (Nicaragua: Secretaría Nacional de Propaganda y Educación Política del FSLN, 1980). The overall picture was that about half of the economically active population was organized in Sandinista unions and that almost 60 percent of the labor force had been unionized in the first year.

[14] Planning Minister Henry Ruiz stressed this point during a one-day seminar on the economy in Managua on April 20, 1980. Ruiz and the Planning Ministry economists emphasized that the Revolution's goal was to increase social services, not to raise salaries, which would fuel inflation. An inflationary spiral was seen as destructive of the class alliance sustaining the Revolution. The Popular Unity experience in Chile was often mentioned as an example of the negative results of a policy of salary increases.

[15] *Barricada*, Oct. 1, 1979, p. 7.

[16] *Barricada*, Oct. 6, 1979, p. 5.

[17] *Barricada*, Oct. 25, 1979, p. 1.

[18] *Barricada*, Nov. 1, 1979, p. 5.

[19] *Barricada*, Jan. 16, 1980, p. 3. Carlos Núñez had earlier had a long meeting with CTN leaders in an effort to persuade them to join the National Inter-Syndicate Commission. *Barricada*, Nov. 12, 1979, p. 1.

[20] The FO, as noted in footnote 13, was a Maoist group which had split from the FSLN in the early 1970s. These incidents were the most divisive as the FO was disbanded; its newspaper *El Pueblo* was closed, and its leadership imprisoned. *Barricada*, Jan. 30, Feb. 2 and 3, 1980.

[21] *Barricada*, Feb. 14 and 20, 1980. The most important confrontation took place at the Fabritex textile plant. The FSLN considered CAUS's demands demagogic. CAUS leaders acted as if the standard of living of the working class was independent of the national economic situation. *Poder Sandinista*, Mar. 13, 1980, pp. 4—5.

[22] *Barricada*, (February 7, 1980), pp. 1 and 6. In June 1980, the revolutionary government approved a wage rise of 125 cordobas to workers earning less than 1,200 cordobas a month. Approximately 300,000 workers benefitted. The private sector opposed backdating the increase to June 1. *Latin America Weekly Report* (June 20, 1980).

[23] The National Inter-Syndicate Commission was formally inaugurated on April 13, 1980, with the CST and the CGT-I.

[24] *Barricada*, Feb. 20, 1980, p. 5.

[25] *Poder Sandinista*, Mar. 20, 1980, p. 3.

[26] *Poder Sandinista*, June 26, 1980, p. 8.

[27] Ibid., p. 6.

[28] *Barricada* Jan. 21, 1980.

[29] *Barricada*, Apr. 16, 1980, p. 4.

[30] *Poder Sandinista* June 26, 1980, p. 7; and *Poder Sandinista*, Apr. 18, 1980, p. 3. Prior to July 1979, there were only two professionals in occupational safety in Nicaragua. *Barricada*, Nov. 1, 1980, p. 5.

[31] The revolutionary government invited a commission from the Pan-American Health Organization (PAHO) to make recommendations on improving health standards in the mines. These were nationalized in November 1979. Miners were officially affiliated to the CST. It was reported that they were militant in their demands for safety and to a lesser degree for salary increases. *Latin America Regional Report*, Sept. 19, 1980; and interview with Manual Gómez, a member of the PAHO delegation.

[32] *The Guardian*, Oct. 9, 1980, p. 17.

[33] The inflation for 1979 was 60 percent. The 1980 rate was expected to be 22 percent, but it was actually closer to 35 percent. Unemployment hovered around 30 percent. *Latin America Regional Report*, July 11, 1980.

[34] The total 1980 budget was U.S. $597.2 million, nearly double the last Somoza budget.

Health and Education each received $77 million U.S. *Latin America Weekly Report*, Apr. 25, 1980

[35] Cuba and Uruguay had higher literacy rates than Nicaragua.

[36] *Barricada*, Jan. 2, 1980, p. 3.

[37] *El Trabajador*, II, No. 10.

[38] *Poder Sandinista*, June 26, 1980, p. 3. The commission was to be funded largely through contributions from enterprises (1 percent of the monthly payroll).

[39] Nicaragua had a mixed economy with three types of enterprises: state, mixed, and private. The Sandinista leadership naturally looked towards state property as the forerunner in the new social relations of production. See Henry Ruiz, "El papel político del APP en la nueva economía sandinista" (Nicaragua: Secretaría Nacional de Propaganda y Educación Política del FSLN, 1980.).

[40] *Barricada*, Dec. 7, 1979, p. 7. Workers' assemblies took place immediately following Robelo's resignation in April. The CST also organized workers' meetings prior to the Revolution's first anniversary to renew their commitment to the Revolution. These assemblies had a mobilizing and educative objective. *Poder Sandinista*, June 26, 1980, p. 3.

[41] *Poder Sandinista*, Jan. 17, 24, and Feb. 29, 1980.

[42] *Poder Sandinista*, June 26, 1980, p. 5.

[43] Carlos Nuñez, "El papel de las organizaciones. . . ," p. 18.

[44] *Barricada*, (July 20, 1980).

[45] *Barricada*, August 24, 1980. Ortega also announced that Edén Pastora would lead a militias brigade to the northern areas of Nicaragua where the counterrevolution was beginning to establish some strength.

[46] *Latin America Weekly Report*, Oct. 3, 1980.

[47] Economic growth for 1980 was 18.2 percent. *Latin America Regional Report*, July 11, 1980.

Chapter 8

The Role of Women
in the Nicaraguan Revolution

SUSAN E. RAMÍREZ-HORTON

In a poor district near Managua, Beatriz took up arms after watching a National Guardsman shoot a brother in the head in his mother's arms. In the
provincial capital of Estelí, Rosario, elderly but determined, left before
dawn every other day to walk the two hours to an *hacienda*, turned into a
rural refuge, to take her turn with other women cooking for the
"muchachos."[1] At a private university in the capital, a bespectacled, jovial
matron told the feared Guard that the mimeograph machine and quantities
of paper and ink in the library under her direction were used to produce a
library bulletin, when in fact they belonged to student militants and were
used to print communiqués against the Somoza regime. Maria Luz decided
to use her university education and leave her daughter with the maids, over
the strong protests of her husband, to begin organizing women in the urban
areas in defense of human rights. She was determined to call the attention of
an indifferent and largely disbelieving world to the daily horrors lived in
Nicaragua. The active participation of these and many other women in the
struggle against a hated government shattered the stereotyped, prerevolutionary image of the meek, home-bound and long-suffering woman.[2]

Indeed, although most women accepted and aspired to live the "ideal"
that society prescribed, only a few middle- and upper-class women were
able to lead such a life before the Sandinist victory of July 1979. To attend
high school and college presupposed a comfortable and progressive family
background. Few realistically could expect to be the chaperoned daughter
of an overly-protective father and then a loving wife and dutiful mother
under the eye of a watchful and jealous spouse. A life dedicated to administering the home and domestic economy, educating the children, and
working for charity and the church was also reserved for the privileged
strata. But, many of the women lucky enough to have been born into and
raised for the good life enjoyed a superficial happiness which actually mask-
ed a deep-seated, often unexpressed, uneasiness, a frustration at times
bordering on desperation.[3]

Ideals of womenhood were one thing, reality for the vast majority of
the female population of Nicaragua, however, was quite another. Most

were not born so lucky. The lives of lower-class Nicaraguan women had always been hard by urban, middle class standards, but they had become in some respects even harder especially since World War II. The growth of the agro-export sector dramatically changed the lives of present-day young women from that of their grandmothers. The growth of cotton, sugar, and coffee exports tied Nicaragua to the world market and brought modern technology and efficient management to the lands on the Pacific coast. But, in human terms this linkage meant the dispossession of small holders as more and more land was appropriated into large holdings to plant cash crops. Formerly independent peasants who lost their small plots or whose holdings proved insufficient to produce enough to support a family joined the salaried rural proletariat, suffering seasonal unemployment. The process of dislocation and the low wages paid farm labor forced peasant women to abandon the garden and the homestead to work in the fields beside their men, further depressing earnings and adding to unemployment. Deplorable conditions in the countryside and lack of opportunity resulted in rural-urban migration that destabilized family life as men left the mother of their children to find work in the city and never returned.[4]

For the women who followed their example, conditions in the cities were little better. Incipient industrialization put artisans out of work, exacerbating the problem of unemployment. Opportunities in the manufacturing sector were insufficient to engage all those who sought jobs. In Managua, less than 20 percent of the economically active female population found employment in industry. Poor women, often alone with children, undereducated and unskilled, had little choice but to work as domestic servants, to take in laundry and ironing, to become "penny capitalists" in the market or along the street, or to turn to prostitution.[5]

To be a poor woman in Nicaragua in the 1970s, after thirty or more years of dependent "development," meant to expect to live to be about fifty. To be poor and female meant a three out of ten chance of never attending school and becoming one of every two over the age of ten who remained functionally illiterate. To be poor also meant to end childhood and adolescence abruptly at or shortly after puberty with a first pregnancy, usually outside of wedlock. To be a woman, aged 34, meant having reached advanced middle age. In the rural areas, such a woman could expect to have been pregnant an average of eight times, although only three or four of her children would still be alive. In the more urbanized Department of Managua, about half of the single mothers of comparable age could count on having three of five children alive. The vast majority would be matriarchs, probably not by choice, with responsibility for maintaining the household.[6]

Even if the women had the knowledge and financial resources to use it, Nicaraguan law, written by men for men, offered little relief. Formally, women enjoyed the legal niceties of being able to own and administer property, apart from that of their husband; and they also had the right to vote. But the former reflected the reality of the relatively small sector that were legally married and had property; the second made little difference given the country's record of manipulated elections.[7]

Somoza's laws regarding marriage were paternalistic and discriminatory. If a woman was unfaithful only once and even in complete privacy, she could be accused of committing "adultery" in the eyes of the law. One act was sufficient cause for her husband to seek a divorce. Infidelity by a man was not "adultery" but "concubinage." Unlike a male, the aggrieved wife could not take legal action unless her husband maintained his mistress in the conjugal residence or "publicly and scandalously." Article 130 of the Penal Code established a theoretical equality of punishment for a spouse who in a fit of passion killed his or her partner and a lover. But this equality was more apparent than real, according to one source, given that the law used the term "adultery," applicable only to female infidelity. Under Somoza's laws, a divorced woman had to wait days to remarry; a man could do so immediately. A mistress could inherit from her lover, but a wife could not inherit from hers. If a husband died intestate, his wife received one fourth of the estate, their children the rest. A concubine or wife in free union inherited half the estate. Such inequalities led at least one lawyer to conclude that, under Somoza's law, "it was better to be a mistress than a wife."[8]

Somoza's laws dealing with female laborers appeared fairer. The labor code provided that women receive equal pay for equal work (Article 105, Section 10). But these laws were seldom observed. Women received less pay for the same work on the excuse that they labored less efficiently. Women on one coffee farm near the capital traditionally picked right alongside the men. Women living with male companions, however, had the beans they picked weighed together with those of their partner. Only the latter appeared in the records. Only he was paid and covered by social security. When women pickers learned of their rights and insisted on being listed and paid apart, owners and overseers refused to give them work, claiming, when they gave a reason at all, that their labor had become too expensive.[9]

Article 107 promised social security protection, but Article 133 exempted an important segment of working women. Domestic servants were not insured and they were excluded from the rule of an 8-hour day and a 48-hour week. Instead, domestic servants typically worked 14-hour days and 84-hour weeks.[10]

Most women, however, were not conscious of these underlying reasons for their poverty, loneliness, and status as second-class citizens. They joined the struggle for a more immediate reason: to rid themselves of Somoza and his National Guard, who, schooled in repression, brutalized the populace in a futile attempt to maintain the old order of privilege for the few. Some women traced their involvement back to the Guard's repressive reaction to a student strike in 1959 and their subsequent involvement in such organizations as "Patriotic Youth" (*Juventud Patriótica*) and "Youthful Renovation" (*Renovación Juvenil*). Others remembered the 1960s, when the Guard questioned and threatened them to find out the locations of the guerrilla bases of operation.[11]

Doña Emperatriz, sitting in a rocking chair at home in the district of San Judas in Managua, cried when she recalled how the Guards broke into her home and led away two of her seven sons. She watched as the Guard bayoneted the eldest for moving too slowly. Both were subsequently tortured and killed in Somoza's jails. At an interview in her home in Estelí, one of the principal urban battlegrounds of the war, Sonia described how the Guard captured, tortured, and killed three of her brothers for conspiring with the FSLN during the September 1978 insurrection. Later, seven blasts from a tank destroyed her home, which she had turned into a refuge for orphaned children. During this interview that became an open forum for the neighborhood as the morning wore on, other women told of how the Guard conducted house-to-house searches to check the knees and elbows of the young. Bruises or scrapes marked a person as suspect and subject to imprisonment or death as Sandinist guerrillas. To make matters worse, guards routinely robbed as they carried out their duties. The chronicle of horrors that occurred in or in front of their homes was endless. Few families escaped untouched.

The courage of women increased gradually as each began to understand the clandestine struggle. Many recounted how they became active, hesitating at first out of fear, afraid to confide in friends and colleagues, unsure who among them were *soplones* (whisperers or informants) and *orejas* ("ears" or spies) in the pay of Somoza. Little by little they realized how many others were also committed and involved and how they could help. For women it was, in some cases, doubly hard to make the first moves. Their husbands and partners objected to their leaving their home and neglecting their duties as housewives and mothers and to the danger that could be brought into the house if they were to be suspected or apprehended. Many, too, had to overcome their own internal misgivings, product of a lifetime of socialization, about what was acceptable action and what was not. For many, joining the resistance was, at the time, the "ultimate expression of rebellion," rebellion not only against the government but the frustrations of their own existence.

Their participation took many forms. Women in the countryside contributed food and served as cooks. Some made flags and bandanas for the rebels. They eventually served as spies and runners, transporting supplies across the country. In the latter two roles, their condition as women, sometimes pregnant and often with their children, worked to their advantage and aided them in avoiding suspicion when stopped by the Guard.

Their urban sisters helped in many of the same ways. Besides collecting food, money, and clothing for the rebel cause, they asked for and received tape recorders, "walkie-talkies," and watches, all improvised material for battle. Some donated wigs and old eyeglasses to disguise activists. Others served as chauffeurs. They offered their homes as safe houses where militants could sleep, eat, or stay to recover from wounds. They helped open holes in the walls of their gardens and patios through which a fleeing comrade (*"compañero"*) could escape. They even learned how to fabricate bombs.

A major step in channeling the individual actions and good intentions of these sympathizers was the foundation in Managua of a national women's organization, the Association of Women Confronting the National Problem (*Asociación de Mujeres ante la Problemática Nacional, AMPRONAC*), in early September 1977. The creation of AMPRONAC was no easy task. Although the founders included well-educated lawyers, journalists and bureaucrats, they had little organizing experience. Because the prevalent idea was that the woman's proper place was in the home, few women's groups existed. The dozen or so AMPRONAC founders, therefore, had little on which to build.[12]

Nevertheless, in the next few months, with the administrative advice of a few reluctant spouses, the organization grew to incorporate working-class as well as other middle-class women around the country. By March 1978, its members numbered over a thousand. As it grew, it became increasingly radical. In time, members were not only mobilizing public opinion in support of human rights, their primary goal, but actively organizing strikes and protest marches against price hikes and tax increases as well. In addition to calling public attention to the disappearance of hundreds of peasants in the north, AMPRONAC members began organizing the takeover of churches to protest abuses and hunger strikes to demand freedom for political prisoners. Disagreement over AMPRONAC's "proper" role and the related issue of whether or not to join the United People's Movement (*Movimiento Pueblo Unido* [MPU]) or the Broad Opposition Front (*Frente Amplio Opositor*) split AMPRONAC in the summer of 1978. The decision to join the MPU turned AMPRONAC into a popular organization that one year later would have an estimated membership of 8,000 to 10,000.[13]

During the last months of the war, women, both affiliated and unaffiliated with AMPRONAC, organized in preparation for the final offensive. They worked alone and in small groups so as not to call attention to themselves and thus were able to perform important support and intelligence services for the FSLN. They began stockpiling food to establish public dispensaries. They gathered emergency medical supplies and recruited doctors and nurses to teach short courses on first aid. In Estelí and Monimbó, they worked out warning codes: banging on pots and pans, and clapping hands, or turning on or off the lights to alert their neighbors to the approach of the Guard. They organized communication networks to send messages to comrades in arms and families of the militants.

When fighting arrived in their neighborhoods, on their streets and blocks, indirect, supportive involvement turned to direct action. Women pitched in to make barricades. One wife and mother bragged that the barricades she and her neighbors built out of sandbags were the strongest and highest in the area. The only thing these women did not do was "take up a rifle."

Younger women, without family responsibilities, either never developed or quickly overcame initial hesitation. Made conscious in school or through friends of the role they had to play in bringing down the regime, they took up a rifle and other weapons to fight in such numbers that by July 1979 anywhere from one-quarter to one-third of the FSLN combatants were female. School girls of 13 and 16 made contact with the underground and often left for the hills (*"montaña"*) without formal farewells. During the day, they made bombs or trained for combat. In the evenings, they engaged in political discussions. Women combatants reported that they were treated with consideration in the camps. They were not sex objects; there was little promiscuity. Men and women shared all duties including cooking. Everyone slept in hammocks. Women were willing and ready to go wherever sent, wherever needed. They rejected old stereotypes, the image of the subservient, dominated woman, suitable only for domestic work and having children. They were forging an alternative ideal, that of an active participant in the defense of a people, nation, and party.[14]

One woman, named Ana María, only 19 or 20 at the time of the final offensive, was given the responsibility of starting the battle against the National Guard holding out in the town of Juigalpa on July 17th, the day Somoza left Nicaragua and only two days before final victory. Her task was to shoot the first rocket at precisely 4 a.m. as a signal for the attack to begin. She recounted how she and a few companions began crawling toward the rear of the Guard headquarters to be in position on schedule; how she shot her rocket and how she was both surprised and delighted at her comrades' immediate response. They shot down the commander in his helicopter as he tried to escape. The battle was over by early afternoon. She heard that Managua had fallen, that Somoza had fled. The next night she and her comrades began marching joyfully toward the capital.

Victory was dear. Mothers lost sons and daughters. Children lost mothers. Not a few women separated from husbands and companions because of their new activism. Material losses, too, caused suffering. But the movement that began as a campaign for national liberation had also brought new self-esteem, a feeling of accomplishment and confidence and the beginning of self-liberation.

The women's movement did not die with the FSLN victory. Recognizing the contribution of women, the FSLN assigned them a part in the continuing revolution so as not to lose women's newly-recognized energies. Women assumed prominent positions in government. Doña Violeta de

Chamorro, the widow of the outspoken critic of Somoza and editor of the opposition newspaper *La Prensa*, was one of the original members of the Junta. Leah Guido and Vilma Nuñez de Escorcia, both founding members of AMPRONAC, were named to head a ministry and to the Supreme Court respectively. Other qualified women accepted responsibilities at all levels of the government.

During its first year in power, the FSLN also encouraged women to involve themselves in its ambitious programs for national reconstruction. Women were asked to participate in the literacy campaign, either as teachers or students. Many volunteers spent five months in remote parts of the country as part of the program. Those who could not leave home because they held regular jobs or had other obligations caught buses in the late afternoon to teach evening classes in outlying districts. Those with few reading and writing skills were encouraged to attend. Raising the literacy rate was seen as a method for training women for work outside the home.

To ease women into the work force and help solve the problem of unemployment, the Ministry of Social Welfare embarked on a program of promoting production collectives (*colectivos de producción*), organized along cooperative lines. These workshops were designed to benefit families by increasing income and to aid the nation by increasing production. The sewing collective of Estelí became a reality when the Ministry responded to the initiative of a group of unemployed women shortly after the end of the fighting. In answer to their petition, they were assigned an empty warehouse and supplied with sewing machines and credit. Soon the clothing they made with materials they purchased wholesale in Managua was being sold in a downtown store. Later, the collective began to fill special orders, like those for the duffel bags carried by the literacy campaign volunteers into the rural areas. Part of the proceeds were earmarked for better working conditions; for new work centers; for emergencies, festivals and vacations; and for social services. The rest was divided among its eighty-nine members according to their production. One member reported that her first month's earnings totaled 500 córdobas.[15] By August 1980, she was clearing 800 per month. After less than a year in operation, the collective looked forward to building its own workshop, with space for a child-care center, a most pressing need for the working mothers at the moment.[16]

Day care centers, called *centros de desarrollo infantil, (CDI)*, were also part of the FSLN plan to overcome the structural problems that had limited the participation of women in national development in the past. The FSLN found that many, if not the majority of the women, even those who actively participated in the two-year popular war, now expressed reluctance to leave home to participate in its programs because they had to watch children. The CDIs, then, were designed to free mothers, aunts, grandmothers, eldest daughters, and others from these tasks. A few such centers already existed in Managua under Somoza, but were inadequate to meet the demand. Since the victory, more than a dozen have been established in Managua, Estelí, and other provincial capitals. In Matagalpa, the CDI, housed in the mansion of a former Somocista congressman, was originally established in November 1979 (less than three months after the FSLN victory) with a donation from Holland. Early in 1980, the Ministry of Social Welfare assumed its funding. The center's staff bathed, fed and attended daily to the basic health needs of fifty-two children. By August 1980, plans to approximately double the capacity of the center were nearing completion.[17]

The literacy campaign, production collectives and child care centers were just the beginning of the government's program for overcoming the legacy of inequality for women. In August 1980, women were being organized according to skills they already possessed (e.g., sewing and artisanry). Governmental plans envisioned the establishment of training workshops (talleres escuelas) to provide on-the-job instruction for women in more complicated tasks. Likewise, with more opportunities for formal study, it was anticipated that women would become managers and professionals, eventually enabling them to replace the male accountants and administrators on whom they depended and to make worker self-management a reality.[18]

According to the official vision, getting the women out of the home would create more demand for additional child-care centers, popular laundries, and popular dining halls. The government hoped that through projects such as these women would develop skills and become more integral members of productive society. Diversification would eventually follow.[19]

The FSLN charged AMPRONAC with raising the political consciousness not only of urban workers but peasants, housewives, and professionals as well. Within two weeks of the July victory, AMPRONAC began recontacting its members who had dispersed to help with the more immediate tasks of the final insurrection. Its original goal of helping to bring down the dictatorship now accomplished, it began to re-emerge with the goal of becoming a mass organization, working to guarantee the accomplishments of the Revolution, and, in so doing, guaranteeing women's freedom. To reflect the new goal, the name of the organization was changed to the "Luisa Amanda Espinoza" Association of Nicaraguan Women (Asociación de Mujeres Nicaragüenses 'Luisa Amanda Espinoza' [AMNLAE]). Luisa, a seamstress, was the first woman killed fighting with the FSLN in 1970. As such, she had become the symbol of the struggle facing the contemporary Nicaraguan woman.[20]

During its first year, an original group of twenty women in Managua and Matagalpa organized chapters of 30 to 100 members in ten departments and set up embryonic organizing committees in five others. In Matagalpa, for example, AMNLAE established six local chapters in the city and one in the countryside. These chapters named representatives to their respective municipal and departmental executive committees. Departmental representatives traveled to national headquarters on a semiweekly basis for planning sessions. In April 1980, AMNLAE counted 17,000 members. By October of its second year, 25,000 women participated in 420 rural and 382 urban chapters. AMNLAE expected to continue to extend its membership into the countryside to reinforce existing ties and to coordinate activities with the provinces through improved communication and training seminars in the capital.[21]

AMNLAE's other activities were many and varied. To promote a new image for women, AMNLAE assumed the responsibility for broadcasting weekly radio and television programs, editing a newspaper, *La Voz de la Mujer* (*The Women's Voice*), and reviewing textbooks and other teaching aids. In conjunction with its organizing tasks, AMNLAE collected detailed information on rural and urban working conditions. With one seat on the Council of State and talented and dedicated lawyers within its ranks, it planned to use this information and its political clout to hasten the replacement of Somoza's antiquated laws to better reflect women's special problems.

AMNLAE also worked in conjunction with government ministries. It sponsored a music festival in November 1979 to raise funds for the literacy campaign. Energetic members in Matagalpa were the ones responsible for soliciting the initial grant from the Dutch government and acquiring a site for the establishment of the first childcare center of that city. AMNLAE also worked with the Ministry of Health to train some of its members to function as public health promoters. These women were destined to play a vital role in neighborhoods and rural districts where health facilities have always been rudimentary at best. Mobile units, specializing in preventive medicine, joined Ministry officials in remote areas to prepare a census, deliver talks on hygiene, and vaccinate the population.[22]

But AMNLAE's job was difficult. Gloria Carrión, one of the organization's national leaders, in a healthy display of candor, complained of a lack of a detailed plan of action and priorities and a lack of coordination with different state ministries which led to the duplication of effort and a waste of precious resources. Moreover, although membership was growing, it was still relatively small, because AMNLAE lacked a true constituency. AMNLAE competed with other mass organizations for members. Peasant women and urban working women saw little need to join when the Association of Rural Workers and the Sandinist Workers' Confederation were already solving their most basic problems. Of those who did join, Carrión estimated that 95 percent were active in other work centers, in the national government, in the political structure of the FSLN, and in the Sandinist Defense Committees with little extra time to dedicate to women's projects.[23]

A lack of funds and communication problems with some of their less-educated, rural sisters also limited activities. Imagine how difficult it was to organize peasant women when some asked what the word "organization" meant! Other affiliated women in departmental capitals and cities wanted to do more, but hesitated to act because they felt disoriented. They clamored for more training, which, for lack of funds, was still unavailable. Further complicating AMNLAE's task were lingering male suspicions of a "women's" organization and a still too vague notion of "liberation" and its consequences.[24] Perhaps in no institution did these doubts and suspicions surface more clearly than in the military, the one institution where women were endeavoring to play nontraditional roles. The female combatants, some pregnant and with children, who chose to remain in the army after the victory brought with them a new mentality, not always shared by their fellows. They rejected sex roles; each member was assigned duty according to ability. There were no prohibitions. Both men and women received the same basic training in physical fitness, combat, arms deployment, arms maintenance, and political theory. Women officers reported no resentment on the part of men when they gave orders.

But in fact, women were not seen as equals. While military men conceded that women combatants won their respect for the excellent job they did during the insurrection and that women would be called on again to defeat a foreign invader, they encouraged women to accept technical and administrative positions. Furthermore, unlike their male counterparts, not all women lived in barracks. Instead, they were allowed to live off-base, usually with the family, giving evidence of lingering chauvinism on the part of some men.[25]

As a result of these and other factors, the percentage of women still in the Sandinist Popular Army (*Ejército Popular Sandinista*) at the end of the first year had dropped to between 8 and 10 percent, as Stephen M. Gorman reports in more detail in chapter 6. This reduction may not be as drastic as it seems, since many women left the army to serve in the Sandinist National Police Force and many still participated in the militia reserves. Furthermore, since July 1979, many more men than women joined the army as a result of an enlistment campaign. Also, although women were ably represented by Dora María Telles[26] and Mónica Baltodano on the thirteen-member general staff, women were underrepresented in the officer corps, as the figures of Table 8.1. indicate in more detail. The explanation for this situation most certainly had to do with attitudes common to some men and women that were inherited from the past and could not realistically be expected to be overcome in one year.[27]

But, if much remained to be done, Nicaraguan women should be congratulated. Many had broken with the traditional bourgeois sterotypes of behavior. They had responded to the national crisis and moved into the forefront, as if the extraordinary situation had given them license to venture beyond the normally accepted boundaries of the feminine domain. After the emergency, they had continued to work to be free to the extent that their situations permitted. They realized that liberation and freedom to work outside the home could also mean a "double day." They knew that action had not yet freed all women from exploitation, subordination, dependency, and inequality. Most were still bound by the prerevolutionary superstructure and harsh economic realities that had conditioned their life chances and roles in the past. But Nicaraguan women conscious of this were working to enlighten their sisters and certain sectors of male-dominated society to forge a creative companionship for a better future.[28]

TABLE 8.1

WOMEN OFFICIALS IN THE SANDINIST PEOPLE'S ARMY

Position	Total Number	Total Women	Percent
Guerrilla Commander	32	3	9
Brigade Commander	18	0	0
Captain	24	0	0
First Lieutenant	96	5	5
Second Lieutenant	61	5	8
TOTAL	231	13	6

Sources: "Comandantes Guerrilleros del Frente Sandinista," Barricada, Sept. 3, 1979, p. 3, "asignan grados en el EPS," Barricada, July 15, 1980, pp. 5 and 14; and Victoria Schultz, personal communication, Nov. 9, 1980.

Notes

[1] Affectionate expression for both boys and girls, for adolescents.

[2] Much of the material in this chapter was gathered during interviews conducted in Nicaragua during August 1980. Because many interviewees requested anonymity, all last names have been omitted in the text. Special thanks are given to Cristiana Chamorro and Deborah Clayton.

[3] Elsa M. Chaney, Supermadre (Austin: University of Texas Press, 1979).

[4] Elizabeth Maier, "Mujeres, contradicciones y revolución," n.p., n.d. [1980], mimeographed, pp. 2-3; Paula Diebold de Cruz and Mayra Pasos de Rappacioli, "Informe sobre el papel de la mujer en el desarrollo económico de Nicaragua," USAID: Oficina de Planificación y Desarrollo, Managua, 1975, mimeographed, pp. 49-50.

[5] In 1950, 14 percent of the economically active population (excluding homemakers) were women. By 1977, the figure had risen to 28.6 percent. Connie A. Montealegre, "A Survey of

Women's Organizations in Nicaragua, 1978," n.p., Jan. 1979, mimeographed, pp. vi-vii; and Nicaragua, Ministerio de Bienestar Social Programa: Mujer en la Revolución, Proyecto: Unidades de producción colectiva y desarrollo integral de la mujer, "Plan General del Proyecto," n.p., n.d., mimeographed, pp. 2-3.

[6] Vivian H. Gillespie, "Análisis de los datos existentes sobre las mujeres cabezas de familias en la Región Central Interior de Nicaragua." n.p., Oct. 1977, mimeographed, pp. 1-3; Maier, "Mujeres," p. 8; Elizabeth Cruz and Rappacioli, "Informe," 3, 7-8 and 11—12; and Patricia Flynn, "Women Challenge the Myth," NACLA's Report on the Americas, XIV, No. 5 (Sept.-Oct. 1980), p. 30.

[7] Hilda Hernández, "La doble explotación de la mujer en Nicaragua." La Prensa, Aug. 11, 1979, p. 2; and Cruz and Rappacioli, "Informe," pp. 14 and 77.

[8] Ibid., pp. 16-18.

[9] Ibid., 14-15, 53, and 69; María Helena Palacios Hernández and Vilma Nuñez de Escorcia, "Algunas reflexiones acerca de la problemática socio-juridica de la mujer en Nicaragua," n.p., n.d., mimeographed, pp. 22-23, 28 and 30; and Pablo Emilio Barreto, "El drama socio-económico de la mujer." La Prensa, Mar. 11, 1979, p. 2.

[10] Cruz and Rappacioli, "Informe," 15.

[11] Margaret Randall, "Gladys Báez: Una mujer en la guerilla." Plural, IX-X, No. 6 (July 1980), pp. 50-51; and "Hablan mujeres de Cua." La Prensa, Nov. 7, 1979, p. 4.

[12] Montrealegre, "Survey," pp. vii-7; Roger Burbach and Tim Draimin, "Nicaragua's Revolution," NACLA's Report on the Americas, XIV, No. 3 (May-June 1980), p. 5; La Gaceta, No. 292, (23 Dec., 1975); and Cruz and Rappacioli, "Informe," p. 80. According to one study, only eight voluntary organizations functioned before 1958. Seventeen more were organized in the 1960s. In 1975, the recognition of the growing importance of women in the national economy prompted the establishment of a Woman's Office in the Ministry of Labor to promote the development of women's organizations as a means of furthering their advancement in general. Within three years, 144 organizations had been identified, representing over 8,000 women or slightly more than 1 percent of the economically active population. Almost half belonged to housewives' clubs, Garden Clubs, 4-H clubs and cooperatives and over half of these were in Managua. The rest were concentrated in the Departments of Zelaya, Chinandega, Chontales, and León. See Instituto Nicaragüense de Tecnología Agropecuária, División de Divulgación Tecnológica, "Programa Educación del Hogar y Liderazgo de la Mujer Rural," n.p., n.d., mimeographed.

[13] Philip Wheaton and Yvonne Dilling, Nicaragua: A People's Revolution (Washington, D.C.: Ecumenical Program for Interamerican Communication and Action, 1980), pp. 29-34; Elizabeth Maier, "Mujeres," p. 20; Asociación de Mujeres Nicaraguenes 'Luisa Amanda Espinoza,' "Organizadas para combatir, organizadas para reconstruir," Managua, 1979, mimeographed (hereafter cited as "Organizadas"); Roger Burbach and Tim Draimin, Revolution," p. 5, and Luis H. Serra, Personal Communication, December 1980.

[14] Burbach and Draimin, "Revolution," 2; Margaret Randall, "Báez," pp. 50-51; [Cristiana Chamorro], "La mujer en el ejército," La Prensa, August 26, 1979, pp. 1 and 9; "La mujer en la revolución," Barricada, August 15, 1979, p. 5; and Phillip Wheaton and Yvonne Dilling, Nicaragua, 30.

[15] One American dollar was equal to approximately 10 córdobas at the official exchange rate in August 1980.

[16] Plan General del Proyecto, p. 10.

[17] Patricia Flynn, p. 31. See Cruz and Rappacioli, "Informe," p. 82 on the day-care centers that existed before 1979.

[18] Plan General del Proyecto, pp. 5-7.

[19] Ibid., 9-10.

[20] "AMNLAE: Hay que profundizar las conquistas alcanzadas," Barricada, Dec. 31, 1979, p. 15. (hereafter cited as "Conquistas"); AMNLAE, "Orientaciones sobre la propaganda de la A.M.N.," Managua, Jan. 1980, mimeographed; "Combativas compañeras de AMPRONAC

inauguran su sede," *Barricada*, Aug. 15, 1979, p. 1; "Nace la Asociación de Mujeres Nicaragüenes," *Barricada*, Sept. 21, 1979, p. 5; "Conquistas"; and "Organizadas," p. 4.

[21] Burbach and Draimin, "Revolution," 22; "Conquistas;" Flynn, 31; Luis H. Serra, Personal Communication, December 1980. The ten departments with chapters are Managua, Matagalpa, Estelí, Jinotega, Chinandega, León, Masaya, Carazo, Rivas and Boaco.

[22] "Nuevas actividades pro-alfabeticización programan mujeres," *La Prensa*, Nov. 5, 1979, p. 5; and "Festival en apoyo a alfabetización," *Barricada*, Nov. 5, 1979, p. 7.

[23] "Conquistas," p. 16.

[24] "Conquistas."

[25] Stephen M. Gorman, "The Role of the Revolutionary Armed Forces in Nicaragua," in this volume.

[26] Dora María Telles was Comandante 002, who participated in the takeover of the National Palace and was commanding officer of León during the final offensive. See Wheaton and Dilling, *Nicaragua*, p. 35.

[27] [Christiana Chamorro], "Ejercito," pp. 1 and 9; Stephen M. Gorman, "Armed Forces;" and Patricia Flynn, "Women," p. 28. Flynn reports that women made up a quarter of the new Popular Sandinist Army and almost half of the police force.

[28] Elizabeth Maier, "Mujeres," 14; Elisa M. Chaney, *Supermadre*, p. 165; and "La mujer batalla por justa dignificación," *La Prensa*, Nov. 3, 1979, p. 9.

Chapter 9

The Churches
in the Nicaraguan Revolution

MICHAEL DODSON
T.S. MONTGOMERY

When Fidel Castro entered Havana on January 1, 1959, the Roman Catholic and Evangelical Churches were unseen and unheard. Both were indifferent to social change, with the Catholic Church adhering to a traditional, sacramentalist view of its role in society, and the Evangelical Churches more concerned with "saving souls" than with saving lives. As the Cuban regime moved toward socialism and into a close alliance with the Soviet Union, the Cuban churches abandoned their indifference in favor of opposition or exile.[1]

When the Sandinistas entered Managua on July 19, 1979, one of the first public events to celebrate victory was a Mass presided over by Archbishop Miguel Obando y Bravo and attended by thousands. Dozens of similar masses occurred in parishes throughout the country. These masses were symbolic of the role played by Nicaraguan churches, both Catholic and Evangelical, in the Revolution. How and why the Nicaraguan churches came to support revolution is the subject of this chapter.[2]

The Second Vatican Council, convened in 1962 under Pope John XXIII, is a benchmark by which to measure the changing character of all churches in Latin America. Prior to Vatican II, national churches presented a uniformly traditional religious image, accompanied by sharply conservative social and political attitudes. Virtually everywhere, including Nicaragua, the Church was an ally of the old order.

This is dedicated to the memory of Maura Clark, M.M., who served the people of Nicaragua for twenty years and who was martyred in El Salvador on December 2, 1980.

The research for this chapter was carried out over a period of more than one year. The authors are grateful to many persons who generously gave of their time and knowledge during this period. Those whose contributions are utilized in the text include Gilberto Aquirre, Álvaro Argüello, Angel Arnaiz, Eduardo Carretero, Antonio Castro, Ricardo Chavarría, Maura Clark, Benajamín Cortés, Evonne Dilling, Peggy Dillon, Miguel D'Escoto, Albino Melendez, Luis Medrano, Loren Miller, Uriel Molina, Patricia Nolan, Miguel Obando y Bravo, Pablo Schmidt, Miguel Vásquez, and Julie Warnshuis. We would also like to thank Peggy Healy, Gary MacEoin, John McFadden, Gustavo Parajón, Tom Quigley and Father Felix Quintanilla, and the Christian Base Community of San Pablo Parish in Managua. Finally, Michael Dodson gratefully acknowledges the support of the Texas Christian University Research Foundation and The Sloan Foundation, which made possible his participation in the project.

In the same year that Vatican II convened, a report of the Catholic Press Association of the United States offered a profile of the Nicaraguan Catholic Church which emphasized its institutional and pastoral weaknesses. The report found priests to be few in number and "poorly formed," the hierarchy unable or unwilling to provide ecclesiastical leadership, and the Church virtually absent in the countryside, where more than half of the people lived. It described the Church as "living in the past," its priests "blind about social problems" and aligned with a government that was "hated by the people."[3] This was a church that openly criticized Castro but never criticized the Somoza regime. The Evangelical Churches were scarcely different, although they tended to be apolitical rather than openly aligned with the regime.

The first signs of change in the Nicaraguan Catholic Church appeared in the late 1960s, stimulated by the historic Latin American Bishops Conference at Medellín, Colombia, in 1968. Medellín sought to apply the reforms of Vatican II to Latin America and it precipitated a dynamic process of reflection and experimentation within the Church. Its bold positions encouraged Catholics and Evangelicals throughout the continent to rethink their faith. Above all, the emphasis on identifying the Church with the poor led to the assumption of a more prophetic attitude toward society and politics.[4]

The prophetic attitude was expressed in a theology of liberation which interpreted the gospel as demanding that Christians be a force actively working to liberate the great majority from poverty and oppression. By the mid-1970s, even where theological reflection was not very sophisticated, the theology of liberation had become the common coin of discourse among progressive Catholics and Protestants. It is within this context that we must understand the transition of the Nicaraguan Catholic and Evangelical Churches from conservative defenders of the status quo to outspoken opponents of Somocismo and even, to a remarkable degree, active participants in the Sandinista Revolution.

Important segments of the Catholic and Evangelical Churches in Nicaragua became revolutionary in the years between 1972 and 1979 by virtue of coming to identify the Christian liberation of their people with the armed struggle led by the Sandinista Front of National Liberation (FSLN). From this vantage point, the post-Medellín evolution of the Nicaraguan Churches differs in significant ways from the experiences of other Latin American countries, where post-Medellín activism took the form of organized clerical movements committed to structural change in society.[5] These movements typically consisted of an avant garde nucleus of priests whose wish to change the Church and society often led to bitter struggles with the Church hierarchies as well as with political authorities. Battling on two fronts, the vulnerability of these movements to pressure from bishops and regimes was accentuated by the absence of popular lay participation.

This deprived them of the strong grass-roots ties which would have given them wider credibility and practical support. Although weak in resources, the Nicaraguan Churches at the base were so strong that they were able to withstand regime and hierarchy pressure and to participate actively in a popular political struggle. The uniqueness of Nicaragua can be explained in terms of four themes:

1 . The emergence of a prophetic point of view following Vatican II and Medellín coincided in Nicaragua with the deepening of anti-Somoza sentiment throughout the country, especially after the 1972 earthquake. The radicalization of the churches coincided with the growing strength and popular acceptance of the FSLN.

2 . While some of its key leaders were Marxist, the FSLN was not, on the whole, antireligious. Indeed, it accepted, even encouraged Christian participation in the Revolution.

3 . The level of repression in Nicaragua and the specificity of its sources in Somoza and the National Guard also distinguished Nicaragua. In many areas, the churches came to be the only source of refuge. By providing refuge, the churches came under attack, and so became a focal point of popular resistance. Following the assassination of Pedro Joaquín Chamorro in January 1978, the churches became crucial sources of refuge for participants, including combatants in the armed struggle, and an important tactical resource for the FSLN, especially in the poorest *barrios* of such cities as Masaya, León, Estelí, and Managua, where repression was the heaviest.

4 . The Catholic Church hierarchy became anti-Somocista, or at least was perceived that way by the people, even though it never became pro-Sandinista. By playing the role of mediator between the FSLN and Somoza in such crises as the taking of the Palace in August 1978, the Church gained credibility with the FSLN. So, in the insurrection the weight of the institutional Church was perceived in the popular imagination as anti-regime. Meanwhile, much of the Evangelical leadership within the country openly embraced the FSLN as the legitimate representative of the Nicaraguan people.

Origins of Church Radicalism

At Medellín, the Latin American bishops called on the Church "to defend the rights of the oppressed," to foster grass-roots organizations, and "to denounce the unjust action of world powers that works against self-determination of weaker nations."[6] In Nicaragua, the churches generally were not prepared to embrace this "option for the poor" and break their ancient alliance with the rich and powerful. There were fateful exceptions to this general picture, however. In 1965, Trappist Father Ernesto Cardenal founded a lay community on the Islands of Solentiname in Lake Nicaragua. About the same time, Spanish Father José de la Jara and a conscientization[7] team began working with families in the Managua barrio *14 de Septiembre*, developing Christian Base Communities (CEBs),[8] a movement that spread to other poor neighborhoods.

By the time of Medellín, Jesuits and students were working in communities in the Departments of Carazo, Masaya, and Masatepe, and a Spanish Capuchin, Father Bonafacio, had begun three-day conscientization courses in Managua with the aim of enlisting students for a Church-sponsored radio school, broadcasting in the North, that provided a grade school education.

The priests and religious who spearheaded these early efforts had in mind a socially conscious church that targeted the poor and they developed their *pastoral*[9] in terms of the poor. In the CEBs popular religiosity, which focused on the sacraments, was unconsciously but inevitably pushed aside in favor of Christian reflection groups that focused on social issues.[10]

The first indication that priests were beginning to take Vatican II seriously came in 1968 with the publication of a Declaration signed by seven Nicaraguan clergy which took great pains to avoid being political.[11] Citing Conciliar documents, the priests called on the government to halt repression and torture, to free political prisoners, and they urged a more just economic order. Also in 1968, the first of a series of national pastoral meetings was held to examine the national situation in light of Medellín. Though it lacked focus and achieved few tangible results, this first pastoral meeting did enable the clergy to begin a dialogue on how to bring change to the Nicaraguan Church. Finally, at about this time Managua's newly named Archbishop Miguel Obando y Bravo took a first step toward distancing himself from the regime by selling Somoza's gift of a new Mercedes-Benz and giving the money to the poor.

Between 1968 and 1970, Christian Base Communities took hold and grew. By the beginning of the new decade, only two of the original seven signers of the 1968 Declaration were still actively working to implement Medellín, but others in the Church were moving in new directions. On returning from a 1971 Bishop's synod in Rome, Monseñor Obando y Bravo was asked if he was going to register for the upcoming elections. His answer was no, he did not wish to dignify the electoral process. To underscore this attitude, the Archbishop avoided both the inauguration of the Triumvirate in 1972 and Somoza's own inauguration in 1974.

In 1971, a second national pastoral meeting was held. Priests attending discovered that they were moving in a more concerted direction. At this meeting, they concluded that evangelization had to be aimed at conscientizing, although just what this meant still had to be worked out. This conference coincided with another development in the life of the Church: the growing activism of Catholic high school and university students. Clergy working with these students were dubbed "the seven priests of Marx," although at the time none would have identified himself as a Marxist. Eleven such students came to one priest and proposed that they live with him and form a community for study and reflection. Several of these students would become leaders in the FSLN.

In October and November 1970, and again in May 1971, Catholic students occupied the Cathedral in Managua to protest human rights violations and the presence of the National Guard on campus. Occupation of the Cathedral was accompanied by occupations of five other churches around the country and was supported by twenty-two priests. A strong statement from the Archibishop's office supported the students' demands while lamenting the involvement of the priests.[12] One result of these protests was that members of the FSLN began seeking out these priests and students to explore possibilities for cooperation between the FSLN and the Church. Between 1970 and 1972, Archbishop Obando y Bravo was drawn repeatedly into political conflict over the strikes at the universities and student occupation of the churches. In these conflicts, the official Church began to take antiregime stands. Moreover, the taking of the churches was a signal to many people "that priests and sisters were beginning to have some solidarity in opposition to Somoza."[13]

It is fair to say that in this early post-Medellín period, these activist Christians had little idea that their gropings toward a prophetic ministry would lead to intimate involvement in a popular revolution. As one participant later observed, however, they were beginning to "see Christ in an active, transforming charity, one that changes the world." And they were beginning to see that political action could be "a means of bringing about the redemptive action of God."[14]

Christian Communities in the Cities

The 1972 earthquake was a turning point in the country's political development and in the political role of the churches. Although considerable tension had developed between the Catholic Church and the government during the preceding two years, in the immediate crisis of the earthquake Church and regime moved closer to one another. In its devastation, Managua was utterly dependent on relief supplies coming in from outside the country. The Church was an important mediator of the relief effort, much of which came from international Church agencies. This rapprochment lasted only a few weeks, until Somoza forced all relief supplies to be processed through offices of his own Liberal Party. This overtly political manipulation of humanitarian aid quickly alienated the Church, and both priests and bishops began to criticize the government once again.

At this time, in the poorer communities of Managua, priests and religious were experiencing vividly the connection between political structures and the suffering of the poor. The Sisters of the Assumption, for example, had lived and worked in one of the neighborhoods destroyed by the earthquake. They relocated in the barrio of San Judas, where they saw at first hand the consequences of official corruption which prevented relief supplies from reaching people suffering great hardship. Their daily experience moved them toward a prophetic interpretation of the gospel and into active sympathy with popular resistance to the dictatorship.

The experience of the Maryknoll Missionaries in the barrio OPEN 3 (now Ciudad Sandino) was similar. A neighborhood of several hundred people prior to the earthquake, OPEN 3 grew rapidly during 1973 with the influx of displaced persons. Here, the Church mediated relief through the Youth Club that had been formed by the Maryknoll sisters. When the government took over the relief effort and the flow of supplies into OPEN 3 virtually ceased, both the Maryknoll sisters and the Christian youth were in a position to see the regime's indifference to the poor and its willingness to profit at the expense of their misery. It was widely understood throughout OPEN 3 that Somoza and his officials were hoarding or selling the relief supplies. As with the Sisters of the Assumption, these Church people took the first steps toward a prophetic interpretation of their religious mission as a direct consequence of living through the effects of systemic political corruption and oppression.

The Christian communities in Managua, particularly in the poorer eastern zone of the city, became a focal point of political protest following the earthquake. In such communities, the Church had to respond to the demands of Medellín from a position of direct participation with the poor under conditions which made it obvious that the source of much of the suffering was the government itself. For them, the structural sin referred to by the Latin American bishops had a very concrete reference—*Somocismo*. Priests, religious, Catholic youth, and ordinary citizens in these communities began to organize their opposition to the regime and, particularly among the youth, there was an opening to the FSLN. From within the Christian Revolutionary Movement, founded in 1971 by Father Uriel Molina in the Parish of Fátima, a number of young Christians entered directly into the FSLN as combatants, while others helped establish a communications network. Thus, it was at the grass roots and on the part of the laity that the Church first became involved with the FSLN and the revolutionary process. Given the political climate within which these developments took place, the activity was increasingly clandestine. The public protests of the pre-earthquake period, such as the seizing of churches, therefore declined.

The Earthquake and the Evangelicals

The Earthquake was an even sharper turning point for the Evangelical Churches than for the Catholic Church in that the Protestants had not experienced the same degree of early ferment. Thus an important difference between the Catholic and Evangelical Churches was that in the Nicaraguan

Catholic Church reflection preceded action; for the Protestants, that order of events was reversed.

Four days after the earthquake, a Protestant doctor, Gustavo Parajón, issued a call via radio for a meeting of Evangelical leaders. Eight responded the first day, and within three weeks twenty denominations were involved in five different relief programs under the newly created Evangelical Committee for Assistance to the Destitute (CEPAD). With hunger the most pressing problem, food kitchens set up in Evangelical Churches and schools and run by 800 volunteers were quickly serving 30,000 people breakfast each day. In cooperation with PROVADENIC, an Evangelical health agency already in existence, three clinics were established immediately in the poorer barrios of Managua. Refugee centers were created around the country not only to provide shelter but also to reunite families. A housing program resulted in the construction of 500 homes. Finally, literacy classes were begun in conjunction with ALFALIT, another existing Protestant agency, and quickly had 400 teachers, although CEPAD withdrew from this program after a month.

Three months after the earthquake, CEPAD changed the last word of its name from "Destitute" to Development" as it began to think in a more long-term context and to focus on the spiritual basis of social action. The guiding principle for CEPAD's work from the beginning was that of service rather than proselitizing.

Gilberto Aguirre, Director of Programs for CEPAD, saw a path leading from the relief work following the earthquake to the first of sixty pastoral meetings that were held around the country between September 1974 and the end of 1980. The first week of study and reflection brought together 300 pastors from three dozen denominations. Such themes as "The Responsibility of the Christian in Latin America" and "The Keys of Liberation" were kept general to avoid Somoza's wrath. The emphasis throughout the retreat was "You're Christian; I'm Christian," which did much to break down traditional sectarian barriers. Substantively, the pastors began to wrestle with the same issues as the Catholic Church: poverty, injustice, and human rights violations.

This conference produced "an explosion" among the Evangelical Churches both spiritually and organizationally. Between late 1974 and the Revolution, twenty-three local CEPAD committees were established throughout the country, all initiated at the local level, and nine regional offices were opened to encourage a decentralized development program.[15]

Full discussion of CEPAD's multiple projects in rural and community development is beyond the scope of this chapter; what is important is that these projects, conceived and implemented at the local level in more than 200 communities, enabled the Evangelical Churches to work, plan, and organize together, at times also in conjunction with Catholics; this experience was vital in the insurrectionary period.

Two years and twenty retreats after the first pastoral week in 1974, a group of fifty clergy and laity gathered for the first "Interdenominational Retreat of Evangelical Pastors" (RIPEN I) to reflect on the "social responsibility of the Church," church unity, human rights, and Christian ethics. Out of that meeting came a document that revealed a clear understanding of the growing political polarization within the country, the array of forces at work, and the social and economic causes of the problems. The document urged "joint action of the government, private enterprise, religious and cultural groups and the citizenry."[16] Though Nicaraguan Evangelicals were not prepared to embrace the FSLN in 1976-77, they were moving in a direction that would culminate less than two years later in strong support for the revolutionary process.[17]

The Growing Radicalization of the Catholic Church

Two public events in the mid-1970s, involving the Catholic Church bear discussion at this point. They occurred a year apart, in December 1973 and 1974. On the first anniversary of the earthquake, the Church hierarchy held a commemorative mass in the central plaza of Managua. Somoza, who had intended to hold a government-sponsored event, cancelled his plans and invited himself to the Church celebration. Meanwhile, the Christian communities of Managua, particularly from such parishes as San Pablo and Fátima, resolved to make their own presence felt at the celebration and to attend with the explicit purpose of expressing a theological position different from that of the bishops. The hierarchy conceived the event as a commemoration of the dead. The Christian communities wanted to focus on the needs of the living. As a former priest who provided live radio commentary said, "The people of God had one set of theological concerns and the bishops had another."[18]

With the assistance of priests, parishoners made hundreds of hand-held placards and carried them secretly into the plaza. As the ceremony unfolded, Somoza and his officials were deeply offended by the statements of the bishops and angered by the display of antiregime slogans. Abruptly he got up and walked out while national guardsmen disconnected the loudspeakers carrying the Archbishop's speech to the audience. In short, while the breach between regime and Church was increasing at this time, the surface picture of regime-Church conflict obscured a still deeper division within the Church between a moderate hierarchy and increasingly prophetic Christian communities.

The second major event, which occurred almost exactly one year later, was the capture by the FSLN of Somocista officials at a Christmas party on December 27, 1974. This event was important in the life of the Church and in the Church's relation to the popular struggle in that the hierarchy played a visible role in mediating this conflict between the government and the FSLN and, even more important, was perceived by many people to be "leaning" to the Frente, even though its leader, Obando y Bravo, presented himself as a neutral go-between. Intentionally or not, the Church gained some credibility with the FSLN during these negotiations.

Perhaps even more important was the effect of the FSLN's success (its ransom demands—including the broadcast and publication of a lengthy FSLN position paper—were met by the government and several political prisoners were freed) on people in the Christian communities. The residents of OPEN 3 were "filled with jubilation" when the report came in over the radio. Said one Maryknoll sister, "it was like hearing our own salvation history" as they listened to the FSLN leaders review the preceding twenty years of Nicaraguan history, detailing injustices of the regime and the struggle of the opposition. With this success the Frente gained stature in barrios such as OPEN 3, Riguero, 14 de Septiembre, and San Judas, while Somoza "lost face" and ordinary people had a glimpse of the possibility that popular opposition could be effective against his regime.

The next three years marked a period of growing popular protest in the poor barrios of Managua and other cities, accompanied by increasing repression by the National Guard. The experience of OPEN 3 illustrates how elements of the Churches moved to active collaboration with the FSLN at this time. University students from the Christian Youth Movement (founded by the Jesuit Fernando Cardenal) came into OPEN 3 to work with the Maryknoll missionaries and their Christian Youth Clubs. Their work was not explicitly evangelical. Based on the assumption that Christian faith was compatible with social action, these study and reflection groups focused on issues concerning the dignity of poor people and questioned the possibilities of achieving such dignity under a Somoza government. Many of these young people went from being anti-Somoza to being Christian revolutionaries.

Alongside this organized youth activity was a series of political struggles between the barrio and the government. During the summer of 1976, the barrio waged a campaign to reduce water prices, which had been raised by the government in poor neighborhoods but not in well-to-do ones. People were astonished to discover the degree of organization that had developed during the preceding two years. The Youth Clubs, the Christian community, the local worker association, and a women's organization pooled their resources to carry out the struggle of the "water fight." Members of the local parish center became leaders in the struggle. The Church used its mimeo machine for announcements and its building for meetings. After nearly three months of struggle, OPEN 3 succeeded in getting a reduction in the price of water. The struggle was a lesson in political organizing; it helped to solidify the politically conscious members of the Christian communities and sharpened their confidence to act politically. For the Church itself, it was a lesson in how to "accompany" the people in the historical process of their own self-determination. As one Maryknoll missionary put it, participation in these struggles "carried the Church into the stream of history."[19]

The Church in the Countryside

More than half of Nicaragua's people lived in rural areas which traditionally enjoyed only limited contact with the institutional Church. In the wake of Vatican II, and particularly after Medellín, the Church began attempting to reach people in the countryside more effectively by creating two notable and closely related programs, the Evangelical Committee for Agrarian Advancement (CEPA), and the Delegates of the Word.

CEPA was created by the Jesuit Order, with the support of the hierarchy, in 1969 for the purpose of training peasant leaders to organize politically their own communities. Initially, the training seminars were offered primarily in the coffee-growing region of Carazo and Masaya, but CEPA later expanded into the north from León to Estelí. They attempted "to integrate biblical reflection and technical agricultural training," and they published a cartoon-like pamphlet entitled "Cristo Campesino" which interpreted political demands such as the right to land as sanctioned by the Christian gospel.[20]

CEPA was created originally as a self-help program designed to enable peasants to meet their daily needs more effectively. In time, these efforts came to center on organization as it became clear to CEPA members that peasants could not improve their conditions without organized, collective political action. When this awareness took hold, it raised the level of theological reflection among people in the Church. They perceived the need to assist peasants in organizing to defend their interests within the context of a society which was controlled by *Somocismo* and fundamentally hostile to peasant interests. In this manner, a number of Christians working in CEPA became sharply politicized and militantly anti-Somocista. When the FSLN created the Association of Rural Workers (ATC) in 1977, some key CEPA workers joined the ATC and became directors of the organization. Other CEPA members joined the FSLN as armed combatants and at least four CEPA workers were killed by the National Guard during this period of increasing radicalization. As this radicalization progressed, the hierarchy became disenchanted and attempted to restrict the activities of CEPA, discouraging it from becoming political and from developing a greater sympathy with the FSLN. When this restriction became too confining, CEPA cut its ties with the hierarchy and became an independent Christian organization. Into the early 1980s, it continued to do the same work, had priests and Catholic youth still working with it, and considered itself to be doing religious work, occasionally in cooperation with the FSLN. By the time of victory, it had become closely allied with the FSLN.

Because of limited resources, the Catholic Church in Nicaragua never was able to put many priests into the rural areas. In contrast, that is where the Evangelicals were the strongest. In the aftermath of Vatican II, a creative response to this problem was to train and authorize lay persons, called Delegates of the Word, to perform many of the sacramental functions. Illustrative of the role the Delegates played in religious change is the experience of the state of Zelaya, the largest department in Nicaragua, comprising much of the eastern half of the country. Entirely rural, Zelaya had been represented by the Church through the Capuchin Fathers. After Medellín, the Capuchins encouraged the selection and training of Delegates in the Christian Base Communities. The Delegates were trained to develop the Christian formation of peasants, focusing on literacy, conscientization, and health. Religious services themselves consisted of dialogues based on biblical texts and focused on pressing needs in the life of the community.[21] By 1975, there were approximately 900 Delegates active in Zelaya. Though the conscious intent of the Capuchin-Delegate program was to give a voice to very marginal citizens in the spirit of Medellín, it was not consciously intended to have political influence.

The political impact of the Delegates of the Word, however, quickly became apparent to the Somoza regime. Indeed, the National Guard saw their activities as subversive and began to harrass them. Peasants disappeared or were killed in areas with a strong Delegate presence. When the Capuchins made an appeal through their bishop to Somoza, the President denied all allegations.

As the Capuchins looked more closely at the political situation, they discovered that some Delegates had made a Christian option to work for the people by working against the regime. Delegates had taken the teachings of Medellín, which formed part of their training, and developed them in an explicitly political direction—without telling the priests. Having repulsed the overtures of the Sandinistas a few years before because their Marxist, irreligious arguments had little appeal, these Christians came to sympathize with, and often collaborated with, the FSLN. The Sandinistas, in turn, had become more open to the Christian bases for political action. The Capuchins realized that there was a political basis for Guard repression, and that they had to make a decision about their own political involvement.

In June 1976, the Capuchins decided to go public against the regime. To avoid censorship, they published a letter outside the country in which they documented the killings and disappearances in the countryside. Widely circulated, the Capuchin letter on human rights violations brought increased international pressure on the regime at a time when pressure within the country also was mounting. The decision to publish the letter illustrates how important elements of the Church came into the opposition to Somocismo and why that opposition took a pro-Sandinista course.

The Delegates of the Word also flourished in some areas of the western third of Nicaragua in the early 1970s, particularly in Carazo and Estelí, where they took part in CEPA training seminars and were radicalized by witnessing the repression of the *campesinos*. As the repression intensified after the earthquake, many of these Delegates became more clandestine in their political organization, which facilitated their collaboration with the FSLN; in the ensuing years, the ties between the Church and the Frente deepened through this connection. Again, some Delegates entered the FSLN as armed combatants.

Finally, in the northern zone of Matagalpa, Jinotega, and Yalí, yet another story of Guard repression and Church radicalization unfolded. When Father Miguel Vásquez took over the parish in 1972, he organized CEBs and courses in Christian conscientization which soon produced enough political organization to lead to conflict between parishioners and the government. The local press labeled them "communists," and at one point the Guard accused the priest of being the leader of a local guerrilla unit. The "guerrilla unit" turned out to be the Christian conscientizaiton team of the parish.

The parish of Yalí was 85 percent rural. There being few priests, the region depended heavily on the Delegates of the Word. In Yalí, 32 CEBs were operating by 1974 under the direction of young Delegate leaders, most of whom were between the ages of 20 and 30. When, by 1975, the Guard decided that these Christian communities were "subversive" and began to persecute the members, some communities began actively collaborating with the FSLN. Over the next three years, the estrangement of the people and the government deepened as churches were searched and occupied by the Guard and as individuals were imprisoned or killed, or disappeared. Religious meetings were broken up or banned altogether. By 1978, most Christians not only opposed the Somoza regime but were pro-Sandinista. This was as true for Evangelicals as for Catholics. At least ten Protestant ministers joined the FSLN as combatants or worked full-time organizing their respective barrios.

In January 1978, the churches consisted of three identifiable elements. A small group remained loyal to Somoza. A larger, nonviolent opposition typified by Catholic Archbishop Obando y Bravo sought a mediator role, believing strongly that Somoza must go but fearing a Sandinista victory. The third group, centered mainly in the Christian Base Communities, was now actively working to bring about a Sandinista victory. Even the moderate position of the Archbishop seemed to further the isolation of the regime and to help set the stage for the insurrection. For example, the bishops' pastoral letter of January 1977 described the atmosphere in the countryside as a "state of terror," pointing to the dispossession of peasant landholders and to direct repression of the Church, "particularly the Delegates of the Word."[22] In May, Somoza's newspaper *Novedades* called upon the Archbishop to clarify the Church's position with respect to the government and to take a stand against subversive elements. In response, the advisory council of the archdiocese defended the Archbishop and described the national scene as one of "institutionalized violence." In November, the Guard burned Solentiname, arresting some of its members and exiling others, and in December the Catholic youth once again seized Churches to protest Guard abuses and demand the freeing of political prisoners. A Spanish priest of the Sacred Heart, Gaspar García Laviana, joined the FSLN as a combatant. Just after the turn of the year a national strike was called.

The Church in the Insurrection

The assassination of Pedro Joaquín Chamorro, January 10, 1978, intruded powerfully upon this panorama of events. In the Christian communities, many people felt that they were now called upon to live out the values of the Gospel in a revolutionary situation. In the barrio of OPEN 3, the youth had occupied the Cruz Grande Church since December 14, but abandoned it on January 10 with the news of the assassination. Stunned, the people of OPEN 3 instinctively drew closer together. Church people in their community now concluded that "the Church was the only place people could speak the truth in Nicaragua."[23] "Speaking the truth" thus became a political act that meant active opposition to *Somocismo*. For many, it also meant active collaboration with the FSLN. In churches and in church schools in such cities as Managua, Masaya, Estelí, and Jinotega, lay people, particularly students, and some priests, pastors and religious, began to assume specific revolutionary tasks in preparation for the general uprising. They made bombs and stored arms; they accumulated supplies and taught courses in first aid; they cleaned and filled baptismal fonts in the Evangelical Churches with drinking water; they published news and organized communications links for and with the Sandinistas.

On September 8, 1978, CEPAD held a meeting to discuss emergency measures in the event of an insurrection, during which one pastor commented, "I hope nothing happens tomorrow, because we aren't prepared yet." The next day, the September insurrection began. As a result of this meeting however, the churches that had not already done so began to stockpile food and medicine in their buildings. During and after the September insurrection, CEPAD cooperated with CEPA and other Catholic agencies on relief efforts in Monimbó and Masaya. In Monimbó not only were the churches supplying food and medical care but also "support to the combatants."[24]

Following the insurrecton, CEPAD organized refugee centers around the country. Every pastor had a Red Cross flag to place outside his church or school. In eastern Managua, the Church of the Nazarene, like many others, painted huge red crosses on the outside walls and served as an important refugee center during the final insurrection. The Red Cross advertised the fact that the flags would be in various locations and asked that they be respected. (Often they were not.)

By the end of 1978, the archdiocese, through CARITAS and CEPAD, began coordinating relief efforts even more closely. In March 1979, CEPAD sponsored a national radio marathon which raised $20,000 for Masaya, a fund that was administered by CRISOL, an ecumenical organization. During the final insurrection, the Evangelical Churches supported the FSLN by providing medicines and, in a more limited way, food. This was especially true in the eastern barrio of Managua, and in Masaya and Carazo.

For many, these actions were accompanied by exceedingly painful reflection on the meaning of religious principles and teachings. They were forced to ask, as one participant put it, "What do we do to live our faith now?" The prospect was frightening indeed, particularly in light of the violence it portended. Yet there was also a sense of a clear spiritual call to face this reality. They confronted "an enormous paradox of God's presence amidst terrible evil."[25] The experience brought the Christian community together in a powerful way. The centrality of prayer in their daily life was dramatically heightened. In September 1978, when the general uprising began, Christians throughout Nicaragua had accepted the need for revolution in the country. When the final insurrection began the following May, they were prepared to fight or to assist the combatants until victory.

The Role of Christians after Victory

Just as churches in Nicaragua were active in the Sandinista-led popular insurrection, so too was there active participation by some parts of the churches after the victory in support of the Government of National Reconstruction. Many Christians actively supported the Revolution and the Sandinista leadership. Others offered cautious and qualified support, while some opposed the Revolution. The government itself took a keen interest in the role of the Church and invited Church support in a variety of ways.[26] Below the surface there were deep-seated fears and divisions within the Church over how and to what degree Christians should accompany the Sandinista Revolution. There appeared to be two pervasive fears among church people who did not wholeheartedly support the Revolution. First, they recalled the example of Cuba, where the churches refused to accept the Revolution, became antirevolutionary and as a result suffered a decline of influence when the Revolution took root and prospered. The Catholic Church hierarchy in particular did not want to "blow the opportunity" in this sense and be pushed to the sidelines in the Nicaraguan Revolution. Then, too, they did not want to merge into the Revolution to such a degree that the Church would begin to lose its own identity, particularly its spiritual identity, and its independence. There were also those who supported the Revolution and identified themselves as Sandinistas, but who were also profoundly anticommunist and concerned that Nicaragua would become a second Cuba.

One of the more notable features of the first year of the Government of National Reconstruction was the presence of a large number of priests in government positions. Ernesto Cardenal was Minister of Culture, and Miguel D'Escoto, a Maryknoll Missioner, was Foreign Minister. Numerous priests also began working in social welfare ministries and the agrarian reform institute. One of the most important policy projects of the new government in its first year was the national literacy campaign, headed by Fernando Cardenal. The participation of priests in high government office was troubling to the hierarchy and caused some friction within the Church and between the government and the bishops.

Direct involvement of the Church was much deeper than priests in government, however, if one considers the Church role more broadly. Pastors in poor barrios reported, for example, that almost all of the Catholic youth in their parishes joined the literacy crusade out of Christian commitment to the Revolution. Some of these consciously incorporated the Bible and Christian teachings into their courses. In both Catholic and Evangelical Churches throughout Nicaragua, one saw posters proclaiming literacy training as a Christian vocation. Many Evangelical Churches, with ALFALIT and CEPAD serving as coordinators, participated with equal zeal in the campaign. Church schools were used extensively to house *brigadistas* and to teach classes. For example, a Christian high school in Jinotega, operated by the Brothers of LaSalle, was a literacy campaign center and source of support to the Revolution, according to its director "as a testimony of the Church in the liberation of the people."[27]

Still, there were many Evangelical Churches with a different theology which opposed the literacy crusade as they mistrusted the Revolution. For them the crusade was too secular and too political. They were particularly alarmed by the way many of the *brigadistas* picked up the language of Marxism and of liberation theology. The Reverend Albino Melendez, Baptist minister and a CEPAD official deeply involved in the development of courses designed to conscientize clergy and laity so that they could participate more energetically in the Revolution," admitted that "within the Evangelical world, a majority still think that the church has to be structurally apolitical." Further, "There is a contradiction between what they say and what they do." In other words, they came to accept the theological position that "God is on the side of the poor," but they did not want the institutional Church to be involved in any way in helping to alleviate that poverty or its byproducts.[28]

There was considerable speculation about the Catholic bishops' stand on the Revolution. Their June 2, 1978, declaration had been pointed to as evidence of their belated but authentic attempt to support armed revolution against *Somocismo*. Some Church people in Nicaragua subsequently doubted that this was the bishops' intention. The bishops were anti-Somoza but did not seem to want a Sandinista government, so they were uncertain after victory how the Church could coexist with the Revolution. Indeed this was the question uppermost in the minds of most Nicaraguan Christians. How could the Church accompany the Revolution? The Latin American bishops assembled at Puebla Mexico early in 1979 spoke of the "people of God" and defined this people substantially in terms of the poor. In this sense, it was clear that the people of God, especially in the poorest barrios of Nicaragua's major cities, were with the Revolution. The bishops feared that they could not control the faithful or their participation in the Revolution. In mid-summer 1980, the priests in government, despite the Vatican ruling barring direct involvement in political life, decided to remain for the time being.

Moreover, the government itself was taking some initiative in areas traditionally reserved for the Church. In August 1980, the religious festival of Santo Domingo was highly publicized and endorsed by the government, which used it as an occasion to urge proper moral and social conduct in keeping with the principles of the Revolution. The government urged that the festival be conducted with the utmost religious seriousness and that drinking not be part of the celebration. By and large the public response was favorable, but rather than reassure the bishops about the government's respect for religion, this event seemed to reinforce their fears of government interference in religious activities, and their own loss of influence among the people.

Perhaps their most profound fear was that there would be a gradual increase of atheism among the people as the government's influence reached into wider and wider areas of social life and that at some point in the future, when it was no longer needed, the government would abandon the Church. Archbishop Obando y Bravo stressed that the Church must be vigilant not to lose its freedom to fulfill its mission in an independent way. From his point of view, one of the most severe challenges faced by the hierarchy was to maintain unity in the Church. He spoke optimistically in this regard, but the forces of pluralism that could lead to disunity in the Church, especially between the hierarchy and the rank and file, were strong indeed.

These concerns were, to a remarkable degree, absent among the Evangelical leadership of the country. Three months after the Victory, 500 pastors gathered for RIPEN II (recall that 50 had attended RIPEN I three years earlier), whose theme was "Pastors in the Reconstruction." Following several days of study and reflection, the 500 (about half the Protestant ministers in Nicaragua) signed a Declaration, at the beginning of which they gave "thanks to God our Father for the victory of the Nicaraguan people and their instrument of liberation, the Sandinista Front of National Liberation."[29] "We are committed," they continued, "to offer cooperation in all the labors, projects, activities, and programs that the government develops for the real benefit of the people; understanding that our participation . . . is related to our fidelity to the Lord Jesus Christ." The 500 saluted the Junta for "its program of government" and said they understood that the end of "this revolutionary process is the formation of the new person (and) of a just and fraternal society in which its inspiration is Jesus Christ." They called on all Christians to "participate in political actions that unite us in the common good; to study . . . the program of government (and) scientific methods of analysis in order to understand how our society works." They called for participation in the Sandinista Defense Committees and for service in programs such as "literacy, health and liberating education." They condemned "all counterrevolutionary intentions"—then, in a more global perspective, also condemned the twenty-year old U.S. economic blockade of Cuba and called on their fellow churches in the U.S. to bring pressure on their government to end it. Clearly, the Evangelicals had come a long way in three years.

Unlike the Catholic Bishops' Pastoral letter, which appeared a month later and carefully spelled out what kind of political system the Church could live with, the Evangelicals threw their unequivocal support to the government and the FSLN as the revolutionary vanguard. The only specific appeal of the Evangelicals was for representation in the Council of State and for greater attention and sensitivity on the part of the government to the special conditions of the Atlantic Coast (which is overwhelmingly Evangelical).[30]

On March 20, 1980, a large and diverse group of activist Christians, both lay and religious, published a pamphlet containing the bishops' pastoral letter of November 17, 1979, along with a brief discussion of the views of pro- and antirevolutionary Christians. Some members of most of the religious orders in Nicaragua, representatives of Christian Base Communities, members of CEPA, faculty of the Jesuit University, faculty of Catholic high schools, communities of religious women, and some Evangelical pastors signed the document. The pamphlet criticized those who feared the government and refused to work actively in support of it. It pointed out that top Sandinista leaders had insisted that religion would not decline in Nicaragua "because the Nicaraguan people are religious and Christian." They noted that Commander of the Revolution Daniel Ortega had said the best arguments the Sandinistas had urging people to take up revolutionary struggle were Christian arguments.[31]

Less than a year after the Revolution, the activist Christians represented by these statements were trying to develop a new "theology of national reconstruction" for Nicaragua that would integrate the Church into the Revolution.[32] Less than two months after victory, some clergy organized a week-long seminar to bring together Church people and members of the FSLN to discuss ways the Church could accompany the Revolution. The seminar was held at the Jesuit Central American University (UCA) and included members of the Junta, Catholic priests, Evangelical ministers, and leaders of Christian communities. The major thrust of the seminar was to encourage critical but sympathetic and active support of Christians in the Revolution. The organizer of the conference, Father Álvaro Argüello, S.J., Director of the Historical Institute at UCA and a strong supporter of the Revolution, was elected by the Association of Nicaraguan Clergy to the Council of State, a broadly representative advisory body on policy to the Junta.

A second major vehicle for linking the churches and the Revolution was the Antonio Valdivieso Center. This center for Christian reflection was established within a month after victory "to keep the revolutionary spirit alive among Christians, to help Church leaders understand the revolution, and to counteract the pressure of rightist businessmen on Church leaders."[33] The Center, named for a sixteenth-century bishop assassinated by large landowners because of his defense of the Indians, was headed by Franciscan

Father Uriel Molina,Nicaraguas leading biblical scholar, and by José Miguel Torres, a Baptist minister. Father Molina, like Father Argüello and many other Christians, had been touched personally by the struggle against *Somocismo*. Both had brothers who died in the fighting. The Center had explicit political goals in concert with the Revolution. It held seminars, published a newsletter, and served as a meeting place for Christians who wanted to support the Revolution. Like the Historical Institute, it sought to document the history of Christian involvement in the anti-Somoza struggle. Because of its strong disposition to involve the Church constructively in the Revolution, the Center devoted considerable attention to courses designed to energize the Christian Base Communities and to provide training for their leaders. Given its strong grass-roots orientation, its independence, and its ecumenical cast, the Center presented a challenge and perhaps a threat to the hierarchy.

Other centrifugal forces were at work in the Church. At the base community level, there were both priests and lay leaders who wanted to promote Marxist-Christian dialogue. The CEPA, now independent of the hierarchy but with a strong presence among Christians in the countryside, was notably promoting such dialogue. Christian communities which were well-developed before victory continued to have vitality but evidenced some selective openings to cooperation with the Sandinistas. Where the Church was weaker, the Sandinista movement had clearly begun to supplant religious practices in community life. The fear among the hierarchy was that this would spread to the more vigorous Christian communities such as those in Estelí, where Sandinista influence was particularly strong. Finally, some of the most effective Delegates of the Word had left their lay ministries and gone into Sandinista organizations such as the ATC, other worker syndicates, or taken leadership positions in the Sandinista Defense Committees.

These defections were seen as a clear threat to the institutional Church. Such people had gone into the Church when they had few other opportunities to experience creative social roles under Somoza. Now the Church seemed to be losing them and thus one of its most valuable resources. Would they maintain their Christian orientation and retain their loyalty to the Church? This was a question of great practical concern to the bishops. These fears were valid, though there was room for disagreement as to what the Church should do about this problem. For large numbers of Nicaraguan Christians, particularly the youth who were subjected to such ruthless persecution by Somoza and who had come to support and participate in armed struggle with the FSLN, the answer would not be fear and mistrust but an active presence in the Reconstruction to assure that the Churches, through their members, not become marginal to the Revolution.

Notes

[1] The notable exception to this phenomenon was the Pentecostal Churches, *none* of whose pastors left after the revolution.

[2] Although more attention is given to the Catholic Church than to the Evangelical Churches, we are interested in the role played by both churches in the revolution. We try to be clear which church we are discussing at any given point in the chapter. Generally speaking, if we do not specify the Evangelical Churches, we are referring to the Catholic Church.

[3] "The Catholic Church in Nicaragua," Report of the U.S. Catholic Press Association, 1962, p. 18.

[4] The concept of a prophetic church is discussed at length in Michael Dodson, "Prophetic Politics and Political Theory," *Polity*, Vol. XII, No. 3 (Spring 1980), p. 388-408.

[5] In Argentina, they called themselves the movement of Priests for the Third World; in Chile, the Christians for Socialism; in Colombia, Golconda; in Peru, the National Office of Social Information (ONIS).

[6] *The Church in the Present Day Transformation of Latin America in Light of the Council* (Washington, D.C.: United States Catholic Conference, 1970), pp. 80-82.

[7] The English term consciousness-raising is not normally associated with the development of political awareness and has a more individualist orientation than does the Spanish term *conscientizacion*. The latter term implies group process and political action, so we use it throughout, translating it as conscientization.

[8] The reference to Christian communities throughout the chapter reflects the language used by Nicaraguans themselves to refer to the very fluid, decentralized nature of church experience from Medellín to victory. Much of the prophetic action of the Church took place in small communities at the local level without sponsorship or, in some cases, even the awareness of the official church hierarchy. Many formal Christian Base Communities (CEBs) were established, but many more grew up spontaneously, carrying Christians into the Revolution without formal Church approval.

[9] The term *pastoral* is widely used in Latin America to refer to all aspects of the priestly or ministerial function of evangelizing. Its Spanish meaning is thus broader than the English usage. We use the Spanish throughout.

[10] It is important to note that during this period the actual number of Christian communities developing along the lines of Medellín was more than fifty parishes; only eight in the eastern zone and three in the western were involved in the process described in the text. But these parishes played a crucial role in the popular insurrection ten years later. In addition, the change to increasingly explicit emphasis on social concerns created conflict within the Christian communities between those who followed Medellín and the Charismatics who persisted in their attachment to popular religious practices. This conflict was never resolved and continued into the 1980s.

[11] "Declaración de Sacerdotes Nicaragüenses," *Cuadernos de Marcha*, No. 17, (Sept. 1968), pp. 31-32.

[12] "Climate of Violence Hits Nicaragua," *NC News Service* (Washington, D.C.: U.S. Catholic Conference, Oct. 1, 1970), p. 2.

[13] Interview with Peggy Dillon, M.M., Ciudad Sandino, Nicaragua, July 29, 1980.

[14] Interview with Ricardo Chavarría, Managua, Nicaragua, August 11, 1980.

[15] CEPAD's 1980 membership included 34 denominations and four organizations, representing approximately 800 churches with 250,000 members, or 96 percent of the evangelicals in the country and 10 percent of the population, an extraordinarily high figure for Latin America.

[16] "Los Evangélicos en Nicaragua: Juicio y Mensaje a la Nación," document signed November 24, 1976, and adopted by the CEPAD Directorate on June 7, 1977.

[17] The process for Evangelicals was slower than for many Catholics in part due to far

lower levels of education and theological training. Many pastors had only a grade school education.

[18] Ricardo Chavarría, August 11, 1980.

[19] Peggy Dillon, M.M., July 29, 1980.

[20] Yvonne Dilling et al., *Nicaragua: A People's Revolution* (Washington, D.C.: EPICA Task Force, 1980), p. 23.

[21] The best and most moving example of this dialogue appears in Ernesto Cardenal, *The Gospel in Solentiname*, Vols. 1 and 2 (Maryknoll, N.Y.: Orbis, 1977, 1978.)

[22] "Mensaje de la Conferencia Episcopal de Nicaragua Renovando la Esperanza Cristiana al Iniciarse el Año de 1977," Managua, Jan. 8, 1977, p. 3.

[23] Peggy Dillon, M.M., July 29, 1980.

[24] Interview with Benjamín Cortés, Managua, February 1980.

[25] Peggy Dillon, M.M., July 29, 1980.

[26] See "Communicado Oficial de la Dirección Nacional del F.S.L.N. Sobre la religión" San José, Costa Rica: DEI, pp. 15. Reprinted from *Barricada*, Oct. 7, 1980, p. 3.

[27] Interview with Eduardo Carretero, Jinotega, Nicaragua, August 8, 1980.

[28] Albino Meléndez, February 1980.

[29] "Declaración de los 500," II Retiro interdenominacional de pastores evangélicos de Nicaragua [RIPON II], mimeographed, Oct. 5, 1979.

[30] Subsequently, the Federation of Christian Businessmen, without CEPAD's knowledge or permission, promoted CEPAD for membership in the Council of State, a move from which CEPAD publicly dissociated itself, meanwhile reaffirming "our militant participation in the revolutionary process." Letter to the Junta, published in *Nuevo Diario*, August 1980.

[31] *Los Cristianos Están Con la Revolución* (San José, Costa Rica: DEI, 1980), pp. 9-14.

[32] *Fé Cristiana y Revolución Sandinista en Nicaragua* (Managua: Instituto Histórico Centroamericano, 1979), p. 151.

[33] Rolando Caetano, "Revolutionary Situation Gives Birth to Nicaraguan Christian Center," *Latin America Press*, Vol. 12, No. 1 (Jan. 1980), p. 7.

Chapter 10

News Media
in the Nicaraguan Revolution

JOHN SPICER NICHOLS

The revolutionary war in Nicaragua was in part a war of words with major battlefields on the front pages of newspapers and television screens both in Nicaragua and the United States. Throughout the insurrection, Anastasio Somoza maintained firm control of the military apparatus. The tanks, artillery, and airpower of the Nicaraguan National Guard exacted a heavy toll on the opposition forces and innocent civilians, but Somoza's inability to win complete control of the channels of communication despite the use of heavy-handed tactics was pivotal in his downfall. Clearly the revolution was the product of a nexus of events and conditions, including the bloodshed, hardship, and sacrifice of hundreds of thousands of Nicaraguan people. But without the constant assault of the opposition press and the failure of the government propaganda machine, the Somoza family might still be in power today.*

The Somozas' ability to stay in power and dominate virtually every aspect of Nicaraguan life was predicated, in large part, on two interrelated factors. First and probably foremost was the Somozas' relationship with the United States. For more than forty years, U.S. action and inaction were crucial in perpetuating the family dictatorship.[1] The actual or perceived threat that the United States would intervene to keep the Somozas in power tended to strengthen the support among the regime's allies, namely the National Guard, and undercut the opposition of its enemies. The second factor was the Somozas' success in preventing an alliance among their domestic opponents. By skillfully playing one opponent off against the others, the Somozas long averted the creation of a large, unified opposition group that could not be controlled by simple repression. The contribution of the Nicaraguan opposition press, primarily the newspaper La Prensa, in disconnecting Anastasio Somoza's link with the United States and building the second link between Somoza's opponents is the focus of this chapter. In addi-

*This research was funded in part by the College of the Liberal Arts (Stanley F. Paulson, Dean and Thomas F. Magner, Associate Dean for Research and Graduate Studies) and the School of Journalism (Robert O. Blanchard, Director) of The Pennsylvania State University. The author also wishes to thank Profesors R. Thomas Berner, Penn State University, and Richard Millett, Southern Illinois University at Edwardsville, for their assistance.

tion the chapter examines the effect of the media's participation in the revolutionary process on the type of media system that evolved after the Sandinista victory.[2]

For a better understanding of the function of the media in the Nicaraguan revolution, two important characteristics that distinguish most Latin American media from their North American and, to some extent, European counterparts should be explained:

Collaborative posture. Unlike the news media in North America and Europe, much of the Latin American media did not develop as a separate institution. Instead, they frequently were founded and continue to serve as collaborators with specialized power contenders in society, usually political factions. While the major North American and European media tend to attack the government regardless of what political faction is in power, the collaborative Latin American media's opinion of the government depends on which faction holds office. For example, if a political faction is out of power, the media that are allied with it usually will attack the other faction controlling the government, bearing a resemblance to the North American-European tradition. But once the opposition triumphs, its allied media become defenders of the new government and criticize the recently displaced faction. The media of this new opposition force, in turn, change from defenders of the government to critics of the government.[3]

Nicaragua offers a classic case of collaborative journalism. It is *not* an example of balanced, dispassionate reporting in which the journalist stands off to the side and reports unfolding events without becoming personally involved in or affecting the outcome of those events. Rather, it is an example of political advocacy in which journalism was used as a tool by combatants to further their causes. The Nicaraguan media were closely allied with political factions before the Revolution and continued to be allied with significant political, economic and religious groups after the FSLN victory.

Limited audience. The Latin American media, particularly the print media, are not very important to the vast majority of the people. While North Americans and Europeans are accurately described as living in a "media society," most Latin Americans, owing largely to widespread illiteracy and scarce economic resources, are unable to use much more than a cheap transistor radio. The Latin American media are better described as *class* media than *mass* media.[4] Thus, the stereotype of a crusading newspaper editor in Latin America inflaming the masses to revolt against an evil dictator does not represent reality. In Nicaragua, where the per-capita number of newspaper copies, radio receivers, and television sets has been among the lowest in the Americas, and the majority of the population was illiterate until 1980, the prerevolutionary media played a significant role only for the privileged classes. And to the extent that the opposition press did affect the broader base of Nicaraguan people, it was not so much for its content, but rather as a political symbol. The latter phenomenon continued to be an important element in post-Somoza Nicaragua.

Prerevolutionary Media

The nation's first newspaper, *El Telégrafo Nicaragüense,* was founded in 1835 by the president of the country, José Zepeda, mostly as a political tool rather than a means of disseminating news.[5] In the following century and a half, most newspapers were founded to espouse the cause of a local *caudillo,* economic or other special interest groups, or, most often, one of Nicaragua's two major political parties—the Liberal or the Conservative. Similarly, the first radio system in Nicaragua was founded in 1931 for purposive ends. The rebel Augusto Sandino frequently destroyed telegraph and telephone lines and disrupted military communications. In response, the U.S. Marines occupying the country at the time built the Radio Nacional network.[6] The heritage of military control of broadcasting affected the ownership and regulation of radio (Nicaragua's most widely used medium) and subsequently television throughout the Somoza family rule, and continued to affect policy under Sandinista rule. Television was founded in 1955 as a commercial enterprise of the Somoza family and its allies.[7]

This tradition of collaborative media especially applied to the major figure in the history of Nicaraguan journalism, Pedro Joaquín Chamorro Cardenal. Chamorro, a product of more than a century of highly partisan Conservative party politics, was the descendant of one of the most prominent families in the country and a long line of important public figures, including four Conservative presidents: general Fruto Chamorro (1854-1855), Pedro Joaquín Chamorro (1875-1879), general Emiliano Chamorro (1917-1921, 1926, and, according to Millett, "Nicaragua's perpetual revolutionary"), and Diego Manuel Chamorro (1921-1923).[8] In 1930, Chamorro's father, Pedro Joaquín Chamorro Zelaya, brought the newspaper *La Prensa,* a forum for the Conservative platform and eventually an international symbol of opposition to the Somozas' and the Liberal Party's dominance of Nicaragua. The younger Chamorro became publisher of *La Prensa* following the death of his father in 1952.

However, long before the younger Chamorro gained the reputation as one of the region's most respected opposition journalists, he had established credentials as a political militant.[9] While a law student at the national university in Managua during the 1940s, Chamorro joined an anti-Somoza political group and as a result of his political activities was arrested and exiled to Mexico, where he completed his legal studies. He returned to Nicaragua in 1948 and continued his political activities. In 1954, he was sentenced to six years in prison for participating in a revolt but was released early. In 1956, he was again convicted, this time for complicity in the assassination of Anastasio Somoza García. After a period of house arrest in 1956 and 1957, he escaped to Costa Rica, from which he ran guns to the opposition in Nicaragua. In 1959, he went to Havana to seek arms from Fidel Castro, who had recently achieved a revolutionary victory in Cuba, but they did not reach an agreement because Chamorro feared that Castro was attempting to dominate the Nicaraguan opposition. Later that year,

Chamorro helped to organize an army to invade Nicaragua from Costa Rica. The invasion force was defeated easily by the Nicaraguan National Guard, and Chamorro again was sentenced to jail. He was freed in 1960 during an amnesty by Luis Somoza and remained out of jail, although not partisan politics, until 1967, when he organized an anti-Somoza demonstration in Managua that erupted into a gun battle between the National Guard and armed demonstrators and resulted in 40 deaths and more than 100 injuries. Chamorro again was arrested but was released forty-five days later, after Anastasio Somoza Debayle, the heir to the Somoza dynasty, had himself elected president of the country.[10]

At this point, Chamorro retired from overt revolutionary activity and concentrated on journalism and more conventional party politics in opposition to Somoza. In addition to editing La Prensa, Chamorro became secretary-general in 1974 of a coalition of opposition parties and groups called Democratic Union of Liberation. Thus, although he won international acclaim for his role as a journalist, it is impossible to separate Pedro Joaquín Chamorro the journalist from the political activist and revolutionary.

The Somozas did not invent censorship and other forms of repression of the press in Nicaragua, although they probably were more zealous and consistent in their application. Long stretches of censorship were common in Nicaragua from 1936 to 1961, including during the political violence in 1954.[11] In that year, Hernán Robleto, prominent editor of the opposition paper La Flecha, and several other journalists were arrested and accused of complicity in an assassination attempt on the president. Robleto described the consequences to the Inter American Press Association:

> My son, who was general manager of the newspapers, was subjected to all manner of torture. On different occasions they fractured his ribs, they have hung him by the feet submerging him in a fetid well. He contracted typhoid fever that had him on the verge of death. He has been blinded for two and three days because they forced him to sit in (front) of a lamp of 1,000 candlepower in order to force him to declare lies.
>
> They assassinated one of our staff members. . . , who on an earlier occasion was exiled to Costa Rica on foot and, as if this were not enough, they stapled his fingers of his hand together so that he would not be able to use a typewriter to write against the Somozas.[12]

During this period, the censorship often was so strict that the newspapers were not allowed to publish the fact that they were being censored. However, according to Pablo Antonio Cuadra, popular Nicaraguan poet, longtime associate of Chamorro and the post revolutionary editor of La Prensa, the newspaper developed a novel means of communicating with its readership. Every time the censors deleted an article from La Prensa, the editors would replace it with a photo of Hollywood star Ava Gardner. Often *La Prensa* would look more like an Ava Gardner fan magazine than a newspaper. But the photographs became a widely recognized symbol of Somoza repression. When the newsboys picked up their newspapers, they would look through them quickly to see if there was an Ava Gardner photo. If there was, instead of shouting "*La Prensa* for sale!" they would simply shout "Ava Gardner, Ava Gardner!" and the people of Nicaragua would know that *La Prensa* had been censored again. According to Cuadra, the Ava Gardner pictures greatly increased both *La Prensa's* circulation and citizen opposition to the Somoza rule.[13]

Government control of the mass media became more subtle as the Nicaraguan presidency descended the Somoza family tree. In the 1960s and early 1970s, the Somozas relied less on formal censorship and other forms of overt repression and more on methods such as hoarding newsprint, withholding advertising, levying heavy taxes on machinery and repair parts for the opposition press, and cutting off official news sources from unfriendly reporters while granting special privileges to cooperative reporters.[14] Yet the most effective control was ownership of the media. An overwhelming majority of the nation's radio and television stations was either owned directly by the Somoza family or its cronies, or controlled by the National Guard. Likewise, the Somozas invested heavily in the country's sparse print media, including outright ownership of the Managua daily *Novedades*.[15] Under the weight of this combination of controls, virtually all of the opposition press collapsed, with one important exception—*La Prensa*.

Perhaps because of his family tradition, his revolutionary fervor or social commitment, Pedro Joaquín Chamorro continued his opposition despite the constant pressure. It was this dogged opposition that eventually made Chamorro a regional *cause célèbre* among press organizations and human rights groups. Somoza resorted largely to petty legal harassment to stem Chamorro's repetitive editorial attacks.[16] However, each legal maneuver and other form of repression by the government brought criticism from regional and international press associations, especially the Inter American Press Association, a Miami-based publishers' organization in which Chamorro served as a director, member of the executive committee, and vice-president of its Freedom of the Press Committee during his twenty years of membership. In 1965, he won the IAPA's Mergenthaler award for his efforts "in behalf of freedom of the press."[17] In addition, Chamorro became a popular lecturer and interview subject in the United States, and in 1977 accepted the prestigious Maria Moors Cabot award from Columbia University, which cited him for "journalistic leadership of those forces opposed to tyranny in Nicaragua."[18] This external support gave Chamorro greater leverage to criticize the Somoza government, while at the same time the deteriorating domestic situation following the 1972 Managua earthquake and increased Sandinista activity made Somoza even more sensitive to the opposition press. Somoza was forced to return to formal censorship in 1974 to end Chamorro's attacks.[19] But the restoration of formal censorship in Nicaragua only raised Chamorro's international image and further tarnished Somoza's. Amnesty International, the Organization of American States, the Carter administration in the United States, the aforementioned press associations, and other groups brought heavy pressure on Somoza to end censorship as part of a package to end human rights violations in Nicaragua. Somoza relented in 1977, which opened the door for some of Chamorro's most acid criticism.[20]

Somoza was trapped in a hopelessly downward spiral. Each time he punished Chamorro for his polemics, he also boosted Chamorro's reputation abroad and eroded his government's support from its most important patron—the United States. Each action or inaction by Somoza inevitably required that he would have to take a harsher action against Chamorro in the future. In effect, Chamorro had beaten Somoza at his own game. In the end, it was Chamorro who had earned the greatest credibility in the United States. For that reason, the assassination of Chamorro in January 1978 produced a wave of international protest against the Somoza dynasty and contributed to the government's downfall.

Of course, the editorial and political opposition of Chamorro and his eventual killing by assassins believed to be sympathetic to Somoza (if not under the direction of Somoza or his lieutenants) also had tremendous domestic impact. Indeed, many Nicaraguan and foreign analysts argue that Chamorro's assassination was the spark that touched off the fires of revolution in Nicaragua. Regardless of the exact effect of his assassination, Chamorro and his newspaper, after almost three decades of opposition, became national symbols for all of the ideologically diverse enemies of Somoza. "I see La Prensa as the republic of paper fighting the dictatorship of steel," said Pablo Antonio Cuadra, the newspaper's associate editor, shortly before the assassination. "We are the only watchdog of the judiciary, the legislature and the executive. When people have complaints, they can only turn to us."[21]

Throughout the decades of their rule, the Somoza family was adept at repressing opposition among the peasant and working classes and coopting potential opponents in the middle classes with large-scale corruption, and by persuading the latter group of the communist or antibusiness threat of the former. The Somoza family's greed during the reconstruction following the 1972 earthquake destroyed the financial advantage of middleclass cooperation with the regime, and La Prensa's increasingly sympathetic coverage of the guerrilla forces helped to alleviate the suspicion of the newspaper's largely middle- and upper-class readers and thus paved the way to a revolutionary alliance.[22]

La Prensa editorially endorsed the formation of a broad coalition of opposition groups that would isolate Somoza and offered its politically moderate readers a steady diet of articles identifying the common ground that they had with the more radicalized opposition forces. The coverage was so sympathetic that the government press office in 1975 released a white paper showing marked similarities between articles and editorials in *La Prensa* and the Sandinista's manifestos, therefore, according to the government, proving "the editor of *La Prensa* and the Sandinista terrorists in Nicaragua are conspiring jointly."[23]

In addition, *La Prensa* effectively used foreign news sources to support its cause. In the late 1970s, an increasing number of U.S. foreign correspondents came to Nicaragua to cover the growing hostilities. A few highly regarded U.S. journalists, such as Alan Riding of the *New York Times,* Karen DeYoung of the *Washington Post,* and Bob Sherman of Jack Anderson's staff, visited clandestine guerrilla camps to interview the Sandinista commanders and analyzed in less dogmatic terms their policy statements.[24] These correspondents and particularly their colleagues who later followed them to Nicaragua were not permanently assigned in Central America and thus were not fully familiar with the background and important issues in the conflict. Chamorro, who was well-known in regional journalistic circles,was happy to supply the visiting correspondents with a briefing. The first stop for virtually all foreign correspondents arriving in Managua was the offices of *La Prensa*—a tradition that continued after the end of the revolutionary war.

The increasingly critical coverage of the Somoza government by U.S. newspapers was magnified many times by the local opposition. For example, *La Prensa,* a subscriber to the New York Times News Service, would take small articles critical of Somoza but buried on the inside pages of the *Times* and splash them across the front page of *La Prensa* under banner headlines. To compound the problem, Somoza found it very difficult either to censor or to discredit such prominent publications from the United States, his reputed ally. Both power-holders and power-contenders took note and began to question the depth of U.S. support for Somoza. The negative publicity via *La Prensa* fanned unrest within the National Guard, Somoza's traditional power base, and encouraged the opposition in the belief that their actions might not bring U.S. intervention after all.

The Media During the Insurrection

When Somoza responded to external pressure and ended censorship in September 1977, *La Prensa* was the only significant opposition voice still alive to take advantage of the situation. The opening assault of *La Prensa*'s new campaign against the Somoza regime was to publish all of the articles that had been censored in the thirty-three months since censorship began. It then followed up with a new blitz of editorials charging the government with corruption, constitutional irregularities and human rights violations.[25] In the afternoons, *La Prensa* would accuse the government or the National

Guard of a serious abuse, such as the torture and killing of innocent peasants, and supplement the charge with gory photos. On the following mornings, *Novedades*, Somoza's paper, would counterattack with photos allegedly showing the bodies of National Guardsmen similarly treated by the guerrillas and with any evidence or rhetoric that might discredit *La Prensa*, Chamorro, or his staff.[26] Sober, objective journalism was not the order of the day.

After the assassination of Chamorro, *La Prensa*'s opposition went far beyond journalistic opposition. Xavier Chamorro, Pedro Joaquin's brother and the newspaper's new editor, turned *La Prensa*'s offices into the head-quarters for the diverse opposition forces. The general strike that followed the assassination was coordinated at the newspaper. Much of the editorial staff was divided into small Sandinista cells that carried out both propaganda and military activities. Many top Sandinista leaders in the postrevolutionary government doubled as reporters for *La Prensa* during this period. They included William Ramírez, later a member of the FSLN Directorate; Bayardo Arce, who became president of Council of State; and Carlos Chamorro, youngest son of the slain editor, who became editor of the FSLN's newspaper, *Barricada*, after serving as Deputy Minister of Culture in the new government.[27]

Recognizing the importance of *La Prensa* as a serious opposition force, the Somoza government retaliated with more than verbal attacks. *La Prensa*'s telephones and telex machines were cut off; its reporters were constantly harassed by the government; several staffers were arrested and beaten; the newspaper's office was the target of repeated machine gun attacks; the government returned to formal censorship under the martial law provisions; and finally in June 1979, *La Prensa* was bombed out of production in a coordinated attack by National Guard tanks, aircraft, and ground forces.[28]

The Postwar Media
The Sandinista victory in July 1979 brought many superficial changes and several substantive changes to the Nicaraguan news media. But close examination indicates that, with the exception of Somoza and his allies, many of the same individuals, groups, and underlying principles continued to govern the Nicaraguan media system. A description of that system and an analysis of its problems and portents follows.

Systems Perspective
Media watchdog organizations such as the Inter American Press Association, International Press Institute, and Freedom House, which tend to dominate the discussion of world media systems, argue that any society that precludes or severely limits government control of the mass communication process has a "free press." Conversely, media systems that are owned or otherwise controlled by the government are labeled "not free." Indeed,

some of these proponents of the North American concept of "free press" claim that all controls from outside the media organization, regardless of source, are dysfunctional; therefore the mass media must be entirely uncontrolled and unregulated to best serve society. The simplistic rhetoric of these groups notwithstanding, all media systems in the world *are* controlled. When defined as the absence of external controls, particularly governmental, which influence the outcome of the journalistic enterprise, freedom of the press does not exist in the world today, never has existed, never can exist and, many might argue, never should exist.

The process of mass communication, by its very nature, requires control. From the infinite number of facts, ideas, and opinions in the world, journalists must select, process and transmit a few to their audiences; these editorial decisions are made in response to a wide variety of political, economic and social forces. In a complex society, the variety of controls comes from numerous sectors of that society; however, one sector (usually, but not always, the government) oft times gains majority control in these media decisions. Latin American governments have been particularly adept in this regard. Some governments use censorship and other overt means of repression, but most use more subtle means such as economic pressures. Regardless of types of control, the fact remains that all media systems in Latin America and elsewhere, even the traditional democracies, are to some extent controlled by their governments. Supporting this view, Frederick S. Siebert, a pioneer in the study of comparative foreign journalism, wrote that not only were controls necessary and always present in a press system, but also that "government has a legitimate function to define the limitations. . . ."[30]

Even if the watchdog organizations' goal of the elimination or substantial reduction of government controls on the media were a realistic possibility, that does not mean there would be a total absence of controls and that media actors could make their decision autonomously. Other sectors of society, such as business, labor, church, political parties, terrorists, and so on, invariably fill the void. In short, controls are always present. The press never can be entirely uncontrolled. The questions, therefore, are not whether controls exist or should exist. Rather, the questions should be: what combination of controls are exercised, by whom, and most important, what impact do they have on society?

Another shortcoming of the watchdog organizations' traditional concept of freedom of the press is that it implies only one type of press system is best for all peoples and nations. Of course, this view does not account for the tremendous cultural, economic, and political diversity in Latin America. Just because a Latin American nation adopts a press system with a combination of controls different than those in the so-called "free press" systems of North America, it does not mean the Latin American system is inappropriate or destructive for that society. By the same token, just because a Latin American nation accepts the North American press structure, it does not mean that type is automatically in the best interests of its citizens.

In their research program on social forces in the mass communication process, the research team of Tichenor, Donohue, and Olien found a strong relationship between the social structure of U.S. communities and the type of function the local newspapers serve for those communities.[31] Small, homogeneous communities with few powerful interest groups and few mechanisms for protecting the social order from disruption that could result from a public dispute tended to have newspapers that avoided conflict and enlisted public support for community goals. On the other hand, the press in larger, more heterogeneous and pluralistic communities tended to shift from a consensus approach to a conflict approach. This latter type of newspaper served the function of initiating social action and maintaining political discourse among a wider variety of interest groups. Thus, according to the research team's findings, more complex and differentiated social systems need news media that report government conflict and thereby contribute to the vitality of the social system. In social systems with a simple, monolithic power structure, conflict reporting would be disruptive for the social system and therefore less likely. More recent research finds evidence of this phenomenon at a national level in the revolutionary society of Cuba. Using descriptive data, Nichols found that as Cuban President Fidel Castro reorganized his government in the late 1970s to include a larger and more diverse power structure and more mass participation in public decision-making, the function of the Cuban mass media also shifted. Reflecting the structural changes in the social system, the Cuban media carried more public criticism of government operation and supplied a forum through which the increased number of sectors in the power structure could advocate their positions.[32]

Nicaragua after the FSLN victory was no exception. Its media system, like all media systems of the world, was subject to numerous and varied controls. Using this systems perspective, the nature and degree of the controls operating in the postwar Nicaraguan media will be discussed and the extent to which that combination of controls reflected the social environment and served the needs of the country will be evaluated.

Official Controls on the Media

Knowing full well the importance of communication in the revolutionary process, the FSLN and the Junta of the Government of National Reconstruction moved quickly to formalize and consolidate their control over the domestic media. After July 1979, they exercised the following controls on the Nicaraguan mass media:

Legal. One of the first official acts of the new government was to promulgate the "Statute on the Rights of Nicaraguans," which declared: "Freedom of information is one of the fundamental principles of authentic democracy." But much the same as in the prerevolutionary constitution of Nicaragua, the guarantee of freedom of expression was not absolute. "The exercise of these freedoms brings with it duties and responsibilities, and consequently may be subject to certain necessary formalities, conditions, and restrictions specified by law," read the bill of rights, followed by a list of general equivocations.[33]

In August 1979, the Junta issued the General Provisional Law on the Media of Communication which elaborated the principles and detailed the exceptions mentioned in the bill of rights. Sections of the law prohibited media content that portray women as sexual objects and promote laziness, subversion, other crime, and human degradation. Violence, pornography, and advertising of tobacco and liquor were specifically banned. In addition to listing types of content that the media must not disseminate, the law also stated the types of content that must be disseminated, such as ". . . to express a legitimate preoccupation for the defense of the victories of the revolution, the process of reconstruction and the problems of the Nicaraguan people."[34] Later, these general provisions were interpreted to preclude the discussion of sensitive political topics such as food shortages, military matters, and the timetable for elections.[35] Nonetheless, the new press law was not rigorously enforced. As in most Latin American countries, the legal provisions were largely a matter of form and other means of media control were more significant.

Ownership. The new press law empowered the government to prevent the economic dominance of the media by any social group, especially former Somoza collaborators.[36] To this end, the revolutionary government nationalized all the media in which Somoza or his allies had financial investments. Thus, following the precedent of the prerevolutionary government, most broadcasting was directly owned by the government or tightly supervised by the military. In 1980, the government declared television a "privileged medium" and converted the nation's two channels, both previously dominated financially by Somoza, into the Sandinista Television System. The Junta and the FSLN also established significant control in the radio medium. Of the 33 stations that returned to the air after the insurrection, 13 were operated by the government. The remaining stations were under private ownership, and several tended to deviate from the official line in their news and commentaries. However, all stations, both government and private, were linked through the National Sandinista Channel, which broadcasted news, and information supporting the literacy campaign and other public affairs content. Although the privately owned stations technically were not required to broadcast material from this Sandinista network, the government strongly encouraged them to air important programs, and the stations usually did.[37]

Similarly, the print media were largely controlled by the new government. Only two privately owned daily newspapers emerged from the revolution—*La Prensa* and *El Nuevo Diario*. The nation's third daily is *Barricada*, the official voice of the FSLN.[38] The first issue of *Barricada*, printed at the facilities of the former Somoza newspaper *Novedades*, appeared in Managua a few days after the Sandinista victory. It was originally staffed by inexperienced journalism students from the national university and an assortment of foreign Marxists whose own revolutions had failed elsewhere in Latin America. As a result, the content was dogmatic, stilted and frequently inaccurate. The top Sandinista leadership privately expressed great dissatisfaction with *Barricada* because its strident political line tended to limit the FSLN's flexibility in innovating new policy and the paper's numerous *faux pas* publicly embarassed the leadership. To improve the quality of the staff and make *Barricada* a respectable newspaper, the FSLN appointed Carlos Fernando Chamorro, youngest son of the martyred editor, as editor. Numerous improvements in the paper were forthcoming.[39]

Union. Probably the most important and controversial control mechanism in Nicaraguan media was the Union of Nicaraguan Journalists (UPN). The union was started informally in 1978 as an underground opposition group of journalists active (both pen and sword) in the overthrow of Somoza.[40] UPN was formalized in the August 1979 press law as a *colegio*, or closed-shop union.[41] Theoretically, all Nicaraguan journalists, both print and broadcast, were to be members of the UPN in order to practice journalism, and in order to be a member, journalists were to be certified by the national university as having completed its journalism training program. Practicing journalists who were not university trained were "grandfathered" and were admitted if, in the opinion of the union, they had good moral character, no criminal record, five years or more of significant professional experience, and no previous involvement with Somoza.[42] Perhaps owing to journalism's unique role in the revolution and the prerevolutionary union membership of several Sandinista commanders and high government officials, UPN's power extended beyond journalism into the operation of the new government. Specifically, UPN held a seat on the Council of State.[43]

The union also demonstrated its power to control the flow of information in Nicaragua when, in early 1980, it expelled from membership Oscar Leonardo Montalván, news director of Radio Mil. Montalván, whose newscasts had the largest audience in the country for nongovernment radio programs, had criticized a Sandinista leader shortly before his expulsion; without union credentials, Montalván could not continue broadcasting on that station.[44] Despite substantial union control, not all journalists joined UPN. Of particular importance, *La Prensa* employed many non-UPN journalists, including most of the top editors.[45] Whether the *colegio* rules would be enforced on the *La Prensa* staff or how the contradiction would eventually be resolved should demonstrate a great deal about the news media system in Nicaragua.

Extralegal Pressures. Because of the effectiveness of the aforementioned media controls, the new government, for the most part, did not resort to censorship and other overt forms of repression characteristic of the Somoza regime. The most notable exception was the closing of *El Pueblo*, the daily newspaper of the Worker's Front, a radical left organization (which included disgruntled former Sandinistas) that, according to the government, was attempting to undermine the Sandinista economic reforms. The newspaper, which had been allowed to publish during the Somoza period but never circulated more than a few thousand copies, accused the Sandinistas of "selling out the proletariat to the local bourgeoisie" and called for "active sabotage of the economic plan in order to bring power back to the hands of the people."[46] In January 1980, the paper was closed and the editors jailed on a combination of charges, including subversion and storing illegal arms.

Official Propaganda. In addition to restricting certain information, the Junta and the FSLN were forceful in encouraging positive information about the revolutionary government. The Directorate of Publication and Press of the Junta and the National Secretariat of Propaganda and Political Education of the FSLN both conducted extensive information programs to enlist domestic support for revolutionary programs. The Sandinista commanders and Junta members frequently held press conferences, granted interviews with local and foreign journalists and appeared on the Sandinista Network program "Face the People" to answer citizen complaints and questions.[47]

Other Sources of Media Control

Although the government clearly held majority control of the media in 1980, it did not have a monopoly. Other important sectors of Nicaraguan society continued to influence the process and content of journalism. Primary among these were the private business sector and the Catholic Church.

During the initial period of reconstruction, FSLN policy was determined to a large extent by the realities of a national economy shattered by the destruction of war and the financial pillage of the Somoza regime. To rebuild the economy and to prevent the flight of additional capital, and of technical, managerial, and business personnel, the FSLN needed the cooperation of the private sector, organized into the Superior Council of Private Enterprise (COSEP). Despite the nationalization of Somoza's huge business empire, about three-fifths of the economy remained in private hands—an important gauge of COSEP's economic power. In addition, COSEP drew substantial external support from the U.S. government and other countries in the hemisphere.[48] In turn, COSEP's influence on the domestic media was largely through the economic and political support of *La Prensa*. Content analysis of Managua dailies during the first two weeks in June 1980 indicated that *La Prensa* was receiving the bulk of nongovernment advertising. Regardless of whether the intent was to prop up a pro-business voice or merely to take advantage of *La Prensa's* large circulation,[49] the impact of the private sector's advertising in *La Prensa* was to maintain the newspaper as an economically viable medium and as an advocate of private sector interests.

In the post revolutionary period, the Catholic Church was the only sector of Nicaraguan society that had popular support approaching or ex-

ceeding that of the Sandinistas. The Church took an active role in the overthrow of Somoza, and consequently several clergymen were appointed to
important billets in the new government, including Father Ernesto
Cardenal, head of the Ministry of Culture, a government division that
shared responsibility for establishing media policy and enforcing the new
press law. However, the Church's greatest impact was in the ownership and
operation of Radio Católico, one of the most important of all the media in
the country. In the summer of 1980, the Church was restructuring its news
programming to offer a significant alternative to government and business-
backed media. Oscar Leonardo Montalván, former Radio Mil news director
who had been expelled from the union and banned from the air, was
heading the revamp of Radio Católico and was serving as its major news
commentator.[50] Because of the Church's support for the Revolution and its
symbiosis with the government, there seemed to be little likelihood that the
government would have the desire or the capability to control the church
media, even if they deviated from the government line. In sum, significant
power bases continued to enforce political and economic diversity in
postrevolutionary Nicaragua. That diversity was manifested in the media of
the country.

The Case of *La Prensa*

The Chamorro family was united in what it opposed but not in what it supported. When *La Prensa* returned to publication shortly after the Sandinista
victory, the Chamorros, missing their patriarch, were deeply divided about
the newspaper's editorial direction. One faction of the family headed by
Xavier Chamorro, who replaced his slain brother as editor of *La Prensa*,
was reluctant to criticize the new government, in the manner typical of collaborative journalism in Latin America. "The new role of the newspaper is
to support the revolution as long as it represents the needs of the people," he
said.[51] Xavier Chamorro was supported in his stance by Daniel Aguirre Solís,
one of the country's most distinguished journalists, the paper's news editor
and president of UPN, and the majority of the staff. The other faction of the
family, headed by Pedro Joaquín Chamorro, the murdered editor's oldest
son and member of the editorial board, favored a probusiness policy, which
would entail criticizing the new government. Pedro Joaquín had the backing
of his uncle Jaime and his father's longtime associate, Pablo Antonio
Cuadra.

For months, the family feud simmered internally, with the exception
that the union added *coletillas* (dissenting footnotes) to *La Prensa* articles
with which it didn't agree.[52] However, in April 1980, the family dispute
escalated into a national crisis when Violeta Bários de Chamorro, the
former editor's widow and, for several months, a member of the Junta, sided with her eldest son Pedro in his efforts to have his uncle Xavier removed
as editor of *La Prensa*. The day after Xavier's dismissal was announced, the

Sandinista-backed union responded by closing down the newspaper. *La Prensa*, the national and international symbol of "press freedom" and resistance against the Somoza regime, had been closed down, in effect, by the government. "When Somoza used to shut down *La Prensa*, it meant that something big, something ugly was about to happen," a Nicaraguan observer told a U.S. correspondent during the strike. "People still feel very nervous when they don't see the paper on the newsstands."[53]

Simultaneous with the dispute at *La Prensa*, the relationship between the FSLN and COSEP deteriorated to its lowest ebb. There was little communication between the groups—most of it hostile. Finally, however, the two opposed groups, realizing that their survival might depend on the cooperation of the other, began negotiations to settle their disagreements. High on COSEP's list of demands was that the *La Prensa* strike should be resolved in favor of the probusiness faction of the Chamorro family as demonstration of the Sandinista's commitment to political pluralism, thus reinstating the only major medium supporting COSEP positions.[54] FSLN negotiators agreed to this point as part of its overall agreement with the private sector representatives, but before the government acted to resolve the *La Prensa* strike, the factions of the Chamorro family settled their differences independently. The family gave Xavier Chamorro 25 percent of the capital invested in *La Prensa*, which he used to start a competing daily, *El Nuevo Diario*. The majority of *La Prensa*'s editorial and technical staff joined him in establishing the paper. In turn, *La Prensa* was allowed to reopen.[55]

On May 26, *La Prensa* published its first issue in more than a month under a banner headline: "We Return Again! *La Prensa* always will be *La Prensa*." But the *La Prensa* that returned was not the same *La Prensa* that Pedro Joaquín Chamorro had edited before the revolution and had earned an international reputation. It had the same name and was published at the same location, but most of the staff and top editors and some of the family members had departed for competing newspapers. Yet neither *Barricada*, edited by Carlos Chamorro, nor *El Nuevo Diario*, edited by Xavier Chamorro, could legitimately claim the *La Prensa* tradition. The real *La Prensa* was a casualty of the revolution it helped to create.

Problems and Portents

The combination of controls governing the Nicaraguan mass media in the postwar period was unique. It was modeled after neither the U.S. nor the Cuban system; rather, it was a hybrid that reflected the special role of the press in the Revolution and other historical, cultural, economic and political conditions in Nicaragua. However, revolution obviously is a volatile process in which the media would be expected to change as the social structure of the country changes. In the future, *La Prensa* would surely be the focus in assessing those changes.

La Prensa emerged from the Revolution as a national and international symbol of human rights. Despite the fact that it was not the same paper that earned this reputation, it continued as the most popular medium in the nation; its offices were a magnet for U.S. congressmen and diplomats, officials from other nations, trade delegations, and so on, and the Inter American Press Association redoubled its campaign to portray *La Prensa* as the last bastion of press freedom in Nicaragua. These domestic and world links are not dissimilar to those existing for the old *La Prensa* and represent formidable protection against greater government intervention. It could be expected that *La Prensa* would use its position of power to continue its traditional function of advocacy journalism. Although it was advocating the cause of a group somewhat different from its prerevolutionary collaborator, *La Prensa* would probably persist in its criticism of the new government. Unlike the U.S. approach, in which the press is supposed to disseminate objective, accurate, and critical information about all contenders for power in society, the Nicaraguan press, including *La Prensa* and all other media, would maintain its traditional role as political tools.

Thus a confrontation between *La Prensa*, or perhaps another nongovernment medium, and the revolutionary government seemed inevitable. Although the FSLN was the first popular government in Nicaraguan history, it faced serious economic problems testing that popular support. Under such conditions, could the FSLN tolerate *La Prensa*'s criticism, or, more important, could it waste a communications resource that could be used to forge a political consensus in the country and to help in critical development projects such as the literacy campaign? Whatever the outcome, the answer lay in the political and economic structure of the country. If the FSLN, for either ideological or practical reasons, maintained a degree of pluralism, alternative voices would be heard in Nicaragua. If the FSLN saw fit to consolidate its power further, not even the special reputation of *La Prensa* would ensure its survival.

The literacy campaign of 1980 also was likely to affect Nicaraguan dynamics. Because of the mass illiteracy before the revolution, *La Prensa* was more important for what it was than what it said. Now, with the impact of more widespread literacy in the country, *La Prensa* might be judged in the future more for its content than its tradition. Thus, how *La Prensa* and other media responded to their new role as mass media rather than class media would be paramount in understanding the Nicaraguan Revolution.

Notes

[1] Richard Millett, *Guardians of the Dynasty: A History of the U.S. Created Guardia Nacional de Nicaragua and the Somoza Family* (Maryknoll, NY: Orbis Books, 1977); Millett, "Central American Paralysis," *Foreign Policy*, 39 (Summer 1980), pp. 99-177; William M. LeoGrande, "The Revolution in Nicaragua: Another Cuba?" *Foreign Affairs*, 58 (Fall 1979), p.

28-50; Thomas W. Walker, "The Sandinista Victory in Nicaragua," *Current History*, Feb. 1980, pp. 57-61 and 84; and Richard R. Fagen, "Dateline Nicaragua: The End of the Affair," *Foreign Policy*, 36 (Fall 1980), pp. 178-191.

[2] While the foreign press was also an important ingredient in the revolution, it will not be discussed in detail due to space limitations. See John Spicer Nichols, "Jet Journalists in the Nicaraguan Revolution" (typewritten manuscript).

[3] Robert N. Pierce with John Spicer Nichols, *Keeping the Flame: Media and Government in Latin America* (New York: Hastings House, 1979), pp. 231-234.

[4] John Ryan Morris et al., *Area Handbook for Nicaragua* (Washington: U.S. Government Printing Office, 1970), DA PAM 550-88, p. 196.

[5] Ibid.

[6] Richard Millett, *Guardians of the Dynasty*, p. 76.

[7] Robert Harris, "Nicaragua—The censor at work," *Index on Censorship*, 6 (Nov.-Dec. 1977), pp. 23-30; and John Ryan Morris, *Area Handbook*, p. 191.

[8] Agence France-Presse et al., "Asesinaron en Managua al líder opositor Chamorro," *La batalla por Nicaragua*, Vol. 1: *Cuadernos de uno más uno* (Mexico: Editorial Uno, 1980), pp. 33-34; Richard Millett, *Guardians of the Dynasty*, pp. 23-46; and Sara L. Barquero, *Gobernantes de Nicaragua 1825-1947*, 2nd Ed. (Managua: Ministerio de Instrucción Pública, 1945.).

[9] Pedro Joaquín Chamorro was the "heir to the Chamorro family's irresponsible revolutionary tradition," according to Eduardo Crawley, *Dictators Never Die: A Portrait of Nicaragua and the Somoza Dynasty* (New York: St. Martins Press, 1979), p. 119.

[10] Pedro Joaquín Chamorro, *Los Somoza: Una Estirpe Sangrienta* (Buenos Aires: El Cid Editor, 1979); Charles W. Flynn and Robert E. Wilson, "An Interview with Somoza's Foe, Now Dead," *New York Times*, 13 January 1978, p. A23; Laurie Johnstone, "Editor Was Honored in U.S.," *New York Times*," January 1978, p. A3; James L. Busey, "Nicaragua and *La Prensa* After Somoza" (typewritten manuscript); and Jerry Knudson, "The Nicaraguan Press and the Sandinista Revolution" (typewritten manuscript).

[11] Richard Millett, *Guardians of the Dynasty*, p. 190.

[12] Inter American Press Association, *Proceedings of the XV Annual Meeting* (San Francisco, 1959), pp. 228-229.

[13] Interview with Pablo Antonio Cuadra, Managua, June 11, 1980.

[14] Jerry Knudson, "Nicaraguan Press," p. 4. Also see numerous examples in *IAPA* (Inter American Press Association) *News*.

[15] John C. Merrill, Carter R. Bryan, and Marvin Alisky, *The Foreign Press: A Survey of the World's Journalism* (Baton Rouge: Louisiana State University Press, 1970), pp. 189-90; and Robert Harris, "Nicaragua—The Censor at Work," p. 28.

[16] See, for example, "Chamorro's civil rights suspended," *IAPA* (Inter American Press Association) *News*, Aug.-Sept. 1974, p. 8 and "Nicaragua," *IAPA Updates*, Mar. 15, 1977, p. 2. Surprisingly, most of the measures that Anastasio Somoza used to repress Chamorro and *La Prensa* in the late 1960s and 1970s were within the letter, although probably not the spirit, of Nicaraguan law. Unlike many Latin American countries which modeled their constitutions after the libertarian constitutions of the United States and France, the Nicaraguan constitution did not make a blanket guarantee of the freedom of speech and the press. Prior censorship of the news media and other suspensions of civil rights were legal under martial law provisions, and most of the criminal and civil charges filed against Chamorro appear to have basis in Nicaraguan prerevolutionary law. These legal restrictions will be compared to postrevolutionary law later. See *Report on the Situation of Human Rights in Nicaragua* (Washington: Inter American Commission on Human Rights, Organization of American States, 1978), pp. 65-68; U.S. Congress, House Committee of International Relations, *Human Rights in Nicaragua, Guatemala, and El Salvador: Implications for U.S. Policy, Hearing before the Subcommittee on International Organizations*, 96th Cong., 2nd sess., June 8-9, 1976, pp. 3-4 and 25; John Ryan Morris, *Area Handbook*, p. 190 and Robert Harris, "Nicaragua—the censor at work," p. 25.

[17] Mary A. Gardner, *The Inter American Press Association: Its Fight for Freedom of the*

Press, 1926-1960 (Austin: The University of Texas Press, 1967), p. 162 and Chamorro, *Los Somoza*, p. 8.

[18] Johnstone, "Editor Was Honored."

[19] "Nicaragua," *Latin American Report*, Jan. 1975, p. 6.

[20] Karen DeYoung, "Politics by Media in Managua," *Washington Post*, Feb. 9, 1978, p. A22.

[21] Andrew Hale, "Death in Managua," *Index on Censorship*, 7 (May-June 1978), p. 57.

[22] An alliance between alienated and disparate sectors of society was a precondition to the previous Latin American revolutions in Mexico, Bolivia, and Cuba. See Samuel P. Huntington, *Political Order in Changing Societies* (New Haven: Yale University Press, 1968), p. 277.

[23] "Nicaragua," *Latin American Report*, p. 6.

[24] Alan Riding, "Respectable Rebels Threaten Somoza Dynasty," *New York Times*, January 25, 1978, p. 4E; Karen DeYoung, "Exiled Nicaraguan Guerrilla Pledges to Depose Somoza," *Washington Post*, Oct. 19, 1978, p. A21; Jack Anderson, "Washington Merry-Go-Round," *Washington Post*, Nov. 1978, p. B7; Interviews with Alan Riding, *New York Times* correspondent, Mexico City, May 26, 1980; Karen DeYoung, deputy foreign editor, *Washington Post*, Washington, July 16, 1980, and Bob Sherman, Jack Anderson's staff, Washington, July 15, 1980.

[25] Jerry Knudson, "Nicaraguan Press," pp. 8-9.

[26] Karen DeYoung, "Politics by Media" and Andrew Hale, "Death in Managua," p. 56.

[27] Interviews with Carlos Fernando Chamorro, editor of *Barricada*, Managua, June 10, 1980; and Manuel Pinell, former *La Prensa* reporter and former editor and current deputy editor of *Barricada*, Managua, June 10, 1980.

[28] Alan Riding, "Newspaper Family Typifies Nicaragua's Divisions," *New York Times*, May 24, 1980, p. 10; and Jack Anderson, "Washington Merry-Go-Round: Nicaragua Press Subject to Somoza's Wrath," *Washington Post*, Nov. 29, 1978, p. C29. Also see numerous articles in *IAPA News* and *IAPA Updates* in 1978 and 1979.

[29] For example, see Raymond D. Gastil, *Freedom in the World: Political Rights and Civil Liberties* (New York: Freedom House, 1979).

[30] Frederick S. Siebert, *Freedom of the Press in England 1476-1776* (Urbana: University of Illinois Press, 1965), pp. 9-10.

[31] Phillip J. Tichenor, George A. Donohue and Clarice N. Olien, *Community Conflict and the Press* (Beverly Hills, California: Sage, 1980).

[32] John Spicer Nichols, "Organization, Control and Functions of the Cuban Mass Media," *Journalism Monograph*, forthcoming.

[33] Pedro Camejo and Fred Murphy, eds., *The Nicaraguan Revolution* (New York: Pathfinder Press, 1979), p. 48. Also see La Dirección de Divulgación y Prensa de la Junta de Gobierno de Reconstrucción Nacional, *Programa de Gobierno*, No. 1: Documentos (Ediciones Patria Libre, N.D.), p. 3.

[34] La Dirección de Divulgación y Prensa de la Junta de Gobierno de Reconstrucción Nacional, *Ley General y Reglamento Sobre Medios de Comunicación*, No. 2: *Serie Legislativa* (Ediciones Patria Libre), pp. 5-6.

[35] "Managua Asks News Checks," *The Times of the Americas*, Sept. 10, 1980, p. 16.

[36] Junta, *Ley Sobre Medios de Comunicación*, p. 5.

[37] Interview with William T. Hines, public affairs officer, United States International Communication Agency, Managua, June 12, 1980. Hines's information was based on unclassified portions of a classified USICA study of the Nicaraguan media.

[38] Several other non-daily newspapers and periodicals also are published by the Junta and FSLN. They include, for example, *Patria Libre* and *Poder Sandinista*.

[39] Interviews with Carlos Fernando Chamorro, Manuel Pinell, and Alan Riding. Riding reported that one of the top Sandinista commanders said, in reference to *Barricada*, "Those presses *(formerly Novedade)* print only shit."

[40] Interviews with Daniel Aguirre Solis, president of UPN, Managua, June 11, 1980 and Manuel Pinell.

[41] Junta, *Ley Sobre Medios de Comunicación*, p. 6.

[42] Interviews with Manuel Espinoza E., press secretary to the Junta, Managua, June 12, 1980, and Aguirre.

[43] Ibid. Also see "Expanded Council of State Inaugurated May 4," *Nicaragua Newsletter* (Embassy of Nicaragua), April 1980, p. 12.

[44] United States International Communication Agency, "Bilateral Communication Relationship: Nicaragua FY 1981," typewritten report, p. 2.

[45] Interviews with Pedro Joaquín Chamorro B. member of editorial board of *La Prensa* Managua, June 10, 1980, Pablo Antonio Cuadra, and several *La Prensa* reporters. Also see U.S., Congress, *Country Reports on Human Rights Practices for 1979, Report to Committee on Foreign Affairs, U.S. House of Representatives and Committee on Foreign Relations, U.S. Senate by Department of State*, 96th Cong., 2d sess., 1980, p. 372.

[46] "Nicaragua: Government hits out at left," *Latin America Weekly Report*, Feb. 8, 1980, p. 6; U.S. Congress, *Human Rights Practices*, p. 372.

[47] Personal observation during June 1980 and interview with Manuel Espinoza.

[48] "Nicaragua: A Revolution Stumbles," *The Economist*, May 10, 1980, p. 26.

[49] The estimated circulation of *La Prensa* in June 1980 was 65,000. Nicaraguan newspaper circulations are not audited, thus estimates vary widely. Nonetheless, all sources, including competing newspapers, agreed that *La Prensa* was the circulation leader.

[50] Interview with William T. Hines.

[51] Interview with Xavier Chamorro, editor of *El Nuevo Diario*, Managua, June 11, 1980.

[52] *Coletillas* added to articles in privately owned newspapers in Cuba by government-backed unions in 1960 foreshadowed the eventual take over of the entire Cuban press by the government. See Robert N. Pierce with John Spicer Nichols, *Keeping the Flame*, p. 86.

[53] Fred Bruning with Larry Rohter, "A Revolution Moves Left," *Newsweek*, May 5, 1980, p. 63.

[54] Confidential sources close to the negotiations.

[55] Alan Riding, "Newspaper Family."

PART V

REVOLUTIONARY PROGRAMS AND POLICIES

The real measure of a revolutionary government is whether or not it works effectively and quickly to implement changes which uplift the condition of the common man. The chapters in this unit discuss revolutionary policy in a number of areas including economics, agrarian reform, literacy education, health care, housing, sports, minority affairs, and international relations.

The chapters on economics and foreign policy give an indication of the difficult practical context in which domestic policy was being implemented. The economically-dependent, nearly bankrupt, and outrageously indebted condition in which Somoza had left Nicaragua meant that the new government was in a vulnerable and delicate position precisely at a time when it was extremely important to implement a variety of potentially costly programs. It was imperative, therefore, to renegotiate the foreign debt on more favorable terms, to attract additional aid and loans on a strictly concessionary basis, to diversify the country's external economic relationship and to try to maintain good relations with the United States (a country which could use its economic power to destabilize the Revolution). Furthermore, it was essential that individuals planning Nicaragua's economy do so with considerable care—avoiding major mistakes which often take place early in a revolution—in order to increase productivity and maximize the amount of resources available to fund social programs.

Given the overwhelming economic problems faced by the country in this period, one could expect that the new government would have been able to accomplish very little in the social realm. In reality, however, the Revolution achieved more social reform in a year and a half than most prerevolutionary Latin American countries had accomplished in decades. Part of this success can be attributed to the fact that such limited budgetary resources as did exist could now be spent honestly and with maximum impact. Then, too, in areas such as housing and land usage, the simple passage and enforcement of laws designed to ease the exploitation of the common man helped considerably.

The real key to the implementation of otherwise utopian projects, however, lay in the voluntary participation of hundreds of thousands of common citizens through the Sandinist popular organizations. It was largely through this vehicle that nationwide innoculation campaigns, urban cleanups and housing projects, a low-budget but surprisingly successful sports program, and so on, were carried out. The most impressive success of all, however, was the massive 1980 Literacy Crusade, which, while costing the government practically nothing, occasioned a spectacular reduction in adult illiteracy and won Nicaragua international acclaim, including a very prestigious UNESCO award.

Chapter 11

The Economics
of the Revolution

E. V. K. FITZGERALD

On July 20, 1979, the leadership of the Frente Sandinista de Liberación Nacional met to decide upon a new stage of their strategy. From the first moments, the scale of the task of organizing the economy and establishing a new state served as a damper on the excitement of victory. Even though "the reorganization was quite rapid in terms of the functioning of the public administration, the reality of the situation in which we had received our country still had to be evaluated and a strategy had to be designed in order to win the new battle which faced us—this time in the economic terrain."[1]

This chapter is concerned with that battle and its apparent outcome during the first year and a half of the new government, a period which includes the immediate emergency measures for the remainder of 1979 and the 1980 Program of Economic Reactivation in Benefit of the People (*Programa de Reactivación Económica en Beneficio del Pueblo, 1980,* commonly known as the "Plan 80"). The phrase "apparent outcome" applies, because only in the longer run, when the shape and destiny of the Revolution are revealed by history and much more material is publicly available on the 1979-80 period than at present, will it be possible to make a reasoned judgement. Nonetheless, the main elements of the economy of the first year are clear, and their analysis provides not only an essential aspect for the nature of the Revolution as a whole, but also has a number of more general implications. Here we shall deal, albeit briefly, with five points: (1) the background to the economic structure; (2) the main economic problems of reconstruction and the resources available to tackle them; (3) the emergency measures of the first few months; (4) the design of Plan 80; and (5) finally, its execution during 1980. All judgements, however, must be regarded as no more than tentative. It is impossible moreover, to understand an economy without reference to the class struggle that takes place within its structure, a structure which is in turn modified by the pattern of accumulation resulting from that struggle; but this task must be left to other chapters.

Background
The Nicaraguan economy[2] in the 1970s exhibited most of the characteristics commonly included in a definition of "underdevelopment." It had a depen-

dent and dual structure, relying on agricultural exports for its dynamic and exhibiting one of the worst income distributions in Latin America. Its degree of industrialization was low, despite the promise of the Central American Common Market, and nutrition so bad that the infant mortality reached 200 per 1,000 live births despite surplus land resources. The nature of the Revolution was both conditioned by, and designed to change this economic structure.

The economy was based on agriculture, about half the land area being dedicated to a wide range of export products, including cotton, coffee, sugar, sesame, bananas and cattle. In addition, the primary sector contained a fishing industry and some somewhat depleted gold mines. This primary agro-export sector had, however, experienced considerable modernization during the previous twenty years, a process which had not only strengthened rural capitalism but had also created a strong rural proletariat. Nonetheless, the other half of the land areas was under peasant production of food crops, mainly maize and beans, which provided the principle source of wage-goods to the economy; these peasants were a key component of the rural social structure, particularly in the mountain areas of the North.

In contrast, industry was of more recent creation, and, if the elementary processing of agricultural products such as that done by cotton and sugar mills are excepted, a result of the Central American Common Market. There were two elements to this: the provision of inputs to and processing of outputs from agriculture, particularly textiles and chemicals; and the typical branches of early import substitution, such as bottled drinks and toothpaste. However, the latter had not made much progress, and in consequence the urban proletariat was not large. The expansion of the tertiary sector was, nonetheless, rapid, both in the modern sector (banking in particular) and in the "informal" activities of retailing and petty services. Thus the urban population was relatively large, absorbing in Managua alone almost a quarter of the total population of some 2.35 million in 1977.

Primary exports were the dynamic element in the Nicaraguan economy: the trade coefficient (the mean of the ratio of exports and imports of goods and services to GDP) was very high, reaching 40 percent by the mid-seventies, and the growth of incomes depended upon price fluctuations in capitalist world markets. Although the United States was a dominant element in the economy, exports did not go exclusively to that country; meat and fish did, but coffee went to Western Europe and cotton to Japan. Imports, particularly of equipment, were, however, of predominantly U.S. origin, and determined the nature of accumulation in the economy.

This accumulation depended, logically enough, on the pattern of ownership. In the first decades of the Somoza era, this became progressively more concentrated on a domestic oligarchy, particularly the landowners. Peasants were proletarianized or pushed out towards the agricultural frontier. Industrialization was closely connected to this group too, so that no "industrial" bourgeoise emerged. Surprisingly, foreign capital did not exer-

TABLE 11.1

ECONOMIC STRUCTURE IN 1978

	Gross Domestic Product		Economically Active Population	
	Million Cordobas	*Percent*	*Thousands*	*Percent*
Agriculture, etc.	3,701	24.7	338.5	45.4
Mining	46	3.1	5.7	0.8
Manufacturing	3,149	21.0	79.0	10.6
Construction	429	2.9	32.3	4.3
Subtotal: Material production	7,325	48.9	455.5	61.0
Government	1,082	7.2	n.a	n.a
Commerce	3,540	23.6	90.7	12.2
Other services	3,041	20.3	n.a.	n.a.
Subtotal: Services	7,663	51.1	290.7	39.0
Total	14,988	100.0	746.2	100.0

Source: Banco Central de Nicaragua, *Informe Anual, 1978, Managua, 1980.*

cise a great degree of ownership in the economy—with particular exceptions such as mining, bananas, oil refining and petrochemicals. During the last decade, however, the Somoza group began to extend its own holdings, using as a vehicle the financial system (both banking and real estate), and encouraged by U.S. "aid" policy; this extension intensified the exploitation of the working classes, alienated the rest of the bourgeoisie, and steadily exacerbated the structural imbalances in the economy.

The 1972 earthquake, which virtually destroyed Managua, only served to make these tendencies more extreme. The Somoza group, with only isolated protest from the bourgeoisie, speculated flagrantly in real estate, embezzled the aid funds, and deployed armed force to crush popular opposition. The international commodity boom granted a brief but illusory strength to the balance of payments, but this increase in resource rents was not used for capital accumulation (let alone economic development), and the poverty of that half of the population living on an annual average of $286 per head (in an open economy with prices similar to those in the USA) contributed to the rising popular unrest. By 1978, the economic model had become unviable and politico-military pressure from the FSLN was uncontainable; all attempts at dependent capitalist development were abandoned, to be replaced by bloody repression and the flight of capital.

TABLE 11.2

DISTRIBUTION OF PERSONAL INCOME, 1977

Income Stratum	Population (thousands)	Share of Income	Annual Income per Head
Top 5%	116	28%	$5,409
Next 15%	349	32%	2,062
Next 30%	698	25%	805
Lower 50%	1,162	15%	286
Total (100%)	2,325	100%	966

Source: UN / ECLA, *"Nicaragua: Repercusiones Económicas de los Acontecimientos Políticos Recientes"* [mimeo] Mexico City, August 1979.

Identifying The Problems

During the July meetings, it became clear that the economic problems could be grouped under four headings, as outlined in the following paragraph. The task of coordinating economic policy and of developing a coherent plan for overcoming these problems was entrusted to the newly-formed Ministry of Planning and within this Ministry to a special division called the "Commission for Economic Coordination," acting as a "staff" to the Junta (which had only a small "cabinet office") and eventually to the FSLN National Directorate on economic matters. From these small beginnings, with one room in the Intercontinental Hotel (the only secure building in Managua), where the new government was quartered in the first days, grew the foundations of a planned economy. From the start, this was a highly cooperative enterprise, involving leaders, cabinet ministers, professionals, and representatives of the popular organizations in a constant series of discussions which were, in effect, working out what the Sandinista philosophy would mean in practical terms when applied to concrete economic problems. The principles of anti-imperialism, basic-needs provision, independent development, income redistribution, and so on, were a useful guide—and an important antidote to expediency—but the specific actions would have to be worked out in a dialectical fashion within the real situation.

The four headings for the economic problems were, first, the immediate repair of the damage from the war and the reorganization of administration; second, the amelioration of food shortages and widespread unemployment caused by the dislocation of the war; third, the renegotiation of the massive external debt built up by Somoza in the last years of his regime; and fourth, the first step in the reconstruction of the economy in a new form. It was clear that there would be little time to solve them, and that if they were not solved, not only would the subsequent economic crisis bear heavily upon the most disadvantaged members of society, but that the progress of the Revolution itself might be threatened. Economic policy had to have, therefore, "one central objective: the defense, consolidation and advance of the Revolution."[3]

The first problem, that of the destruction of war itself, was in itself almost overwhelming. The 50,000 dead in the years of war were equivalent to 2 percent of the population, and a greater proportion (possibly 5 percent) of the workforce; many of the 100,000 wounded would require long-term care; and there were an equal number of orphans to look after. In purely financial terms, the United Nations[4] estimated that the direct damage to infrastructure, plant, equipment and inventories was US$ 481 million. To this should be added at least $1.5 billion (US) in capital flight (much of it due to the Somoza group) during the previous year, including the last-minute extraction by *Somocistas* of the remainder of the Central Bank reserves. The dislocation of war meant that little cotton and maize had been sown in 1979, while industrial production had virtually ceased. Gross domestic product in 1979 was 24 percent down from 1978, itself a decline from 1977; in fact, real output per head was only just above that of 1962. The financial system was bankrupt, with enormous foreign liabilities and no real domestic assets. The lack of sowing, the slaughter of herds, and general rural disruption meant not only immediate food shortages but also a serious foreign exchange problem until 1981, when the next full cotton crop could be exported. In physical terms, the centers of a number of provincial towns had been bombed (with particular attention to hospitals), roads were impassable, houses burnt, communications disrupted, and records lost. Even the most optimistic observers felt that it would take several years and billions of dollars to repair the damage; even the center of Managua had remained unrebuilt since 1972.

The second problem was that of food shortages and unemployment. There was clearly a structural problem of malnutrition and underemployment in Nicaragua, the product of dependent capitalist growth model, which could only be solved in the longer term. But the disruption of the war meant that there were severe shortages of even the most basic foods such as maize, beans, flour, milk, and eggs, without which the population would simply starve before the end of the year. In addition, about a third of the workforce was now unemployed, meaning that they had no incomes in order to buy what little food there was. This was, of course, the social consequence of the first problem, the dislocation of production. Food would have to be obtained from abroad and distributed to the poorest until the next harvests in the autumn of 1980; some means of getting income to the unemployed until the economy recovered and their jobs opened again would also have to be designed.

The third problem was the external debt. The Somoza government, the

Somocista banks, and the associated companies had managed to build up an external debt of $1.650 billion (U.S.); most of it was with the U.S. commercial banks, and much in the form of short-term suppliers' credits; it had mainly been accumulated during 1978 and 1979 itself. There were also some dubious debts (connected with arms purchases and illegal transactions), but it would be necessary to recognize and repay most of this enormous sum, equivalent to about $4,000 per family and larger than the entire national income for 1979, if trading with the capitalist world were to be continued. The payments of amortization and interest due and overdue for 1979 alone were larger than remaining export income, so that some form of rescheduling was clearly necessary. The problem was how to obtain this without falling into the clutches of the International Monetary Fund (IMF) or some similar "supervisory" organization.

Fourth, and most significantly, it was necessary to start on the process of reconstructing the economy, to achieve what had not been done before—economic development as opposed to growth, social justice as opposed to exploitation, an adequate insertion into the international division of labor as opposed to dependency. Although it would take many years to effect a full transition, the urgent tasks of "reactivation" should not be allowed to impede a new direction, or be used as an argument for leaving "development" until later. On the contrary, reactivation of production within the existing structure would make the developmental task even harder, as domestic interest groups reestablished their positions and financial control by the United States over the economy became possible. In sum, it was only a completely new direction that would give meaning to the eighteen years of fighting, the decades of struggle, and the thousands of dead. The people had not risen and faced the guns of the National Guard in order to restore "Somocismo without Somoza," nor did people quite have Costa Rica in mind when speaking of "a new Sandinista Economy."

Mobilizing Resources

The picture, then, was daunting in the last days of July as the planners, many of them exhausted from the battlefield, gathered to work out some sort of economic policy. There were, however, two major positive points: the potential strength of the "Reconstruction State" itself; and the combination of overwhelming popular support for the FSLN, little opposition to the JGRN among the middle class and bourgeoisie, and considerable international sympathy for Nicaragua.

The new state, quite apart from having a new political form (described elsewhere in this volume), had a new economic nature as well. Indeed, the state under Somoza had played a reduced role in the economy (directly, that is, for clearly it was crucial to the maintenance of low wages, and so on); there were few public enterprises, social services were extremely limited; and the government undertook little investment except in roads.

Now, the state would naturally become the central element in the economy insofar as it was to be planned and social services (particularly health and education, but also housing, public transport, utilities) were to be expanded. In addition, the prevention of the complete bankruptcy of the economy (or rather the possibility of its continued operation in a condition of technical bankruptcy) would require direct state control of the financial system—banking and foreign trade in particular. In fact, the nationalization of the financial system was complete, taking in the banks under the Nicaraguan Finance Corporation (CORFIN), the insurance companies under the Nicaraguan Insurance and Reinsurance Institute (INISER), and external trade under the Ministry of External Commerce. In addition, state corporations were rapidly set up in order to organize the rational use of primary resources, particularly the Institute of Natural Resources (IRENA), the National Corporation of Mines and Hydrocarbons (CONDEMINAH), the People's Forestry Corporation (CORFDP), and the Nicaraguan Fisheries Institute (INPESCA). These developments were, to a great extent, inevitable and dictated by circumstances.

The advantage, an irony of history perhaps, was that the enormous properties of Somoza and his direct associates became state property. This was not nationalization in the normal sense, since these enterprises were already "part of" the state; in a very real sense Somoza could have echoed the claim of Louis XIV that "L'ètat, c'est moi." These properties, which formed the basis of the People's Property Area (APP) and which almost all came under either The Nicaraguan Agrarian Reform Institute (INRA) or the People's Industrial Corporation (COIP) included about half of the large farms of over 500 hectares in the country (see Chapter 12 on land reform), a quarter of all industry (including a number of dynamic firms), large construction companies, hotels, real estate, shops, an airline and a fishing fleet, and so on. This was, in effect, the dynamic center of the economy, precisely that which had been built up into a giant monopoly-capital "holding" by the dictator. It presented the opportunity to change the economic structure from within, without the necessity for immediate further changes in ownership. In the traditional terminology of socialism, the state already possessed the "commanding heights" of the Nicaraguan economy.

The overwhelming popular support for the FSLN was, however, the main strength of the government in its economic policy. In a general sense, popular acquiescence is obviously helpful to any government, particularly a reformist one, but in this case, the "mass organizations" were to be an integral part of the policymaking and implementation mechanisms. This was particularly important in the context of the immediate problem of an unreformed public administration in the first months, and subsequently in relation to the need for support for governmental policy towards the private sector within the factories and farms. For example, the Sandinist Defense Committees (CDS) carried out much of the administrative work of clearing rubble, distributing food, issuing identity documents, etc., in the first

TABLE 11.3

STATE PARTICIPATION IN THE ECONOMY, 1980

	Public sector (%)	Capitalist sector (%)	Small producers (%)
Production			
Agriculture	21	29	50
Manufacturing	25	45	30
Construction	70	5	25
Mining	95	5	—
Subtotal: Material production	25	37	38
Services	56	22	22
Gross domestic product	41	34	25
Commerce			
Production for export	26	59	15
Exports	75	25	—
Imports	45	55	—
Internal trade	30	35	35
Accumulation			
Fixed investment	82	13	5
Credit granted	100	—	—
Credit received	40	40	20
Employment			
Economically active population	21	26	53

Source: MIPLAN (The Nicaraguan Ministry of Planning).

months. The Reactivation Assemblies organized by the workers were essential to getting private enterprises operating again. In the longer term, this participation was formalized by integrating representatives of the mass organizations into the Programmatic Coordinating Commissions (sectoral "cabinets" supervising the ministries) and the sectoral planning commissions. Support, or at least nonopposition, from the middle classes and the anti-Somocista bourgeoisie was also essential, because it allowed the government to build up a new form of organization for the economy and strengthen the economic administration of the state sector itself without having to take on the whole of the production system.

Finally, Nicaragua could count upon considerable sympathy abroad. This was reflected in the generous donations from voluntary organizations, offers of technical cooperation from all over the world, and considerable aid proposals from the major international organizations. In the particular case of the United States, a decision was made to avoid what the State Department saw as the mistake made twenty years before with Cuba, and provide finance.

Despite the scale of the problems, then, the economic planners embarked upon their task with some optimism.

The First Steps

During the first six months of the new administration, considerable progress was made on the four problems we have identified.

The repair of the immediate destruction was undertaken at once. The repairing of streets and rebuilding of houses was mainly organized by municipalities and CDSs and completed with remarkable speed. The agricultural cycle could not be accelerated, of course, but emergency food-crops were immediately sewn in the cotton fields and student brigades mobilized to get in as much of the coffee crop as possible. As much foreign aid as feasible was mobilized to organize a rudimentary hospital service, and replace burned-out buses and restore communications. The foreign reserves of the Central Bank were replenished by lines of credit from Latin American central banks and from the IMF, although this latter organization was rather less generous than it had been to Somoza. In fact, these "immediate repairs" were carried out more rapidly than anticipated, reflecting both the enthusiasm of the populace and the sad fact that, so to speak, the hovels of the poor were almost as easy to put together again as they had been to destroy. Observers reaching Nicaragua by September were amazed at the air of "normalcy" that already prevailed.

The problems of food shortages and open unemployment were still there, however. A vast quantity of imported foodstuffs, mostly financed from foreign donations, had to be distributed up to the middle of 1980, when domestic production could come onto the markets. It was decided to organize this in conjunction with work schemes for the unemployed in order to accelerate reconstruction, to make sure that the food got to those who most needed it, and to maintain a sense of dignity among those who were not only unemployed through no fault of their own, but had actually suffered the most in the war itself. These aims were combined in the "food-for-work" scheme, which involved direct payment in kind for work on public reconstruction projects. Although this was seen as a temporary expedient, it was remarkably successful, and in fact work for repairing the damage of the 1972 earthquake, for new water and drainage schemes for slum areas, and for rural penetration roads was being undertaken as well by early 1980. However, it was clear that the domestic production of food and the reopening or creation of permanent jobs would be the objective in the medium term.

With Mexican support, the negotiations with a committee representing the foreign creditors was begun in Mexico City in September. The decision to deal with the "hardest" part (the commercial debts) first was a risky one, but once it was made clear to the bankers that this was the only chance that they had of recovering their loans, and that Nicaragua intended to subordinate debt policy to the economic plan rather than the other way around, the negotiations proceeded steadily. But the negotiations took longer than anticipated, the first stage concluding only in August of 1980. However the terms, based on five years' grace and an interest rate of less than 7 percent (the difference between this and LIBOR being capitalized over the succeeding years), were such as to have justified the Nicaraguan decision. The next steps, that of the multilateral and bilateral debts, were expected to be easier per se (being with ostensibly "aid" institutions) and could be only on easier terms than those obtained from the bankers. The negotiations were also made less difficult, however, by the decision not to make excessive requests for new finance (the ECLA had estimated the requirements for 1980 alone as $1 billion (U.S.), but disbursements of only $250 million were planned for) or even to accept all the offers of finance from multilateral organizations. The only major difficulty was the U.S. attitude, which steadily hardened, particularly as the promised $75 million in new loans had successively more outrageous political conditions attached to them as the months went by. The irony is that these loans were destined in large part for the private sector.

In all, some $490 million in loans had been signed by the end of 1979. Of these, $344 million were for investment projects and $147 million for "rehabilitation"; that is, repair of war damage to the APP and the private sector. However, it should be noted that of the investment loans, $178 million (over half) were in fact loans signed with the Somoza regime, but now reassigned to conform with the new economic objectives of the Revolutionary Government. The main lending agencies in both categories were the IDB and the IBRD, and the terms were uniformly "soft." In total, it was intended to disimburse all the rehabilitation credits and some $223 million of the investment loans in 1980, making a total gross inflow of $370 million, no more than a third of the value of the war damage and capital flight suffered by the economy in the previous two years. The sum total of donations—about $72 million in the second half of 1979 and another $25 million anticipated for 1980 (mainly for the Literacy Crusade)—was very gratefully received, but hardly matched the magnitude of the problem.

The resolution of the fourth problem, that of establishing a new framework within which economic reconstruction could take place, was started in September 1979 with the formulation of a broad economic strategy for the five-year period leading up to mid-1984. It was clear that the first "normal" agricultural cycle would be 1980-81, so that the immediate reactivation would take two years at least. In addition, the lead-time for new investment projects meant that new capacity (it should be remembered that productive investment in Nicaragua had virtually ceased since 1972) and thus a modified production structure could not be expected until 1983-84 at the earliest. In fact, it would not be until 1984 that per-capita incomes reached their 1977 levels again—although they would be considerably better distributed by then, of course. Other changes, such as land tenure, industrial organization, and the establishment of new trading patterns would also take some years. In consequence, although the 1980 Economic Program would have to be a short-term document in view of future uncertainties, it would have to contribute to the achievement of long-term goals.

The sectoral planning commissions were established by October, and started their work almost without training or data. However, the very process of analysis generated both these virtues in a remarkably short space of time, aided by the facts that Nicaragua is a small country and the Sandinistas have intimate practical knowledge of it. Over 200 people worked on the Program, but the vast majority were from the sectors themselves, ranging from cabinet ministers and comandantes to workers' leaders and secretaries, all of those caught up in the excitement of constructing what was, in effect, the first programmatic document of the new government: the *Programa de Reactivación Económica en Beneficio del Pueblo*.[5] The FSLN National Directorate assigned one of its own members, Henry Ruiz, to head the Ministry of Planning (MIPLAN) in December 1979, recognizing its importance thereby as the central economic authority and giving it the leadership of a man whose intellectual qualities and guerrilla experience peculiarly qualified him for the job.[6]

Plan 80

Despite its short length (140 pages), the *Programa de Reactivación Económica en Beneficio del Pueblo* is an important document because it represented the first "programmatic" statement of Sandinista objectives since the *Programa de la Junta de Gobierno de Reconstrucción Nacional de Nicaragua* of the Junta itself on July 9, 1979. About 50,000 copies were printed, and it was being sold in supermarkets as late as September 1980 even though it had been issued in January. More relevant, popular versions were circulated for discussion by popular groups, cartoon summaries were printed in the newspapers and shown on television, and it provided the basis for economics courses in the universities. However, perhaps the most interesting form of dissemination for discussion was the arithmetic workbook used in the Literacy Crusade; it is less well known abroad than *El Amanecer del Pueblo*, (the Dawn of the People) reading and writing primer, but *Cuaderno de Educación Sandinista de Operaciones Prácticas* (Workbook of Practical Exercises in Sandinist Education), subtitled *Cálculo y Reactivación: Una Sola Operación* (Calculation and Reactivation a Single Operation), provides for the teaching of simple calculations as applied to the daily life of workers and their families.

The "Plan-80," as it is popularly if inaccurately known, had as its prime objective the "Defense, Consolidation and Advance of the Revolution." Its long-term aim was to create the New Sandinista Economy, which would permit a "just, free and fraternal human life in our country," based upon "the social welfare of the most dispossessed within the objective realities of the country." The specific economic expression of the revolutionary process in the 1980-81 period was made up of four points: (1) "reactivation" of the economy by emphasizing the basic needs of the population; (2) "dynamization" of the operating structure of the state through administrative reform, financial control, and popular participation; (3) strengthening of "national unity" based on workers, peasants, artisans, and professionals, and an attempt to integrate the "patriotic businessmen"; and (4) the start on the "transition to the New Economy." It was recognized in the Plan 80 that "reactivation" would involve the use of installed production capacity and the reallocation of the surpluses generated thereby, and that it would take at least two years.

The material production targets were related to the recovery of production levels in 1978; in these terms, the "degree of reactivation" programmed for 1980 was as follows: agriculture, 80 percent; manufacturing 87 percent; construction 136 percent. Public services would "recover" by 137 percent (basically due to new welfare provision) private services by 77 percent. In all, Gross Domestic Product was expected to recover to 91 percent of its 1978 level, but material production would be held back by agriculture, for the reasons we have discussed above. Exports would be similarly constrained, but were expected to reach a value of $524 million during 1980 even though most of the normal cotton and meat exports (worth nearly $200 million) would not be available. There would, therefore, be a considerable expansion of GDP as a whole (22 percent) but material production would only rise by 10 percent over 1979.

Apart from the temporary expedient of the "food for work" schemes, employment would recover with production in 1980-81; only in the longer run could productive investment create new workplaces. Open unemployment in the autumn of 1979 had been estimated at 33 percent of the workforce; the average for 1979 was estimated to be 28 percent and the target for 1980 was 17 percent.[7] This would require the generation of 50,000 jobs in agriculture, 10,000 in industry, 15,000 in construction and 20,000 in services; a total of some 95,000 jobs in a comparatively short time.

Although the major accumulation drive could only start in 1982, when reactivation would be complete, it was necessary to undertake considerable investments in construction and agriculture to get the economy moving at all. A total of some 2,230 million córdobas ($223 million U.S.) in public investment would be required, since the private sector was not expected to invest very much in plant although they would replace inventories. In consequence, capital formation would have to reach 16 percent of GDP, a considerable burden for a still weak economy.

Assuming that these production targets could be met (they were feasible in technical terms, but did depend upon the cooperation of the private sector and a considerable organizational capacity in the public sector), the major problem lay on the side of demand management in general and income redistribution in particular. The objective was to reflate the economy while redistributing income downwards, without creating such enormous imbalances as would destabilize the economy. The consequences of domestic inflation and balance-of-payments deficits in terms of black markets, food shortages, and labor unrest on the one hand, and external vulnerability on the other, would be serious. The experiences of countries such as Chile and Cuba in their early years were taken very seriously. In consequence, it was decided to operate what at first sight seemed to be a "conservative" policy of restrictions in wages, tax increases, and exchange controls. In fact, this policy was not conservative at all, but rather a radical concept. On the one hand, what was proposed was the *programming* of demand as well as supply, in other words a Kaleckian rather than a Keynesian approach. On the other, the stability so gained could be used as a "breathing space" to prepare for radical reforms.

In specific terms, this meant that the total wage bill could only be raised in line with the availability of wage goods, especially food, in order to avoid an inflation that would most hurt the poorest. Within this wagebill, there would be a considerable expansion even if wages were not raised because of the expected increase in employment. In addition, it was intended to raise rural wages more rapidly than urban wages in order to work towards the long-term objective of narrowing the income differentials between town and country. In consequence, the redistribution of the wage bill would make it difficult to increase urban wages by very much. The expansion of popular living standards would be in the form of the "social wage," therefore government expenditure on health, education, housing, and social services would have to increase, but to contain this within reasonable limits of expenditure, large-scale popular voluntary participation would be necessary. The increase in public expenditure, on investment as well as services, was to be paid for by profit-receivers and higher-income earners, rather than by the poor, through greatly increased taxation, which would raise tax pressure (tax revenues divided by GDP) from 9 percent in 1978 to 14 percent in 1980. Finally, control of foreign exchange would allow the planners to allocate such expenditures to essential supplies such as oil and foodstuffs, and thus prevent the conversion of local currency incomes or financial assets into imported luxury goods. The demand management program therefore, was to be both stabilizing and redistributive: the targets were a very small increase in money supply (the domestic fiscal deficit was to be 312 million córdobas, less than 2 percent of GDP), a balance of payments deficit on current account of $249 million (U.S.), and an inflation rate (GDP deflator) of 22 percent, as opposed to 60 percent in 1979.

This somewhat ambitious task would depend upon both an efficient public sector administration (which was now responsible for finance, trade and investment) and the support of the private sector (which accounted for 75 percent of material production) if it was to succeed. For the former, a specific "program of state transformation" was included in Plan 80, which pointed out that not only did the unbalanced expansion of government expenditure pose a threat to stability, but that an efficient state was necessary in order to push forward to deeper reforms in the future. The planning system (headed by MIPLAN but involving the whole public sector) would be central to this, but the imposition of financial control over enterprises, worker participation in policy-making, and massive training schemes were also seen as vital. The cooperation of the private sector, too, was stressed as essential to the Program. Although the "subject" of economic strategy was clearly defined as the workers and peasants, the private enterprise sector was invited to cooperate in return for guarantees of reasonable profits and security of ownership so long as the law was obeyed and activities such as tax evasion, capital flight, and speculation were avoided.

The combination of state expansion, political mobilization, wage restraint, income redistribution and the transition to a planned economy, within an unstable international situation, was obviously going to be a tense one: in fact Chapter III of the Program (which expounds its economic logic and explains the "three balances": demand and supply; external payments; and fiscal-financial accounts) was entitled "Dynamic and Tensions of the Reactivation." The Program had been designed so as to minimize the probability of failure, but there was no guarantee of success.

Plan 80: Results

At the time of writing,[8] it was too early to give a complete evaluation of the economy in 1980. However, some of the broader outlines were more or less clear by then and provided the basis for a partial evaluation of Plan 80. The complete evaluations carried out on a quarterly basis by MIPLAN were, of course, confidential. However, the published data shown in Tables 11.4 and 11.5, which represent the best estimates of out-turn in 1980, do give a reasonable picture.

As can be seen, the main targets of production recovery appear to have been met: agriculture reached 76 percent of its 1978 level (80 percent in the Plan); industry was at 82 percent (87 percent in the Plan). This was mainly due to the unexpectedly good response of peasant farmers and cooperatives to price incentives and technical assistance for maize on the one hand, and the positive response of the industrial APP and medium manufacturers on the other. Overall, the GDP was back to 83 percent of its 1978 level in 1980, slightly less than planned (91 percent); in part this was due to the inability of the construction sector to keep up with the somewhat ambitious public works program, and in part to the midyear decision to restrain government

TABLE 11.4

GROSS DOMESTIC PRODUCT
(billions of Córdobas at 1980 prices)

Output	1977	1978	1979	1980
Material Production:				
Agriculture, etc.	6.24	6.42	5.45	4.90
Manufacturing	6.36	6.37	4.63	5.24
Construction & mining	1.96	1.16	0.42	0.76
Subtotal	14.56	13.96	10.51	10.90
Services				
Commerce	5.97	5.11	3.19	3.86
Other	7.44	6.69	5.57	6.58
Subtotal	13.41	11.80	8.76	10.44
Gross Domestic Product	27.96	25.76	19.28	21.34
Expenditure				
Investment				
Fixed capital	6.19	3.44	1.40	2.90
Inventories	0.82	—0.56	—1.75	0.50
Subtotal	7.01	2.88	—0.35	3.40
Consumption:				
Government	2.56	3.15	3.46	4.48
Basic	10.41	9.99	7.42	9.15
Other private	10.84	10.56	7.03	9.44
Subtotal	23.83	23.70	17.91	23.07
Gross Domestic Product	27.96	25.76	19.28	21.34

Source: MIPLAN. The figures for 1980 are not, therefore, the planned ones but rather the expected outcome toward the end of the year.

expenditure in order to maintain the macroeconomic balance. In addition, the cotton farmers did plant in the early summer, ranchers were restocking their herds, and all but a few manufacturers (hampered by lack of export markets to El Salvador, or, as in the case of the cotton oil mills, by lack of raw material) had opened their factories. Despite the growing tension between the private sector and the state throughout 1980, there were no significant lockouts, strikes, land invasions, serious cases of capital flight, or substantial departures of skilled personnel. On the production side at least, the reactivation was working.

TABLE 11.5

BALANCE OF PAYMENTS

[millions]

	1977	1978	1979	1980
Exports (FOB)				
Traditional products*	414	428	408	320
Others	222	218	208	150
Subtotal	636	646	616	470
Imports (CIF)				
Petroleum	105	89	76	165
Equipment	193	114	46	105
Others	464	392	308	700
Subtotal	762	595	430	870
Imports (FOB)	704	553	389	787
Visible Balance	−68	+93	+227	−317
Invisible Balance	−125	−127	−138	−88
Donations	11	9	72	23
Current Account Balance	−182	−25	161	−382
Net Entries of Capital:				
Public	196	43	209	—
Private†	−71	−242	−339	—
Subtotal‡	125	−199	−130	213
Variation in Reserves	+57	+224	−31	−169

Source: MIPLAN, September, 1980.

    *Cotton, coffee, sugar and meat.

    †Includes "errors and omissions," (i.e. capital flight) before July 1979; after that date it includes credits to banks for support of private sector.

    ‡A negative sign reflects an increase.

Plan 80 was premised not only upon getting production going again but also upon the control of demand in what was still a market economy and a substantial redistribution of the income generated by that economy. But even more urgent than this was the need to get new investment projects going. In the event, public works projects, particularly roads, moved more slowly than planned due to the advent of the rainy season in May, before the new Ministry of Construction was fully capable of acting as the country's construction company—it having been decided for obvious reasons to do without large "international" (i.e., mainly U.S.) consultants and construction firms. Productive investment, particularly for machinery in productive sectors (e.g., cotton harvesters, fishing boats) went more rapidly than planned. The result was a total public investment in 1980 of about $200 million (U.S.), below target but still equivalent to 13 percent of GDP—a considerable achievement. This investment was not all funded from abroad, as had been programmed, and required extensive use of the nation's own exchange reserves, which as a consequence, despite generous support form Mexico and Venezuela in the matter of oil imports, were placed under considerable pressure by the end of the year. Moreover, the lack of foreign loans to the budget meant that taxes had to be raised by more than planned, reaching an average of 16 percent of GDP. However, in spite of these efforts, a deficit rather larger than planned was generated by the fiscal sector. This overrun required considerable constraint on credit to the private sector, particularly commerce, as well as generating a money supply in excess of the program. The fact that inflation (as measured by the GDP deflator) for 1980 was only 30 percent reflects the success of the efforts at demand management.

Meanwhile, rural wages were raised rapidly, but although the overall open unemployment rate was down to 15 percent by mid-1980 and serious shortages in rural seasonal labor developed towards the end of the year, urban wages were not raised, and actually fell slightly in real terms between January and September. That this did not lead to widespread strikes is a tribute to the unions' understanding of the situation; nonetheless, the continued high level of professional and capitalist incomes, however necessary in order to maintain the "alliance," generated growing tension. In fact, these "upper decile" incomes were being continually eroded by inflation, public-sector salary ceilings, and import restrictions which limited the availablility of consumer goods upon which to spend higher incomes. In addition, the sharp reduction of urban rents, the extension of the health service, the expansion of employment, and the control of basic food prices (which rose farther than the average), let alone the effects of the Literacy Crusade, lead to a considerable nonmonetary increase in working class living standards. In consequence, the demand side of the economy moved broadly along the lines proposed by the Economic Program; although the details (which were hard to measure given the lack of monthly or quarterly income estimates in any case) did show sharp divergencies (in matters such as sugar shortages), these were always corrected in a comparatively short time due to the relatively small size of the economy (which allowed information to move easily and decisions to be implemented rapidly) and close cooperation within the government's economic team. Finally, the balance of payments was kept under reasonable control during the year; although imports (at $870 million c.i.f. as opposed to $773 million) were 13 percent above forecast, due to the excessive "leakage" through the Central American Common Market, the year did end with only a modest decline in reserves.

Conclusions

As was pointed out at the beginning of this chapter, it is extraordinarily difficult to evaluate economic policy so soon after the event. In a country embarking upon a process of radical transformation, it is almost impossible, because short-term economic management is not an end in itself, but rather part of a longer project, the content of which may be confidential and the outcome which remains to be seen. At the superficial level, the immediate aims of the emergency program and the 1980 economic program had been met by the end of that year. In addition, the period of stability had allowed the FSLN to build up a number of organizations capable of confronting the more difficult tasks and challenges that had to come.

However, in Plan 80 itself, and increasingly during the year, it was evident that the socio-economic equilibrium was unstable. Obviously, a political reaction by the domestic bourgeoisie or by the United States could have destabilized the economy during 1980, and that threat did not diminish. Equally important, the next steps in the social transformation processes would inevitably have a serious impact on the economy. Less obviously, but also equally important, the need to impose a coherent economic policy in the next steps, to support a higher rate of state accumulation and a lower inflow of foreign funds, would impose much greater strain upon the "alliance"—this time due to the inevitable reduction of the profitability of capital rather than ideological threat. What the reaction of the United States to the construction of socialism in Nicaragua, let alone in Central America as a whole, would be was hardly a comforting prospect. But this was a prospect already at the head of the economic planners' agenda in 1980.

Clearly this is not the place to make predictions about the future. Nonetheless, it would be reasonable to say that the FSLN, having learned much from the study of economic instability in the first years of other revolutions, was able to apply these lessons with a degree of success which would at least ameliorate the difficulties that lay ahead.

Notes

[1] Preface to the "Plan 80" (see below), by Comandante Henry Ruiz, Minister of Planning. Author's translation.

[2] There is no good bibliography on the economy of Nicaragua: the main official statistics can be found in the *Informe Anual* of the Central Bank of Nicaragua, while the best general introduction to the recent socio-economic structure is, of course, Jaime Wheelock, *Imperialismo y Dictadura* (Mexico: Siglo XXI, 1975).

[3] Plan 80, p. 11.

[4] UN /ECLA, op. cit.

[5] Although usually referred to as a "plan," it could not properly be called one because Nicaragua was not yet a centrally planned economy.

[6] Comandante Modesto had a degree in mathematics and had spent ten years living and fighting with the peasants in the northern mountains.

[7] All these figures include adjustments for the "permanent employment equivalent" of seasonal jobs in agriculture.

[8] November 1981; the data is taken from the 1981 Economic Program (*Programa Económico de Austeridad y Eficiencia: 1981, Año de la Defensa y la Producción*, Managua: MIPLAN).

Chapter 12

Nicaragua's Agrarian Reform: The First Year (1979-80)

DAVID KAIMOWITZ
JOSEPH R. THOME

From its beginnings in the early 1960s, the modern Sandinista movement considered the overthrow of the Somoza regime only as a starting point in a long process of social transformation. From the ashes of a corrupt and unjust system would emerge a society working on behalf of all, particularly the workers and peasants. For an agricultural country like Nicaragua, this meant, among other things, an agrarian reform.

Agrarian reform has long been considered a necessary process for achieving more developed and equitable societies in Latin America. And responding to decades of external and internal pressures, many Latin American countries have indeed enacted agrarian reform legislation. But in only a handful of cases have the respective governments gone beyond a lip-service approval of reform to actually provide the political and economic support necessary for achieving any substantial structural change. By contrast, the Nicaragua Government of National Reconstruction not only considered agrarian reform as a key element of a new economic policy whose ultimate purpose was to create a just and egalitarian society,[1] but also backed its concepts with action. Within weeks of its victory, the new government drastically altered the land tenure structure in Nicaragua through the wholesale confiscation of the landed estates owned by Somoza and his allies.[2] It is the purpose of this chapter to review and analyze the crucial first year of this agrarian reform.

The Development of Nicaragua's Rural Structure
Nicaragua's economy has always been very dependent on its agricultural sector. In most years, more than 70 percent of the country's foreign ex-

We would like to thank Roberto Gutierrez, Ligia Elizondo, Peter Marchetti, Orlando Nuñez, and Carmen Diana Deere for their invaluable assistance. We would also like to thank the Land Tenure Center at the University of Wisconsin for making this project possible. All opinions and errors, however, are, of course, our own.

change came from agricultural production, particularly cotton, coffee, sugar, and meat. If the *processing* of agricultural products is included, the agricultural sector accounted for almost 35 percent of the country's gross domestic product (GDP).[3] According to the 1971 census, nearly a million people, or 52 percent of the population, lived in the rural areas.[4] In addition, more than 45 percent of the economically active population (EAP) depended upon agriculture for its livelihood.[5]

The agro-export model of development in Nicaragua had its roots in the great expansion of coffee cultivation in the late 1800s. With coffee, Nicaragua became definitely integrated into the world market, selling agricultural exports to buy the manufactured and other goods it needed. The development of a profitable market for coffee greatly raised the value of land, leading to the dispossession of sharecroppers, renters, independent peasants, and Indian communal landholders, and creating a demand for an available work force to work on the coffee plantations. Land ownership thus became more concentrated, and dispossessed small farmers had little choice but to work on the coffee plantations.[6]

The expansion of coffee production might eventually have brought about the establishment of modern capitalist production in the countryside. This did not occur, however, for a number of reasons. In the early 1900s, the United States supported a series of conservative governments whose social base lay among the traditional livestock *hacendados*. The coffee growers found themselves without the institutional support necessary for their expansion. This problem was exacerbated by the low coffee prices brought on by the Great Depression in the 1930s.[7]

Not until the Korean War, with its accompanying demand for raw materials, did Nicaragua's agriculture regain a high rate of growth. The introduction of cotton to the Pacific coast marked the beginning of modern, commercial farming in the country. Cotton acreage expanded markedly from 1950 to 1970, once again resulting in the forced removal of small-scale grain farmers from their holdings as well as a dramatic increase in the demand for seasonal labor. In 1973, of the 228,000 workers employed during the cotton harvest, only 26,000 had year-round employment.[8]

Agro-expert production, including sugar and beef as well as cotton and coffee, boomed through the mid-1970s, providing the economy with a dynamic, high-growth sector and making possible a rapid rate of capital accumulation. Reliance on export crops, however, made Nicaragua dependent on the volatile world markets for primary commodities. Export crop production aggravated the problem of seasonal unemployment since coffee, cotton, and sugar all have their harvests concentrated in the period from December to March. Because of a high level of dependence on imported pesticides and machinery, and other foreign inputs, the contribution of modern export production such as cotton to the balance of payments was often much less than it appeared.[9] Since Nicaragua had little in the way of modern techniques or infrastructure, it was forced to compete in the world market on the basis of its cheap labor, a feature which had to be constantly reenforced for the traditional agro-exporting system to function.

With the expansion of agro-export production, food production for domestic consumption was pushed onto the poorest lands, often on the agricultural frontier. The overwhelming bulk of government assistance went to export crops and most domestic food production became concentrated in the hands of small producers who lacked the resources to produce capital-intensive export crops or to modernize their production. Basic food production thus tended to stagnate and imports and prices to rise.[10]

The resulting social structure was characterized by a highly skewed distribution of assets and income, with vast rural poverty coexisting with great concentrations of wealth. Thus, 1.4 percent of the total number of farms controlled 41.2 percent of the farmland, while, at the other extreme, 50 percent of the farms, all under 7 hectares (17 acres), controlled only 3.4 percent of the land.[11] Many of these small farms were on the agricultural frontier, isolated from access to roads, drinking water, electricity, education, and health services. In addition, a large number of rural families owned or controlled no land whatsoever.

Seasonal unemployment affected the majority of rural workers (both the landless and those with small plots), with steady work available only during the 3-4 month peak agricultural period. In 1972, the annual average income of the poorest 50 percent of the rural population was $35 per capita.[12]

Somoza and the War

As the rural poor became increasingly impoverished, one family was becoming increasingly rich. When Anastasio Somoza García first became president in 1936, the Somoza family had practically no agricultural holdings, but by 1979 they were the largest landholders in the country. In addition, the Somozas controlled the only two meat-processing plants licensed to export, three of the six sugar mills, 65 percent of the commercial fishing, 40 percent of the commercial rice production, and the largest milk-processing plant. Moreover, the Somozas had controlling interests over a wide assortment of companies involved in processing, selling, and transporting agricultural inputs and goods.[13] Needless to say, the Somozas were proficient at using the state apparatus to their own benefit; during World War II, for example, many coffee plantations owned by German immigrants were confiscated by the government and transferred through various means to the Somozas, making them the largest coffee growers in the country.[14]

The problem, of course, was not just one family. Around the Somozas a whole social structure developed. The military dictatorship of Somoza created strata of military and civilian functionaries who controlled the development of the country in pursuit of the sole goal of enriching themselves and building their private empires.

Conditions for the rural poor had been worsening for some time, but the 1979 war brought the entire economy to the verge of collapse. Due to the dislocation and destruction of the war, agricultural production fell 37 percent in 1979. The cotton harvest was only 20 percent of that of a normal year. Corn was down 33 percent, beans 29 percent, and rice 37 percent. It is estimated that up to 300,000 cattle were either slaughtered or smuggled out of the country. Much agricultural machinery was destroyed or sabotaged by Somoza's followers before they left the country. Material damages in agriculture alone, not counting the value of lost crops, came to almost $30 million.[13]

The Process of Agrarian Reform, 1979-80

1. Initial Goals and Policies

For some time before the final victory in July 1979, the Sandinistas and other anti-Somoza groups had maintained that the maldistribution of land, insufficient production of basic grains, low standards of living, and other economic and social ills could be resolved only through basic changes in the economic structure, such as agrarian reform.[16] The Sandinista Front (FSLN) also realized that the success of both its military operations and any subsequent social restructuration was to a large extent dependent on the support and participation of organized workers. The FSLN thus promoted the organization of rural workers and landless peasants into workers' committees. By 1978, these committees had grown strong enough to found the Rural Workers Association (ATC) as a national organization.[17]

Land invasions and other peasant actions during the war also affected subsequent agrarian reform policies and programs. As early as June 1979, for example, organized peasants in the Province of León began to invade large and mostly Somoza-owned estates in those areas liberated or controlled by the Sandinista forces. Once the lands were occupied, the peasants, often acting under Sandinista Front supervision or guidance, began to organize communal or cooperative forms of tenure. Known as Comunas Agrícolas Sandinistas (CAS), they were subsequently formally incorporated into the agrarian reform program.[18] To a lesser extent, this experience was duplicated in various regions of Nicaragua, creating a situation to which the new government of National Reconstruction had to respond.

Upon the overthrow of the Somoza regime in July of 1979, the new government wasted no time in setting about its most immediate tasks of reactivating the economy and reconstituting it into a mixed system, including both private and state enterprises, and redistributing income within the limitations of Nicaragua's economic possibilities.[19]

In the crucial agricultural sector, the government's goals were to increase production and at the same time begin a process of agrarian reform that would transform the land tenure structure in Nicaragua and provide the rural population with different forms of access to land, credit, technical assistance, and other indispensable services. According to the government program, the first stage of this reform process would include the acquisition of all the lands owned by Somoza, his family, and his military officers and followers, as well as those lands owned by delinquent taxpayers, lands obtained illegally from the public domain, and all abandoned or uncultivated lands. Once acquired by the state, these lands could be held and worked only through associative or group forms of farming, such as production cooperatives or state farms; they would not be redistributed as individual, private parcels.[20]

Complementary agrarian reform measures such as land and water use controls, rent controls, credits for the private sector, and better wages and conditions for the rural workers would also be provided. Finally, these and other general policies and goals would be subsequently defined and operationalized through a comprehensive agrarian reform law.[21]

2. Implementing the Reform: Land Redistribution

While, as we have seen, some reform activity was carried out during the course of the war, the agrarian reform was not officially proclaimed until after the final victory. Decree No. 3, of July 20, 1979, authorized the Attorney General to "intervene, requisition and confiscate all the properties of the Somoza family, and of the military and government officials." Once so acquired, these properties were to be transferred to the agrarian reform authorities.[22] Complementary Decree No. 38, of August 8, 1979, speeded up the process by giving the Attorney General power to suspend any transaction or temporarily seize (intervene) any property or business belonging to persons or corporations affiliated with the Somoza regime.[23]

Acting under these powers, the Attorney General, by November 23, 1979, barely five months after the victory, had confiscated without compensation 1,500 farms with a total area of approximately 800,000 hectares (2 million acres), representing over a fifth of Nicaragua's cultivable land.[24] Moreover, most of these lands were in large, modern, and highly productive farms situated along the populated Pacific coast, an area with excellent soils and access to both national and international markets.[24]

This circumstance or dynamic to a large extent determined the course of the Nicaraguan agrarian reform and made the Nicaraguan experience almost unique among revolutionary processes. Few, if any, governments have been able to start an agrarian reform with an almost costless and instant nationalization of vast and productive landholdings. Even more unique, this was achieved without alienating the bulk of the landowning class, most of whom despised the Somoza clan. Moreover, the very fact that the government had to swallow such a large morsel all at once gave the large landowners a certain measure of security, at least for a while. The new government now had to face the problem of organizing these holdings and restoring their productivity. As we shall see, INRA, the Nicaraguan Institute of Agrarian Reform, did indeed concentrate on managing the confiscated estates, as well as servicing the small peasants, administering 4 million hectares (10 million acres) of public domain lands, most of it in virgin forests along the Atlantic coast, and other complementary measures.[26] Thus, as of mid-July 1980, INRA had acquired only an additional 200,000 hectares (500,000 acres)[27] of land, some through confiscation and the rest through expropriation with compensation of lands not subject to confiscation under Decree No. 3 but which had nevertheless been occupied by peasants or temporarily seized or intervened by the government.[28]

To direct the agrarian reform, the Nicaraguan Agrarian Reform Institute (INRA) was formed in August 1979.[29] INRA initially used the resources of the old Nicaraguan Agrarian Institute, Somoza's ineffective agrarian reform agency, and INVIERNO, an integrated small-farmer rural credit program which had been sponsored by the U.S. Agency for International Development. In addition, INRA counted on many dedicated agrarian technicians from the ranks of the Sandinista Front.

Although INRA was in charge of managing the reformed sector and providing services to the small peasant sector, there was also a Ministry of Agriculture which continued to exist separately. As INRA began to take on more and more general responsibilities for the agricultural sector, the two institutions were merged in January 1980 into a new Ministry of Agricultural Development (MIDA).[30] INRA continued to be the most dynamic element of the Ministry, and Comandante Jaime Wheelock, the original head of INRA and a member of the Sandinista Front, became the new Minister.

3. The State Sector

Once the land had been acquired, a decision had to be made about its disposition. Having decided not to divide the land into small parcels, the government opted instead for the development of state farms and production cooperatives. Most confiscated farms had been operated for years as large, capital-intensive enterprises. Their parcelization could have resulted in a major drop in production, besides representing a qualitative reversal in the limited modernization of Nicaragua's agriculture.[31]

As can be seen in Table 12.1, the state, or "people's sector," in 1980 accounted for a substantial percentage of the total agricultural production. In addition, INRA administered five of the six sugar mills, and an assortment of agricultural and input operations. Finally, more than 50,000 workers, or 13 percent of all agricultural laborers, worked full-time in the reformed sector.[32]

INRA's major responsibility was to manage the reformed sector. To meet this goal, eighteen regional offices were set up, one in each province plus two special offices on the Atlantic coast. The expropriated farms

TABLE 12.1
PRODUCTION OF AGRICULTURAL PRODUCTS
(by form of ownership in 1979-80)

Crop	State Sector (INRA) (%)	Small Producers* (%)	Large Producers (%)
Cotton	20.0	18.0	62.0
Coffee	15.0	30.0	55.0
Livestock	15.0	73.0	12.0
Corn	8.7	87.2	4.4
Beans	17.0	79.1	3.8

Source: CIERA elaboration, 1980.
  *The Ministry of Agricultural Development defines small producers as those with a family income of less than $1,800 per year. These producers usually own less than 15 hectares of land.

themselves were converted into "state production units," or UPEs. These UPEs were combined into 170 production complexes, which in turn formed 27 agricultural *empresas*, or enterprises.[33]

In addition to the INRA division in charge of state farms, other INRA departments or sections administered important agrarian reform activities. The most important of these was AGROINRA, which managed all the vertically integrated agroindustrial operations, including the processing facilities for coffee, cotton, milk, sugar, fruits, and vegetables; the stockyards; the sugar, tobacco, and rice plantations; the pork and chicken farms; and the production of animal feed. The Service Department of INRA was put in charge of managing the tractors and other machinery for the state sector, as well as a number of irrigation and transportation projects operated by INRA. PROAGRO, another department of INRA, controlled the distribution of such agricultural inputs as seeds, fertilizers, and pesticides for the reformed sector.[34]

A major effort was made to improve the living conditions of the state-sector workers. Small health units, schools, and housing projects were established. Small stores were opened for selling basic necessities at controlled prices. In general, the emphasis was on increasing the supply of social goods rather than raising salaries, though these also were improved.[35]

Production cooperatives called Sandinista Agricultural Communes or CAS were also organized. As of late 1980, there were about 1,327 of these cooperatives, of which a third were on land leased to the peasants by the government and two-thirds on land rented or lent to the CAS by private farmers.[36]

Originally formed on invaded lands in the León area, the CAS had become a semispontaneous form of organization created by the peasants to take advantage of the increased accessibility of credit and land. A group of twenty-five or thirty peasants would get together, rent land collectively, and request credit from the government for their living expenses and working capital during the growing season. At the end of the season, the bulk of the CAS's income would go to paying back the loans while the remainder was divided up among the peasants.

The structure of the CAS tended to be relatively informal and flexible. The members met frequently and worked out production plans and problems with the governmental agencies and the ATC. Often a smaller coordinating committee was elected by the members to direct the day-to-day functioning of the farm. Most Sandinista Agricultural Communes were formed on farms which had previously been rented or sharecropped out to peasants. Few Sandinista Agricultural Communes exceeded 35 hectares (88 acres) in area.[37]

A small number (ten or fifteen) of Sandinista Agricultural Communes were formed by peasants who pooled their own land to form the cooperative. Where this occurred, it was usually the result of a long period of political work with the peasants concerned dating back to before the triumph of the revolution. These CASs were usually much better organized and had more formal structures. They were, however, the exception and not the rule.[38]

TABLE 12.2
STRUCTURE OF THE REFORMED SECTOR

	No. of Units	Average Acreage (hectares)	No. of Rural Workers	Average No. of Permanent Workers per Unit
State Farms	1,200	644.2	35,358	29.5
Sandinista agricultural communes	1,327	42.0	13,402	10.1
	2,527		48,760	

Source: CIERA elaboration, Aug. 1980.

4. Problems of the Reform

INRA had to face innumerable problems during its first year of operations. Many of the farms were in ruins and had been abandoned by owners and workers fleeing the war. The ministries were only beginning to reorganize themselves and take charge of their functions, and there was a limited number of people with much experience in public administration or farm management. In addition, there was little experience in agricultural planning, as Nicaragua had never previously attempted to plan its agricultural development in a systematic way. The information system the government had inherited was incomplete and the available statistics often erroneous.[39]

The first months of the agrarian reform were thus somewhat hectic and disorganized. The government tried to work quickly to plant cereal crops to take the place of the lost cotton crop and to feed the thousands of people left hungry from the war. But this was a difficult task with no regular supplies of seed or fertilizer and no organized management on the farms. In this initial period, the peasants themselves often took the initiative by identifying lands for confiscation and putting them into production.[40]

The problems were not all technical. Many social institutions, such as worker discipline, which were often based on repression under the old regime, tended to collapse in its absence. In some places, productivity declined because workers decided to cut their hours. With the increased availability of land, peasants had less need to work as agricultural laborers. This, combined with the death of many young workers during the war and the end of the traditional practice of using Salvadorean and Honduran labor in peak seasons, helped create sporadic labor shortages. Finally, during the first part of the year, the government also had to contend with extremist groups who were urging agricultural workers to occupy lands not subject to confiscation or to strike for higher wages which were impossible to meet given the economic situation of the country.[41]

5. Planning and Participation

The state sector component of the agrarian reform process became more consolidated toward the end of 1979. By then, the system of state production units and complexes was begining to function. In January, the government officially published its Plan for Economic Reconstruction for 1980.[42] This was the first time the government had set out a clear program for the reconstruction of agriculture and the role to be played by its major components: the state sector, the small peasant sector, and the private commercial farm sector.

The most important objective for agriculture set out in the plan was to recover the overall levels of production of the years prior to 1979-80. The plan set out goals for each major crop and provided the resources for sufficient credit and agricultural inputs to meet the production goals. Plan 80 specifically acknowledged the great economic significance of the social changes in the countryside and laid out mechanisms for the participation of agricultural workers and their organizations in defining and implementing the plan.[43]

Plan 80 exemplified the government's strong commitment to the active participation of agricultural workers in agrarian reform. Such participation, however, was conditioned on the existence of a strong workers' union or association. In the past, any attempt to organize had been repressed by Somoza's National Guard. Only a few church groups had been semi-tolerated; they formed the nucleus of most of Nicaragua's original peasant associations and cooperatives.[44]

The Sandinista Front had worked with peasants ever since its founding in the early 1960s. Still, it was not until 1976 that the Sandinistas formed the first Agricultural Workers Committees among the coffee workers in the Department of Carazo. Their original demands were mostly economic: higher salaries and better living and working conditions.[45]

In 1977 and 1978, the committees spread and began to take an active role in denouncing the repression. On March 25, 1978, the committees organized the Association of Rural Workers (ATC). During the war, the ATC played an important role on a number of fronts, and many *campesinos* were killed fighting against Somoza.[46]

When victory came on July 19, 1979, the ATC was organized in only four provinces: Managua, Carazo, Chinadega, and Masaya. It grew quickly from that point on, soon becoming the mass organization of the entire Nicaraguan peasantry. By July 19, 1980, the ATC had a paid membership of nearly 100,000.[47]

Reflecting the four basic forms of production in the countryside, different types of union locals were established to represent the state-farm workers, the private-farm workers, the small independent peasants, and the peasant cooperative members. These local unions and base committees were in turn organized into municipal committees with their own elected executive councils. Delegates from these councils belonged to the departmental assemblies, which in turn elected the departmental executive councils. The highest-level leadership unit in the ATC was the National Assembly, which gave the general orientation for the Association and selected its national executive committee. Prior to the first National Assembly in December 1979, there were over 600 local meetings to discuss the work to be accomplished at the Assembly and to elect its delegates.[48]

While maintaining a very close working relationship with the government, the ATC still managed to function as an independent organization representative of the peasants, which did not hesitate to criticize the bureaucracy, policies with which it disagreed, or unreasonable working conditions. In February of 1980, for example, an ATC-organized demonstration of over 60,000 peasants demanded that the government not return any of the temporarily intervened lands, that small producers be pardoned of certain past debts, that agricultural workers be allowed greater participation in the running of state farms, and that the old Somoza labor code be replaced. The government responded by expropriating the lands in question and promising solutions to the other problems.[49]

As of September 1980, three ATC delegates were members of the Council of State, Nicaragua's new legislative assembly. In addition, the ATC was represented in the national council of the Ministry of Agricultural Development, in the National Agricultural Council, and in many advisory and technical councils of various ministries. It also maintained representatives in the administrative structure of each agricultural *empresa*, production complex, and state farm.[50]

Within each state farm, meetings were regularly scheduled with the workers to discuss work schedules, production problems, or other concerns the workers might have. Other meetings were occasionally held to discuss the annual plan of the farm or major government campaigns. Special "Assemblies of Commitment" were also organized by the ATC to discuss the specific goals and progress of each individual farm on the eve of the first anniversary of the revolution. On the private farms, the ATC organized assemblies to monitor any decapitalization, violations of the labor code, or hoarding in which the owner of the farm might be engaged.[51]

6. The Small-Farm Sector

The incorporation of the small producers and seasonal agricultural workers created a number of special problems for the agrarian reform. The state sector alone could not be expected to incorporate the majority of these peasants. Yet the consolidation of the revolution depended on a strong political alliance between the small peasants, the other agricultural workers, and the urban workers. To win their political support and to raise their production and standards of living, a number of measures targeted at the small producers were undertaken.

The most immediate change was a drastic increase in the amount of credit available to small producers. Under Somoza, over 90 percent of all agricultural credit had gone for export crops, produced mostly by large farmers, while most agricultural producers received no credit at all.[52] By contrast, in 1979-80 agricultural credit became available for practically anyone who requested it. INRA expanded the old INVIERNO program into a new department called PROCAMPO to provide services for small peasants. Together with ATC and the National Development Bank, PROCAMPO organized national, provincial, and local credit committees to approve loans and assure their availability to peasants who were illiterate and without any form of collateral.[53]

To promote the most efficient administration and use of this credit, PROCAMPO and ATC encouraged the organization of credit and service cooperatives.[54] Twelve hundred of these co-ops were organized in 1979-80, and they received over 50 percent of the agricultural credit distributed during that period.[55]

This improved access to credit was not achieved without problems. Functionaries of the National Development Bank (BND) expressed concern about the prospects for recuperating monies lent to small producers for the 1980 crop season. This was especially true for the agricultural frontier, an area of rapid expansion where large numbers of peasants received credit to produce basic grains in marginally accessible areas. MIDA—INRA, BND, and ENABAS were thus faced with the simultaneous problems of recuperating loans and providing adequate marketing, transportation, and storage services for the corn and bean harvests.[56]

The government viewed production cooperatives such as the Sandinista Agricultural Communes as the best solution to the continuing problem of the subdivision of land into smaller and uneconomical plots. Cooperatives would make possible a more comprehensive planning of the agricultural sector.[57] This process of cooperativization, however, would be strictly voluntary and would proceed by stages, beginning with credit, marketing, and service cooperatives, and only later involve production cooperatives. The first production cooperatives would be mostly on rented lands, but eventually, it was hoped, small peasants would pool their own lands as well. Economic incentives, along with constant persuasion, were the mechanisms foreseen to stimulate these changes. In credit, for example, the government offered Sandinista Agricultural Communes a 7-percent interest rate; credit and services cooperatives paid 8 percent; and individual farmers had to pay 11 percent.[58]

Other agricultural policies designed to favor small peasants were the nationalization of all marketing channels for agricultural exports, direct government purchase and sale of basic grains, and the control of rents. State-operated foreign trade companies were established for exporting coffee, cotton, sugar, meat, and fish, as well as for importing pesticides, fertilizers, and other agricultural inputs.[59] State control over foreign trade gave the government direct control over this strategic sector of the economy and made it possible to tax that sector directly. It displaced a whole set of intermediaries who in the past had taken advantage of the peasants' lack of education and marketing power to make high profits at their expense. The Nicaraguan Basic Foods Company (ENABAS) was organized for similar reasons to purchase a portion of the basic food harvest from small peasants and market it in the towns and cities. The formation of ENABAS gave the government some control over consumer prices for basic foodstuffs and the ability to limit the effect of any artificially created food shortages. However, most of the internal marketing of basic foods remained in private hands.[60]

Rent controls for agricultural lands were also established to benefit small producers. Maximum rents were set at $21 (U.S.) per hectare for cotton land, which had formerly rented for more than $140 per hectare, and $7 per hectare for cereal-producing lands.[61] Although the government attempted to prevent the eviction of peasants from lands they had previously rented and to allow peasants to rent land not put into production by the owners, these measures were not fully successful.[62]

To coordinate the programs involving small producers and to develop guidelines for policy in this area, the government created the National Committee of Small Peasant Production. This committee included PROCAMPO, the National Development Bank, ATC, the Ministry of Planning, and the Nicaraguan Basic Foods Company (ENABAS). The national committee developed working definitions of who was a small producer, studied crop production costs upon which state purchasing prices could be based, set credit guidelines, and worked toward smoother coordination of the different agencies involved with small producers.[63]

7. The Private Sector

Despite the government's confiscation of Somoza properties, private sector continued to play a predominant role in the agricultural sector. Large, private, commercial farms concentrating on such export crops as cotton, coffee, cattle, and sugar still accounted for 64.5 percent of Nicaragua's cultivable land.[64] And, as could be expected, a tense and sometimes contradictory relationship developed between this private sector and the new revolutionary government.

The government repeatedly expressed its desire for a mixed economy with an active private sector. But the rules of the game were now different: the private sector could no longer exploit and mistreat its workers, and it was expected to bear its share in the reconstruction of the economy.

The commercial farmers, for their part, had been unhappy with Somoza's personal monopolization of the economy and repressive government. Most looked forward to a government in which "non-Somoza" businessmen would have a leading role. But they looked with apprehension at a government whose basic commitment was now to the poor and dispossessed. Consequently, they often supported opposition parties, such as the Nicaraguan Democratic Movement or the Conservative Democratic Party, even though they were reluctant to be publicly identified as opponents of the government. Some large farmers tried to avoid complying with the government reform legislation. They refused to rent out their lands for the prices dictated under the rent control law or to provide their workers the benefits required by law. For the most part, however, the private sector complied with the agrarian reform laws and tried to adjust to the new framework.[65]

The commercial farmers and cattle ranchers belonged to their own associations, such as the Coffee Producers Union and the Livestock Owners Federation, which were grouped together as the Nicaraguan Agricultural Producers Union (UPANIC). UPANIC in turn was one of a number of business organizations belonging to the Superior Council of the Private Sector (COSEP), which coordinated private-sector negotiations with the government. Conscious of the government's need for private-sector investment and production, commercial farmers often drove a hard bargain in their negotiations with the ministries. While many small farmers were members of UPANIC affiliates, its leadership and political position were in the hands of the large producers.[66]

The government used various mechanisms to respond to private-sector demands and to orient this sector toward its new role. UPANIC, for instance, was assigned one seat in the Council of State, Nicaragua's new legislative assembly, and also allowed to participate in various governmental technical commissions.[67] Economic incentives were among the government's most important policy instruments toward the private sector. Low interest credits were made available, and a coffee stabilization fund was established to shelter coffee producers against the instability of the world market.[68] Many of the large commercial farmers, particularly in cotton, actually benefited from the rent control law, since over 40 percent of the cotton was grown on rented lands. Indeed, even personal income and company profits were taxed at low levels during the first year in an attempt to stimulate private investment.[69]

At the same time, certain limits and controls were placed on the private sector. Salaries were increased substantially. The average agricultural wage went from $1.70 to $2.20 per day at the end of the first year.[70] Agricultural workers obtained the right to decent food at the workplace. Serious measures were taken to eliminate occupational health hazards, such as pesticide poisoning, that were common on the private farms. In general, social legislation was enforced for the first time in Nicaragua's history.

The government took the initiative in planning private-sector activity. Acreage quotas were established for cotton crops and various stimuli used to assure their fulfillment. The government also began to rehabilitate Nicaragua's coffee plantations, long plagued with low yields and a fungus disease that ran rampant when control measures broke down during the war. The Ministry of Agricultural Development began to take infested farms out of production and to promote new, higher-yield coffee plants.[71]

Conclusions

Nicaraguan's agrarian reform accomplished more during its first year of operation than most agrarian reforms achieve over much longer periods. Approximately one-fourth of the agricultural sector was socialized through the organization of state farms and production cooperatives. Credit and technical assistance to the small and medium producer were substantially improved and state marketing channels established to secure more stable and fairer prices to both producer and consumer. At the same time, large commercial farmers maintained their access to credit and to other governmental services. Rural workers were organized into a strong national union, and began to receive better wages and to participate in governmental policy formulation and implementation. The necessary institutional framework for effective agricultural research, planning, and administration began to be developed. Finally, production levels by the end of 1980 were, with the exception of cotton, nearly equal to prewar levels for export crops, and at a par or higher for basic grains for the internal market.[72] These accomplishments were all the more impressive given the widespread destruction and crop failures facing Nicaragua at the end of the war.

But Nicaragua still had a long way to go. No matter how efficient its government operation, it might take Nicaragua ten to twenty years to consolidate its revolution in the countryside and provide a satisfactory level of living for all. Recurrent problems still facing Nicaragua by late 1980, such as seasonal unemployment, dependence on world markets, and low productivity, were deeply rooted in a social and economic structure developed over Nicaragua's history. Restructuring society is no easy task, particularly for a small, poor country.

Indeed, the very effort to change this structure produced its own tensions and problems which may find only partial solution in this generation. By December 1980, for example, INRA still faced the challenges of developing proper forms for organizing worker participation in the new state enterprises, finding the correct mix of work incentives and noncoercive means of worker discipline, and creating mechanisms for preventing or adjudicating conflicts between permanent and seasonal laborers.

The success of the agrarian reform during its first year to a large extent depended on INRA's ability to impose an orderly and controlled process and to maintain a delicate balance between the state sector, the rural workers and peasants, and the large commercial farmers and ranchers. How long could this balance be maintained? If the state incorporated too many permanent workers into its state farms and through its services increased the profits to the small producer, the commercial farmer might face serious labor shortages during the peak harvest periods. On the other hand, some large landowners were reluctant during 1979-80 to enter into sharecropping or rental agreements with small producers, and in certain cases even evicted tenants and sharecroppers. This created increased pressure for land from landless peasants and workers, and resulted in some land invasions. The Minister of Agriculture responded to these pressures by proposing the expropriation with compensation of unused or abandoned lands.[73] But such ad hoc measures did not go to the root problems, and by year's end the government had not yet enacted a comprehensive agrarian reform law to clearly establish the rules of the game.

Aside from land invasions, other tensions between the government and peasants and rural workers surfaced during the first year of agrarian reform. These included demands for higher wages which strained the government's anti-inflationary and nondeficit spending policies. Finally, ATC, the Rural Workers' Association, was at year's end still trying to determine how far it could support the revolutionary government without losing its independence and representativeness.

These and other problems are inherent in any dynamic process of social change. Still, Nicaragua faced the decade of the 1980s with justifiable optimism. Relatively underpopulated but well endowed with natural resources, it had a high potential for agricultural development. Moreover, ATC and the Government of National Reconstruction enjoyed massive popular support and shared a common outlook on the basic policies and programs for Nicaragua's unique process of social change. The rural workers and peasantry could thus look forward to the future with the hope of eventually overcoming the many difficulties they faced.

Notes

[1] Ministerio de Planificación, *Plan de Reactivación Económica en Beneficio del Pueblo* (Managua, 1980), pp. 11 and 15.

[2] Nicaraguan Institute of Agrarian Reform (INRA), "Objetivos y Alcances de la Reforma Agraria Nicaragüense" (Managua, n.d.), p. 6.

[3] Food and Agriculture Organization (FAO), *Nicaragua: Misión de Identificación y Formulación de Proyectos (Managua: Programa de Cooperación Técnica, 1979), p. 9.*

[4] LIC-INRA-USAID, "Agrarian Reform Support: A Project Paper," first draft (Managua, July 1980), p. 28.

[5] FAO, *Nicaragua: Misión de Identificación*, p. 10.

[6] Jaime Wheelock, *Imperialismo y Dictadura* (Mexico: Siglo XXI, 1974), pp. 13-19.

[7] Ibid.

[8] Charles-Andre Udry, "Nicaragua after the Overthrow of Somoza," *Intercontinental Press*, Oct. 9, 1979, p. 947.

[9] Sociedad Cooperativa Anónima de Cafeteros de Nicaragua, "Impacto de la Devaluación en el Sector Cafetalero y Solicitud al Banco Central" (Managua, 1979), p. 3.

[10] FAO, *Nicaragua: Misión de Identificación*, p. 14.

[11] Ibid., p. 19.

[12] Ibid., p. 20.

[13] "Pide Nicaragua Asistencia Técnica en Pesquería," *Diario de las Américas*, Sept. 25, 1979, p. 6; Eduardo Cue, "Despots's Land Now Communal," *San Juan Star*, Aug. 19, 1979, p. 2.

[14] Alejandro Bendaña, "Crisis in Nicaragua," *NACLA*, 12:6 (Nov.-Dec. 1978), p. 8.

[15] "Pushing Ahead with the Rural Revolution," *Latin America Weekly Report*, Aug. 22, 1980, p. 9: United Nations Economic Commission on Latin America (ECLA), "Nicaragua: Daños Humanos y Materiales y Responsabilidades de la Comunidad Internacional," in *Notas sobre la Economia y el Desarrollo de América Latina*, no. 301 / 302 (Sept. 1979), pp. 5, 6.

[16] INRA, "Objetivos y Alcances," p. 6

[17] Roger Burbach and Tim Draimin, "Nicaragua's Revolution," *NACLA*, 19:3 (May-June 1980), p. 5.

[18] Orlando Nuñez, "Formamos 400 Brigadas," in *Nicaragua; Un País Propio*, by Pablo González Casanova et al. (Mexico: UNAM, 1979), p. 112.

[19] Ministerio de Planificación, *Plan de Reactivación*, pp. 11-12.

[20] Gobierno de Reconstrucción Nacional, "Primer Programa de Gobierno," in *1979, Año de la Liberación* (Managua: República de Nicaragua, Difusión y Prensa, 1979), pp. 11-12.

[21] INRA, "El Programa de Gobierno y Nuestra Reforma Agraria" (Managua, n.d.), pp. 1 and 2.

[22]*La Gaceta—Diario Oficial* (Managua), año 83, no. 1, Aug. 22, 1980, p. 5. The whole decree consists of two articles contained in seventeen lines.

[23] Ibid., no. 6, Sept. 3, 1979, p. 42. Due to several abuses in its implementation, this decree was revoked by Decree no. 172 on November 21, 1979. *Barricada* (Managua), Nov. 22, 1979.

[24] Comandante Jaime Wheelock, Minister of Agriculture, interview, November 23, 1979.

[25] Salvador Mayorga, Vice-Minister of INRA, lecture, February 10, 1980.

[26] Ibid.

[27] Comandante Jaime Wheelock, Minister of Agriculture, transcript of press conference (Managua, July 17, 1980), pp. 1, 2.

[28] Roger Burbach and Tim Draimin, "Nicaragua's Revolution," p. 19.

[29] Decree no. 26, *La Gaceta—Diario Oficial* (Managua), año 83, no. 3, Aug. 24, 1979, p. 21.

[30] Aníbal Yañez, "Cabinet Changes Ratify FSLN Course since July Revolution," *Intercontinental Press*, Jan. 19, 1980, p. 8.

[31] INRA, "Objetivos y Alcances," p. 4

[32] Data from Centro de Investigación y Estudio de la Reforma Agraria (CIERA), Aug. 1980.

[33] Jaime Wheelock, press conference of July 1980, pp. 2, 3.

[34] INRA, "Estructura del INRA y Definición de Funciones" (Managua, 1979), pp. 4-8.

[35] Jaime Wheelock, "No Hay 2 Reformas Agrarias Iguales" (interview), *Nicarahuac* (Managua), no. 1 (May-June 1980), p. 65.

[36] Peter Marchetti, "Participación e Implementación de las Políticas de Reforma Agraria: Los Casos de Chile y Nicaragua" (paper presented at V Conferencia de Sociología Rural, México, 1980), p. 24.

[37] Interview with Peter Marchetti, Managua, Nicaragua, August, 1980.

[38] Interview with Orlando Nuñez, Madison, Wisconsin, June 1980.

[39] Ministry of Agricultural Development (MIDA), "Proyecto: Centro de Investigación de la Reforma Agraria" (Managua, June 1980), p. 6.

[40] Marion Brown and Peter Dorner, lecture, October 1979, Madison, Wis.

[41] Alan Riding, "Managua Junta Warns of Steps by Extremists," *New York Times*, Oct. 16, 1979, p. 7.

[42] Ministerio de Planificación, *Plan de Reactivación*.

[43] Ibid., pp. 43-47.

[44] Rural Workers' Association (ATC), "Asamblea Nacional Constitutiva, Memorias" (Managua, 1980), p. 17.

[45] Ibid., pp. 16, 17

[46] Interview with Justino Arceda, Madison, Wis., March 1980.

[47] Peter Marchetti, "Participación e Implementación," p. 11.

[48] ATC, "Asamblea Nacional Constitutiva," pp. 47-51; Burbach and Draimin, "Nicaragua's Revolution," p. 22.

[49] Roger Burbach and Tim Draimin, "Nicaragua's Revolution," p. 19; ATC, "Plan de Lucha" (Managua, n.d.), pp. 1-4.

[50] INRA, "Apuntes sobre la Organización de las Unidades de Producción Estatal y Complejos Estatales" (Managua, n.d.), pp. 3, 5.

[51] Interview with Peter Marchetti, August 1980.

[52] Peter Marchetti, "Participación e Implementación," p. 13.

[53] Comité Nacional de la Pequeña Producción Agropecuaria (CNPPA), *Definición de la Política Institucional de la Revolución Sandinista para el Pequeño Productor Agropecuario* (Managua: CNPPA, 1980), p. 3.

[54] INRA, "La Revolución y el Campo" (Managua, n.d.), p. 23.

[55] Peter Marchetti, "Participación e Implementación," p. 24.

[56] LTC-INRA-USAID, "Agrarian Reform Support," p. 11.

[57] INRA, "Revolución y Campo," pp. 23-27.

[58] CNPPA, *Definición de la Política*, p. 10.

[59] FAO, *Nicaragua: Misión de Identificación*, p. 22.

[60] Ibid.

[61] Decree nos. 230 and 263, *La Gaceta—Diario Oficial* (Managua), año 83, nos. 6 and 28, *Feb. 7, and Feb. 8, 1980*, pp. 266, 267; and 24, 25, respectively.

[62] Jaime Wheelock, press conference, June 1980.

[63] CNPPA, *Definición de la Política*, pp. 1-14.

[64] Data from CIERA, August 1980.

[65] "Nicaraguan Private Sector Baulks at Reconstruction Plans," *Latin America Weekly Report*, Dec. 21, 1979, pp. 1-2.

[66] Cristopher Dickey, "Sandinistas Act to Keep Business Sector Favor," *Washington Post*, Apr. 29, 1980.

[67] Roger Burbach and Tim Draimin, "Nicaragua's Revolution," pp. 16—17.

[68] Decree no. 85, *La Gaceta—Diario Oficial* (Managua), año 83, no. 16, Sept. 22, 1979, p. 121.

[69] Orlando Nuñez interview, June 1980.

[70] Peter Marchetti interview, August 1980; note, however, that the rate of inflation in 1980 was approximately 35 percent.

[71] "7,155 Manzanas de Café Renovadas," *Barricada* (Managua), May 9, 1980.

[72] "Pushing Ahead," *Latin America Weekly Report*, Aug. 1980.

[73] Jaime Wheelock, press conference, June 1980.

Chapter 13

The Nicaraguan Literacy Crusade

VALERIE MILLER

In August of 1979, with the violence of war less than a month behind them, the young government of Nicaragua took on what to many outsiders seemed an impossible task. They proposed to plan, organize, and complete a literacy campaign involving more than one-half million people—all within only 12 months. Prospects for success seemed bleak. Somoza had left the country destitute, war damage was heavy, food in short supply, psychological trauma widespread, health conditions grim, and the new government had no experience in public administration. How in that environment could a national program of such magnitude and scope even be contemplated, much less implemented?

There were several pragmatic reasons for its immediate consideration. First, the young government wanted to prove its commitment to the poor by initiating programs which would immediately benefit them and involve them in the process of reconstruction. With no public money available, any national project of this type would have to depend on volunteer labor and the ability to capture the interest of the international community for financial support. A literacy campaign not only filled those pragmatic requirements but responded to other more important needs as well.

Devastated by war and dictatorship, Nicaragua faced an international debt of 1.6 billion dollars. The majority of her people lived in poverty. Yet the nation was rich in agricultural potential. Lands were fertile and abundant. If international cooperation could be obtained to renegotiate the debt and to approve reasonable credit terms, Nicaragua possessed the real possibility of breaking the traditional patterns of underdevelopment. If the human energies of the country could be mobilized for national reconstruction and a means found to promote popular participation, the foundations for a system of equitable development could be established. Motivated by this challenge, the new leadership oriented its policies and programs toward the poorest sectors of the population. They understood that such a developmental strategy, in large part, depended upon the participation of an educated populace—people able to analyze, plan, think and create; people motivated by a sense of social responsibility rather than personal gain. A literacy campaign, implemented through a volunteer teacher corps, was seen as a fundamental first step in achieving these aims. Such a program would provide an opportunity for people to develop the skills and attitudes necessary to meet the development challenge.

In addition, a literacy campaign would give the many young people who had fought and suffered the traumas of war a constructive way to make the transition from the past to the present. It would provide them with a concrete means to channel their energies positively into building the new nation and into developing a commitment to the poor. The successful completion of such a program would also establish the credibility and capacity of the government to direct and manage national development.

But there was another reason that moved the new government to undertake such a venture—a reason that was echoed throughout the nation. Over 40,000 Nicaraguans had been killed in the war. Their sacrifice had led to the overthrow of Somoza and given the country an opportunity to build anew. The government and revolutionary leadership pledged to honor their memories by working to transform the system of inequities inherited from the dictator. The Crusade was seen as a first means to redress those injustices and pay homage to the dead. Each person learning to read and write would become a living tribute to the sacrifice, commitment, and hope of those who had given their lives in battle. Through the achievements of the living the memories of the fallen would be made immortal. The campaign was named in their honor—The National Literacy Crusade: Heroes and Martyrs for the Liberation of Nicaragua.

"River of Popular Knowledge"

Probably the best way to understand the significance of the Nicaraguan Literacy Crusade is through the words of people directly involved in the process. The following quotations were chosen because together they provide a sense of the Crusade's history and spirit. They come from a variety of sources: governmental documents, newsbroadcasts, personal interviews, and newspaper articles. While perhaps not truly representative in a "scientific" way, they convey a sense of how the campaign touched some people's lives and reflect the struggle and hope of the new nation.

> In Nicaragua we are fighting for justice . . . for social transformation.[1]
>> Carlos Fonseca Amador   October 1970
>> Founder FSLN

> A thorough reform of the objectives and content of national education will be undertaken so that a critical and liberating process of education can be designed and become a key factor in the humanist transformation of Nicaraguan society . . . a national literacy campaign will be launched . . . programs of liberating adult education will begin in order to allow full par-

ticipation in the process of national reconstruction and development.[2]

> First Proclamation of the   July 1979
> Government of National
> Reconstruction

Literacy is fundamental to achieving progress and it is essential to the building of a democratic society where people can participate consciously and critically in national decision-making. You learn to read and write so you can identify the reality in which you live, so that you can become a protagonist of history rather than a spectator.[3]

> Fernando Cardenal, S.J.   February 1980
> National Coordinator
> Nicaraguan Literacy Crusade

High school and university students will be organized into the Popular Literacy Army and will take up their arms of pencils and primers and do battle with ignorance . . . in the process they will learn about country life and participate in the activities of peasant families.[4]

> Ministry of Education   March 1980

Dear Mom and Dad,   May 1980
. . . The mosquitos are driving me crazy. Whenever I talk they fly into my mouth. They say the mosquito nets are coming soon. I hope so . . . I'm learning a lot. I now know how to milk a cow and plant vegetables. The other day I was with Don Demesio roping a steer, but I'm so stupid that I frightened the thing and we had to work twice as hard to catch it again. . . . The rains are constant. The soles of my boots came unglued and I had to sew them with a needle they use to make sacks with. . . .[5]

> Love, David [age 15]

It's difficult sometimes. Tomasita is smart and wants to study but her baby cries a lot and she can't put him down. I visit her three times a day just on the chance she'll be free but . . . she's only on lesson 4. . . . Camilo doesn't seem to assimilate his sounds very well. Of course he does need glasses. He's 67. . . . Socorro and Joaquina are way ahead on lesson 14 but Julio left to pick coffee and Catalina's in bed with malaria. . . . Vicente has improved incredibly since he fell off his mule. He was really a lazy bum before. But now, with his broken arm, he's quite serious and dedicated, even though he's had to learn to write all over again with his left hand.[6]

> Guadalupe, age 16   May 1980
> Brigade: Enoc Ortez
> Reporting to her teaching supervisor

Eight ex-national guardsmen crossed the border from Honduras yesterday and murdered the literacy teacher Georgino Andrade.[7]

> Newsbroadcast, Managua   May 19, 1980

Doña Auxiliadora, what does ignorance mean to you?

Ignorance means that I don't know anything about who I really am or very much about this world that I live in.

Why do you want to learn to read and write?

Well . . . to wake up my mind.

And you, Asunción?

Learning to read and write . . . we're going to be able to participate more in the benefits of agriculture. Now we're going to have the tactics, that's what I call them anyway, the tactics to work the land better. Somoza never taught us to read—it really was mean of him, wasn't it? He knew that if he taught the peasants to read we would claim our rights. Ay! But back then, people couldn't even breathe. You see, I believe that a government is like a parent of a family. The parent demands the best of his children and the children demand the best of the parent, but a governor, like a parent, that does not give culture and upbringing to the child, well that means he doesn't love his child, or his people. Don't you agree?[8]

> Literacy Class, Masaya   May 1980

The Literacy Crusade is like the source of a river of popular knowledge which no one will stop.[9]

> Alicia, Urban volunteer   May 1980.

The Literacy Crusade is indoctrination. It's an attempt to domesticate the minds of the poor.[10]

> Alfonso Robelo   May 1980
> Millionaire Industrialist
> Opposition political leader

Do you know I am not ignorant any more? I know how to read now. Not perfectly, you understand, but I know how. And do you know, your son isn't ignorant any more either. Now he knows how we live, what we eat, how we work and he knows the life of the mountains. Your son, ma'am, has learned to read from our book.[11]

> Don José, a peasant farm-worker   July 1980
> worker speaking to the mother
> of his literacy teacher

The Literacy Crusade taught us two things. One, what our own children are capable of doing and of becoming. Two, what our country is like and how gentle and how poor our people are in the countryside.[12]

> Mable, the middle-class   August 1980
> mother of three literacy
> teachers, Managua

The panel of judges designated by the Director General of UNESCO to grant the 1980 prizes for distinguished and effective contribution on behalf of literacy . . . has unanimously chosen for first prize—the National Literacy Crusade of Nicaragua.[13]

> UNESCO, Paris, France   September 1980.

Challenge and Legacy

In August 1979, UNESCO was far away. The challenge to be confronted by the campaign was mammoth and the responsibilities heavy. The Crusade was charged with overcoming and transforming the educational legacy left by Somoza—a legacy of disparity, repression, and high levels of illiteracy. Under the dictatorship, the educational structure had been stagnant and corrupt. It had served to maintain inequitable political and economic power relationships and employed a system of rewards which promoted graft and incompetence. The educational disparities that the system engendered were stark. Of the approximately 7 percent of elementary school-age children who actually entered primary grades in 1976, over half dropped out within a year.[14] Two-thirds of the students enrolled were in urban areas.[15] During the 1970s, official statistics revealed that in rural areas only 5 percent of those who entered primary school finished; in the cities the figure reached 44 percent.[16] In 1977, only 17.5 percent of the total high-school-age population (13-18) was enrolled in secondary school and 8.4 percent of the 19-24 age group attended institutions of higher learning.[17]

Teaching standards were abysmally low, opportunities for professional development restricted, and incentives for excellence nonexistent. The system rewarded certain selected officials at the top with opportunities for advancement, international scholarships, and graft. Some functionaries, for example, received phantom teaching positions which allowed them to collect double salaries. In rural areas, political favorites were assigned to village schools and then allowed to play hooky most of the year. Teachers who questioned the system were fired and activist student groups were the subject of surveillance and repression.

In this overall context, it is not surprising that among the population over 10 years of age illiteracy reached upwards of 50 percent and soared to over 85 percent in some rural areas.[18] Illiteracy was both a condition of the nation's underdevelopment and a direct product of Somoza's economic and political policies. The logic of the system made the promotion of universal literacy irrational. It was neither economically necessary for the functioning of the system nor politically advisable for its maintenance.

The dictatorship's economic model depended upon large numbers of unskilled, docile farm workers. Peasants functioned strictly as field hands and had no technical, managerial, or administrative responsibilities. Education for these groups, therefore, was neither required nor encouraged by the economic system. The expansion of educational opportunities for these sectors was discouraged also by the regime's political structures, which served as one-way channels of authority and control. Participation by the community in decision-making was not part of the system and therefore an informed citizenry was unnecessary. Moreover, as Asunción explained, "Somoza never taught us to read. He knew that if he taught the peasants to read we would claim our rights."[19] Literacy would have given people like Asunción access to information that might have led greater numbers of Nicaraguans to organize against the dictator sooner than they did.

Somoza did authorize some adult educational programs—the "Plan Waslala," for example. This literacy project was named after a town in the North that in the mid-seventies had been the site of a feared concentration camp where the Guard tortured and killed hundreds of peasants. According to an official government report in 1978, the "Plan Waslala" was designed as part of a regional counterinsurgency operation. It assigned over 100 "literacy teachers" to the mountains of Matagalpa between 1977 and 1978. Their principal task was to act as security agents searching out and identifying peasants sympathetic to the FSLN.[20]

The Spirit of Inspiration

The spirit which inspired the 1980 Literacy Crusade and had defeated the creator of "Plan Waslala" grew out of the liberation struggle begun by General Augusto César Sandino in the 1920s. Despite the difficulties involved in setting up an education program during battle, General Sandino held a firm commitment to teaching his men the basics of literacy. When possible, he tried to provide learning opportunities for them; as he explained in the following description:

> When General Pedro Altamirano first joined us he did not know how to read or write but . . . during the fighting and only because I insisted on it, Altamirano learned. He stumbled and mumbled as he went along and yet despite his age, he has made great strides since then. Now, as amazing as it may seem, he actually knows how to type—even if it is only with one finger.[21]

Widespread learning, however, was limited by the demands of war and by a critical shortage of people available to teach.

Over the years, universal literacy became a priority concern of San-dino's revolutionary descendants. In the 1960s, Carlos Fonseca, the founder of the FSLN, took up the General's challenge. Following Sandino's example, he instructed his men not only to teach people the tactics and strategies of battle, but also the skills of reading and writing. Small clandestine literacy efforts were conducted throughout the long years of struggle. In early July 1979, just two weeks prior to the victory over Somoza, the *Frente* chose a team of Nicaraguan educational experts to begin the actual planning of a national literacy program. By the 19th, the day of victory, they had com-pleted a draft proposal calling for the immediate organization of a nation-wide campaign. Fifteen days after the triumph, the new government named a coordinator to organize and direct the program; eight months later, Nicaragua's Literacy Crusade was launched.

On March 24, in town plazas across the nation, over 55,000 high school and university students proudly displayed their Crusade uniforms—blue jeans, grey peasant shirts, and rubber rain boots. Standing with their classmates and teachers, they pledged to carry out their respon-sibilities as literacy volunteers with honor and respect. Flags waved, bands played, mothers cried, and kids, shouting and laughing with excitment, scrambled for transportation. Some climbed into buses or trucks; others boarded boats or trains. The roads were clogged for three days. As the caravans of volunteers passed through towns and villages, people waved and offered up bananas and oranges and words of encouragement. Up into the mountains and back into the jungles, the corps of volunteers continued their journey. Some were dropped off along the wayside and some went on to road's end. With their brightly colored napsacks bulging, they trudged off into the hills. A few groups got lost and most got blisters. Some were welcomed warmly, for others it took longer. The Crusade had begun.

Society in Transformation

To understand the nature of the campaign and appreciate its ac-complishments, the Crusade needs to be placed in the context of a society engaged in a process of profound transformation. From the beginning of the liberation struggle, it had been clear to the revolutionary leadershp that the institutions and structures of the old society had not met basic human needs nor served the interests of the majority of the population. They believed that the only way to address the nation's urgent development requirements was to embark upon a course of rapid social transformation. Such a course implied transforming not only the structures and systems inherited from the dictatorship, but also the interests the dynasty represented and the values and cultural traditions it had attempted to legitimize.

Implicit in this process of transformation was the vision of a new socie-ty and of an education model which would help bring about its realization. According to revolutionary thinking, that vision rested principally on the intelligent, creative involvement of a new kind of citizen in new participatory forms of social organization. Essentially, it called for the formation of the "new man" and the "new woman," a revolutionary citizenry inspired by goals of community service rather than individual gain, motivated by such values and attitudes as "sacrifice, humility, love, discipline, cooperation, creativity, hard work, and a critical consciousness." The new social order meant creating a different set of institutions which would respond to the interests and needs of the majority—the nation's peasants and laborers. The design of the system seemed to imply a network of economic enterprises and political structures managed and directed by workers and community members. These organizations would work closely with government to set priorities and to plan and coordinate national development. (The first manifestation of this system was the variety of mass citizen organizations that had emerged in the course of the liberation struggle).

Education in such a context was seen as serving as a catalyzing force to energize and propel transformation and guarantee effective citizen participation in the design and management of the emerging structures. The words of Junta member Sergio Ramírez underscored that position:

> We are teaching the poor and disenfranchised to read and write not out of charity, but rather so that they will be prepared both politically and technically to become the genuine authors of development and the only legitimate owners of the Revolution.[22]

The realization of this vision therefore depended upon the creative and active involvement of precisely those sectors of society that Somoza had marginalized. Education would have to provide the poor and disenfranchised with opportunities to acquire skills and knowledge so that they could assume leadership responsibilities. Only then could they fully become what Father Fernando Cardenal, the National Coordinator of the Crusade, called "Architects of their own destiny . . . the protagonists of history rather than the spectators."

> We believe that in order to create a new nation we have to begin with an education that liberates people. Only through knowing their past and their present, only through understanding and analyzing their reality can people chose their future. Only in that process can people fulfill their human destiny as makers of history and commit themselves to transforming that reality.[23]

> Fernando Cardenal S.J.

> The function of knowledge is but one—to transform reality. . . .[24]

> Bayardo Arce
> Member of the FSLN National Directorate

The basic function of education in the New Nicaragua, then, was liberation. Its basic purpose was to transform reality—to help people critically understand their world in order to take an active creative part in improving it. Education, in this context, involved a frontal attack on the inequities inherited from the dictatorship and on the passivity and subservience the system had engendered. As such, revolutionary education needed to focus on people recovering their sense of dignity and self-worth, taking charge of their lives both as individuals and as community members, learning to become knowledgeable decision-makers and to function as responsible citizens with rights as well as obligations. Following the principles of the renowned Brazilian educator, Paulo Freire, it implied people working together in community to acquire an understanding of society's economic, political, and social forces in order to act upon them and transform them for the common good.

Purpose and Objectives

The overall purpose of the Crusade was to help people become involved members of their community, committed to social transformation and to participating as informed citizens in the political, economic, social, and cultural life of the nation. At the practical level, the program was designed to assist participants in acquiring basic skills in reading, writing, mathematics, and analytical thinking. In the process, people would gain an elementary knowledge of history and civics as well as an appreciation of themselves and their culture. The campaign was also intended to sensitize the general public to the problems and rights of the poor, to promote social commitment, and to prepare citizens for their responsibilities in meeting the challenge of national development. To provide for the special learning needs of the Miskito-, Sumo-, and English-speaking populations, a separate series of Crusades was planned to begin in October 1980.

Specifically, the campaign proposed to eliminate illiteracy as a social phenomenon. Such a proposal involved first reducing the actual illiteracy rate to between approximately 10 and 15 percent; second, setting up an extensive program of adult education after the Crusade; and third, expanding primary school facilities throughout the country. But, while eliminating illiteracy was the most obvious goal of the program, others were of similar importance. They also were aimed at rooting out inequities and laying the foundations for the new society. These other goals were to encourage an integration and understanding between Nicaraguans of different classes and backgrounds; (2) to promote political awareness and a critical analysis of underdevelopment; (3) to provide participants with a working knowledge of the nation's new development programs and structures; (4) to nurture attitudes and skills leading to increased creativity, production, cooperation, discipline, and analytical thinking; (5) to forge national cohesion, consensus, and commitment to social service; (6) to strengthen the channels for economic and political participation and to consolidate the mass citizen organizations; (7) to recover, record, and disseminate the history and popular culture suppressed by the dictatorship, and (8) to conduct basic research studies necessary for future development planning.

How to translate these complex goals into an effective program of action—that was the question facing the Crusade's staff in August 1979. That question and many more kept the team working twelve- to fourteen-hour days, seven days a week. What did it imply to equip tens of thousands of volunteers? Where did you find 60 or 70 thousand boots, raincoats, lanterns or mosquito nets? How did you pay for them? How did you locate the vehicles to transport that many people all on the same weekend? How many water purifying tablets did 60,000 people consume in a five-month period? How many bandages? There were moments at the beginning when the challenge seemed overwhelming but as Fernando Cardenal explained,

> . . . the lessons of the war provided us with a special source of strength and inspiration. During the insurrection, we had learned to take unimaginable risks and to dare against what seemed impossible odds. We learned about organizing and to trust and appreciate people's extraordinary capacity for daring, creativity, and perseverance. We were confident, therefore, that we could translate that spirit into the basis for the Literacy Crusade but, in August, we just were not quite sure how . . . in one year, we learned a lot.[25]

Strategies, Structures, and Methodologies

From that experience and steadfast faith in people's creative capacities emerged the strategies, structures, and methodologies of the Literacy Crusade. The war and its heroes also served as an inspiration in another way. The program borrowed terms associated with the struggle and adapted them to the campaign. The Crusade, for example, was also known as the "War on Ignorance." Volunteer teachers were called "Brigadiers"—troops of the "Popular Literacy Army." Organized into "Squadrons and Brigades," these "literacy warriors" named each of their army units after a fallen combatant. On one level, this choice of military terminology was designed to inspire a sense of seriousness and responsibility in the teenage volunteers and to help them understand that the campaign required the same kind of dedication, selflessness, and discipline that the war had demanded. But at another level, the choice took on a deeply spiritual meaning. The young volunteers, by calling forth the names of the fallen dead, kept alive their memories and their courage. In moments of frustration and doubt, the memory of their sacrifice inspired greater commitment and compassion. As one volunteer wrote in his diary,

It's true that right now I don't like being here . . . but so many
compañeros have fallen for this cause. . . . For all those who
never said they were going to die for their country, but who
simply did, for them, I have to love people; for them, I have to
continue the struggle.[26]

The specific means to carry out the literacy struggle was based on a
strategy of carefully coordinated community participation supported and
financed by international solidarity—the same strategy used in the war. Just
as in battle, victory over illiteracy rested on people working together with
dedication and creativity for a common purpose. That strategy guided all
levels of the program from fund-raising to the design of the campaign's
structures and methodologies.

Funding for the massive effort was gathered principally outside the
country from donations made by church organizations, international
development agencies, solidarity groups, and sympathetic governments.
The World Council of Churches and the countries of Switzerland, Sweden,
Holland, Britain, and the Federal Republic of Germany were among the
most generous donors. To collect funds inside Nicaragua, the Crusade instituted a program of Patriotic Literacy Bonds. The popular organizations
and governmental institutions also contributed by sponsoring such activities as raffles, bake sales, dances, song fests, poetry readings, and con-
certs. Peasants' groups and students' associations collected "pennies for pencils." On an individual level, people from both the private and public sector
contributed one day of wages for each month of the campaign. This joint
funding strategy proved successful. Approximately $10 million (U.S.) in
cash and goods were collected. The Crusade met expenses without having
to use public funds.

The same guiding principles of participation, creativity, and internationalism which influenced the structures and strategies of the Campaign
were reflected in the program's educational philosophy and methodologies.
Once again, the experience of the war served as a teacher. The educational
philosophy underlying the entire Crusade was based on a belief which had
been tested and verified under fire. It rested on a profound trust in human
potential and creativity and on an appreciation of learning as a dynamic
participatory process of action and reflection. Two critical experiences
established the basis for this understanding: the clandestine literacy programs conducted during the struggle, and the small study and planning
groups carried on throughout the war. The tremendous creative capacities
of people demonstrated during the fighting deepened that understanding.
From these experiences and philosophy, important educational approaches
and principles had been derived. The value of small-group study, peer
teaching, and collective problem-solving had clearly been established, as
had the importance of creative self-directed learning—the ability to acquire
and apply knowledge with initiative and imagination. The understanding

gained from this shared national experience provided the foundation for the Crusade's educational program. Besides the profound influence of the liberation struggle, the program's methodology and materials were also influenced by the work of Paulo Freire and further enriched by a personal visit he made to Nicaragua in October 1979. An analysis of literacy efforts in Cuba, Peru, Guinea Bissau, São Tomé, and other countries provided further insights.

During September and October, with these experiences as a foundation, the Crusade's curriculum staff designed the basic primer and accompanying materials. In November and December, they tested the package in a series of pilot projects and revised it accordingly. The materials consisted of the basic literacy primer *Dawn of the People;* a teacher's manual, the *Teacher's Guide for Literacy Volunteers;* and an arithmetic workbook, *Math and Economic Reconstruction: One Single Operation.* During the course of the Crusade, teaching games that stressed learner creativity were also developed and distributed. The primer had a three-part organization: (1) the history and development of the Revolution, (2) the socio-economic programs of the Government of National Reconstruction, and (3) civil defense. It consisted of twenty-three lessons, each with accompanying photographs and writing exercises. Some of the lesson themes were "Sandino, guiding force of the Revolution; Work is the right and duty of every citizen;" "Spend little, save resources and produce a lot—that is Revolution;" "The FSLN led the people to Liberation;" " With organization, work, and discipline, we will be able to build the nation of Sandino."

The methodology devised for using the primer consisted of a multistage process based on a dialog and phonetics approach. Each lesson began with a discussion about a photograph. The dialog exercise was considered the key to the entire learning process, and of great political import, for it provided participants with the skills to analyze and create. As Fernando Cardenal stated,

> This initial step is highly political for it offers people the power of the word. By expressing their own opinions about their lives, their history, and their future in dialog with others, they begin to develop and strengthen their power of creativity and analysis . . . for any education that merits the name must prepare people for freedom—to have opinions, to be critical, to transform their world.[27]

The FSLN representative to the Crusade, Carlos Carrión, expressed a similar opinion:

> The literacy methodology is intrinsically political. How? It's not just that we speak of Sandino or of Carlos Fonseca, or of the Frente Sandinista. The most political, the most revolutionary aspect of this literacy approach is the fact that we are providing scientific knowledge and analytical skills to our brothers and

sister in the fields and factories who do not know how to read or write—the skills to reason, think, compare, discern, and the ability to form their own human and political criteria.[28]

Following the dialog, a series of phonetic exercises were provided to acquaint participants with each lesson's syllable families. Reading and writing practice concluded the lesson.

A national training program was designed to prepare the volunteers in the use of the methodology and for the new type of educational role they would be expected to play.

> You will be a catalyst of the teaching-learning process. Your literacy students will be people who think, create and express their ideas. Together, you will form a team of mutual learning and human development. . . . The literacy process is an act of creation in which people offer each other their thoughts, words, and deeds. It is a cultural action of transformation and growth.[29]

In order to equip people to be facilitators of such an educational process, the training program stressed small-group study, collective problem-solving, peer teaching, and educational methodologies which promoted participation and creativity. Role plays, debates, simulations, group discussions, and a variety of forms of artistic expression were techniques commonly used.

To accomodate the massive training needs, a decentralized four-tiered program was designed. The program depended on a multiplier effect. Beginning with a core group of 80, four months later it concluded with a teacher corps of over 80,000. In December and January, the core group, 80 teachers and university students, was trained. In February, that group prepared 600. In early March, the 600 trained approximately 12,000, of which most were teachers, and in mid-March, the 12,000 prepared tens of thousands of University and high school students. In order to supplement their original training, Saturday workshops were conducted for volunteers by their teaching supervisors. A daily radio program broadcast on all national radio stations provided further educational orientation.

To support the immense teacher corps required a massive organizational network. Once again, lessons learned in battle proved valuable. Following the wartime strategy, a structure was set up that was based on extensive popular participation coordinated and directed by a central collective leadership. The Crusade was made up of a nationwide network of governmental institutions, popular organizations, citizen groups, professional associations, and religious organizations, and was directed by one central executive body, the National Coordinating Board. The Board was responsible for planning, administering, and managing the Crusade. Although most of its members lacked public administration experience, the Board maximized its own capacity and creativity by working in teams and using a system of collective problem-solving.

In order to guarantee maximum involvement and cooperation among participating organizations, two national planning and evaluation congresses were held and a National Literacy Commission was established. The Board organized the congresses to assess the accomplishments and identify the weaknesses of the program in order to improve its operations. They originated first at the community level and extended upward to the township, county, and state, finally culminating in two nationwide conferences. It is estimated that over 100,000 people participated in the process. The Board set up a National Literacy Commission composed of representatives from each participating organization in order to plan and coordinate program activities. To fill out the organizational network, the National Board established local Board offices and set up Literacy Commissions in each of the 16 state capitals and 144 county seats. Subcommissions were organized in townships and urban neighborhoods.

Citizens' groups, workers' associations, and public institutions formed the organizational backbone of the campaign. Their tasks were many. They coordinated the national literacy census in which over 1,400,000 people were canvassed. They also conducted fund-raising events and arranged for accomodations, food distribution, transportation, and supplies for Brigadiers and staff. Two groups had especially heavy responsibilities. The Sandinista young people's association was in charge of organizing the rural teacher corps—the Popular Literacy Army (EPA)—and recruiting its volunteers. To prepare the new recruits for the rigors of rural life, the group set up an outward-bound program in conjunction with the Boy Scouts and held a seminar series to discuss current events, governmental programs, and educational and developmental theories. In the field during the Crusade, the association was responsible for maintaining both enthusiasm and discipline. ANDEN, the National Association of Nicaraguan Educators, had the responsibility for organizing and coordinating the almost 10,000 teachers who participated as educational supervisors. Two to three teachers were assigned to each squadron of thirty volunteers in order to provide them with technical support and guidance. Teachers were also in charge of supervising the administration of the literacy examinations given to determine whether a participant had successfully mastered reading and writing skills.

For organizational purposes, the Crusade was divided into two main teaching fronts—urban and rural. EPA was the principle force in the rural areas, though other groups added to its strength. The Farmworkers' Association (ATC) joined the educational army with their contingent of teaching troops the Peasants' Literacy Militia (MAC), and the Sandinista Labor Federation (CST) sent a small corps from their "Laborers' Literacy Militia." A Brigade of some 400 Cultural volunteers supplemented the rural forces—gathering histories, legends, songs, and poems of the country people, and organizing cultural events with them. Brigades of medical students, about 750 in all, attended to volunteer health care needs. Parents organized

EPA 2, which arranged for sending provisions and for family excursions to visit the troops. A specially formed mothers' association helped supply the teacher corps and their students with food and clothes as did a network of government institutions.

Before joining EPA, volunteers had to obtain parental permission to participate in the five-month campaign. In the field, they were separated according to sex and organized according to school. In general, they lived with peasant families, sharing their days and tasks. The volunteers spent mornings working with the peasants in their daily activities. Late afternoons and evenings were dedicated to preparing lessons and conducting small learning groups. In the final weeks of the campaign, teaching was intensified and volunteers spent every available hour tutoring their peasant students.

In the cities, the volunteer corps was made up of two groups—the Laborers Literacy Militia directed by the CST, and the Urban Literacy Warriors organized by the Women's association and the Sandinista community defense committees. Their forces; some 25,000 strong, consisted of housewives, factory workers, governmental employees, professionals, and working students. They taught in homes, churches, factories and offices; even a national brewery and the onion stall in the Managua market became thriving centers of study. In the urban areas, literacy work with adults was complemented by educational programs for children. The Quincho Barrilete project provided special study in literacy, culture, and sports for child street vendors; and the "Rear Guard" program served as a type of summer day-camp for school children between 4 and 12.

A spirit of international cooperation was evident at every level of the Crusade's structure. The Dominican Republic, Spain, and Costa Rica sent delegations of teachers specifically to work in the program. Cuban teachers assigned to teach primary school in remote areas worked in the campaign after classes. Individuals from all over the world volunteered as Brigadiers and dozens of educational experts from the Americas worked as technical advisors. In the National offices in Managua, for example, the international staff came from Argentina (2), Chile (1), Colombia (4), Costa Rica (1), Cuba (4), El Salvador (2), Mexico (2), Honduras (1), Peru (1), Puerto Rico (1), Spain (4), the United States (3), and Uruguay (2).

"The River of Popular Knowledge:" Conclusions and Beginnings

For nearly twelve months, the National Literacy Crusade galvanized the country's attention and energies. The campaign reached deeply into Nicaraguan society and laid the foundations for political and social transformation. Approximately a quarter of the population had been immersed in the intense learning experience, and directly or indirectly through family and friends, the campaign touched almost the entire nation. Its achievements were extraordinary by any measure. Some 400,000 Nicaraguans mastered elementary reading and writing skills, studying their history and revolution in the process. By 1981, that number was expected to reach 500,000. Basic illiteracy was reduced from 50 percent to 13 percent. Fundamental skills and experiences were acquired which would serve as a force for national development. Through the Crusade over 50,000 urban young people and their families had learned about rural poverty and peasant culture. Close to 20,000 teachers and members of the National Literacy Crusade and participating organizations learned similar lessons and also confronted their assumptions about education. More than 25,000 urban dwellers who served as literacy teachers in the cities acquired a new understanding of their community and workplace. In the course of the campaign, volunteers participated in a nationwide malaria control program and in countless local community development projects. They also provided valuable information for future national developmental planning. Literacy Brigades conducted several surveys collecting important agricultural data; Cultural Brigades recorded thousands of stories, legends, and histories to be developed into educational materials; and Medical Brigades made a national inventory and distribution map of rural diseases to be used for improved health programming.

The campaign had been a project of many dimensions, or levels. On one level, it had been a social and cultural exchange program which had brought citizens together to learn about each other, and in the process to develop a new understanding of themselves, their relationship to the world, and their culture. On another level, it had been a program of economic education and job training, teaching people about underdevelopment and the pressing challenge of reconstruction, and providing them with skills necessary for more effective participation in the workplace. On even a further level, the campaign had been a political project to forge national unity and to demonstrate the commitment and abiltiy of the new government to respond to the needs of its principle constituency, the poor. By doing so, it had earned legitimacy and credibility on a national and international scale. But perhaps the greatest political significance of the program was found in its role as a developmental project. As part of the government's overall developmental strategy, the Crusade helped lay the basis for redistributing the nation's power and wealth. By attacking illiteracy and inequity, the Crusade directly confronted some of the major obstacles that barred large sectors of the population from effective participation in national development. With the skills, knowledge, and attitudes gained during the campaign, these sectors and the popular organizations to which many of them belonged were better prepared to participate in the transformation of Nicaraguan society and in the political and economic structures that transformation was bringing. As such, the Crusade established the foundation for restructuring the very basis of national power.

The campaign was not without its costs, however. The massive nature of the Crusade affected the quality of teaching skills acquired by the volunteers. If a gradual regional approach had been used, a better training program would have been possible. Instead of relying on quickly prepared primary school teachers, a campaign organized by regions would have allowed an experienced training team to conduct the program. Implementing the campaign so soon after victory also had its consequences. The Crusade had to rely heavily on organizations and institutions with almost no experience in administration or management. In the long run, however, both these disadvantages also had their positive sides. The nation's teachers received training in new educational approaches and were given the opportunity to put them into practice, while institutions and organizations were able to develop their managerial capacities and improve their operations. But the Crusade provoked a strong reaction and the cost to human life was high: Somoza supporters and ex-National Guardsmen assassinated nine literacy volunteers.

The remarkable accomplishments of the Crusade were testimony to the creative power and potential of the popular organizations and the hundreds of thousands of individual Nicaraguans who participated in the program. The success of the campaign also clearly demonstrated the capacity of the government to inspire and mobilize large sectors of the population and to organize and administer national development programs. However, the achievements gained through the Crusade were extremely fragile. Without constant and extensive reinforcement, the skills, attitudes, and organizational competencies acquired would quickly dissipate. Acutely aware of this possibility, the newly formed Vice-Ministry of Adult Education designed an immediate follow-up program. Self-directed community learning groups were set up, reading and writing materials provided, and a special radio program produced and broadcast to motivate and direct further study. Before leaving their sites, volunteers, with the assistance of their supervisors, had selected and trained either an outstanding literacy graduate or a literate member of each community to serve as the learning group coordinator. One person was also chosen for each valley or township to coordinate and supervise the groups in the surrounding area. Popular organizations were called upon to give assistance to the followup program. This resultant community learning network provided the bridge between the Crusade and the formal program of the Vice-Ministry which would begin following the gathering of the coffee and cotton crops in March. Reading and writing continued. The Crusade had ended, but "the river of popular knowledge" proceeded on its journey.

Notes

[1] Carlos Fonseca Amador, speech given after escape from Costa Rican jail, October 1970.

[2] Government of National Reconstruction, *First Proclamation* (Managua: July 1979), p. 6.

[3] Fernando Cardenal S.J., interview with author, Managua, February 3, 1980.

[4] Cruzada Nacional de Alfabetización, *La Alfabetización en Marcha*, (Managua: Ministry of Education, 1980), p. 3.

[5] "Diario de un Brigadista," *El Brigadista*, Managua, July 1980, p. 5.

[6] Guadalupe Rivera, interview with author, Valle de Enoc Ortez, Nicaragua, May 30, 1980.

[7] Newsbroadcast, Radio Sandino, Managua, Nicaragua, May 19, 1980.

[8] Auxiliadora Rivas and Asunción Suazo, conversation in literacy class, Masaya, Nicaragua, May 4, 1980.

[9] Marcos Arruda, "Total Warfare against illiteracy in Nicaragua," report for World Council of Churches, Geneva, Switzerland, November 1980, p. 9.

[10] Alfonso Robelo, interview with the author, Managua, Nicaragua, May 30, 1980.

[11] Lorena DiMontis, "Los Brigadistas Aprenden a Leer de los Campesinos," *La Prensa*, July 17, 1980.

[12] Mabel Somarriba, interview with author, Managua, Nicaragua, August 27, 1980.

[13] UNESCO, "Premio Nadezhda K. Krupskaya, Premio Asociación International de Lectura y Premio Noma 1980—Proclamación," Paris, UNESCO, September, 1980, pp. 1-2.

[14] Ministry of Education, *La Educación en el Primer Año de la Revolución Popular Sandinista* (Managua: Government of National Reconstruction, 1980), p. 31.

[15] George Black and John Bevan, *The Loss of Fear* (London: World University Service, 1980), p. 18.

[16] Ministry of Education, 1980, p. 31.

[17] Ibid.

[18] Ibid.

[19] Interview with Auxiliadora Rivas.

[20] Ministry of Education, *Plan Waslala*, (Managua, 1978).

[21] *Alfabetización en Marcha*, p. 1.

[22] Sergio Ramírez, "La Crusada en Marcha," Bulletin no. 4, Managua, Apr. 1980, p. 8.

[23] Fernando Cardenal, interview with the author, Managua, August 20, 1980.

[24] Bayardo Arce, speech Universidad Centroamericana, Managua, November 15, 1979.

[25] Fernando Cardenal, S.J., interview, August 20, 1980.

[26] "Diario de un Brigadista," p. 5.

[27] Fernando Cardenal, S.J., August 20, 1980.

[28] Carlos Carrión, speech before First Literacy Crusade Congress, June 17, 1980.

[29] Cruzada Nacional de Alfabetización, *Cuaderno de Orientaciones* (Managua: Ministry of Education, 1979), p. 1.

Chapter 14
Health Care
in Revolutionary Nicaragua

THOMAS JOHN BOSSERT

Passing signs proclaiming "The Revolution is Health," I wandered into a health center in one of the major towns in the Central Highlands. I was genially welcomed by the energetic and busy nurse, who easily incorporated my interruption into her more pressing activities—giving me a detailed description of the local health programs while at the same time assisting the rest of the health center staff and village volunteers in search of vaccines, food supplements for infants, and materials for latrine construction. Her programs included finishing the third phase of the national polio vaccination campaign, sponsoring tetanus vaccinations in the local elementary school (which she reported had already reached 75 percent of its target population), promoting a sanitation campaign that had installed 300 latrines in six months, and initiating a local census of the children under 5, mothers and pregnant women—the population most "at risk" medically. She and other members of the health center staff also delivered weekly "health talks" informing the community members about how best to care for their own health through nutrition, sanitation, and prenatal care.

I had been in health posts in Nicaragua before the revolution and what impressed me most was the amount of new activity and the excitement and enthusiasm of all those involved. This health center was now engaged in activities it had not done before. It was not only distributing more vaccines and food supplements than it had under Somoza but it was integrating these activities into the newly formed community organizations: the Sandinista Defense Committees (CDS), the local Council of Reconstruction, and the new Nicaraguan Women's Association (AMNLAE). For the first time on a large scale, the government was encouraging communities to participate in activities to improve their health conditions and was supplying many of the needed materials—milk, vaccinations, latrine construction materials. What is more, there was an incredible openness among the health staff and the

Research for this study was supported by a Post-Doctoral Research Fellowship from the Tinker Foundation. It involved visits to Nicaragua for short periods in 1975 and 1976 and six weeks of interviews with government officials in 1980. I am indebted to Mark Rosenberg, David Parker, Thomas W. Walker, James Kurth, and Terri Shaw for comments and suggestions.

volunteers, an awareness of other activities related to health and a willingness to explore the failings and problems of their own programs. This was just a beginning—the task was great and the solutions not yet clearly established.

The sign over the small health center—"Revolution is Health"—posed a difficult question: what kind of health care is revolutionary? On the face of it, the answer appears deceptively simple. The public health system of the Somoza regime was so extremely inequitable, and so clearly emphasized curative hospital care rather than sorely needed preventive programs, that a new approach which brought more equal distribution of services and began to emphasize preventive programs would be revolutionary for Nicaragua. However, in comparison with other countries, it is difficult to specify a particular health policy as revolutionary, because existing revolutionary regimes have quite different approaches and because even the least reform-minded regimes, such as that of Guatemala, have begun to adopt new policies that represent a more equitable distribution of health services. Indeed, there is now a general commitment by both revolutionary and nonrevolutionary regimes to the achievement of several goals embodied in the internationally approved "primary care approach."[1] These goals may be summarized: (1) the achievement of greater equality of access to health services, both by increasing services to lower classes, and, most important, by providing access in the rural areas where large populations previously had no access at all; (2) a decisive commitment to improved preventive measures such as provision of clean water, sanitation, nutrition, immunizations, maternal and child health—activities which are more likely to improve health than are physician-oriented curative services; (3) considerable participation of communities in establishing local health priorities and implementing local health programs. A fourth, less explicit goal is to achieve the objectives of equity, prevention, and participation within a relatively restricted national health budget. This last goal in part recognizes the limited contribution of health services to improved health levels of a population.[2] It is likely that expanded production and more equitable distribution of wealth have a greater impact on health than do health services themselves.

While all national governments are officially committed to these goals, one could expect a greater commitment from revolutionary regimes to at least the first three goals of greater equity, prevention, and participation. If we consider revolutionary regimes to be those ideologically committed to achieving economic equity, popular participation, and rationally planned allocation of goods and services, these health goals fit the general commitments. There is no doubt empirically that revolutionary regimes such as those of China, Cuba, and Tanzania have made remarkable progress toward the achievement of these health goals—far greater progress than most nonrevolutionary regimes.[3]

A central issue, however, is raised by the fourth goal: a restricted health budget. Revolutionary commitment may be measured in terms of a willingness to devote national resources to a social service such as health. Provision of more health services could be seen as both a means of redistribution of wealth and as a response to popular demand. As such, it moves toward achieving economic equity while also gaining popular legitimacy. Following this logic, the Cuban revolution appears to have chosen to devote considerable resources to the provision of high levels of health care. However, few regimes are capable of making this choice, which, even for revolutionary regimes, means a sacrifice of other sectors. Furthermore, it seems unwise to devote massive resources to the health sector in the absence of clear evidence that health service expenditures are the most cost-effective means of improving health. Also, to assume that provision of health services contributes to a regime's legitimacy is problematical. Health services are a costly means of redistributing wealth and of responding to popular demand, and they will become more costly if regimes are to respond to accelerating demands for higher-quality care. Effective policies to increase production are likely to be a more useful means of gaining legitimacy.

The Nicaraguan revolutionaries, then, were faced with the problem of restructuring the Nicaraguan health system in such a way as to achieve equity, prevention, and participation within a relatively restricted budget. Their task was difficult under any circumstances. It was complicated by the severe problems of the health system they inherited from Somoza.

Health and Health Services under Somoza

There is little doubt that the health conditions of Nicaraguans during the Somoza dictatorship were extremely poor, although they were not notably worse in Nicaragua than in other comparable Central American countries like Guatemala and Honduras. Life expectancy was 53 years, and infant mortality, often taken as an indicator of the general health status of the whole population, was estimated at the extremely high rate, between 120 and 146 per 1,000 live births.[4] Guatemala and Honduras had similar high rates, while by contrast wealthier and progressive Costa Rica had a life expectancy of 70 years and infant mortality of 29 per 1,000. As in Guatemala and Honduras, preventable diseases were the principal causes of death; diarrhea and infectious diseases accounted for 31.4 percent of all deaths and over 50 percent of infant mortality. Nutrition levels were also extremely low, contributing to mortality from other causes: 66 percent of children under 5 years of age were estimated to have some degree of malnutrition.

At first glance, the Somoza health system appears not to have been severely inadequate to the task of caring for the rather small population of 2.3 million. In 1977, there were fifty hospitals and clinics with a total of 4,675 beds, or 2 beds per 1,000 people. In 1975, it was estimated that there were a total of 1,357 doctors in Nicaragua, a fairly high average of 6 per

10,000 people. These figures compared very favorably with Guatemala and Honduras and not far below those of Costa Rica. Budgetary figures suggest that Nicaragua's health budgets were somewhat higher than those of Guatemala and Honduras, although they were considerably lower than those of Costa Rica. Nicaragua was spending between 15 and 20 percent of its national budget on health, or 2 to 4 percent of the GDP, compared to Costa Rica which spent around 30 percent of its national budget, or 5 to 6 percent of the GDP.[5]

Nicaragua, however, had an extremely inequitable health system. Like most public health systems, the Nicaraguan system did not serve the upper class—those who could easily afford private medical care and who could go to the United States for specialized treatment. Nevertheless, the system tended to favor the better-off middle classes in urban areas. For instance, the Social Security Institute (INSS) which, like most Latin American social security agencies, provided a significant portion of the medical care in the country—an estimated 40 percent of the health sector expenditures—served no more than 10 percent of the population.[6] This 10 percent was almost entirely urban employees in fairly secure jobs. While the public hospital system was officially responsible for both urban and rural areas, it overwhelmingly favored the former, a phenomenon not unusual in Central America but perhaps more extreme in Nicaragua. In 1973, over half of the hospital beds in the country were in the three major cities and only five health facilities with beds were in rural areas. Even the most simple facilities—the health centers without beds—were much more prevalent in urban than in rural areas. Only 35 of the 119 health centers were in rural areas and most were staffed with untrained auxiliary nurses. While Managua had only 25 percent of the population, 50 percent of the physicians and 70 percent of the professional nurses worked there. Urban areas had averages of more than 11 physicians per 10,000 population, while the countryside had 2.5 or fewer. Provision of potable water was also skewed toward urban areas, where most habitations had direct water connections, while only 14 percent in the rural areas had any access at all to potable water.

Inefficiency of the hospital system, again, is not unusual for Central America, but may have been even more extreme in Nicaragua. In spite of the large number of hospital beds in the country, there were only 4 reported hospital discharges per 1,000—compared to 26 discharges per 1,000 in Honduras.[7] Most health facilities were in extremely poor condition, lacked necessary equipment and medicines, and had very low utilization rates.

A general problem of public health systems in Latin America is that usually two major institutions are responsible for health facilities—the Ministry of Health and the Social Security Institute. This dual system often leads to duplication of services and tremendous inefficiencies. The Nicaraguan system was unusual in that it not only had this dual character but was actually even more fragmented. In addition to the Ministry of Health, which was primarily responsible for preventive medicine and small clinics, there were autonomous governing boards for each public hospital (nineteen Social Assistance Boards [JLAS]) and another national agency responsible for financing hospital construction through the national lottery (National Social Assistance Council [JNAPS]). This fragmentation added to the confusion in a sector which also had the Social Security Institute, an autonomous water and sewer agency, and military hospitals. Furthermore, even the Ministry of Health was fragmented internally with several vertically-run programs that functioned with relative autonomy. Like most other institutions in Nicaragua, the fragmented health system was dominated by personal associates of Somoza. His wife, Doña Hope, headed the hospital sector, and his last Minister of Health was one of his personal physicians.

What really set Somoza's Nicaragua apart from other Central American countries was that there was no major attempt to improve the system and redress the inequalities. In the early 1970s, Guatemala, Honduras, and Costa Rica began significant new programs that emphasized primary care and preventive activities for their extremely underserved rural areas. These programs actually did shift the expenditure patterns of the governments, demonstrating a major commitment to public-health programs for rural areas which was not apparent in Somoza's Nicaragua, where only a few small primary care programs were initiated in the late 1970s.

Insurrection and the Destruction of the Somoza Health System

The period of insurrection beginning after the assassination of Pedro Joaquín Chamorro had several implications for the future health system. It marked a period of brutal destruction of hospitals, raised the need for curative and rehabilitative services for those wounded in the war, weakened the capacity of the Somoza government to maintain even the inadequate services that existed, and inhibited small reform initiatives. On the positive side, it also marked a period of construction within the insurrectionary forces of a cadre of physicians and a model of volunteer community services.

During the period of intense struggle to control the major cities, the National Guard bombed many health facilities, resulting in the almost complete destruction of four major hospitals and considerable damage to several others. This destruction of already existing curative facilities led the new government to give considerable emphasis to reconstruction of hospitals.[8] Furthermore, during the war systems of supply and maintenance, never very effective, were allowed to deteriorate further as much of the materials and transportation were diverted toward supplying the National Guard.

The war also produced a tremendous number of casualties that required curative and rehabilitative services. After the Sandinista victory, three new centers for rehabilitation were created, but the need was much greater than these centers could meet. Some war victims were sent to Cuba, Spain, Costa Rica, and East Germany for special treatments, and teams of plastic surgeons visited from the United States.

The period of insurrection was also one in which part of the medical profession played a visible public role in opposition to Somoza. Although the traditional association of physicians, the *Colegio de Médicos*, was strongly Somocista (its president was one of Somoza's personal physicians), a second physician organization, more closely associated with the medical school of the National University, was openly opposed to the Somoza regime. This organization, the *Federación de Sociedades Medicales de Nicaragua*, however, was extremely weak and apparently did not play the radicalizing role that its counterpart in Cuba did.[9] The more important opposition came from the health workers' union, FETSALUD, which was dominated by nonphysician hospital staff. FETSALUD organized several long strikes in hospitals during the last years of the Somoza regime. While these strikes did not fully disrupt services, they did rally popular support in opposition to Somoza.

During the insurrectionary period, the Sandinista army, as well as other popular organizations, did attract and incorporate in its ranks many medically trained people. Physicians abandoned their practices to join the guerrilla fronts and care for the wounded. Medical students joined the organizing efforts and engaged in training of paraprofessionals. These activities not only involved care for the insurrectional military forces but also marked the beginnings of a popularly-oriented volunteer health system which would be expanded and institutionalized after the victory. As one official claimed: "The National Guard obliged us to create a cadre of health volunteers in each neighborhood." These volunteers were trained by medical students and nurses to treat the wounded, to organize community activities for emergency health needs, and to attempt to organize longer-term efforts to establish clean water supplies and sanitation. The health volunteers were part of the neighborhood Civil Defense Committees (CDC) which attempted to limit the damage of war in each locality and provided support for the guerrilla activities. At the end of the war, these community organizations were formalized as Sandinista Defense Committees (CDS) and the health volunteers were given responsibility for health activities in each committee.

First Steps Toward Building a New Health System

Even before the new Nicaraguan leadership left Costa Rica, it declared its commitment to improving the health of Nicaraguans. The government's program stated that the new regime would "stimulate and organize popular participation to solve the major national problems: hunger, unemployment, malnutrition, illness, illiteracy and housing—the despicable results of fifty years of *Somocismo."* One of the first acts of the government was to unite the fragmented health organizations of the Somoza period into a single system under the authority of the Ministry of Health. This gave the Ministry direct control over not only the hospitals in the two Social Assistance systems (JLAS and JNAPS) but also all of the Social Security (INSS) hospitals, ending the duplication of facilities and the preferential medical care for the small percentage of the population covered by Social Security. Furthermore, the new reorganization of the Ministry did away with the variety of semiautonomous vertical programs, all of which were to be fully integrated into the administrative structure of the Ministry.

During the first months, much of the activity of the Ministry was consumed by the need simply to respond to the most immediate pressing demands and to gain an understanding of the system. Most decisions appear to have been made through collective processes in innumerable meetings. No clear regular hierarchy of administration emerged and many officials were rotated from position to position before they found a more or less stable set of responsibilities. It was soon clear that central planning would be difficult in the absence of good information about the existing health system.

Following the Government's theme that emphasized reconstruction, the most immediate and pressing needs appeared to be for physicians and hospital care.[10] During the first months, the Ministry assessed the damage done to hospitals and almost immediately began reconstruction of the worst damaged. They were aided in these tasks by donations from West Germany, Sweden, and Switzerland. Also, in response to an international commitment of solidarity, the Ministry assumed responsibility for international brigades of more than 500 physicians who arrived from many countries.

There was a clear popular demand for these services. In sharp contrast to the underutilization of the Somoza health facilities, the government now found itself flooded with people in the hospitals and clinics around the country. People claimed that these services were now "theirs," and not Somoza's. The Ministry estimated that while the Somoza health system covered only 30 percent of the population, in the first few months of the Revolution the Ministry services were covering around 70 percent. Furthermore, the people were not simply waiting for the government to supply services. Many communities were using local resources—often the confiscated homes and goods of Somoza supporters who had left the country—to provide hospital beds, medicines, office equipment, refrigerators, and even buildings for clinics and warehouses. In spite of the willingness to use local resources for these facilities, this activity only increased the demands for the Ministry to supply the facilities with trained personnel (especially physicians), medicines, and other supplies for curative-oriented services.

The Ministry, however, did not devote itself entirely to curative activities. In the early months, the regime initiated three major programs in preventive medicine. It began a widespread vaccination campaign against polio, measles, and other infectious diseases, which reached an estimated 85 percent of the target population. In the first six months, a sanitation campaign distributed 4,200 latrines—twice the number the Somoza regime distributed in all of 1978. Using materials supplied by UNICEF, the Ministry established 250 centers for oral rehydration for the treatment of diarrhea. These centers, located in health facilities all over the country, provided an easily administered solution of salts and sugar which is perhaps the most effective and inexpensive means of reducing mortality from diarrhea.

The Ministry also took charge of the training of all health personnel. One of the early decisions was to encourage the medical school to increase the number of graduates from 50 per year to around 500. This decision may have been ill advised, since physicians only increased the demand for curative care; however, plans were made to increase the preventive medicine component of medical education and to discourage the pursuit of esoteric specialties. Efforts were also begun to improve the training and expand the number of nonphysician health workers, especially nurses and lab technicians. Since an estimated 70 percent of the auxiliary personnel in the Ministry had received no formal training, the Ministry also began an in-service training program for all auxiliaries.

Health activities were coordinated with other Ministries. The Ministry of Health contributed educational materials, first-aid instructions, and medicine for the *brigadistas* of the literacy campaign. Course materials on health were prepared for the regular instructional program of the Ministry of Education. The Ministry of Health coordinated with the Agrarian Reform Agency's program of mobile health units and with the Ministry of Labor on occupational health and safety.

Perhaps the most significant feature of the new health system was the open commitment to the participation of the community in health programs. As suggested earlier, the CDS and other mass organizations like the Association of Farm Workers (ATC), the Nicaraguan Women's Association (AMNLAE), and the local Councils of Reconstruction supported the activities of the Ministry of Health. From all reports, this participation was enthusiastic. Through these popular organizations the Ministry implemented its immunization campaigns, promoted the installation of latrines, distributed food supplements, and completed a census of children at risk. These organizations began their own initiatives in providing materials, labor, and equipment for construction of health posts and for preventive programs. They also took responsibility for assuring that price controls for some food items were respected. While it is clear that popular participation was more prevalent in some areas than others—rural areas were still weakly organized—and that the Ministry was often unable to respond to popular organization requests for supplies, equipment and manpower, the government clearly made a significant commitment to achieving massive popular participation at a level rarely achieved in other countries.

A final area of concern for the new regime was the improvement of planning and administration, which proved to be a major task. As noted above, the health system under Somoza was particularly inefficient and poorly administered. The information systems, essential for good planning and administration, were probably worse than those in other poor Central American countries like Guatemala and Honduras. The autonomous hospital boards each had different reporting and budgeting processes making comparisons and cost-effective analysis even more difficult than it is in other countries. Corruption and "phantom salaries" further undermined the reliability of past budgets. Although under United States AID prodding there had been one major effort at health planning in the mid-1970s, its results were never made public and the planning infrastructure collapsed during the insurrectional period.

When I was in Nicaragua, the health system still suffered from a lack of systematic information about details of its basic aspects: numbers of beds, types of facilities, medical supplies, and personnel. The inaccuracies of the Somoza system in this respect were compounded by war destruction and the spontaneous creation of new "hospitals" and clinics by the local community-based efforts.

In the absence of such specific data, health planning was practically impossible and efforts in this area were postponed. The one ministry official with any planning experience was still in charge of the ministry's planning office, but his major task was only to implement the Interamerican Development Bank loan for health-facility construction.

Shortage of administrative skills was also a problem. While many people in the Somoza ministry stayed on to contribute to Revolution, the most important decision-making positions at all levels tended to be taken over by a new group of officials with little administrative experience and almost no training in public health. Many, including the first Minister of Health, Dr. César Amador Kuhl, a neurosurgeon, were private physicians with highly technical specialties. Others were young recent graduates from medical school.

The lack of administrative and public health experience was partially compensated for by an enthusiastic collective decision-making process that particularly marked the early months of the regime. Workshops for both national and regional officials were held at least once a month. One workshop that I attended laid the basis for an information system that would support the administrative needs of the regional officials as well as provide information for future planning and programming at the national level. The meeting also allowed the regional officials to voice their concern with growing discontent over inequalities in the salary scales. It was clear that no firm hierarchy of administrative decisions had yet been established and that the national level was not rigidly imposing a predetermined policy on the regional offices. The effort emphasized the collective nature of the enterprise of problem-solving and decision-making. This process was later viewed as having a considerable cost in terms of time and efficiency, but it did contribute to knowledge sharing in the initial period when few could claim expertise or authority for decision-making. While efforts were being made to reduce the numbers of meetings and to establish some administrative skills and hierarchies, the decision-making process was developing so as to retain some of the benefits of collective involvement in programming Ministry activities.

The new health policy was first initiated without clear budget guidelines. By February 1980, however, the Ministry was beginning to draw up a budget for that fiscal year. The basis for the budget was the 1979 Somoza budget projections. It was clear that the budget allocation for the health sector would not be significantly higher than that allocated by the Somoza government. The revolutionary health policy would have to achieve its goals within these rather restrictive budgetary constraints.

Part of this budget was supported by international assistance. Immediate support from several European countries assisted in the reconstruction of hospitals destroyed during the war. UNICEF provided the materials for the oral rehydration program. CARE, the Red Cross, the World Food Program and others began several emergency feeding programs. In the first three months of the new regime, more than $1.6 million in medicines was received.

International agencies also began contributing to long-term efforts to improve the health services. Two AID loans that had been negotiated under Somoza had hardly been implemented. Almost $7 million remained to be renegotiated for health and nutrition purposes targeted toward primary care and rural areas. All of a previously signed $20 million loan from the Interamerican Development Bank remained and was to be spent mainly on construction of rural health posts and centers. In addition, the technical assistance of the Pan American Health Organization was increased to $1.5 million for 1980.

Revolutionary Health Policy

The new regime had clearly made progress toward achieving the goals of equity, prevention, and participation within a reasonable budget restraint. They made major advances over the previous regime's extremely inadequate system. More Nicaraguans, especially those in the lower classes, were being served in the hospitals and clinics. Immunization campaigns and other preventive programs were more widespread than they had been under Somoza. An extensive system of popular participation in health activities had begun. Furthermore, all this activity was apparently accomplished within a national budget not significantly greater than that of the Somoza regime. There remained, however, some critical problems which suggested that the initial policy was not as clearly oriented toward equity and prevention as it might have been. Although some activities were targeted for rural areas, by far the major emphasis was on providing care in the urban areas, leaving the urban-rural imbalance observed under Somoza virtually intact. In addition, while the revolution had begun preventive primary care programs (such as those of our energetic nurse cited above), such programs were still severely restricted in relation to the expenditures on curative care, especially for urban hospitals.

The central question for this analysis is why, when they had a chance early in the regime, did the Nicaraguan revolutionaries not choose to give greater emphasis to equity and prevention. One reason has to do with the apparent general policy commitment of the regime to restore basic services to their prewar status. Most government programs in other areas, not only health, emphasized "reconstruction" in 1980. The National Plan of Reconstruction clearly reflected this orientation. It included few original new programs, but rather was based largely on programs that were planned during the last two years of the Somoza regime. This general policy appeared to respond to the immediate demands from the crucial urban and semiurban areas from which the Revolution had drawn its initial and most important political support. In the health sector, it was this population that appeared to be flooding the hospitals which they now considered to be rightly theirs, and it was in these areas that the most widespread spontaneous creation of popular clinics occurred. In order to consolidate its base of support in the early period of the regime, the Nicaraguan revolutionary government emphasized an immediate response to this demand.

A second reason for this policy is in part the result of the administrative disarray during the initial period. The lack of administrative control implicit in this period made it necessary not to overextend the limited administrative capacity of the Ministry. Just getting a grip on this vast institutional structure was a difficult task for the incipient administration. In this confusion, two elements contributed to a lack of decisive commitment to prevention and equity. First, there was no clear budget or planning during the first six months. Choices were made without regard to trade-offs and implied future costs. Decisions to rebuild urban hospitals and train more physicians were made without analyzing how much they would cost in the long run and how much they would take away from the possibility of achieving equity and prevention. A demonstration of this lack of an appreciation of trade-offs occurred when the Ministry finally began drawing up its budget in February 1980. It was soon found that simply maintaining the previous budget for existing and reconstructed hospitals would require the entire Ministry allocation of the National Budget. When this constraint was discovered, the Ministry had to begin searching for ways to cut hospital expenses in order to free funds for at least some of the ambitious preventive programs under consideration. The government was beginning to learn how difficult it is to achieve equity and prevention within reasonable budgetary constraints.

During the initial period of administrative confusion, a second condition shaped health policy. The new team of policy-makers was made up almost entirely of physicians whose training was primarily curative-oriented. Furthermore, very few of the top-level officials had received any training in the preventive-oriented public health field. Without clear indications of the need for trade-offs, physicians as policy-makers are especially likely to respond to a demand for curative care.[11] I found an illustrative example of this orientation during a discussion of the potential contribution of the Harvard School of Public Health to the Nicaraguan revolution, when a high official suddenly changed the theme, urging me to assist him to obtain high-cost, high-technology cancer treatment equipment. He did not realize the incongruity of the request, nor the continual drain on the Ministry budget such an investment implied.

What was the potential for a change in health policy toward a greater commitment to equity and prevention? A shift in policy would have been difficult. Already in February 1980, there were growing pressures to increase, not decrease, the emphasis on hospital care in urban areas. These demands, somewhat ironically, were in part the result of the unification of the health sector under the Ministry of Health. The Ministry, having united twenty-three separate semiautonomous institutions, inherited twenty-three separate salary scales. In some cases, the salary differential for personnel with the same qualifications was 300 to 400 percent. This situation soon resulted in an intense demand for an equalization of the wage scales, a demand which could only be achieved through increasing the lower salaries and thereby increasing the total cost of the hospital sector.

The unification of the health sector also had the consequence of increasing popular pressure to raise the overall level of curative services to the relatively high standards and high costs of hospitals that had belonged to the Social Security Institute. Those who previously had benefited from these privileged services found it difficult to accept less adequate services in the unified system, and they made public their complaints. The public outcry—voiced by both the government and opposition press—put tremendous pressure on the Ministry to place more emphasis on these traditional curative services.[12]

There were, however, some reasons to expect that the initial policy could change significantly in the future. Growing awareness of budgetary constraints and the need to limit costs in the hospital sector in order to achieve goals of prevention and equity, as well as a growing administrative capacity to manage new programs, were likely to have an impact on policy-making. Perhaps a more potent source of change could come from a more active participation in health policy by the Sandinistas, the FSLN, who would have the political capacity to restrict responses to popular demands in urban areas and to resist physician preference for curative policies.

During the first months of the new regime, the health sector was not a priority sector for the FSLN. Few FSLN members were assigned to the Ministry. Gradually the FSLN increased its presence in the Ministry, until by mid-1980 the neurosurgeon who had been Minister had been replaced by

Leah Guido, a Sandinista leader who was not a physician. Also, in the *Junta de Gobierno*, Daniel Ortega of the FSLN assumed greater responsibility for health activities.

The FSLN, more than the physicians in the Ministry, had an interest in imposing its national austerity program and enforcing trade-off choices in the health sector. With pressing needs for national resources in productive sectors and concern for restrictions on foreign exchange, the FSLN could reorient Ministry priorities away from high-cost, low-effectiveness curative services and toward more equitable, more preventive programs. Also, using its greater influence in mass organizations, the FSLN could place emphasis on channeling popular participation toward preventive activities and away from the creation of new clinics. Such efforts, for instance in the Farm Workers' Associations (ATC), had achieved a widespread recognition of the need for workers to increase production while restricting demand for wage increases. A similar effort directed toward health activities in popular organizations could relieve the explosive demand for hospital care by redoubling the kind of preventive activities that occupied the nurse at this chapter's beginning.

The Nicaraguan Revolution has taught us the difficulty of achieving revolutionary goals in health policy. It had achieved great advances over the Somoza regime's health policies, but it still faced difficult choices if it was to achieve greater emphasis on preventive programs and equal distribution of services. In 1980, the Revolution was still in progress; its truly innovative stages were likely to come in the future.

Footnotes

[1] There is a growing literature on international health and primary care. See, for example, World Health Organization and United Nations Children's Fund, *Primary Health Care* (Geneva: World Health Organization, 1978); World Bank, *Health Sector Policy Paper* (Washington, D.C.: World Bank, 1980).

[2] See Tomas McKeown, *The Role of Medicine: Dream, Mirage or Nemesis?* (Oxford: Basil Blackwell, 1979); also, Davidson R. Gwatkin, Janet R. Wilcox, and Joe D. Wray, *Can Health and Nutrition Interventions Make a Difference?* (Washington, D.C.: Overseas Development Council, 1980).

[3] On Cuba, see Ross Danielson, *Cuban Medicine* (New Brunswick, N.J.: Transaction Books, 1979); and Vincente Navarro, "Health, Health Services, and Health Planning in Cuba," *International Journal of Health Services*, II, 3 (1972), pp. 397-432. On China see Victor W. Sidel and Ruth Sidel, *Serve the People: Observations on Medicine in the People's Republic of China* (New York: Josiah Macy, Jr. Foundation, 1973); and Pi-chao Chen, *Population and Health Policy in the People's Republic of China* (Washington, D.C.: Smithsonian Institution, 1976). On Tanzania, see Oscar Gish, *Planning the Health Sector: The Tanzanian Experience* (London: Croom Helm, 1975).

[4] Nicaraguan health figures from República de Nicaragua, Ministerio de Salud Pública, *Proyecto de mejoramiento de servicios rurales de salud*, and *Informe sobre el estado de salud en Nicaragua 1974-1977* (Managua, 1977); Junta Nacional de Asistencia y Previsión Social,

Anuario Estadístico 1974 (Managua, June 1975); Office of International Health, United States Department of Health, Education and Welfare, *Syncresis: The Dynamics of Health. An Analytical Series on the Interactions of Health and Socioeconomic Development: Nicaragua* (Washington: U.S. Government Printing Office, 1974).

⁵ Comparative budgetary figures from Thomas Bossert, *The State and International Agencies in Central America: Comparative Health Policy-Making* (in progress).

⁶ Interview with the Director of INSS, Reinaldo Antonio Téfel, February, 1980. See also Mark Rosenberg, "Social Reform in the New Nicaragua" (unpublished manuscript, 1980).

⁷ Ministerio de Salud Pública, *Proyecto*; República de Honduras; and Ministerio de Salud Pública y Asistencia Social, *Memoria Anual 1978* (Tegucigalpa, 1979).

⁸ República de Nicaragua, Junta de Gobierno de Reconstrucción Nacional, Ministerio de Salud, *La salud en Nicaragua antes y después del triunfo de la revolución* (Managua, 1980).

⁹ See Ross Danielson, *Cuban Medicine.*

¹⁰ Following figures from Ministerio de Salud, *La salud en Nicaragua*, and *Boletín Informativo*, Nos. 1-7 (1979-80).

¹¹ On this issue, see Antonio Ugalde, "The Role of the Medical Profession in Public Health Policy-Making: The Case of Colombia," *Social Science and Medicine*, 13C,² (June 1979), pp. 109-119.

¹² Various issues of *Barricada, La Prensa, Nuevo Diario.*

Chapter 15

Housing Policy
in Revolutionary Nicaragua

HARVEY WILLIAMS

Rapid growth and urbanization in developing countries has put considerable strain on the economic and political organizations concerned with providing basic necessities to an expanding and shifting population. The area of provision of shelter and services, requiring extensive capital expenditures and providing little direct or immediate economic return, has presented a particularly difficult challenge. Nicaragua, with its recent natural and social upheavals, provides an interesting case for examination.

General Background

In mid-1980, the Population Reference Bureau estimated Nicaragua's population at 2.569 million. The fertility rate (47 per 1,000 population) was the highest in Latin America. Although the mortality rate (12 per 1,000 population) was also high, the rate of natural increase (3.5 percent) was still the highest in Latin America and represented a considerable increase over the average rate of 2.78 percent between 1963 and 1971.[1] In spite of this, the population density of approximately 45 per square mile was the lowest in Central America.

The Inter-American Development Bank (IDB) noted that the agricultural sector, the basis of the Nicaraguan economy, generated more than two-thirds of the merchandise exports and had shown consistent growth over the preceding fifteen years. At the same time, rural-to-urban migration had been heavy. The economically active population in agriculture had declined dramatically, from 67.7 percent in 1950; to 59.6 percent in 1963; to 46.4 percent in 1971; to 42 percent in 1978. At the same time, the population living in places of 20,000 or more inhabitants had increased from less than 30 percent in 1960 to 48 percent in 1973, to 55.5 percent in 1978.[2]

The process of urbanization in Nicaragua had been dominated by its capital, Managua, a classic example of a primate city.[3] Managua's popula-

Research for the preparation of this article was supported in part by the Center for Latin American Studies, Stanford University, and by a professional development grant from the University of the Pacific. The author acknowledges the kind and extensive cooperation of the people of Nicaragua.

tion passed 50,000 in 1940 and 250,000 in 1963, and its estimated population at the end of 1972 was over 400,000.[4] In more recent years, it had grown at an average annual rate exceeding 8 percent. With an estimated 1980 population of 650,000, Managua accounted for more than 60 percent of Nicaragua's total population increase for the period. Managua was nearly ten times as large as Nicaragua's second city, León.

Housing conditions in Nicaragua were poor. According to data from the national housing census of 1963, the government had calculated a housing deficit of 181,700 units, and it was estimated the demographic growth alone would increase the deficit by an average of 10,000 units per year for the next ten years. In reviewing the data from the 1971 national census, the Nicaraguan Demographic Association noted the following housing conditions: 61 percent had dirt floors; 36 percent lacked access to potable water; 59 percent had no electricity; 46 percent had no sanitary facilities (even a latrine); 68 percent had only one or two rooms; and in 23 percent five or more persons lived in a single room. While acknowledging the construction of 58,114 housing units and extension of electricity and other services over the 1963-71 period, the Association pointed out that only the growth of access to potable water increased more rapidly than the new demand created by demographic growth.[5]

Developments Following the 1972 Earthquake

The earthquake of December 1972 caused enormous destruction in Managua. Approximately 8,000 were killed. Of the total estimated urbanized area of 33 square kilometers, over 80 percent was damaged. The older central core of the city, representing 40 percent of the area, was almost totally destroyed. Some 75 percent of the housing stock was destroyed or seriously damaged, leaving about 250,000 persons without shelter. The total value of losses was estimated by the Central American Institute of Business Administration (INCAE) at $844.8 million (U.S.).[6]

The 1972 earthquake affected the urban development of Managua in several ways. First, the nearly complete destruction of the central core, its subsequent demolition, and the government's interdiction against new construction there until an urban reconstruction plan could be developed accelerated the trend toward decentralization and deconcentration. The narrow streets, congestion, high-density housing, and small commerce found in other cities was no longer to be found in Managua. Second, the earthquake destroyed much of the older housing. In most cities, such housing has been converted into high-density tenements, or *vecindades*. In Managua, this possibility was eliminated. Finally, the disaster increased the housing deficit by some 40,000 units. The IDB reported that the "earthquake exacerbated the urban housing deficit, which increased 78 percent in 1973, to 115,720 units."[7] Whether one uses the term "housing deficit" to refer to merely the demand for shelter, or employs a broader definition which includes infrastructure and support networks, the earthquake added to an already serious national problem.

It was decided that Managua would be rebuilt on the same site rather than relocated. Various governmental agencies took the responsibility for planning and directing the reconstruction efforts, with little success and without controlling corruption and private interests. While spontaneous settlements and organized land invasions, so common in other Latin American cities, were greatly restricted by the government, very little central planning was evident in the commercial and housing construction sector. The government's infrastructure projects, particularly the construction and improvement of a system of circumferential and radial roads, had an indirect influence on construction, but most such construction was determined by individual decisions and market factors. While some private land holders sold whole or subdivided parcels at various locations around the city, others withheld sale or development hoping for greater profits as Managua extended itself around and beyond them. This pattern of development gave Managua a strange and unique appearance, as was noted by a member of a visiting Cuban delegation:

> The already sprawling capital was totally dispersed by the '72 earthquake. The various sections were rebuilt in haphazard fashion. There's no such thing as the urban conglomerate we're accustomed to seeing, but rather built-up areas separated by empty lots, giving the impression of a suburb.[8]

The government's attempt to control the quality of construction with the adoption of an earthquake code modeled after that of California met with little success. The high cost of conforming and the bureaucratic problems involved in inspections and obtaining building permits discouraged most builders, and it was soon discovered that enforcement of the code was sporadic and usually directed only at those foolish enough to apply for building permits.

Post-Earthquake Housing Construction: The Public Sector

Actual housing construction occurred in three areas: the public sector, the formal private sector, and the informal private sector. The public-sector construction took place under the direction of the Housing Institute (INVI). In the period 1959-72, INVI had completed only 7637 low-cost housing units.[9] In the period 1973-78, aided by significant financial support from international resources, many damaged units were repaired, and over 27,000 new units were completed. Most of these were constructed in Managua, although 3,100 units were completed in other cities to accomodate refugees.[10] Nearly half of the Managua housing projects were represented by the 11,132-unit Las Américas projects. The Las Américas projects, financed by USAID, were inexpensive and hastily built wooden structures with dirt floors and no indoor services. These were designed as temporary housing for urban workers, to be converted later to permanent, completely serviced units. The conversion process was still far from completion in July 1979.

INVI housing was designed to meet the needs for the low-income population, but in its distribution of housing (with the exception of the Las Américas projects) INVI was criticized for favoring military and governmental personnel, and other political favorites, over lower-income families. In 1974, INCAE conducted a sample survey of low-income neighborhoods which revealed that 96.7 percent of the Las Américas residents and 91.3 percent of the residents in privately constructed housing met their definition for low-income-families (household income of 1,200 córdobas or less per month, estimated to include 70 percent of Managua's population), while only 71.4 percent of the INVI housing residents did.[11] This suggests some support for the argument that a considerable percentage of the low-income public housing did not accomodate the low-income population.

The contribution of the public sector to the reduction of the housing deficit was not substantial. In spite of the large quantity (much of which did not meet minimum housing standards), the construction did not even replace the earthquake losses, while the estimated increase in the deficit from demographic growth was greater than twice the INVI construction.

The Private Sector

Housing construction in developing countries is extremely difficult to estimate because so much of it is done without going through formal channels (even where these exist). While records of public-sector housing construction are usually available and fairly accurate, private-sector construction reports leave much to be desired. Housing construction by private construction companies will be referred to as the "formal private sector;" construction by home owners or self-employed skilled and semiskilled laborers will be referred to as the "informal private sector."

The Formal Private Sector

During the later years of the Alliance for Progress, the strategy of promoting private housing construction through savings-and-loan associations in Latin America gained popularity. Capitalization from international sources such as USAID and IDB was not uncommon. In 1967, USAID approved a loan to Nicaragua in the amount of $3.7 million (U.S.) for the development of savings-and-loan associations. Between 1967 and the end of 1972, loans from these associations financed the construction of 3,077 housing units. These units were designed for middle-class families and had an average value more than four times that of the average value per unit of INVI housing constructed during the same period.[12] Very few of these middle-class housing units were destroyed by the earthquake. Although there was considerable damage to many, they were all insured as a mortgage requirement, and nearly all were restored in a reasonable period of time.

After a slow start due to government restrictions and confusion relating to the new seismic code and proposed urban plan, the construction sponsored by savings-and-loan associations continued at a pace somewhat greater than during the previous period. Approximately 3,500 units were completed by the end of 1975, and an estimated 11,000 units by 1979. Nearly all of this housing was constructed in several fully serviced tracts located on the outskirts of Managua.

The Informal Private Sector

Although there has been a considerable amount written describing the organization of Latin American low-income urban neighborhoods, the actual contribution of the low-income residents to their own housing construction is rarely documented. Data from Nicaragua indicated that the informal private sector accounted for a substantial percentage of the total, but exact figures were not given.[13] Using the figures for housing stock following the earthquake (20,000 units), plus the documented and estimated construction (35,000 units), and subtracting this figure from the demand created by the estimated 1980 Managua population, it can be concluded that more than 50,000 housing units were constructed in Managua by the informal private sector. While this is significantly more than the combined construction of the public and formal private sectors, it is not unusual.[14]

The INCAE survey of low-income housing sheds considerable light on the production of the informal private sector. The Somoza government was quite intolerant of squatters, and large-scale organized land invasions were virtually unknown. Of the 977 families interviewed, only 5.3 percent were classified as squatters. Those who lived in *cuarterías* (single-storied building of adjoining single-room rental units facing a common patio area) represented 8.3 percent. Other renters represented 13.3 percent, and families sharing or borrowing represented 15.6 percent (the latter is a reflection of instability and housing shortage only fifteen months after the earthquake). More than half (57 percent) were classified as homeowners; and 10.7 percent of the 977 families lived in INVI housing. Most of the squatters, and most of the rental units (including nearly all of the *cuarterías*) were located near the old urban core, whereas the majority of the owner-occupied housing was located beyond the periphery.[15]

The large majority of the squatters lived in marginal areas, in small, very densely populated groups. In most areas, the housing was so irregularly constructed and dense as to severely limit vehicular traffic. The typical squatter's shelter was constructed by the family of occupancy, and was a free-standing one-room unit made of unfinished lumber, with a roof of zinc-coated metal and a dirt floor. Surprisingly, most had access to electricity (although frequently pirated) and many had piped potable water. Since the earthquake, there had been some increase in more isolated squatters' housing, particularly in areas near the old central core where partial destruction left vacant lots.

Cuarterías were much less concentrated than squatter's settlements, and there were infrequently more than one on any block. They generally served as short-term residences. The 1974 survey showed that nearly 80 percent of the *cuartería* families had not resided there in 1972. And while nearly 35 percent of the other families had lived in the same house since before 1965, none of the *cuartería* residents had.[16] Interestingly, in 1974, *cuarterías*, relative to the squatters' shelters, were better constructed and well-serviced. Of the survey sample, all had potable water and electricity, and over 95 percent had sewage connections.[17] This relatively positive situation in 1974 was partially a function of the *cuarterías* being located near the developed central area, and was due in part to the destruction of most of the worst *cuarterías* by the earthquake. Many newer but less-well-serviced *cuarterías* had been constructed since that time by the informal private sector.

Even prior to the earthquake, migration to Managua was putting pressure on the densely populated central core. A number of land holders and speculators had opened tracts of land beyond the periphery of the city, selling small unimproved plots to low-income families. Down-payments and monthly quotas were generally low and within the reach of families with some regularly employed members. It was estimated that about 20 percent of the city's population had lived in these neighborhoods in 1972 and that these areas had absorbed the bulk of the increase in population since the earthquake.[18]

Nearly all of these developments were *repartos ilegales* (illegal subdivisions), meaning that the subdividers had not complied with the regulations of the urban code, had not provided any services beyond the designation of roadways, and had not paid taxes owed on the land. The Somoza government was concerned about this unplanned and uncontrolled increase, particularly because of the demand which was created for extensive networks of services. The government maintained that the subdividers should be responsible for the costs of provision of services, either by installing services directly, or by paying the taxes owed so that the government could use these funds to cover the cost of installing services. The subdividers maintained that they would not be able to pay the taxes owed until they sold the plots of land. But many residents withheld payments to the subdividers when promised services were not installed, causing the subdividers to claim that they still could not pay the taxes or provide the services. For political and practical reasons, little was done to force payment from the subdividers and the government bore the costs of service network installation where they were completed.

Most of the owner-occupied housing in the *repartos ilegales* was constructed by the family, with occasional outside help. While not as well constructed as the INVI housing, the quality was considerably better than that of the squatter settlements. There also was observed a strong tendency for owner-occupied housing to be upgraded by the residents, and the quality of construction and access to services increased over time. Although there were some special loan programs for housing construction and improvement available to low-income families, their impact was very limited. More than 90 percent of the low-income families who obtained loans for construction or improvements used noninstitutional sources.[19]

An analysis of the Managua post-earthquake housing development based on the foregoing information reveals that an estimated 85,000 units were constructed. Of these, roughly 15 percent were fully serviced middle- and upper-class housing constructed by the formal private sector, 15 percent were fully serviced public-sector housing for lower-middle-income familes, and 15 percent were temporary, marginally serviced emergency public-sector housing for low-income families.

The remaining approximately 55 percent was accounted for by the informal private sector, and consisted primarily of low-income owner-constructed and occupied units with limited services, plus some squatter settlements and new *cuarterías*. This activity did little to reduce the calculated housing deficit, while other factors made the situation worse. Following the 1979 triumph, the new Ministry of Housing and Human Settlements (MINVAH) reported that 4,149 houses in urban centers were damaged severely or destroyed in the prolonged Popular War;[20] and heavy flooding in the northeast coastal area left 30,000 persons homeless in late 1979. Thus the new Government of National Reconstruction and MINVAH faced an extremely serious housing situation during the first year.

Urban Development and Housing Policy
under the Government of National Reconstruction

Following the defeat of the Somoza government in mid-1979, the Government of National Reconstruction developed policies and implemented programs directed toward the defense, consolidation, and advancement of the Revolution through its Program of Economic Reactivation in Benefit of the People. The program identified the following as major objectives for MINVAH:

(a)   Initiation of a territorial ordering of human settlements with the goal of reinforcing production, improving the life conditions of the population centers of the interior of the country. . . .

(b)   Planning and massive construction of popular housing in the city of Managua in order to attend in part to the deficit inherited from the Somoza dictatorship. . . .

(c)   To impel an *Urban Reform* that permits the distribution of the benefits of urbanization to all social sectors. . . .[21]

When MINVAH policies were examined at the end of the first year of the new government, the most evident fact was that the policies were still in a state of development. Both within the Ministry and in its relationships with other sectors of the government, policies were still being discussed and developed, and organizational relationships and responsibilities were still being formalized. As of September 1980, there was no formal policy statement. Interviews with MINVAH personnel in May and September 1980 plus two informal documents provided by the Ministry are the primary sources of information for this summary and analysis.

Following the major objectives set for it by the Ministry of Planning, MINVAH directed its attention to developing policies in three major areas: national development, urban reform, and housing.

National Development

MINVAH recognized its responsibilities within the programs of national and regional development. These programs were directed toward economic reactivation and development, particularly in the agricultural and agro-industrial fields. The Ministry of Agricultural Development (MIDA) and the National Institute of Agrarian Reform (INRA) had been identified as the agencies of primary responsibility for these programs. MINVAH described its role as one of cooperating with these institutions in the overall planning, and of taking the responsibility for the planning and development of the actual housing developments and their supportive infrastructure.

In these activities, the Ministry proposed to work closely with the representative organizations, the Programmatic Coordinating Committees (CPC), at the national, regional, and sectorial level. MINVAH identified several organizational relationships between itself and other institutions requiring greater clarifications and agreement. It suggested that Managua be designated as a special case by the Ministry of Planning and that a special CPC be created to study its development plan.

Urban Reform

Most of MINVAH's responsibilities and structure had been inherited from two agencies of the previous government, the Vice-Ministry of Urban Planning (VMPU) and the National Housing Bank and its National Housing Institute. It should not be surprising, then, that its policies in urban reform and housing had been developed more elaborately than those in the relatively new area of national development. MINVAH identified urban reform as a key element in the new government's program. "The process of national transformation and reconstruction has two fundamental complementary pillars that ought to work in close coordination: the Agrarian Reform and the Urban Reform."[22] Urban reform policies were described as having two key components: the regulation of urban and suburban land use, and the resolution of the immediate housing needs of the urban popular sectors.

Regulation of Urban and Suburban land. Urban reforms were defined as an instrument of the State which would be used to alter the system inherited from the previous regime so that the benefits of urbanization would be accessible to all. In particular, MINVAH identified the free-market system of property ownership and exchange as the basic factor responsible for irrational urban development. It declared that urban land represents a social need to which everyone has a right, and that it should not be a commodity subject to the vagaries of the market place. For that reason, policies were to be developed which would strengthen the state's control over urban land use, tenure, and transfer. The several policies included reforms which would tax the value added to property through urban development and capital investment by the state, appropriate land for the common benefit of the people, establish limits of private ownership of land, regulate urban growth and land utilization, and create a Land Bank.

MINVAH cited as the principal goal of urban land regulation the elimination of private profit generated from increases in market value. Nonetheless, it included private property under collective administration. State property would consist of property formerly controlled by the State, property confiscated since the revolution, and other properties donated or otherwise to be acquired. Individual property under collective administration would consist of property in *repartos ilegales,* squatter settlements, and *cuarterías.* Among policies to be considered further were the prohibition against the sale of individual property held under collective administration, and the freezing of prices of land held as private property.

As part of the effort to promote some of these policies, the Junta of the Government of National Reconstruction issued Decree no. 138, the Law Concerning Donations of Property within the Remains of the Urban Center of the City of Managua.[23] This law provided strong encouragement and incentives for the donation to the state of properties within the nearly destroyed city center. All past-due taxes were to be excused; all costs of transfer were to be borne by the State; and a 10-percent tax credit was to be granted to the donor. With greater direct control of the land, the Junta felt that it would be able to promote the redevelopment of the urban center which still had intact much of the pre-earthquake infrastructure. According to MINVAH, the law had a moderate effect. By May 1980, after the time limit for donations had expired, the state controlled almost half the urban core area. Some 10 percent of this had come from donations, representing about 1,000 of the 6,000 parcels. Work had already begun on a housing project, and a large park had been established.

In addition to these donated properties, MINVAH estimated that approximately 3,500 houses had been confiscated through the country. Many had been owned by those in the Somoza regime. Others were confiscated when review of the savings-and-loan associations' mortgage accounts revealed that certain favored persons had been allowed to default on their payments without losing possession.

Programs for the Satisfaction of Immediate Housing Needs. MINVAH proposed several policies in response to the needs of the low-income urban residents. Only two months after the triumph, the Junta announced Decree no. 97, the Law of *Repartos Ilegales.*[24] This law placed all *repartos ilegales* under the control of the state, to be administered by MINVAH. Thenceforth all land-purchase payments were to be made to the Ministry of Housing rather than to the subdivider. An account was established for each *reparto.* The law stated that although the subdividers had no further jurisdiction over the land, they were to be held responsible for complete infrastructure installation. If the payments from the residents were not sufficient to cover infrastructure costs, the subdivider was to be held liable. (In the unlikely case that payments exceeded costs, the surplus was to be returned to the subdivider.)

In January 1980, the Junta published Decree no. 2, the Rental Law, which established rent controls.[25] All rentals up to $50 per month (U.S.) were reduced by 50 percent, and those between $50 and $100 per month were reduced by 40 percent. For all other rentals over $100 in Managua ($50 elsewhere), the maximum allowable annual rent was set at 5 percent of the assessed value of the property, or, if the house had been financed by the National Financing System (SFN), the rent charged could not exceed the mortgage payment. The law restricted the landlord's ability to evict tenants and prohibited collection of rent in advance or suspension of electrical or water services. Houses without sanitary facilities could not be rented. A later decree restructured mortgages owed to the SFN, reducing the interest, excusing up to eighteen months of nonpayment and allowing an extension of the repayment to a maximum of twenty years.[26]

Proposed policies of MINVAH placed a very heavy emphasis on the participation of the residents through the mass organizations, particularly the CDS (Sandinist Defense Committees). Each neighborhood had a central committee made up of the representatives of the many block CDS. The proposed policies required that all requests for support for community improvements be processed through the CDS. It was the responsibility of the CDS to promote the cooperation of all residents in the planning and installation of community improvements. Since funds for improvements were to be generated from the land payments now directed to MINVAH, it was also the responsibility of the CDS to promote and encourage prompt and regular payments.

Housing Policy

Housing policy was seen as an integral part of the broader national program for social and economic reforms. Housing was defined broadly to include not only shelter, but also "the infrastructure, the material, the streets and other urban services and spaces which serve them and which articulate them to the rest of the community and to the urban structure."[27] At the same time, MINVAH took care to clarify the relative position of housing within the range of national economic and social needs. It was accepted that items of higher priority in social and economic reform would leave relatively few financial resources with which to confront the tremendous growing housing deficit, and the similarly expanding need for creation and improvement in the broad range of supportive infrastructure.

The emerging housing policies seemed to have been formulated to confront what the United Nations had identified as the three fallacies of urban development: the fallacy of priority to economic efficiency rather than social development; the fallacy of uncoordinated, piecemeal, remedial action; and the fallacy of *laissez-faire*, "the expectation that somehow urbanization will take care of itself."[28] The new policy strongly emphasized integrated planning and programs which complemented each other as well as those of other ministries and agencies. Thus housing programs were not to be developed in isolation, but rather were to be parts of long-range plans for economic, social, and political development. Although a similar approach had been articulated by VMPU under Somoza's regime, very little of the planning had become reality.[29] After only one year, MINVAH had accomplished more than its predecessor, both in terms of policy development and project initiation.

General Policy Aims. Most of the housing policy aims reflected two principles: integrated planning, and maximization of limited resources. Housing programs which addressed the needs of the workers in the productive sectors were emphasized, as were programs which integrated urban marginal populations and which reinforced the political development of the mass organizations.

Rather than proposing extensive construction of housing by the public sector, the policies of MINVAH proposed structural reforms and long-range developments which would not require massive capital expenditures. While some public-sector housing was proposed to meet immediate emergency needs, most policy stressed planning to reduce the costs of self-help community construction and to promote efficient use of available resources. A program of "densification" called for controlled and planned utilization of urban land to reduce dispersion of the population over a large area so that the cost of the infrastructure could be reduced. Housing developments would be proposed to fill in the vacant spaces created by the earthquake and by the irrational hodge-podge expansion which followed, and priority would be given to maximizing the utilization of the existing infrastructure, such as that within the old central core, rather than to the creation of new networks. New housing would be designed to promote progressive social development. Projects and programs which reinforced community support and interaction, such as apartment units and individual units with communal social and recreational areas, were to be given priority over those which followed the traditional separation and individuality of the residences.

MINVAH proposed programs that would investigate the development of appropriate technology, which would encourage utilization and adaptation of local materials and by-products for construction, and which would promote the development of local industry for the production of construction materials. Programs were proposed for research and the training of technicians who would be made available to CDS for assistance in planning and implementing community development. Consistent emphasis was placed on the involvement of the mass organizations, particularly the CDS, in all phases of housing activity.

Several proposals for structural innovations were made by MINVAH. A Land Bank was proposed for the better control of land use. It was proposed that the resources of the National Financing System (SNF) be extended to a broader range of housing and that the SNF be responsible for the development of financing policies which would be rational, effective, flexible, and low-interest. Support of the Materials Bank was proposed so that construction materials could be made easily available at reasonable prices. In addition, the Ministry proposed continued support for the development of Urban Service Centers—satellite aggregations of health services, schools, child-care centers, and other social services.

MINVAH proposed close coordination of housing policy and urban reform policy through programs for the consolidation of *repartos ilegales,* the renovation of *cuarterías,* and the consolidation or relocation of squatter settlements.

Program Implementation. One year after the defeat of the Somoza regime, several housing policy decisions were in the process of being actualized. Reconstruction and repair of nearly 5,000 of the low-income houses destroyed or damaged in the War of National Liberation was approaching completion. At one of the sugar refineries, the construction of 100 houses for workers had been initiated in cooperation with INRA, and the construction of 500 houses for mine workers of the eastern coast was underway. In the city of León, a 554-house low-income project was under construction and a second project of 200 houses was about to be started.

In Managua, the first project for the consolidation of a squatter settlement was past mid-completion. In the *barrio* José I. Gómez, 463 houses were being constructed in an open pattern with communal areas between them. One-half of the houses had been constructed on open land adjacent to the existing neighborhood. The CDS had been active in the preparation of the land and in supporting the governmental construction teams. Plans called for moving the residents from the old houses into the new or into temporary shelters while the old area was demolished. The ground was to be prepared and the remaining houses constructed for those living in temporary shelters. This project demonstrated MINVAH's policies of active mass organization participation and of minimal dislocation in dealing with the problems of squatters' settlements. Wherever possible, squatters' settlements were to be rebuilt on or near their present locations. Also in Managua, ground had been broken for a low-income housing project of

1,800 houses, and plans were progressing for governmental construction of 550 multistory units in the old central core area. Both projects were intended to serve persons presently living in squatter settlements which had been evaluated as too precarious to be upgraded.

The experience gained during the emergency repair and reconstruction activities had demonstrated the viability of the CDS in housing and community development, and had shown that the concept of a Materials Bank was effective. Several CDSs in Managua, Masaya, and other cities were actively engaged in planning or implementing community development projects with MINVAH support, and Urban Service Centers were being completed in several barrios.

Notably absent from both policy and programs were "sites and services" strategies, suggested by many as one of the most reasonable and efficient ways of developing low-income housing.[30] In the "sites and services" approach, the government is usually responsible for the acquisition and subdivision of an area, the installation of community infrastructure, and the provision of a parcel of land with minimum service connections (and sometimes a basic shelter) for each family. The residents are responsible for expansion and improvements. MINVAH suggested that such programs might be developed in the future, but only within a community organization program. The inherent potential of such programs to promote individualism and discourage community participation[31] were to be avoided by careful planning and consideration.

Some Comparative Perspectives

While there was no denying that the Nicaraguan situation was unique, and that there were few recent Latin American examples which were even similar, certain parallel situations in Nicaragua, Cuba, and Chile provided comparative perspective.[32] MINVAH policies appeared to have drawn heavily upon these examples in developing the Nicaraguan response. Resemblances to Cuba and Allende's Chile included emphasis on an integrated national development plan with agrarian reform as a key element; concentration on rural population for efficient agricultural production; early establishment of rent control; control of speculation in land and housing construction; extension of services and infrastructure to the masses; and governmental control of land development emphasizing rational use and densification. The similarities between Cuba and Nicaragua, especially the rent-control law and the common emphasis on revolutionary defense committees in both countries, had led some to suggest that the Nicaraguan policies were replications of those in Cuba. Closer examination revealed that while there were similarities, there were also significant differences. Nothing in the MINVAH policies, for example, called for the establishment of micro-brigades for construction of workers' housing as had been done in Cuba. The Nicaraguan policies stressed a slow, long-range development plan, whereas the early Cuban policies emphasized heavy public investment in housing construction. Although there were constraints on speculation by the private sector, private-sector construction was not only tolerated but encouraged in Nicaragua. And whereas early Cuban policy provided compensation and lifetime pensions to former urban property owners, Nicaraguan policy required former urban property owners to compensate the state for necessary improvements.

Problems and Prospects

Although progress had been made by the new government and MINVAH through the first year, several problem areas impeded development and implementation of housing policy. These lay in the areas of organization, popular support, and financial resources.

Organization

The Revolution had been successful in its major objective: the defeat and expulsion of the Somoza government. But the government which came to power under the JGRN inherited an organizational structure ill-equipped to initiate radical reforms. Most of the higher-ranking officials of the former government had left the country, and those at all levels who remained with the new government had had little experience developing change-oriented programs under the highly centralized and conservative Somoza regime. The new government had to reorganize most ministries and governmental agencies and to create several new ones. With new organization and new personnel, the process of developing roles and responsibilities during the first year made policy formulation and implementation difficult. This was further complicated by the lack of a Sandinist political tradition. The efforts to develop the definitions and directions of the new Nicaraguan nationalism continued at all levels through the first year, and at times led to internal opposition and divergent policies. MINVAH documents reflected the lack of completely developed and formalized organizational interrelationships. Although this was not atypical for revolutionary situations, it made notable progress during the first year rather difficult.

Popular Support

The JGRN, and MINVAH in particular, placed very strong emphasis on the support and cooperation of the mass organizations, especially the CDS, in the implementation of its programs. But there were major impediments to the successful operation of the CDS, especially in low-income neighborhoods. First, there was no tradition of mass-organization participation beyond that enforced by the Somoza regime in its own behalf.[33] The popular view of the Nicaraguan, as presented by journalist Pablo Antonio Cuadra, includes characteristics which do not foster group affiliation: egoistic, superficial, lacking in mutual trust, and with a concern for things foreign.[34] Second, many of the residents of low-income neighborhoods were not affiliated with the more active and structured mass organizations of women (AMNLAE), workers (CST), and civil employees (UNE). This was due to the high rates of unemployment, to the large percentage of self-employed, domestic, and personal-service workers, and to the relative isolation of many of these neighborhoods. These conditions were similar to others which had been studied in Mexico and Guatemala.[35]

The grass-roots nature of the CDS required considerable effort on the part of a limited number of skilled organizers. Initial reports described CDS as active and effective in a broad range of activities.[36] But others reported that initial enthusiasm had diminished, that there were instances of conflict and bossism, and that emphasis was shifting from CDSs as contributors to policy and decision-making to CDSs as implementers of governmental mandates.[37] Investigations by the author in low-income neighborhoods provided some support for the latter view, but there was observed a wide range of activity rather than any consistent pattern. The level of activity and effectiveness of each CDS appeared to be largely a function of the quality and quantity of local leadership, and the degree of outside support from political activists.

Unofficial reports and personal investigation revealed that a very low percentage of the residents of *repartos ilegales* had registered with MIN-VAH and were making their required payments. It was suggested that this was not so much a demonstration of lack of cooperation or CDS inefficiency as it was evidence of severe economic constraints: these residents were particularly hard-hit by changes in the economy and, unlike renters or those buying homes through the SNF, they had not had their payments reduced by government decree. MINVAH expressed confidence in the CDS, and was clearly and strongly dedicated to maintaining CDS involvement as a key component of the programs to respond to the immediate needs of the marginal neighborhoods, but lack of widespread support through active and well-organized CDSs made full implementation of MINVAH policies problematic.

Financial Resources

While all areas of the government were severely constrained by the nearly bankrupt situation inherited from the Somoza regime, MINVAH faced special problems. Housing and infrastructure demanded heavy investments of capital and, because this area was not seen as a direct contributor to economic growth, it received low governmental priority. During the Somoza regime, Nicaragua had received considerable international assistance for the housing sector. Although the JGRN had received some support from similar sources, the amount was far short of that extended to the former government. Since the MINVAH received the payments from the owners in *repartos ilegales*, and since the former savings-and-loan associations came under government control through the SNF, there was some hope of financing part of the housing development from these internal sources. But neither of these represented large capital resources, and the

SNF funds had not yet been designated for housing. Thus implementation of MINVAH policies and programs was severely restricted for lack of financial support during the first year.

Conclusion

The new revolutionary government inherited from the Somoza regime a housing deficit which had increased under the previous government despite considerable expenditures and international assistance. The situation of the low-income population, largely neglected by the Somoza government, was particularly difficult. During their first year, the Junta and the Ministry of Housing confronted the problem by beginning to develop policies and programs of national development, urban reform, and housing. These policies and programs were seen as integral parts of the new government's plan for economic recovery and were identified as having the long-range goal of bringing the benefits of urbanization and modernization to the masses. The new policies stressed governmental control, particularly in the area of urban development, and emphasized redistributive programs utilizing strong mass organization support and involvement.

Several decrees had been issued in support of these policies, including rent control and the nationalization of squatter settlements and *repartos ilegales*. Although some public housing construction, repair and improvement had been undertaken, problems of organization, popular support, and financial resources had impeded immediate reduction of the housing deficit. Unless such problems were reduced, it seemed unlikely that the housing situation, with its low governmental priority, would improve dramatically. The tremendous pressures of urban growth and the high natural increase rate placed additional severe constraints on progress in this area. Past experience and the current situation suggested that the housing deficit would continue to be one of the most difficult challenges to the new government.

Notes

[1] Population Reference Bureau, *World Demographic Patterns* (Washington: Population Reference Bureau, 1980); and Jaime Incer, *Geografía Ilustrada de Nicaragua* (Managua: Librería y Editorial Recalde, 1973).

[2] Inter-American Development Bank (IDB), *Economic and Social Progress in Latin America: Annual Report 1973* (Washington: IDB, 1973); Banco Central de Nicaragua, Censos Nacionales (Managua: Government of Nicaragua, 1972); and Gerald Breese, *Urbanization in Newly Developing Countries* (Englewood Cliffs, N.J.: Prentice-Hall, 1966).

[3] Gerald Breese, *Urbanization*.

[4] R. W. Kates, J. E. Haas, D. J. Amaral, R. A. Olson and R. Ramos, "Human Impact of the Managua Earthquake," *Science*, 182 (1973), pp. 981-90.

[5] Asociación Demográfica Nicaragüense, "Situación Demográfica en Nicaragua," n.p., n.d., mimeographed.

[6] Instituto Centroamericano de Administración de Empresas (INCAE), "Evaluación

Preliminar de Daños Causados por el Terremoto de Managua del 23 Diciembre de 1973," Doc. No. NI / PL-004, INCAE, 1973.

[7] IDB, *Economic and Social Progress in Latin America: Annual Report 1974* (Washington: IDB, 1974), p. 358.

[8] Julio García, "Managua: Impressions to Remember," *Granma Weekly Review*, Aug. 3, 1980, p. 5.

[9] Martyn J. Bowden, David Pijawka, Gary S. Robff, Kenneth J. Gelman and Daniel Amaral, "Reestablishing Homes and Jobs: Cities," in *Reconstruction Following Disaster*, edited by J. Eugene Haas, Robert W. Kates and Martyn J. Bowden (Cambridge, Mass.: The MIT Press, 1977), pp. 69-145.

[10] IDB, *Annual Report 1973*.

[11] INCAE, "Low-income Family Housing Situation: Managua, 1974," Doc. No. NI / PL-009, INCAE, 1974.

[12] Martyn J. Bowden et al, "Homes and Jobs."

[13] INCAE, "Housing Situation"; Martyn J. Bowden et al., "Homes and Jobs"; and Patricia B. Trainer, Robert Bolin, and Reyes Ramos, "Reestablishing Homes and Jobs: Families." in Haas, Kates, and Bowden, *Reconstruction*, pp. 147-206.

[14] John D. Herbert, *Urban Development in the Third World: Policy Guidelines* (New York: Praeger, 1979).

[15] INCAE, "Housing Situation," p. 9.

[16] Ibid., p. 13.

[17] Ibid., p. 41.

[18] Martyn J. Bowden et al., "Homes and Jobs."

[19] INCAE, "Housing Situation."

[20] Ministerio de Vivienda y Asentamientos Humanos (MINVAH), "Evaluación de daños de edificios, causados durante la guerra civil en ocho ciudades de Nicaragua," (Managua: Gobierno de Reconstrucción Nacional, 1979, mimeographed).

[21] Ministerio de Planificación, *Plan de Reactivación Económico en al Beneficio del Pueblo* (Managua: Secretaría Nacional de Propaganda y Educación Política del F.S.L.N., 1980), p. 109-10.

[22] MINVAH, "Conclusiones del Seminario sobre Políticas, Funciones y Alcances del Ministerio de Vivienda y Asentamientos Humanos," (Managua: MINVAH, 1980).

[23] La Junta de Gobierno de Reconstrucción Nacional (JGRN), "Ley Sobre Donaciones de Inmuebles del Casco Urbano Central de la Ciudad de Managua. Decreto No. 238." *La Gaceta: Diario Oficial*, 84.

[24] JGRN, "Ley de Repartos Ilegales. Decreto No. 97." *La Gaceta: Diario Oficial*, 83, Sept. 1979.

[25] JGRN, "Ley de Inquilinato. Decreto No. 2." *La Gaceta: Diario Oficial*, 1, Jan. 1980.

[26] JGRN, "Decreto No. 377." *La Gaceta: Diario Oficial*, Apr. 1980.

[27] MINVAH: "Conclusiones," 30.

[28] United Nations, *International Social Development Review* (New York: United Nations Department of Economic and Social Affairs, 1970), p. 14.

[29] William Gelman and Jesús H. Hinajosa, "Managua: Un Resúmen del Programa de Reconstrucción Post-Terremoto," *Revista Interamericana de Planificación*, 10 (1976), pp. 40-62.

[30] D. J. Dwyer, *People and Housing in Third World Cities: Perspectives on the Problem of Spontaneous Settlements* (London: Longman, 1975).

[31] John D. Herbert, *Urban Development*; and John Lea, "Self-Help and Autonomy in Housing: Theoretical Critics and Empirical Investigators," in *Housing in Third World Countries*, edited by Hamish S. Murison and John Lea, (New York: St. Martin's Press, 1980), pp. 49-53.

[32] Jorge E. Hardoy and Oscar A. Moreno, *La Reforma Urbana en América Latina* (Buenos Aires: Instituto Torcuato Di Tella, 1972); and Susan Eckstein, "The Debourgeoisement of

Cuban Cities," in *Cuban Communism* (3rd Edition), edited by Irving Louis Horowitz (New Brunswick, N.J.: Transaction Books, 1976), pp. 443-74.

[33] Roger Burbach and Tim Draimin, "Nicaragua's Revolution," *NACLA's Report on the Americas,* XIV, No. 3 (May-June 1980), pp. 2-35.

[34] Pablo Antonio Curada, *El Nicaragüense* (San José, Costa Rica: Editorial Universitaria Centroamericana, 1978).

[35] Antonio Ugalde, *The Urbanization Process of a Poor Mexican Neighborhood* (Austin: Institute of Latin American Studies, The University of Texas at Austin, 1974); and Bryan R. Roberts, *Organizing Strangers* (Austin: The University of Texas Press, 1973).

[36] Roger Burbach and Tim Draimin, "Nicaragua's Revolution"; and Thomas W. Walker, "The Sandinist Victory in Nicaragua", *Current History* (Feb. 1980); pp. 57-84.

[37] Roger Burbach and Tim Draimin, "Nicaragua's Revolution"; and Jorge G. Castañeda, *Nicaragua: Contradicciones en la Revolutión* (México: Tiempo Extra Editores, 1980).

Chapter 16

Sport and Revolution in Nicaragua

ERIC A. WAGNER

Sport might appear to be an unusual topic to be covered in an examination of a sweeping social revolution. Yet the close, symbiotic relationship between sport and society, the openness and the joy with which all Nicaraguans are willing to talk about sport, and the pervasiveness of sport throughout all levels of society make it an area of inquiry both amenable to examination and an institution that is a microcosm of society.

Sport is used for social integration and social control. In nations that have just undergone the chaos of revolutionary war, a fervent commitment to sport and success in it (as, for example, happened in Cuba) helps stabilize fragile and fragmented social institutions and leads to greater social stability. Sport is particularly helpful in dealing with youth, since sport is attractive to them. The average Nicaraguan in 1979 was under 15 years of age, and young people played a major role in the Revolution. In a sense, then, sport helps to "buy time" for the necessarily slower processes involved in socio-economic development.

Sport is also an institution that may prove useful to follow as the social revolution in Nicaragua runs its course. Unlike the economy or social welfare, sport can have its structure, its organization, and even its values changed with rapidity.

Given the pervasiveness of sport in Nicaraguan society, and its relatively low cost (the national budget for sport was less than half a million dollars in 1980), one might expect to find clear evidences of a new social order in the institution of sport well in advance of discernible changes in other social institutions.

Evolution of Sport in Nicaragua

In sports, Latin American countries reflect dominant colonial or quasi-colonial influences in the late nineteenth and early twentieth centuries. In Nicaragua, the presence of the United States dominated the first part of the twentieth century. As a result, baseball is Nicaragua's predominant sport. It is played by all social classes, whether urban or rural.

By 1950, baseball had a wide impact on Nicaragua's people. Small towns as well as big cities had teams, and many open areas became baseball fields. Poorer people saw baseball as an avenue out of poverty and sought to become good enough to play in the major leagues in the United States. A few did make it, such as Dennis Martínez of the Baltimore Orioles and Albert Williams of the Minnesota Twins. Some of the teams in the bigger cities became semiprofessional, and the best players spent most of their time playing baseball. For these select few, baseball became an occupation rather than a recreation.

The quality of baseball improved steadily throughout the century, with Nicaraguan teams participating in numerous international competitions. A high point in Nicaraguan baseball came in 1972, when the Nicaraguans hosted the world baseball championships. The Nicaraguan team tied for second and beat the champion Cuban team in a classic game. Edgard Tijerino Mantilla in *El Mundial Nica* described these championships in terms of pervasive national excitement and pride.[1] Much of this excitement continued to the Revolution, with David J. Wilhelm talking about "overenthusiastic...local baseball fans" when a United States baseball team played in Nicaragua in 1977.[2] Nicaragua even had its own baseball factory, in Masaya, and a children's dispensary there was named after a baseball player, Roberto Clemente, who died while bringing relief supplies to Nicaragua in the wake of the devastating 1972 earthquake.

For many men in Nicaragua, Sunday was not so much the day of church but the day of baseball and other sports activities. And baseball had made substantial inroads into some of the most traditional sectors of the society. Among the poorest of the rural agricultural workers, in little towns like San Juan Oriente near Masaya, baseball was a matter of enormous interest. On forms filled out by poor workers seeking employment in Managua, one often saw the phrase "I am crazy about baseball." Even among the Miskito Indians of the Atlantic coast, an area which had not yet been integrated into the mainstream of Nicaraguan life in the 1970s, and where there was still distrust of things Nicaraguan, baseball had made inroads. Mary Helms, in studying the Miskito village of Asang on the Coco River, notes that Sundays, while centered on church activities, also often included baseball games. In games with neighboring villages, young people went to see and be seen; baseball games were occasions where young people could meet and court one another.[3]

Other sports were also enjoyed by Nicaraguans prior to the revolution. Soccer and boxing were popular, particularly among the lower classes. Some poor people saw boxing as a way to achieve success, and a few professionals did succeed. Both rural and urban people swam, with rural families sometimes going on weekend outings to swimming holes. Volleyball and basketball were quite common sports for both men and women, while kickball was played only by women.

In order to examine the level of participation in various sports, data were gathered from 2,337 applications for employment in Managua.[4] As can be seen in Table 16.1, baseball was definitely the most popular sport. A national sample would have shown baseball as even more dominant, since rural areas were strongly involved in baseball. It is clear, though, that a

TABLE 16.1

Sport Participation in Nicaragua

Sport in Which Participate	Number of Respondents	Percent of Respondents
None	837	35.8
Baseball	688	29.4
Soccer	196	8.4
Volleyball	179	7.7
Swimming	167	7.1
Basketball	155	6.6
Ping-pong	125	5.3
Track, running	88	3.8
Chess	86	3.7
Softball	58	2.5
Boxing	58	2.5
Kickball	37	1.6
Sports (in general)	26	1.1
Karate, judo	23	1.0
Physical exercise	21	0.9
Tennis	21	0.9
Billiards	20	0.9
Weightlifting	17	0.7
Fishing	17	0.7
Cycling	11	0.5
Gymnastics	10	0.4
Walking	9	0.4
Motorcycling	4	0.2
Yoga	4	0.2
Handball	3	0.1
Bowling	3	0.1
Checkers	2	0.1
Hunting	1	0.1
Equitation	1	0.1
	2867	122.8

(Because of multiple responses, the number of respondents does not add to 2,337, nor do the percentages to 100.)

large number of sports were represented in Nicaragua. When the rates of participation were broken down by sex, the author found that 75 percent of the males reported sport activity, while only 34 percent of the females did so. In terms of social class, 76 percent of middle-aged and upper-class respondents participated in sport, and 62 percent of working and lower-class respondents did so. Thus the revolutionary goal of equal sport participation for both sexes and social classes had a long way to go. The data, which primarily reflected the prerevolutionary level of sport participation in Nicaragua, although gathered in mid-1980, show that the revolutionary goal of mass participation was not yet a reality.

In prerevolutionary Nicaragua, it is apparent that there were far more sporting activities for men than for women, and for urban than for rural dwellers; rural dwellers played baseball, and not much else. And while class lines may have been blurred somewhat in sporting activities, it is apparent that middle- and upper-class Nicaraguans had more opportunities to participate, and more sports from which to choose, than did the masses.

Sport and Revolution

Philosophy and Goals of Sport

During the first year after the triumph of the Sandinistas, the two primary goals of the sports program of the revolutionary government were (1) to foster the mass involvement of all the people in Nicaragua, and (2) to encourage the actual participation in sport of all sectors of the society, young and old, rural and urban, rich and poor, female and male. According to Edgard Tijerino, the Director of the Nicaraguan Institute of Sports, "the first step was to give a push to the masses, in other words, those sectors that never had access to sports."[5] Tijerino noted that the new government was more interested in the participation of the people in sports activities than in a select group of "high-performance" athletes who might win a Pan American or world championship. "It interests us that the marginal sectors see that they have access to sports . . . that now they can participate in sports activities."[6]

The Junta of the Government of National Reconstruction recognized sports when it decreed in Point 39 of the *Statute on the Rights of Nicaraguans* that "Nicaraguans have the right to enjoy the highest levels of physical and mental health. The state has an obligation to adopt measures to achieve . . . [the] intensive and systematic development of sports through the creation of all types of facilities."[7] And in the 1980 plan for economic reactivation, the government said it would support sport strongly with the preparation of sports fields all over the country in coordination with local authorities and popular organizations.[8]

With the Nicaraguan government so short of financial resources, and with so much to be done to rebuild the country after the devastation of the War of Liberation, why was attention being given to the development of the sports program? The answer seems to lie in the great emphasis that the Nicaraguan government placed on supporting the masses of people, and on the need for mobilizing and unifying the people as quickly as possible. As Raúl Noda, the Cuban technical adviser to the Nicaraguan Institute of Sports stressed, "Sport is important to the revolution in terms of 'massification' and mobilization of the people."[9] As stated on mimeographed materials sent to the local sport committees, "sport is a weapon of the Revolution." The essence of Nicaraguan sport, and the essence of the Nicaraguan Revolution in the first year, was mobilization.

One of the interesting aspects of the Nicaraguan Revolution was the lack of government support for professional sport. In the past, boxing had existed as a professional sport, and baseball was semiprofessional. In 1980, while not directly prohibiting professionalism, the government was not making its facilities or financial resources available to anyone connected with professional sport. According to Edgard Tijerino, "what is being dealt with is that in professional sports there isn't formation of the athlete. On the other hand, in amateur sports we can mold the athlete and educate him, not use him. The Nicaraguan Revolution is never going to use an athlete."[10]

While the government obviously championed amateur rather than professional sports, it was not clear that the people were totally supportive of this course of action. The three major newspapers, *Barricada*, *El Nuevo Diario*, and *La Prensa*, had substantial sports sections. However, a content analysis by the author over a period of several weeks in 1980 showed that they varied considerably in their sports coverage. *Barricada*, the FSLN newspaper, emphasized local amateur sports events, with a good deal of coverage of women's sports, and paid very little attention to international professional sport. The other two newspapers, independent of the government and with larger circulations, gave very substantial coverage to major-league baseball in the United States and to professional boxing. Nicaraguan professionals, such as baseball players Dennis Martínez and Albert Williams and world champion lightweight boxer Alexis Argüello, received extensive coverage. Professional baseball games from the United States were even broadcast on television, and the early-morning radio sports program, which lasted half an hour, reported the scores and standings of major-league baseball teams in the United States. Many Nicaraguans knew an enormous number of facts about professional baseball in the United States, and followed it avidly.

Nonetheless, the revolutionary goal of deemphasizing professionalism seemed to be gaining a foothold. If one looked at changes in baseball during the first year of the revolution, there seemed to be some movement away from professionalism. Baseball had added players and workers to its group of directors, so there were changes in its management and direction. Before the Revolution, some teams with paid players sponsored by commercial concerns played during the week as well as on weekends. With the Revolution, some of these good, paid, semiprofessional players went to other countries. In revolutionary Nicaragua, the bigger cities had unpaid amateur teams which played only on weekends.

One might have expected that in revolutionary Nicaragua, baseball (associated with "Yankee imperialism") might have been replaced by a more Latin American sport such as soccer. But as yet this was not the case. There seemed instead to be a real interest on the part of all concerned to support

TABLE 16.2

ORGANIZATION OF NICARAGUAN SPORTS

```
                    ┌──────────────────────┐
                    │  Ministry of Culture │
                    └──────────┬───────────┘
                               ▼
                    ┌──────────────────────┐
                    │  Advisory Committee  │
                    └──────────┬───────────┘
            ┌──────────────────┴──────────────────┐
            ▼                                      ▼
┌────────────────────────┐            ┌────────────────────┐
│ Institute              │◄──────────►│     Olympic        │
│ of Sports              │            │    Committee       │
│                        │            └─────────┬──────────┘
│ 1. Administration      │                      ▲
│ 2. Sports Activities───┼──────────►┌────────────────────┐
│ 3. Physical Education  │           │ National Sports    │
│    and Recreation      │           │ Federations (16)   │
│ 4. Voluntary Sports    │           └────────────────────┘
│    Committees (CVD'S)  │
└───┬────────────────────┘
    │           ┌──────────────────────┐
    └──────────►│ Departmental Sports  │
    │           │      Councils        │
    │           └──────────────────────┘
    │        ┌──────────────────────┐
    │        │ Sport                │◄──────────┐
    │        │ Federation           │           │
    │        │ Committees           │───────┐   │
    │        └──────────────────────┘       │   │
    │      ┌──────────────────────┐         │   │
    └─────►│ Voluntary Sports     │         │   │
           │     Committees (CVD'S)│        │   │
           └──────────────────────┘         │   │
              ┌──────────────────────┐      │   │
              │ Local Sports         │◄─────┘   │
              │ Volunteers           │          │
              │ (Various Sports)     │          │
              └──────────────────────┘          │
```

and enhance the preferences of the mass of people, and the majority of the Nicaraguan people were enamored of baseball. Baseball continued as the major sport.

The Organization of Sport

Before the revolutionary insurrection, a separate administrative structure for sport did not exist, though there was a General Directorate of Physical Education and Sport within the Ministry of Education. The revolutionary government established an Institute of Sports under the Ministry of Culture. Separate from the Institute of Sports was the Nicaraguan Olympic Committee, headed by Moisés Hassan, a member of the governmental Junta. An advisory committee of the Ministry of Culture, composed of members from the Institute of Sports, the Olympic Committee, and others, served as a watchdog for both the Institute of Sports and the Olympic Committee. The function of this advisory committee was "to direct the orientations of the revolution in the area of sports."[11] (See Table 16.2 for an organizational chart of Nicaraguan sports.)

The postrevolutionary Olympic Committee was elected in January of 1980 by an assembly endorsed by the directors of the sixteen Nicaraguan sports federations. In addition to Hassan as President, the committee included as Vice-Presidents the coordinator of the basketball federation, a director of the baseball federation (who was also the Minister of Defense), a member of the cycling federation (who was also Vice-Minister of Planning), and a member of the track federation. The treasurer was a planning advisor in the Ministry of Education. A number of other people, including the Director of the Institute of Sports, were also members.[12] It was clear that sport, while short of financial resources, was of special interest to high government officials.

The Institute of Sports, established in September 1979, was organized into four main departments: Administration, Sports Activities, Physical Education and Recreation, and Voluntary Sports Committees. The Department of Administration was in charge of all the materials, donations, aid, and contacts with the government. The Department of Sports Activities coordinated sixteen sports federations, concerned with track and field, chess, baseball, basketball, soccer, boxing, billiards, cycling, judo, weightlifting, motorcycling, swimming, tennis, softball, ping-pong, and volleyball. The Department of Physical Education and Recreation operated mainly in local neighborhoods organizing inexpensive games for youth that did not require sports equipment. The Department of Voluntary Sports Committees fostered sport for the masses in the local neighborhoods.

Under the National Institute of Sports were departmental sports councils, one in each of Nicaragua's sixteen departments. (Not all of the departmental councils had been organized by mid-1980.) Connected to each departmental council was a departmental committee for each of the sixteen sport federations, which coordinated departmental activities and championships, and served as a connection to the national sport federations.

The most exciting part of the organization of sports in postrevolutionary Nicaragua was the voluntary sports committees (CVDs) at the neighborhood level. The CVDs were organized under the neighborhood-level Sandinista Defense Committees (CDSs) that developed during the insurrection. The fundamental purpose of the CVDs was to involve the masses in sport. It was hoped that the CVDs were "going to supply future sports leaders . . . with a more collective mentality."[13]

It was on the level of the CVD that most of the real action regarding sports was taking place in 1980. By September of that year, there were perhaps 200 CVDs organized in Nicaragua. Of that number, 82 were in Managua, 15 in Chinandega, and about 20 in Atlantic coast towns. The remainder were mostly in other cities; very few CVDs had been formed in rural areas. Officials of the Institute of Sports noted that in 1980 they were concentrating on urban areas, and hoped that in 1981 they would be able to turn their attention to organizing CVDs in rural areas. Nonetheless, the organization of the CVDs occurred far more quickly than anyone had anticipated; a number of them seemed to have been organized more or less spontaneously, particularly in Managua neighborhoods. Raúl Noda, the Cuban technical adviser on sports who was also in charge of coordinating the CVDs (and a previous head of the Havana sports committee), commented that it had taken Cuba four to five years to reach this level of organization; he felt that the reason this organization had occurred much more quickly in Nicaragua was that the people were more mobilized because of mass popular involvement in the insurrection.[14]

Many were involved in neighborhood sport committees. In addition to a supervisor and general coordinator, there were supposed to be people responsible for publicity, sport and recreational installations, sport activities, recreational activities, sport equipment and material, and record-keeping. There were also supposed to be people responsible for each of the sixteen sports, though not every sport was represented in every neighborhood committee. That the system was organized and working was evident from the substantial amount of sport activity; tournaments had already been held in baseball, soccer, and basketball, and others were in the planning stages.

One of the most important CVD activities was providing recreation for children. These activities were organized under the "Plan de la Calle" (Plan of the Street), and obviously modelled after the Cuban plan of the same name. The street plan contained numerous examples of games for children, and had as its object the satisfaction of the need for movement in children and of forming from the earliest ages good social habits and the love of sport.[15] Specific objectives were (1) to make possible through different games the participation of masses of youth in recreational activities that would satisfy the needs of their age; (2) to facilitate a program of extracurricular activities as a continuity to physical education programs; (3) to develop through games and sports socially acceptable habits, such as respect for established laws, discipline, self-control, collectivism, and a sense of responsibility; (4) to use dynamic elements in a child's free time to help contribute to physical, social, and intellectual development; and (5) to give an opportunity to children to help contribute to socio-political and ideological development.[16]

By late 1980, growth of the neighborhood sports committees had been slowed by a lack of sports equipment. There were not enough bats and balls of various types, nor were there adequate sports facilities. It was difficult to get government funding for sport because the limited financial resources of the new government were being channelled toward more pressing problems such as the lack of jobs, health, housing, and education. In spite of this, some of the neighborhood sport committees had cleared their own playing fields and had held raffles and other fund-raising events to purchase needed equipment and uniforms. All of the people involved in these committees were volunteers.

Sport Facilities

According to Edgard Tijerino, the Director of the Nicaraguan Institute of Sports, the main problem facing the promotion of sports in post-liberation Nicaragua was that "the revolution received a country without an inheritance of sports installations."[17] Aside from numerous handmade baseball fields, there were very few sports facilities. Nicaragua in 1980 had only one decent gymnasium, the Polideportivo España in Managua, which held only 1,500 spectators. There were no cycling velodromes, and only eight running tracks. In metropolitan Managua, where more than half a million people lived, there were only 2 stadiums, 1 gymnasium, 26 soccer fields, 48 basketball courts, 42 baseball facilities, and 27 volleyball courts.[18] And many of these facilities were inadequate. The largest stadium, for instance, was unusable, having been severely damaged in the 1972 earthquake and left unrepaired thereafter.

During its first year, the revolutionary government took substantial steps toward rectifying the deplorable lack of sports and recreational facilities. Perhaps the most notable achievement, and one that is symbolic of the commitment of the government to help the people, was the construction of a recreational park in central Managua. Utterly destroyed by the 1972 earthquake, most of the heart of Managua had never been rebuilt by the Somoza government, though it had received hundreds of millions of dollars in aid after the earthquake. In the summer of 1979, when the Sandinistas achieved power, the weed-covered rubble stretched for block after block, a wasteland symbolic of governmental indifference. By November 1979, just four months later, workers were swarming over the area, beginning construction of a recreational park. By August 1980, the park was nearly completed. It covered more than forty city blocks, and contained basketball, volleyball, and tennis courts, strolling areas, concession stands, colorful playground equipment, and a host of other recreational facilities. Named after a 10-year old student leader and revolutionary martyr who had been killed by Somoza's troops, the Luis Alfonso Velásquez Flores Park not only had provided thousands of jobs for workers but also had demonstrated graphically that the government cared.

Another project that was being planned in 1980 was the reconstruction of the main stadium in Managua. It was hoped that repairs, which were estimated to cost about $5 million, could begin in 1981. The plans called for the Junta of Reconstruction to fund this project, like the Park before it, as part of its program for combatting unemployment. Neither the recreational park nor the stadium received funds from the Institute of Sports, though the latter was consulted and did give technical advice.

The most substantial plans for sports facilities were being developed by the Managua sports council. According to the Director, Enrique Portocarrero, fourteen sports centers were planned for metropolitan Managua. Plans called for the government to provide all the materials, and the labor during the week, since it needed public-works projects for employment. On the weekends, it was hoped that neighborhood committees would volunteer their labor. Estimates were that it would take five years to complete these sports centers, which were planned to serve from 20,000 to 60,000 people each. While the facilities in each center were not planned to be identical, it was expected that a typical one would contain four basketball courts, four volleyball courts, one soccer field, one track, one gymnasium, one children's park, two baseball fields, and sanitary services. Most of the sports centers were to be built in the poor sections of the metropolitan area.

Sport Participation

In 1980, baseball was clearly the dominant sport. As Edgard Tijerino noted, "Everyone, even with a ball of rags, plays baseball in this country." On Sundays, busses were crowded with men and boys in baseball uniforms of every color. From early morning to evening, baseball fields and even some undeveloped open spaces were occupied by teams. Sometimes a large crowd watched; other times there was only a small number of spectators.

Other sporting activities were also in progress. Along with baseball games on Sundays, there were soccer games, though they were not nearly as numerous. There was a sport unit in the military forces, with emphasis on recreational sport for physical training and discipline. A few soldiers were running substantial distances, with the author occasionally accompanying them. The military and the police were represented in sport competitions, and were developing teams. The Managua police chief, a sports enthusiast, was actively supporting police participation. Nicaragua had developed two annual marathons. One was organized to commemorate the successful guerrilla retreat from Managua to Masaya in June 1979. Run over the same fairly flat route, this marathon was won by a Cuban in 1980. The second, the Carlos Fonseca Marathon, was to be run over the rather steep route from Darío to Matagalpa. Women, who seemed to be increasingly involved in many sports, often played volleyball and basketball. The first women's basketball championship was to be held in the fall of 1980. Nicaragua participated in the 1980 Olympics in Moscow, though her athletes won no medals. There were fourteen people in the delegation, with boxing, track, and swimming represented.

Conclusion

In sports, the Revolution did not represent a complete break with the past. While the structures and the organization of sport, and the projected involvement of the masses in a large number of sports were new, the affection for baseball and the Nicaraguan passion for sports were a continuation from the past.

Much remained to be done. Rural areas had not yet seen much revolutionary sports activity. There were still few sports opportunities for women. Facilities were completely inadequate, especially for the poorer areas of the cities and the countryside. Financial support for sports was almost nonexistent, given the presence of other more pressing national needs. But it was also obvious that the revolutionary government was clearly committed to providing opportunities for sports participation to all members of the society. While resources were scarce, neighborhoods, departments and the national level were all actively being organized, primarily with volunteers. Many top government officials were involved, and a number of government ministries were cooperating. The fundamental revolutionary goals of "massification," participation, no support for professional players, and mobilization were all evident at the various levels of sport organization.

Sport was rapidly coming to reflect a more egalitarian and participatory society. Gone was the Managua Golf Club, and the social privilege it embodied. Gone were sports facilities which were available only to a select few. Gone was the almost exclusively male orientation to sports. Evidence of a new social order was everywhere. Posters encouraged the "massification" of sports. Facilities accessible to the poor were planned. Women were organizing their own sports programs, and receiving support from the government. The social goals of collectivism and mass participation and mobilization being fostered by the government were nowhere more evident than in the neighborhood sports committees. After just one year, sport did portray the new Nicaragua.

Notes

[1] Edgard Tijerino Mantilla, *El Mundial Nica* (Managua: Imprenta Copiaco, 1973).

[2] Daniel J. Wilhelm, "Tropical Baseball: Staying Well in Nicaragua," *The Physician and Sportsmedicine* June 1979, pp. 141—145.

[3] Mary W. Helms, *Asang: Adaptations to Culture Contact in a Miskito Community* (Gainesville: University of Florida Press 1971), pp. 84, 223.

[4] Of the 2, 337 people, 92 percent lived in the Managua metropolitan area. Eighty-six percent were working or lower class and 14 percent were middle or upper class, while 74 percent were male and 26 percent female. Sixteen percent were under 19 years of age, 41 percent were 20 to 24 years of age, 22 percent were 25 to 29 years of age, 15 percent were 30 to 39 years of age, and 6 percent were 30 or older. Thus this group of people was more representative of urban, male and older people than a representative national sample would have been. Grateful thanks are expressed to Ricardo Chavarria for his assistance in gathering these data.

[5] Edgard Tijerino M., interview in Managua, Nicaragua, September, 1980.

[6] Ibid.

[7] Pedro Camejo and Fred Murphy, *The Nicaraguan Revolution* (New York: Pathfinder Press, 1979), p. 52.

[8] Ministerio de Planificación, *Plan de Reactivación Económica en Beneficio del Pueblo* (Managua, 1980), p. 110.

[9] Raúl Noda, interview in Managua, Nicaragua, September, 1980.

[10] Edgard Tijerino M., interview.

[11] *Diario de las Américas,* "Altas Figuras del Gobierno en el Comité Olímpico Nicaragüense," (Miami, January 29, 1980).

[12] Ibid.

[13] Edgard Tijerino M., interview.

[14] Raúl Noda, interview.

[15] Ministerio de Cultura—Instituto Nicaragüense de Deportes, *Plan de la Calle* (Managua, January 10, 1980); Ministerio de Cultura—Instituto Nicaragüense de Deportes, *Tercer Folleto de Recreación. Plan de la Calle* (Managua, July, 1980).

[16] Ministerio de Cultura, *Plan de la Calle* (January 10, 1980).

[17] Edgard Tijerino M., interview.

[18] Enrique Portocarrero, interview in Managua, Nicaragua, September, 1980.

Chapter 17

The Problematic of
Nicaragua's Indigenous Minorities

PHILIPPE BOURGOIS

There are marginalized ethnic minorities in almost all countries of the American continent. In many cases, these exploited indigenous populations constitute national minorities and require an effective process of decolonization in order to achieve full cultural and economic emancipation. Not all ethnic groups necessarily qualify as distinct nationalities, of course, and not all national minority movements automatically represent the exploited classes. Nationhood is born out of the historical, cultural, and political economic formation of a people; it implies a collective consciousness and is usually expressed through struggle. When a population constitutes a distinct nationality, however, and is included in a dominated fashion within the frontiers of a larger state, the feasibility of a liberation strategy based on the creation of autonomous administrative and cultural structures becomes a central issue. In order to determine whether regional autonomy will actually benefit the poor majority, however, the dynamics of the class struggle must be carefully examined. Narrowly nationalistic sentiments are too frequently amenable to manipulation. The right to self-determination should not be seen as an abstract value that legitimizes all secessionist movements. The validity of the demands of an ethnic group ultimately has to be judged by their class content if the struggle for the interests of the oppressed is the primary concern.

In Nicaragua, the first continental state in the western hemisphere in which a popular, anti-imperialist revolution triumphed, ethnic minorities constituted between 5 and 7 percent of the total population. Their significance, however, is greater than their numbers. The precedent the Nicaraguan government would set in its relations with its non-Ladino

The material for this article was collected during nine months of residence in Nicaragua during which time I worked for the *Centro de Investigaciones e Estudios de la Reforma Agraria* and the *Cruzada Nacional de Alfabetización*. I would like to thank the *compañeros* in both these institutions who made this experience possible. The Miskitu and Sumu people and the Sandinista National Liberation Front have earned my highest respect and admiration. The interpretations and errors presented in this article, are of course, strictly my own.

population would have profound ramifications for liberation struggles throughout Latin America. For example, in Guatemala the Maya constitute over half of the population and many are engaged in the armed struggle. Similarly, in countries such as Bolivia, Peru, and Ecuador, the indigenous sector is both numerically significant and politically volatile. Finally, the area inhabited by the ethnic populations of Nicaragua—known locally as the Atlantic Coast—has age-old cultural, geographic and economic ties with the Caribbean, a region budding with progressive social movements.

The Sandinista National Liberation Front (FSLN) was conscious of the historical importance of the example it was setting and assigned priority to the integration of the Miskitu, Sumu, Rama Amerindians, and the Creole Carib Afroamericans into the Revolutionary process.[1] The full participation of Nicaragua's ethnic minorities in the construction of a larger socialist state, however, would be a long-term project since they had been the victims of a particularly noxious complex of economic exploitation and cultural domination, whose tentacles, albeit decaying, persisted as the major obstacles to their complete cultural and economic enfranchisement. In all cases, the decolonization of a significant segment of a nation's population is necessarily arduous. With the leadership of the Sandinistas, however, Nicaragua became one of the few countries in the world capable of accomplishing such a task.

The Revolutionary Problematic

The necessity for a dynamic national program for minorities in Nicaragua must be understood in the context of the regional class struggle developing in the Atlantic province of Zelaya where the ethnic populations reside, and the historical experience of these indigenous peoples. The province of Zelaya, whose boundaries coincide with the Nicaraguan half of the Mosquitia, spans over half of the nation's territory but contains only nine percent of its population. It is by far the most economically underdeveloped zone. This is the direct legacy of the region's past, which conforms almost caricaturally to the classic Third World scenario of the pilferage and rape of the natural resources of a virgin territory by nonnationals. The sacking of the Mosquitia was begun by British settlers in the seventeenth century, was continued by North American companies under the direct supervision of "Yankee" marines at the turn of the twentieth century, and ultimately was systematized by international capital under the auspices of the Somoza dynasty.

On the eve of the Sandinista Revolution, therefore, the local inhabitants—the Costeños—found themselves left with a ravaged environment devoid of the most basic physical and economic infrastructure. There was no access by road to Zelaya; there were few schools; medical facilities were virtually nonexistent; what limited industry remained continued to be dedicated to the extraction of natural resources entailing minimal secondary processing: mining, fishing and lumber.

Within one year of the Sandinista triumph, the structural prerequisites for the decolonization of the Atlantic Coast had been fulfilled: (1) the gold and copper mines were expropriated and placed under the administration of the Nicaraguan Corporation of Mines and Hydrocarbons; (2) most of the lumber companies came under the aegis either of the People's Forestry Corporation or the People's Industrial Corporation; (3) Somoza's fisheries were transfered to the Nicaraguan Fisheries Institute; (4) the cattle ranches formerly owned by the dictatorship's most prominent local representatives came under the jurisdiction of the Nicaraguan Institute for Agrarian Reform (INRA); (5) the Nicaraguan Institute for Natural Resources and the Environment was created as maximum authority for the supervision of the rational exploitation of the country's natural resources by both the private and public sectors; and (6) the Nicaraguan Institute for the Atlantic Coast was founded to coordinate and plan regional economic development projects. Strides toward the economic transformation of the Atlantic Coast were taken, but the most arduous task lay ahead: the total eradication of the racist local class structures that had suffocated the region for so many years. In this domain also, there was significant progress. Within four months of the Sandinista victory, MISURASATA, the indigenous mass organization, was founded with the support of the FSLN to lobby for the interests of the Miskitu, Sumu, and Rama peoples. Furthermore, MISURASATA occupied a seat on the Council of State, the maximum legislative body of Nicaragua, conjoining the most important sectors of the nation such as the church, the army, political parties, mass organizations, and business associations. On August 1, 1980, the Council of State passed a law establishing bilingual education—Miskitu-Spanish and English-Spanish—in Miskitu and Creole communities. The National Literacy Campaign launched a second literacy project in Miskitu, Sumu, and English on August 31.

The political importance of a bilingual language policy should not be underestimated. Language, more than anything else, symbolizes ethnic identity. The fact, therefore, that the one-year-old Sandinista government, despite its devastated economy and crippling foreign debt had allocated the resources necessary for teaching literacy skills to approximately 60,000 illiterate Miskitu, Sumu, Rama, Creole, and Carib in their native tongues gave an indication that ethnic minorities would no longer be second-class citizens in Nicaragua. Furthermore, the manner in which the campaign was organized was designed to promote grass-roots leadership among the indigenous peoples. Due to the shortage of educated Amerindians, seminars were set up in the communities to train minimally educated people how to teach their neighbours to read and write. The bulk of the education campaign, therefore, was carried out by the village dwellers themselves.

Despite these notable initial achievements, one year after the Sandinista victory, the full incorporation of the Atlantic Coast into the Revolution remained an unresolved challenge. Serious cultural animosities persisted; a general mistrust or, at best, apathy vis-á-vis the Revolution prevailed among important sectors. The situation was exacerbated by the region's geographical isolation (the only access was by air or boat) and, more important, by the linguistic barriers. Only one-third of the *Costeños* spoke Spanish as a maternal tongue and over 50 percent in northeastern Zelaya spoke virtually no Spanish at all. The result was a communications gap between the populations of the Atlantic and the Pacific, culminating in a mutual misunderstanding, rife with racist stereotypes.

This alienated relationship, however, was not solely the consequence of logistical difficulties; nor was it merely the product of 45 years of Somocista dictatorship. Rather, it was the legacy of over 300 years of internal colonialism and international neocolonialism combined with a sharpening of local class tensions. The *Costeños* had lived too long under a demeaning yoke of ethnic discrimination and economic marginalization at the hands of their fellow Ladino Nicaraguans to be persuaded in a short period that the new Ladino-dominated central government meant to aid them. Similarly, the Ladino national majority had been convinced for too many centuries of their cultural superiority to be able to sensitize themselves overnight to the reality of their ethnic minorities. Furthermore, certain elements of the formerly pro-Somoza local *Costeño* Ladino elite were determinedly attempting to reestablish their faltering hegemony by skillfully shifting to Sandinista stances. In addition, not even the indigenous movement itself was exempt from infiltration by individuals in leadership positions tainted by former association with the *Somocista* regime.

Origin of the Ethnic Conflict:
The Struggle between Spanish and British Colonialism
The profound cultural antagonism between the Pacific and Atlantic provinces of Nicaragua arose out of their distinct historical experiences and social formations. It had its roots in the diametrically opposed trajectories of Spanish and British colonialism in the region.

On the Pacific Coast during the sixteenth century, the Spanish alternated between a policy of systematic extermination campaigns and one of enslavement of the aboriginal population. Indeed, the decimation of the Amerindians in western Nicaragua was particularly brutal. Large numbers were shipped off as slaves to the plantations of the West Indies and the mines of Peru. During the seventeenth century, immense cattle farms were established under the *encomienda* system with the native population working essentially as slaves on the Spanish-owned *haciendas.*[2]   The Spaniards, however, were unable to penetrate into the eastern half of Nicaragua, where the Sumu and Miskitu waged ferocious battles in defense of the sovereignty of their territory. An eighteenth-century British document comments:

> Their love of liberty added to their natural bravery impelled them to maintain, in sovereign independency the possession of their mountains, valleys, woods, lakes, and rivers, against the superior art, arms and even cruelties of Spain.[3]

The English, vying with Spain for hegemony in the New World, took advantage of the valiant combativeness of the Amerindians of Nicaragua's Caribbean coast to forge an alliance with strategically located groups of them against the Spanish Crown. This relationship began as early as 1589, when French, Dutch, and English buccaneers established refuges on Pearl Lagoon and the Coco River, whence they preyed on Spanish ships. The Miskitu inhabitants of the Caribbean shore were excellent sailors and fishermen; the pirates, therefore, depended on them as guides, food collectors, and boat hands. An eyewitness reports:

> The buccaneers...associated the Mosquito Indians as Fellow adventurers in their Spanish expeditions into the South Seas...[receiving]...the warmest protection of the Mosquito Indians as being Spain's most implacable enemies.[4]

The pragmatic basis of this partnership was recognized with no illusions in a 1789 report by a British colonial envoy: "One common interest united them [the Miskitu] with their new friends, the English, having one and the same common enemy, [the Spanish]...."[5]

Through the trade relations established with buccaneers, and later with merchants, the Miskitu people obtained muskets and machetes, thereby becoming, during the late seventeenth century, the major military force of the Central American Caribbean coast. The aboriginal forms of Miskitu "government" were decentralized and flexible. The Mosquitia had been divided into a series of autonomous subtribal and regional units dominated by local groups of elders. The English pursued a policy of systematically reinforcing Miskitu nationalism and, in 1687, in a maneuver to legitimize their annexation of the region, the English crowned one of the many Miskitu tribal leaders "King of the Mosquitia" at a ceremony presided over by the Governor of Jamaica. The Miskitu King's domain formally extended along 410 miles of the coast, from Cape Honduras (today, the Honduran town of Trujillo) to the San Juan River (currently the Nicaraguan border with Costa Rica.[6] The Miskitu, however, are said to have collected tribute from subjugated populations as far south as Chiriqui lagoon in Panama. In all their dealings with the Miskitu, the English were careful to employ a rhetoric emphasizing their respect for the "inviolable autonomy" of the "Amerindian Nation." A description of the founding of the first British fort in the Mosquitia is indicative of the ironic contradiction characterizing the "independent" status of the Miskitu kingdom:

> [We]...mounted it [the fort] with cannon, hoisted the Royal
> flag and kept garrison to show that this independent country of
> the Mosquito Shore was under the direct sovereignty and pro-
> tection of Great Britain.[7]

Regardless of motive, the British presence in Nicaragua presented a
sharp contrast to the ravages of the Spanish invasion on the Pacific Coast.
Perhaps most important, permanent settlers never arrived in the Mosquitia
in great numbers. The few that came, rather than attempting to subjugate
the local population, imported slaves of African origin.

Unlike the western half of the country, therefore, primitive accumulation did not take place on a large scale on the eastern Coast. Large plantations never took root because of the insecurity caused by Spanish raids. In
fact, in the spring of 1780, all the British-owned sugar plantations of the
"Mosquito Shore" were burned by Spanish soldiers, and in 1787 the English
government signed a treaty promising to evacuate its subjects from the
territory.[8]

Britain Exits; North America Enters
The expansion of North American capitalism brought about significant
changes in the structure of imperialist domination in the Mosquitia. The
abolition of slavery in British territories in 1822, the independence of Central America from the Spanish Crown, the wane of British colonial interest
in the Americas, and the increasingly aggressive penetration of North
American capital in the region all contributed to the precipitation of a crisis
for the fragile Miskitu government. The Nicaraguan declaration of independence and statehood in 1838 implied imminent doom for the relative
administrative autonomy that the Mosquitia had enjoyed as British pawns
in the struggle for colonial power between Spain and Great Britain. In the
wake of independence from the Spanish Empire, a tide of nationalist sentiment surged throughout the new nations of Central America. The British
presence on the Latin American continent was perceived as an unacceptable
infringement of Central America's sovereignty. Tensions rose and open
fighting errupted. As late as 1848, British troops disembarked in San Juan
del Norte to burn the Nicaraguan flag.[9] Finally, in 1860, under pressure
from the United States, the British signed a treaty in which they renounced
all claims to the Nicaraguan coast. A "reserve of the Mosquitia" was
established which formally brought the Miskitu kingdom under Nicaraguan
jurisdiction, granting, however, a certain degree of autonomous self-
government to the Miskitu people. The semi-independent status of the
Reserve was repeatedly defended by the local inhabitants. In 1877, the
Amerindian King rejected a proposal for the integration of the Mosquitia as
a province of Nicaragua. One of his most resounding arguments was "the

religion, customs, manners, and laws of Nicaragua are in no way compatible."[10]

Miskitu self-rule became a dead letter in 1894, however, when General Rigoberto Cabezas militarily occupied the Atlantic zone, deposed the King, and forced the Amerindian leaders to sign a declaration of allegiance to Nicaragua. The Mosquitia was officially renamed the province of Zelaya.

More important than the semantics of international treaties or troop mobilizations was the escalated penetration of North American capital in Central America during the late nineteenth century. Nicaragua assumed particular economic and geopolitical importance because of the prospects for the digging of an interoceanic canal through Nicaragua. The Caribbean coast with its easily accessible reserves of gold and lumber, its soil suitable for banana production, became a center for North American investments. Moreover, the indigenous population, because of its history of conflicts with the Nicaraguan Ladinos, welcomed the presence of the North Americans in much the same way that they had attached themselves to the buccaneers and the British. Indeed, even though Panama was finally chosen as the site of the interoceanic canal, United States economic interests became so important in the region that in 1912 several thousand "Yankee" marines disembarked on the Atlantic Coast to protect North American profits.

A mere half century after the signing of the 1860 British-Nicaraguan treaty, therefore, Nicaragua, having previously been a victim of Spanish Colonialism became a neocolonial ward of the United States, and the Mosquitia, having passed from being a subordinated British "ally," became a North American capitalist enclave, still lacking a right to self-government.

Ideological Ramifications of the Miskitu Colonial Experience

From the point of view of the *Costeños*, the immediate enemy and the culprits responsible for all their tribulations were the Nicaraguan Ladinos. The independence of Central America and the consolidation of the Nicaraguan nation-state had resulted in the abolition of Miskitu self-rule. The *Costeños*, therefore, never differentiated between their fathers' enemies—the Spanish-born *conquistadores*—and their new legal rulers—the Nicaraguan-born bourgeoisie that seized power in 1838.

This equation is reflected to this very day in the local term for non-Amerindian and non-Afroamerican Nicaraguans: "the Spanish." The continued use of the term "Spaniard" symbolically expresses the hatred that persists from so many centuries of bitter warfare and colonial outrage. Echoes of the observations of an eighteenth-century British colonist are still evident:

> The Mosquito Indians, so remarkable for their fixed hatred of the Spaniards, and attachments to us . . . have invariably transmitted from father to son the strongest and clearest ideas of

their independency of Spain and its subjects, accompanied with sentiments and conduct of the most implacable hatred and revenge towards the whole Spanish race, in retaliation of the enormous cruelties universally attending their first conquest and domination in America.[11]

Equally important in the collective consciousness of the Miskitu people was their mystification of the former existence of an Amerindian King. In popular discourse, the existence of a King and an autonomous Reserve had served to focus discontent with Ladino domination. There persisted a feeling of having been wronged when the King was "dethroned" and his territory annexed to the Nicaraguan state in 1894 by General Cabezas' troops.

Another popular expression of disenchantment was the widespread rumor of a secret clause in the 1860 treaty that gave the Miskitu people the right to opt for independence from Nicaragua after a lapse of 80 years. Those who still favored the secession of the province of Zelaya from Nicaragua had built a veritable mystique around this "secret clause." It had become a rallying symbol for legitimizing a thrust for independence and for focusing discontent with the Nicaraguan government. Occasionally, during holiday celebrations the British flag was hoisted as a symbolic, albeit ironically confused, demand for independence from the Nicaraguan state.

The implacable opposition of the Amerindian population to Spanish colonial penetration manifested itself as well in their resistance to conversion to the Catholic religion. To the Miskitu, the Catholic religion symbolized Spanish imposition and was met with unequivocal rejection. It was not until the arrival in 1849 of the Moravian Church, a protestant faith from Germany, that Christian proselytizing took root in the Mosquitia. By 1900, scarcely half a century later, the majority of the Miskitu and Sumu communities had abandoned their traditional religion in favor of the Moravians. Adherence to the Protestant faith was an expression of opposition to "Spanish" domination. Significantly, today in blatant contrast to the deeply rooted Catholicism of the Ladino population of Nicaragua, the majority of the Costeños have maintained a firm adherence to the Moravian Church. Even though perhaps 25 percent of the Miskitu have since entered the Catholic Church—again significantly, through contact with North American and not Ladino missionaries—there is a profound equivalence between "being Miskitu" and belonging to the Moravian brotherhood. The Moravian faith, therefore, has developed into what could be called a national religion. Unfortunately, the Moravian Church is by no means unequivocally progressive. Certain of the less principled Moravian leaders severely compromised themselves by cooperating with the Somoza regime. Throughout the first year of the Revolution, the sermons broadcast by the Moravian Church from Honduras were almost openly counter-revolutionary.

The Period of Neocolonial Domination

During the early twentieth century, unlike the rest of Nicaragua, the Mosquitia enjoyed a frenzied boom of relatively highly paid jobs. Of course, no permanent capital investments were made by the companies, and the wages disappeared overnight as a function of the depletion of natural resources and "busts" in the international market. For example, in 1926 the Bragman's Bluff Lumber Company located in Puerto Cabezas was the biggest employer in all of Nicaragua, with 3,000 wage earners in the sawmill alone.[12] Today, there are probably not 3,000 people earning steady wages in all of Puerto Cabezas. These are long-term dynamics, however; the immediately visible effect of the North American presence was easy cash.

Furthermore, the war against the United States troops in defence of the national sovereignty led by the hero of the Nicaraguan Revolution, Augusto César Sandino, coincided with the Great Depression. The Costeños did not have the benefit of a sophisticated analysis of the world economy; therefore, the drastic reduction in operations of the foreign export firms due to the collapse of the international market was locally interpreted as the result of the raids of Sandino's army against the North American companies. These factors rendered it difficult for the Costeños to perceive Sandino as a national hero or to understand the anti-imperialist foundation of the Nicaraguan Revolution.

During the dark years of the Somoza dynasty (1936-1979), the region was more or less abandoned by the Nicaraguan government. The mahogany and pine forests had long since been stripped; the banana plantations had been decimated by plagues and hurricanes. Possibilities for easy profits were limited; consequently, Somoza did not interfere in the region. The government's presence took the form of a handful of abusive and corrupt bureaucrats and minor military officers; the central government was most notable for its absence, a situation which suited the local population. What few job opportunities remained were provided by the international companies. The notable exception to the National government's "noninterference" in the region, was the Nicaraguan Institute for National Development (INFONAC), which expelled entire Miskitu communities from their ancestral lands under the guise of the rationalization of national forestry resources.

Since there were relatively few of the infamous Nicaraguan National Guardsmen stationed in the area, repression was light and in the Miskitu-dominated half of northern Zelaya, there was no fighting whatsoever. The Costeños, therefore, did not experience the nightmare of the genocidal Somocista dictatorship, nor did they participate in the rigors of the Sandinista combat. They heard about the brutal fighting and repression on the radio, but rarely if ever saw or felt it.

The Sandinista Triumph

The Sandinista Revolution reached the Mosquitia almost immediately. On July 19, 1970, handfuls of raggedly dressed "bearded men" began entering the Miskitu communities, declaring them—in a language most could not understand—to be free from the tyranny of Somoza and North American imperialism. The initial reaction of the *Costeños* was to treat the Revolution as just another power struggle between two equally dangerous armed factions of "Spaniards."

The Sandinista fighters, for their part, were also profoundly baffled by what they found: an apathetic, if not openly hostile, population who refused to understand that they were the victims of imperialism or that General Sandino was a heroic figure. There were no FSLN members of Sumu or Rama descent, and but a mere handful of Miskitu ancestry. The FSLN, therefore, lacked cadres who could speak the same language as the indigenous population and who could understand their modes of expression and thinking.

From the outset, the Revolution faced the problem of establishing direct contact with the *Costeños*. Unfortunately, the opportunistic "Spanish" residents of the region were immediately receptive. They had formerly wielded power in the bureaucratic structures of the Somocista government, and with the triumph of the Sandinistas they promptly set about reestablishing themselves in new positions of privilege. They took advantage of the initial cultural disorientation of the Sandinistas to befriend them and to defame the Amerindian majority, who had always been their implacable class and ethnic enemies. A series of local crises erupted, exacerbating the mutual misperception the ethnic minorities and the Sandinistas had of each other. To many Miskitu, it did not appear that the Revolution was changing fundamentally the local structures of inequality.

The Founding of MISURASATA

A conflict immediately arose over the right of the existing indigenous mass organization, ALPROMISU, to continue to operate. ALPROMISU, the Alliance for Progress of the Miskitu and Sumu People, had been founded with the support of the Moravian Church in 1973. Most of its leaders, however, had been bought off by the Somoza machine.

There existed, nevertheless, a small nucleus of Miskitu students educated at the National University in Managua, who had been opponents of the dictatorship. Some of them had even contacted the Sandinistas in Costa Rica. In fact, their political orientation was not well defined; it was not clear to what extent they supported the Revolution.

These young, educated Miskitu commanded a notable degree of support among the poor majority of their people and they assumed leadership of ALPROMISU on July 19 as the former corrupt directors fled to Honduras and Miami.

In the heat of the personal politicking and mutual distrust that characterized the first days after the triumph, several of the new Miskitu leaders were arrested for fomenting a separatist movement. It took several weeks to disentangle the situation, and it was not until November 11 that Commandante Daniel Ortega, a member of the Junta of National Reconstruction and the National Directorate of the FSLN, arrived in Puerto Cabezas to supervise the dissolution of ALPROMISU and the founding of a new indigenous mass organization to be named MISURASATA (the Unity of the Miskitu, Sumu, Rama and Sandinistas). By this act, the formerly excluded Rama were incorporated formally into the organization and, most important, the Amerindian peoples officially joined the Sandinista Revolution.

The arrested leaders were reinstated and within the next six months MISURASATA grew into the single most powerful force in northern Zelaya. An indigenous revitalization movement stressing the dignity of the Amerindian identity began gaining momentum. The policy of MISURASATA was to lobby energetically for basic economic and cultural demands. For example in the economic domain, a fishermen's union was organized and the prices paid by the Nicaraguan Fisheries Institute for shrimp, lobster, and turtles were renegotiated to a higher level. Similarly, an agreement was made with the Nicaraguan Institute for Natural Resources and the Environment that 100 percent of the revenue of the lumber logged on communal lands would be reinvested in the communities. In the cultural domain, MISURASATA presented the previously mentioned bilingual education law to the Council of State and provided cadres to prepare materials for the indigenous language literacy campaign.

The Class Struggle and the Amerindian Revitalization Movement
Two dimensions of MISURASATA's ethnic revitalization movement must be differentiated. On the one hand, by emphasizing the historically rooted distinct national identity of the Miskitu people, it challenged—at least superficially—the goal of the Sandinistas to consolidate the Nicaraguan nation-state and to increase the integration of the Miskitu in the national polity. At the same time, however, a reaffirmation of the indigenous identity promoted the local class struggle by representing the interests of the peasant producers and asserting the dignity of the poorest, most oppressed sector.[14] Indeed, over the past 100 years, the class struggle in the Mosquitia has manifested itself through an ethnic confrontation between Amerindian agriculturalists and Ladino merchants.

At the time of the Sandinista triumph, over 90 percent of the Miskitu, Rama, and Sumu peoples were impoverished, semiproletarianized (i.e., agriculturalists who earned a significant portion of their income from wage labor) and(or) artesanal fishermen (i.e., fishermen who employ traditional techniques and equipment.).

As periodic wage workers in the mining, fishing and forestry industry, they were invariably relegated to the poorest-paid, most demeaning jobs. In fact, in the gold and copper mines, they were subject to a quasi-apartheid domination. The safe, well-paid supervisory positions were held by Ladinos and in some cases by Creoles. All the highly dangerous, poorly remunerated jobs underground in the mine shafts, on the other hand, were staffed by Miskitu and Sumu. As ultimate insult, they were forbidden to enter the housing complexes and mess halls of the European managers and engineers.

As rice and bean producers, the Miskitu, although they generally had access to the essential means of production—land, machetes, and axes—had their surpluses appropriated from them by the local merchant class. This was because the terms of trade for agricultural products were artificially skewed in favor of the regional mercantile elite, who held a monopoly over the means of transportation and the circulation of locally available capital. In fact, often the merchants were able to institute highly unequal patron-client relationships by trapping agriculturalists in permanent debt obligations.

In addition to this universally despised local merchant class, governmental employees also formed part of the regional elite during the Somoza years. Members of this elite defined themselves as Ladino regardless of actual ethnic origin. Formerly, when Amerindians rose in the local class echelon, that is, when they acquired a little capital and entered the grain purchasing business or managed to obtain a higher education and became teachers or governmental agronomists, they tended to deny the values of their cultural heritage. They lost the ability to speak their maternal tongue and associated exclusively with the "Spanish." At the same time, they were rejected by the Miskitu population because the Amerindian culture with its communal form of land tenure, its institutions of reciprocal labor exchange, and its ideology of mutual aid, would not accept the existence of economic inequality. In fact, Miskitu culture was incompatible with capitalism. As a privileged class, therefore, the Ladino and Ladinized populations of the Mosquitia were fervently opposed to MISURASATA and the indigenous movement.

It was precisely to create a new and nobler life for the exploited peasants and workers that the FSLN overthrew the Somoza dynasty and ousted North American imperialism. A series of policies were implemented to undercut the monopoly that the Ladino merchants maintained over the marketing system. There appeared to be no objective contradiction, therefore, between the welfare of the indigenous peoples and the construction of socialism in Nicaragua. In fact, as an exploited class they stood to benefit greatly from the economic programs of the Sandinista Revolution, securing the following: (1) subsidies on farm implements and inputs; (2) free technical aid; (3) guaranteed crop purchases (in some cases at prices 500 percent higher than before the Revolution); (4) easily accessible cheap credit; and (5) help with the organization of production and commercialization cooperatives.

Despite these apparently compatible ethnic and class dynamics, tensions between the Sandinistas and significant sectors of the Amerindians continued to exist and even augmented. In part, this was due to the persistence of historically related superstructural contradictions, but it is perhaps best understood as a consequence of the regional class struggle. The implementation of the revolutionary policies and programs resulted in the proliferation of new governmental agencies in the Mosquitia. This increased the power of the bureaucratic sector of the regional elite whose status was determined by their strategic positions in the local governmental agencies. The Ladinos, because of their superior education and their cultural savvy, had privileged access to employment in the new and expanded governmental institutions. There were even cases of former Somocista bureaucrats adroitly insinuating themselves into local positions of power. These unsavory elements tended to reproduce the racist, colonial relations of dominance that characterized the former regime.

Significantly, that sector of the Miskitu population most directly threatened by, and in competition with, this newly reemerging local Ladino elite was the better educated leadership of MISURASATA. MISURASATA, of course, was setting the tone for the Amerindian nationalist movement. Its leaders were the first to point out that, while the Somoza regime had abandoned their people to a marginalized peace, the favorable Sandinista social reforms were being administered either by unfamiliar young "Spanish" cadres from the Pacific region, or by the local Ladino elite who had always been their implacable enemies.

Towards Amerindian Participation in the New Nicaragua
Although the situation of the ethnic minorities in the Mosquitia is a complex and profound problematic, the FSLN was determined to smooth out the age-old superstructural tensions and confront the newly emerging class contradictions between Ladinos and Amerindians. At the national level, the Sandinista leadership revealed a genuine capacity for self-criticism and reevaluation in public declarations on the challenges faced by the Revolution in the Atlantic Coast. The right of the Amerindian minorities to maintain their cultural integrity and to have a mass organization to articulate their needs was repeatedly reaffirmed.

Many of the local FSLN representatives stationed in the Mosquitia however, were newcomers from the Pacific provinces. Consequently, the most difficult, and perhaps the most important, dynamic for them to understand was that the Revolution need not feel threatened by an Amerindian cultural revitalization campaign.

To understand the potential consequences of the indigenous rights movement, the dialectical relationship between the reaffirmation of the dignity of the Amerindian identity, the development of the local class struggle, and, ultimately, the consolidation of Nicaragua as a nation had to be fathomed. By showing the indigenous peoples of Nicaragua that their heritage would not only be respected but also promoted, and that they would no longer be subject to the domination of a local Ladino elite, the primary reason for a successionist movement would be removed.[15] By emphasizing, therefore, what would appear to contradict national unity—the distinctive identities of the ethnic minorities—a greater trust and sympathy for the central government would actually be fostered, the local class struggle would be promoted and the dignity of the peasants asserted. On the other hand, of course, the danger existed that opportunistic Amerindian leaders could manipulate this ethnic consciousness in a destructive manner for personal ends.[16]

Under the Somoza state structure, the Atlantic Coast had been an enclave of international capital, primarily North American, and an internal colony of Nicaragua. With the expropriation of the foreign firms and the determined commitment of the Sandinistas to implement economic programs for the benefit of the exploited classes, the material prerequisites for the construction of socialism on the northeastern Atlantic Coast of Nicaragua had been guaranteed. Threats to the actualization of the goals of the Sandinista Revolution in the region persisted, however. For historical reasons, and as a result of the form the class struggle had taken, the Amerindians defined themselves antagonistically to the Ladino population that dominated Nicaragua. In other words, one could argue that they constituted an oppressed national minority.

In the particular case of the Mosquitia, however, secession was not the solution. In fact, independence from Nicaragua would definitely be detrimental to the interests of the indigenous minorities. North American capital would immediately overwhelm the region. As one of the young leaders of MISURASATA explained, "Independence for us today would throw us right back into the arms of the American companies." Furthermore, Nicaragua, the state which was "colonizing" the Amerindians was itself in a stage of transition to socialism and was determined to eradicate all vestiges of internal oppression.

Small fragmented Third World countries are in the interest of international capital. It was imperative, therefore, that the Amerindians consolidate their participation in the Sandinista Revolution rather than separate from it. This would only happen, however, when they ceased to feel threatened culturally, economically and politically by the Ladinos. A potential solution would be to establish locally autonomous governmental structures fully administered by the Costeños themselves. By the same token, whereby ethnic reaffirmation would result in a more integrated Nicaraguan national identity, regional autonomy for northern Zelaya could cement a firmer national unity in Nicaragua.

Notes

[1] In 1980, the Miskitu in Nicaragua were estimated to number between 90,000 and 150,000; the Sumu probably did not exceed 5,000; the Rama were 1,000; and the Creole and Carib, between 25,000 and 30,000. The population of Zelaya was approximated at 220,000, and the total population of Nicaragua was 2.4 million.

This paper will not discuss the Afroamerican population with whom the Revolution has had certain difficulties during the first year (see footnote 14). Neither will the ethnic Chinese be analyzed despite the fact that they dominated local wholesale commerce in the Atlantic Coast.

[2] Jaime Wheelock Román, *Raices Indígenas de la Lucha Anticolonialista en Nicaragua* (Mexico: Siglo Veintiuno, 1974), pp. 25, 26, and 57.

[3] Robert White, *The Case of the Agent to the Settlers on the Coast of Yucatan; and the Late Settlers on the Mosquito Shore, Stating the Whole of his Conduct, in Soliciting Compensation for the Losses, Sustained by each of His Majesty's Injured and Distressed Subjects* (London: T. Cadwell, 1789) p. 45.

[4] Ibid., p. 78.

[5] Ibid.

[6] No author, *Further Papers Relating to the Arbitration of His Majesty the Emperor of Austria in the Differences Between the Government of Her Britannic Majesty and the Government of the Republic of Nicaragua Respecting the Interpretations of Certain Articles of the Treaty of Managua Signed on the 18th of January 1860* (London: Harrison & Sons, 1881), p. 61.

[7] White, *The Case of the Agent*, p. 47.

[8] Ibid., p. 59.

[9] Jorge Jenkins, "Antecedentes Históricos de la Explotación de Recursos Naturales en la Costa Atlántica de Nicaragua," in *Programa Forestal Reporte y Análisis de Resultados, Versión Preliminario,* (Managua: Banco Central de Nicaragua, 1975), p. 161.

[10] *Further Papers*, p. 57.

[11] White, *The Case of the Agent*, p. 45.

[12] Thomas Karnes, *Tropical Enterprises the Standard Fruit and Steamship Company in Latin America* (Baton Rouge and London: Louisana State University Press, 1978), p. 115.

[13] Not a single Rama was present at the founding of MISURASATA, and they continue to remain extremely marginal to the organization.

[14] The class composition of the Afroamericans concentrated in southern Zelaya is different. Within the black population, in addition to a disproportionately large lumpenproletariat, there exists a local *petit* bourgeoisie with a relatively high representation of North American-educated intellectuals and professionals. As members of an English-speaking, urban culture, the Creoles benefitted most from the capitalist enclave structures. Consequently, they were severely and immediately affected by the temporary disruptions in the economy caused by the withdrawal and(or) expropriation of the foreign firms. The Creole-Carib mass organization SICC (Southern Indigenous Creole Community), unlike MISURASATA, did not choose to adhere to the FSLN and was avowedly separatist in its orientation. In general, there was a stronger strain of anticommunism and a greater attachment to North America among the Creoles than among other *Costeños.*

In late September and early October 1980, economic activity in Bluefields, where the Afroamerican population is concentrated, was halted for three days by a series of local demonstrations and acts of vandalism, protesting the presence of "communist" Cuban primary school teachers and doctors in the town.

[15] This is the same train of logic that led Marx to conclude that the only way of uniting the British and the Irish working classes was for the British proletariat to support the independence struggle of the Irish. Karl Marx and Frederick Engles, *The Selected Correspondence of Karl Marx and Frederick Engles, 1847-1867* translated by Dona Torr (New York: International Publishers, 1942), p. 229.

Similarly, Lenin wrote in 1914:

> It remains unexplained why Russia cannot try to 'strengthen' her ties with the Ukranians . . . by granting the Ukranians freedom to use their own language, self-government and an autonomous diet. Is it not clear that the more liberty the Ukranian nationality enjoys in any particular country the stronger its ties with that country will be?

V.I. Lenin, *On the National and Colonial Questions* (Peking: Foreign Lanuage Press, 1975), p. 5.

[16] This was probably what precipitated the arrest in February 1981 of several of the leaders of MISURASATA who apparently were planning to establish a separate government in the Mosquitia. According to newspaper reports (Barricada 1981 and *Nuevo Diario* 1981) they intended to demand a representative on the Junta of National Reconstruction, four additional seats on the Council of State, and the right to 80 percent of the revenues generated in the Mosquitia. A crisis erupted in the community of Prinzapolka resulting in the deaths of eight people: four soldiers, who had come to detain and question a local MISURASATA leader, and four members of the local community.

All the MISURASATA members were released shortly thereafter despite the fact that the leader, Steadman Fagoth Muller was found to have had links to Somoza's secret service prior to the Sandinista victory. Fagoth subsequently broke with MISURASATA and joined   right-wing former National Guardsmen and Somoza supporters in Honduras. He emitted rabidly "anti-communist" statements on the clandestine radio station *"15 de Septiembre"* and gave a series of semi-hysterical press conferences in Tegucigalpa and Miami decrying the "persecution" of the Miskitu by the "Sandino-communists:"

"Nicaraguans, if you have a piece of bread, don't ever give it to a communist. It is better that you give it to your dog because your dog is noble." *Foreign Broadcast Information Service, 1981,* Vol. VI, No. 099, p. 25.

Chapter 18

The Foreign Policy
of the Nicaraguan Revolution

ALEJANDRO BENDAÑA

Al Compañero Presidente
Kenneth Kaunda

En Zambia y Nicaragua
hemos logrado cruzar el río

Que canten las guitarras!
Que canten los tambores!
otros ríos habrá que saltar
en Namibia, El Salvador
en Africa del Sur, en Guatemala
que se abra el corazón
en Zambia, en Nicaragua!

Lusaka, Zambia
Abril, 1980

Daniel Ortega*

Only 41 days after the FSLN's triumphant entry into Managua, with the
country in ruins and hundreds of emergencies to address, the Government
of National Reconstruction took the momentous decision to incorporate
Nicaragua into the Movement of Non-Aligned Countries. Fully aware of

---

The author wishes to stress that he wrote this chapter in his personal capacity and not in
his formal role as a member of the Nicaraguan delegation to the United Nations.

* "Nicaragua, Año 1," *Cuadernos del Tercer Mundo* 39 (Aug.-Sept. 1980), p. 43.

In Zambia and Nicaragua
we have managed to cross the river
Let the guitars play!
Let the drums sound!
other rivers are yet to be crossed
in Namibia, El Salvador
in South Africa, in Guatemala
let us open our hearts
in Zambia, in Nicaragua!

the significance and implications of such a step, the new Sandinista authorities knew that a radical reorientation of Nicaragua's international posture was a logical consequence and an immediate necessity of a revolution fought to attain genuine national independence. Joining the non-aligned countries was a signal to the world that Nicaragua had undergone more than a simple change in government and that a revolution was underway

Inevitably, Nicaragua's presence at the Havana Conference in September 1979 caused some consternation, as had the presence of a delegation of FSLN commanders at the anniversary celebration of the Cuban Revolution some weeks earlier. The U.S. and Nicaragua's northern Central American neighbors could only look askance at the nonaligned movement whose anti-imperialist thrust seemed, in Washington's view, to be assuming an anti-U.S. and pro-Soviet stance under the chairmanship of Fidel Castro. It was a major shift from the days, years, and decades during which Nicaraguan foreign policy had been pegged to, and often decided in Washington's "Foggy Bottom." As Somoza recalled from exile,

> I stood back to back with the U.S. and gave my friend and ally all the support I could muster. . . . [no] president anywhere supported the policies of the United States more devoutly than I did. The record will show that no such loyalty existed anywhere.[1]

For the first time in Nicaraguan history, Nicaraguans themselves defined their own foreign policy in exercise of their newly obtained freedom and right to self-determination. In destroying the dictatorship, the Sandinista Revolution broke the image of Nicaraguan servility to foreign interests. Nicaraguans earned the sovereign right to be present in Havana in solidarity with the states whose own principles and objectives coincided with those of the Revolution itself. Comandante Daniel Ortega, member of the Junta of the Government of National Reconstruction, explained in his message to the Conference:

> We are joining the Non-Aligned Movement because we see in it the broadest organization of the Third World States that play an important role and exercise increasing influence in the international arena and in the people's struggle against imperialism, colonialism, neocolonialism, apartheid, racism (including Zionism) and other forms of oppression; because they are for active peaceful coexistence, against the existence of military blocs and alliances, for the restructuring of international relations on a just basis and for the establishment of a new international economic order. In the Sandinista Revolution there is no alignment; we have a conscious and total commitment to meet the aspirations of the peoples that have attained their independence and those that are struggling to do so. That is why we are in the Non-Aligned Movement.[2]

The Non-Aligned program of support for the right of the peoples of Puerto Rico, Belize, Palestine, Western Sahara, Namibia and East Timor to self-determination and independence; its demand for a restructuring of the world's unjust and neocolonialist commercial and financial structures; its insistence on the right of nations to control their own natural resources and freely define their own social and political systems: these were all points consistent with Sandinista ideology and which henceforth were incorporated and defended in the Revolutionary Government's foreign policy. In taking these positions, Nicaragua's new authorities were carrying out the Program of Government of July 9, 1979 that called for "an independent non-aligned foreign policy" and "solidarity with the democratic nations of Latin America and the rest of the world."[3]

Adopting a progressive foreign policy was both a break with and culmination of past experience. Sandinistas felt that identification with the non-aligned was a logical outgrowth of a long history and deep tradition of national struggle for independence—a history dating back to native Indian resistance to Spanish conquest and colonialism, and a tradition best embodied in General Augusto C. Sandino's struggle against U.S. occupation and colonialism. Nicaragua's nationalist leadership believed that Sandino's contribution to the July 19th victory derived not only from his personal example, but also in his pointing out that the ultimate goal of building a popular democracy in Nicaragua would only be achieved through an anti-imperialist strategy. Indeed, during over four and a half decades of Somoza family dictatorship, a string of antigovernment movements failed to take Sandino's precept into account and ultimately proved failures. Guided by Sandino's political thought, the FSLN, and in particular its principal founder Carlos Fonseca Amador, correctly perceived that the symbiotic relationship between the Somoza dynasty and U.S. power made it possible and necessary to wage a broadly based anti-imperialist war of national liberation in order to topple the dictatorship, and clear the way for democracy.[4]

To the anti-imperialist component in Sandinista thought was added an internationalistic corollary. Sandino and his successors believed that the Nicaraguan struggle was part of a single worldwide struggle for freedom. By the same token, Sandinistas recognized the importance of international support for Nicaraguan liberation. And from Sandino's time onward, the Nicaraguan popular struggle received such support. In the months preceding the ouster of Somoza, a Sandinista diplomatic offensive, led primarily by the Group of Twelve, complemented the military offensive at home in bringing about the isolation of the dictatorship and winning over Latin American governments to the side of the insurgents. These initiatives, coupled with the mobilization of peoples in an international campaign of support, proved instrumental in blocking the U.S. plan, presented at the Organization of American States (OAS) in June 1979, to send an interventionalist force to Nicaragua to keep the Sandinistas from coming to power.

Following victory, it became the moral and political duty of the Revolutionary government, guided by Sandino's thought, to reciprocate that support through its diplomacy.

Internationalism was also a question of self-defense. There could be no escaping the fact that the Somoza family and its allies persisted in attempts to undermine or reverse the Revolution. The elaborate family support network built up over the years in Central and South America, reaching into the U.S. Congress, right-wing circles, and Cuban terrorist groups continued in existence. It was fed not only by Somoza's massive fortune—disguised and protected behind a legal multinational facade—but also by reactionary sectors and regional oligarchies determined to defend their privileges, therefore having a vested interest in the Nicaraguan Revolution's failure, in the destruction of the dangerous and perhaps contagious example of a generous, broad-based revolution. Moreover, Nicaraguans were all too aware that throughout history successful revolutions and attempted counterrevolutions had gone hand-in-hand. The steady right-wing drift within the U.S. and the resurgence of the Cold War in the months following the Nicaraguan victory made the task of consolidation and reconstruction all the more difficult. Membership in the Non-Aligned Movement and cultivation of broad international support for Nicaraguan self-determination offered some protection against the possibility of destabilization and interventionist policies. International solidarity, therefore, continued to be instrumental in consolidating Nicaragua's newly won soveriegnty and with it the right to build a just society free from foreign interference. Sandinista foreign policy set out to maintain and broaden the international base of support for the revolution.

By the first anniversary celebration, Nicaragua had more than doubled the number of countries with which it enjoyed diplomatic relations. Bonds of friendship and cooperation with old friends were strengthened as relations became particularly cordial with Mexico, Cuba, Panama, Costa Rica, Venezuela, Ecuador, Jamaica, Peru, Grenada, Federal Republic of Germany, Spain, the Netherlands, and Sweden. New and good relations were established with the Soviet Union, the German Democratic Republic, Poland, Bulgaria, and practically all the socialist countries in Eastern Europe, including Albania. A particular effort was made to develop bonds with Africa because of the many aspirations common to Nicaragua and the peoples of that continent. Relations were established with Mozambique, Angola, Zambia, Tanzania, Algeria, and other African countries including Zimbabwe, at whose independence ceremony Comandante Daniel Ortega was present. In Asia, Nicaragua established relations with India. With Vietnam, diplomatic relations were merely formalized as they had long existed between two peoples brought together by a common trajectory of struggle. In 1981, particular efforts were made to strengthen ties with other countries in Asia. Although there were no formal relations with the People's Republic of China, commercial ties existed and Nicarguan government officials visited that country.

From the outset, diversity in diplomatic relations figured as a keynote of the Revolution's foreign policy. The point was not merely to prove that Nicaragua was now free to establish relations with any nation, but more important, to use old and new diplomatic ties to encourage a genuine and independent understanding of Nicaraguan and Central American realities on the part of other governments and political forces. The point was to neutralize interventionist sectors in the U.S. and elsewhere which were intolerant of pluralism and prone to confuse a people's will to independence with international communist conspiracies. The FSLN pursued the same objective on a party basis, joining, for example, the Permanent Conference of Political Parties of Latin America (COPPPAL) sponsored by Mexico's ruling Institutional, Revolutionary Party (PRI) and participating as observers at meetings of the Socialist International. The results were clear comments of support for the Nicaraguan Revolution as exemplified in a resolution adopted at the Congress of the Socialist International, which stated its belief "that the victory and the achievements of the Nicaraguan revolution reflect the hopes for social change in the whole region."[5] At the same time, worldwide organizations in solidarity with the Nicaraguan people continue to work actively in promoting popular understanding.

Another purpose of the strategy of diplomatic diversification was to attain economic independence for Nicaragua. Such a goal seemed incongruous in view of the fact that large amounts of external economic assistance were required to reconstruct the economy following the destruction of the country by Somoza. A U.N. commission calculated war-related damages of $480 million (U.S.) to the economic infrastructure, with another $670 billion contracted on terms impossible to meet. The agricultural cycle had been interrupted and the gross domestic product decreased by 25.1 percent in 1979.[6] From the outset the Government made it clear that aid was welcome from all corners, but with no strings attached. In October 1979, the United Nations General Assembly unanimously adopted a resolution recommending assistance to Nicaragua. Prestige and political backing made it possible for Nicaragua to obtain donations and credits on concessionary terms.

The same combination provided the Government a solid bargaining position for renegotiating the foreign debt. Contrary to many predictions, the Sandinista Government made good on its pledge to recognize the foreign debt, although not on terms that might hamper the Revolution's commitment to social reform and redistribution of income. Requests by private commercial banks for immediate payment of past-due interest and for the involvement of the IMF prior to renegotiations were rejected. After long and difficult negotiations, an unprecedented agreement was reached in September 1980 responsive to Nicaragua's needs and ability to pay. The *New York Times* described the terms as "extremely favorable to Nicaragua and representing a pattern for other third world countries."[7]

In line with the quest to assure an economic underpinning to its newly won independence, the Nicaraguan Government oriented its foreign economic policy towards the diversification of trade relationships. Finding additional markets for Nicaraguan exports—cotton, coffee, sugar, and meat—and new sources of imports and technology were part of the critical task of reducing the economy's dependence on structures dominated by U.S. banks and multinational corporations. Nationalizing foreign commerce and creating a Ministry of Foreign Commerce were also means to that end in that they helped the Nicaraguan state to rationalize trade and gain the best possible terms. Such a concern was also apparent in the Nicaraguan government's promotion of a restructuring of the Central American Common Market away from its traditional subservience to multinational interests and towards a greater orientation to popular and regional interests. Beyond the pecuniary objectives lay strategic ones; diversification lessened the vulnerability of the Revolution to any use of trading and credit restrictions as instruments of political pressure.[8]

If it is evident that a sovereign and independent foreign policy had earned the Nicaraguan Revolution considerable successes and prestige, it is also true that the defense of revolutionary principles had carried certain costs and posed difficulties. Right-wing elements within and outside Central America seized on Nicaragua's international positions to attack the Revolution. Distorted accounts of Nicaragua's international posture played a part in the campaign to isolate Nicaragua and break the broad domestic and international support enjoyed by the Revolution. When, for example, a government delegation travelled to the Soviet Union and Eastern Europe, Nicaragua was quickly labeled communist and accused in the U.S. media of signing a secret military pact with the U.S.S.R.[9]

No aspect of Nicaraguan diplomacy stirred more controversy than its policy of upholding fraternal relations with Cuba. The Nicaraguan Government made no apology for its friendship with Cuba. Nicaraguans pointed to Cuban assistance, principally teachers and doctors, as a model of the type of no-strings-attached aid it desired. Government leaders did not deny that Nicaragua, engaged in the formidable task of meeting the basic human needs of its population over a short period of time, could profit from the experience of the only thoroughgoing social revolution in Latin America, in terms of both its achievements and its mistakes.

Another controversy arose over the Nicaraguan decision to abstain on U.N. votes on the Afghanistan question in January and November of 1980. Although not in agreement with the presence of Soviet troops in Afghanistan, Nicaragua took the position, shared by India, that a punitive resolution alone would not contribute to peace in the area. A concern at the time of the first vote was that the condemnation of the Soviet Union would provide a rationale for the escalation of the U.S. military presence in Southeast Asia; subsequent events bore that fear out. Speaking at the U.N. in October 1980, Foreign Minister Miguel D'Escoto reiterated Nicaragua's support for the right of the Afghan people to self-determination and called for regional negotiations. Once again, however, Nicaragua's decision not to follow the lead of the U.S. was interpreted as evidence that the country had drifted into the Soviet bloc.

Relations with Colombia became strained in February 1980 when the Nicaraguan Foreign Ministry envoked the defense of territorial integrity to declare invalid the 1928 Barcenas Meneses-Esguerra Treaty between the two countries. Under the terms of the treaty, Nicaragua had handed over to Colombia the San Andrés and Providencia islands along with the surrounding keys located off Nicaragua's Atlantic coast. In its White Paper, the Nicaraguan Foreign Ministry contended that the treaty had been signed and ratified under pressure during the U.S. occupation of Nicaragua. The territorial transfer was invalid, not only because it was signed by a puppet government incapable of defending national sovereignty, but also because, from the legal standpoint, it was at variance with the provisions of the National Constitution in force at that time.[10]

The Somozas, in due regard to their relations with Washington and investments in Colombia, had never bothered to seriously seek redress of that injustice. To the Sandinista Government, however, it became a matter of priority since it touched on nationalist sentiment and because there were more than 50,000 square miles of national maritime territory involved. Although Colombia refused to recognize or negotiate the Nicaraguan claim, both countries continued to enjoy satisfactory relations.

The same cannot be said for relations with certain Latin American governments in light of Nicaragua's forceful stand in defense of human rights. Dictatorships did not take kindly to Nicaraguan denunciations and accused Managua of interfering in the internal affairs of other states. The Nicaraguan government maintained that the defense of human rights and respect for non-intervention were two fundamental principles of its foreign policy—principles that had been upheld by Sandinista diplomats during the struggle against Somoza and which afterwards continued in force. The Nicaraguan Government condemned the massive repressions in El Salvador, Guatemala, and Bolivia, in the latter case by denouncing the military coup of July 17, 1980. At the U.N. and the OAS, Nicaraguan diplomats were active in promoting international campaigns to isolate the Bolivian Junta and in defending the right of the Salvadorean people to define their own future.

With respect to the Salvadorean struggle, both the Nicaraguan Government and the FSLN rejected the accusations of Sandinista intervention and explained that the best contribution that Nicaragua could make to the Salvadorean struggle was to consolidate its own revolution. Mindful of Washington's frustrated attempt at intervention in Nicaragua in June 1979, Nicaraguan officials warned that any intervention in El Salvador could turn all of Central America into a Vietnam. None of the five republics could remain unaffected by developments in the region. For Nicaragua, there was no certainty that any counterrevolutionary intervention would stop at

Salvadorean borders, any more than there was any guarantee for El Salvador and Guatemala that the example of a successful revolution in Nicaragua would not have a domestic effect.

An indication of the importance attached to the regional situation is the fact that respect for regional self-determination became a basic criterion of Nicaraguan relations with the U.S. In this, as in other aspects of its diplomacy, the Nicaragua Government considered that its objectives were best achieved by a principled yet pragmatic disposition. Upon assuming power, the Government of National Reconstruction signalled to the U.S. its wish to develop the best possible relations and to heal the wounds inflicted as the result of Washington's historical complicity with Somoza. The hope was that Nicaraguan-U.S. relations could develop into a model of mutual respect between a revolutionary nation and the dominant power of the western hemisphere. Recognition was given to the Carter Administration for its efforts to bring about a change in traditional policies. Nonetheless, as the debate and the delay over the U.S. aid package underscored, powerful interests within and outside the U.S. government sought to slander and damage the only popular and democratic government Nicaraguans had ever enjoyed. Foreign Minister D'Escoto defined the course of future relations with the United States as dependent on the co-relation of strength between the realists and the interventionists within the U.S. "We wish to be friends," he said, "but we will never sell out, nor will we ever compromise in our sacred task of building a new, free, and sovereign Nicaragua."[11]

The truism that a nation's foreign policy is the extension of its domestic policy applies to Nicaragua. The Sandinista commitment to political pluralism at home found its counterpart in a foreign policy seeking to maintain friendly relations with as many countries as possible. Within the framework of a revolution upholding the necessity of total liberation, the task was not always easy. Herein lay the originality and the challenge of the Nicaraguan "model."

Notes

[1] Anastasio Somoza and Jack Cox, *Nicaragua Betrayed* (Belmont, Mass.: Western Islands, 1980), pp. 77–78.

[2] *Discursos Pronunciados en la VI Conferencia de Jefes de Estado o de Gobierno de los Países No Alineados, La Habana 3—9 Septiembre 1979* (Havana: Editorial de Ciencias Sociales, 1980), p. 585.

[3] *Programa del Gobierno de Reconstrucción Nacional* (Managua: Ministerio de Educación, 1979), p. 6.

[4] Carlos Fonseca, *Escritos* (Managua: Secretaría Nacional de Propaganda y Educación Política, 1979); José Benito Escobar Pérez, *Ideario Sandinista* (mimeograph).

[5] Resolution of the Fifteenth Post War Congress of the Socialist International, Nov. 16, 1980 (mimeo); see also COPPAL, *Boletín Informativo*, 5 (1980).

[6] United Nations Economic Commission on Latin America, *Nicaragua: Economic Repercussions of Recent Political Events* (E / CEPAL / G1091, Sept. 1979).

[7] *New York Times,* Sept. 9, 1980; *Financial Times,* Sept. 16, 1980.

[8] Bayardo Arce, *Romper la Dependencia: Taréa Estratégica de la Revolución* (Managua: Secretaría Nacional de Propaganda y Educación Política, 1980).

[9] See, for example, the Evans and Novack column in the *Washington Post,* Aug. 1, 1980.

[10] Ministerio del Exterior, *Libro Blanco sobre el caso de San Andrés y Providencia* (Managua: Ministerio del Exterior, 1980).

[11] Naciones Unidas Asamblea General, *Acta Taquigráfica Provisional* (A / 35 / PV.28, Oct. 8, 1980).

PART VI

SOME INTERNATIONAL CONSIDERATIONS

This last part does not pretend to be comprehensive. There are many relevant international themes which might have been examined. Unfortunately, space limitations allow us to cover only three of the more important ones. In their chapter, Mitchell Seligson and William Carroll III delve into the Costa Rican role in the Sandinist victory. They contend that the somewhat ambiguous but generally favorable attitude of the Costa Rican electorate toward the Nicaraguan insurrection lead to policies on the part of the Costa Rican government which basically reflected such attitudes. They maintain that Costa Rican policy toward the insurrection played a very important role in the victory of the FSLN. Max Azicri compares and contrasts the Cuban and Nicaraguan revolutions, finding a number of similarities as well as some very significant differences. Throughout his study, he wonders whether Nicaragua's unique attempt at pluralistic popular democracy could be retained under mounting domestic and foreign counter-revolutionary pressure. Finally, Susanne Jonas examines the impact of the reemerging Cold War on U.S.-Nicaraguan relations. She describes the interplay of powerful conflicting interests in the United States during the prolonged Congressional battle over the infamous $75 million. Although she sees ominous possibilities for Nicaragua during the new and clearly hostile Reagan Administration, she also identifies possible constraints on aggressive U.S. behavior.

Chapter 19

The Costa Rican Role
in the Sandinist Victory

MITCHELL A. SELIGSON
WILLIAM J. CARROLL III

On July 17, 1979, Anastasio Somoza, scion to the dynasty which ruled
Nicaragua since 1936, was driven from office. Researchers are only now
beginning to investigate systematically the factors which contributed to his
downfall. Inquiry is focusing on two central areas: (1) the weaknesses of the
Somoza regime, and (2) the strengths of the Sandinista movement. This
chapter takes up the latter, dealing with one major strength of the movement, namely the assistance it received from Costa Rica at crucial points in
the civil war.[1] Our thesis is that a number of decisions taken by the Costa
Rican government in the twilight years of the Somoza regime were taken in
the context of deep-seated hostility between the governments of Costa Rica
and Nicaragua and that this hostility can be traced back to the early years of
Central America's independence from Spain. That these decisions did not
consistently favor the Sandinistas can be traced to a concern on the part of
Costa Rica over the impact that a guerrilla victory ultimately might have
upon it, particularly insofar as the Sandinistas were perceived as a
communist-led movement.

Historical Roots of Hostility: 1824-1927

As early as 1824, Costa Rica and Nicaragua came into conflict. In that year,
the Nicaraguan province of Nicoya was annexed to Costa Rica, becoming
what is today the province of Guanacaste. The loss of this region has been a
bone of perpetual contention between the two countries. Some years later,
in 1842, Costa Rica revealed its distaste for dealing with other countries in
the Central American region and its particular lack of affinity for Nicaragua
by refusing to send representatives to the Central American confederation
talks being held in that country. Throughout the first half of the nineteenth
century, Thomas L. Karnes notes, "Costa Rica reinforced its tendencies of
late colonial times toward localism, neutrality, and a realization that it was
better to be separated from the quarrels of the other four."[2]

Despite its efforts to remain aloof from her neighbors, Costa Rica's first
violent international dispute found it in conflict with Nicaragua. In 1856,

Costa Rica invaded Nicaragua in an effort to put an end to William Walker's unappreciated intervention in Central American affairs. However, since Costa Rican troops crossed the Nicaraguan border without a declaration of war, Nicaragua's President Rivas was prompted to call "on the entire civilized world to note that his country was being attacked without provocation" and to declare war on Costa Rica. Costa Rica suffered a bitter defeat and heavy losses at the hands of the combined forces of Walker's North American mercenaries and Nicaraguan troops, and was forced to withdraw.

By 1858, the two neighboring nations were again on the verge of war, this time in a dispute over possession rights to the San Juan River, long believed to offer a possible transisthmian route. Open warfare was averted only by the timely intervention of El Salvador and Guatemala, who pressured Costa Rica into signing the Jérez-Cañas Treaty.

The remaining years of the nineteenth century were much calmer, although difficulties did emerge during the period of 1893-1909, during the rule of José Santos Zelaya. During this period, Nicaragua's frequent military incursions into neighboring republics only served to reinforce the antipathy between the two countries.

The first indications of Costa Rican support for the Sandinistas came during Augusto C. Sandino's struggle against the U.S. Marines' occupation of Nicaragua. During this period, Costa Rica frequently served as a jumping-off point for armed incursions northward. The failure of the Costa Rican government to prevent such activity was attributed to problems of effectively patrolling the difficult terrain along its northern border. No doubt there is an element of truth to this claim, but in the context of the historically strained relations between the two countries, it is difficult to accept it as the complete explanation. Nicaragua was able to repay Costa Rica for its failure to stop the Sandinista raids of the 1927-1933 period through its open support for ex-Costa Rican president Calderón Guardia's attempt to regain control of Costa Rica. He had been granted asylum in Nicaragua after the 1948 civil war, during which José "Pepe" Figueres took control. In December 1948, Calderonistas, armed and supported by Nicaragua, invaded Costa Rica. Action by the Organization of American States (OAS) helped avert a full-scale war between the two nations.

Costa Rica was to repay Nicaragua's action of 1948 in 1959. That year, a key antagonist of the Somozas, Pedro Joaquín Chamorro, later editor of the opposition newspaper "La Prensa," haunted the dynasty from Costa Rica. Chamorro and approximately 150 rebels invaded Nicarargua from a base in Punto de Llorones in Costa Rica. This invasion was the opening volley in a battle which was to last until the downfall of the Somoza regime. By the late 1960s, clashes between the Nicaraguan National Guard and Sandinista units became frequent along the Costa Rican border. Civilians in the border region often claimed that the Nicaraguans were being overly zealous and were illegally crossing the border into Costa Rica. Then Nicaragua began harrassing truckers crossing the Nicaraguan-Costa Rican border, and tension mounted.

Renewed conflict arose once again in late 1976, when President Anastasio Somoza accused Costa Rica of diverting water from the San Juan River and thus violating stipulations of the Jérez-Cañas Treaty. Relations worsened considerably when, a short time later, Costa Rica seized three Nicaraguan tuna boats and their crews for fishing inside territorial waters. Not to be outdone, Nicaragua responded by impounding two Costa Rican boats.

Then in October 1977, after a lull of almost a year following the combat deaths of two of its principle leaders, the FSLN went on the offensive, attacking the National Guard barracks in the remote San Juan river town of San Carlos, near the Costa Rican frontier. National Guard reinforcements already in the area were able to force the Sandinistas to retreat across the border, but not before a much more serious incident took place. Claiming "hot pursuit," the Nicaraguan air force strafed three Costa Rican boats inside the latter's national territory. Aboard one of the boats was Costa Rican security minister Mario Charpentier, accompanied by a group of journalists. The hostile act immediately received wide media coverage and led to a vigorous protest by Costa Rica, which further strained the worsening relations between the two countries.

Costa Rican Policy toward the Insurrection: 1977-1979

Following the San Carlos raid, the Costa Rican government granted asylum to eleven members of the FSLN who had participated in the operation and had escaped to Costa Rica. While such a humanitarian gesture on the part of Costa Rica was not unprecedented, the action brought immediate charges from Nicaragua that its southern neighbor was providing sanctuary for Sandinista guerrillas. The Somoza newspaper, *Novedades*, claimed that the invasion of San Carlos occurred with the knowledge and acquiescence of the Costa Rican authorities. The situation failed to improve when a meeting of Central American heads of state in Guatemala City, called on October 31 to discuss the border conflict and other topics, was conspicuously not attended by Costa Rica's president Daniel Oduber.

As Oduber's term in office drew to a close in May 1978, the FSLN guerrillas began to have doubts about the availability of Costa Rica as a safe haven under his successor, Rodrigo Carazo Odio. As a candidate for office, the firm anticommunist Carazo had pledged to recall the Costa Rican ambassador to Moscow. Later, as President-Elect, it was reported that he promised the Nicaraguan foreign minister that he would take action against those FSLN elements operating in Costa Rica.[3] Once in office, however, Carazo seemed to have a change of mind, granting asylum to a high-ranking FSLN leader in June 1978. He may have begun to have second thoughts, though, when Somoza responded to this action by sending reinforcements to the Costa Rica border in a show of strength.

As the year wore on, the strategic importance of Costa Rica as a nearby sanctuary for continuing the struggle against Somoza was further underscored by the return of influential Nicaraguans who had been exiled there. *"Los Doce, "* a group of prominent and well-respected intellectualls and professionals, arrived in Managua from San José in July, having been allowed back by Somoza who hoped "to improve his image in the United States."[4] However, matters did not improve for Somoza since the group immediately called for an antigovernmental front to include the *Sandinista* guerrillas, causing popular outbreaks of violence in major cities. But perhaps the most significant exile to return was Edén Pastora Gómez, who as "Comandante Zero" led a force of twenty-five guerrillas in atacking and holding the Nicaraguan National Palace for forty-eight hours in late August. Costa Rica acted at this time in a somewhat ambiguous role as it offered to have its ambassador in Managua mediate between Somoza and the guerrillas, while publicly announcing that Pastora Gómez would be free to return to Costa Rica whenever he wished.

Costa Rica's concern that a total Sandinista victory in Nicaragua could have a decidedly destabilizing effect on its welfare, and that instability along the northern border would grow, resulted in offers from Costa Rica in September 1978 to mediate the Nicaraguan crisis. This diplomatic effort had little chance to unfold, however, as the gesture was withdrawn by mid-month following new violations of Costa Rican territory by Nicaraguan aircraft in "hot pursuit" of suspected guerrillas. The fact that Somoza denied these violations to the news media did not prevent Costa Rica from calling for an OAS team to investigate its complaint. Concurrently, as the mood in Costa Rica swung away from efforts at mediation, the opinion that Somoza must go at any cost became more prevalent. This increased hostility is illustrated by the official Costa Rican decision at the time to expropriate a 15,000-hectare Somoza estate in Guanacaste, and by ex-President Figueres's call for arms to be shipped to the Sandinistas.

Costa Rican fears of a communist takeover in Nicaragua again surfaced in November 1978. Official policy towards the guerrillas became at best ambivalent as the government in San José initiated cleanup operations to rid the northern border areas of the FSLN. The operation netted about fifty suspected insurgents, some of whom were actually deported to Panama. In addition, a force of some 200-300 Sandinistas marshaled in Panama was denied passage through Costa Rica. Significantly, the change in policy by San José was seen to damage the chances of the FSLN unleasing a planned new offensive against Somoza from the Guanacaste region. Yet during this same period, Costa Rica's official line regarding the guerrillas became even more ambiguous as Costa Rica broke off diplomatic relations with Nicaragua in response to a serious armed conflict between Costa Rica and Somoza forces at the border.

As the year 1978 waned, the final offensive hinted at by the FSLN still failed to materialize. There is sufficient information to suggest that this inaction was due in large part to the intermittent cleanup operations Costa Rica continued to conduct in the border regions. The policy at this time, however, may not have been entirely of Costa Rica's own choosing. On December 26, angered by increased cross-border attacks, Somoza closed the frontier with Costa Rica, threatening to invade the country unless the government in San José stepped up its anti-Sandinista operations. This action precipitated a Costa Rican call to the OAS asking for protection against Nicaraguan invasion. It also led to serious discussions in San José as to whether or not the country should build up its armed forces. Its realization that the Civil Guard was no match for an armed attack begs the question of how the Carazo administration realistically expected these same forces to contain or eradicate an ever-growing and more professionally organized guerrilla force. The policy of rounding up suspected FSLN members was at best never intended to be more than a safety-valve measure to keep Somoza's National Guard at arm's length. The notion becomes even more plausible when threats of a surgical strike into Costa Rica by the National Guard are taken into account.

The ambivalent nature of Costa Rican priorities concerning the Somoza crisis continued on into 1979. Early in the year, "Operación Jaque Mate," aimed at ridding the frontier environs of the FSLN, was launched by San José. But like those that preceded it, the action lacked serious content and was largely ineffective and symbolic. For Costa Rica, the real concern was still the disruption which the continued presence of Somoza brought to the entire region. Short of the unlikely event that mediation would force the dictator out, the Carazo administration realistically concluded that the FSLN was the only viable means of terminating the dynasty.

By never effectively eliminating the Sandinista presence along the border with Nicaragua, whether by design or inability, Costa Rica did provide a valuable asset to the guerrillas in the final takeover of the country. Because he could never be certain that a new and larger offensive was not about to break over the southern border, Somoza found it impossible to concentrate entirely on retaking the cities captured by the guerrillas. He could no longer collect and employ his forces against the rebel centers one by one, as he had done so successfully during the rebellion of the previous September. Whenever this strategy was attempted, FSLN units would invade from Costa Rica, obliging Somoza to detach his special 3,000-man force to prevent the loss of the southern provincial capital of Rivas.

One large guerrilla column of about 300 troops, which crossed over from Costa Rica in May 1979, caused Somoza to call for an emergency meeting of the OAS. Angered by the continued transgressions, and by Carazo's attempts to persuade other Latin American nations to break all ties with Managua, Somoza threatened to invoke the Inter-American Treaty of Reciprocal Assistance in order to obtain military help from other OAS members. Pressure originating from within his own cabinet as well as from segments of the private sector encouraged Carazo to back off from his self-appointed diplomatic initiative; these elements feared the possibility of Somoza lashing out against Costa Rica in retaliation.

By June, as matters rapidly deteriorated for Somoza, the FSLN was allowed to set up a governmental Junta-in-Exile in San José. What normally would have been a diplomatically deplorable manoeuvre by Costa Rica, that of openly fomenting the downfall of a sitting government outside its own territory, now brought immediate recognition for the Junta by various nations, so low was the international public opinon of the Somoza regime. Costa Rica was among the first to extend formal recognition to the Junta, first as a belligerent force to be considered on an equal par with the Somoza government, then as the rightful representative of the Nicaraguan people. Until the final FLSN military victory however, Costa Rica never forgot its underlying preoccupation that a communist power might fill the vacuum which an ouster of Somoza would create. As late as the downfall itself, on July 17, the Carazo administration still pursued the ambiguous policy of providing a public base of operations for the rebel Nicarguan government while trying to convince the Junta that it should toe the official Washington line and broaden its base to include conservatives.

Once Somoza was out, Costa Rica no longer had a hostile force threatening to invade across its northern frontier. Attention could be turned from matters of armed strength to more pressing political and economic considerations. Despite the internal criticism Carazo faced because of his handling of the Nicaraguan crisis, Costa Rica could be content that it had played an important role in removing the hated Somozas from the region. Without the continued use of sanctuaries along the border, and the moral support of the majority of the Costa Rican people, the FSLN might have been denied victory altogether.

Public Opinion and Foreign Policy
An historical deterministic position could well read the events of the past 100 years as making inevitable the Carazo government's "tilt" in favor of the Sandinistas. The complex and harsh realities of political life, however, make such reasoning unacceptable. Carazo had to have more than history behind him when the decided to conduct his foreign policy in the manner outlined above. Since it involved the stability of the Isthmus, the real possibility of outside intervention (from the United States, or from Venezuela and(or) Panama), and, perhaps most important, the distinct possibility that Costa Rica might eventually find itself at war with a militarily far more powerful adversary, President Carazo needed to be sure that public opinion was squarely in his corner. Overwhelming public support for a strong stand on Costa Rica's part undoubtedly would have encouraged a firm, even strident foreign policy vis-á-vis Somoza. On the other hand, ambivalence in public opinion almost certainly would have encouraged a far more moderate approach. We do not claim, however, that

there was a one-to one correspondence between public opinion and Carazo's foreign policy. Rather, our view is that public opinion was fraught with ambivalence, and that this ambivalence was reflected in Carazo's actions.

It is clear that serious cross-pressures were influencing public opinion. Indeed, it would be appropriate to characterize the Costa Rican people as caught in an "approach-avoidance dilemma." On the one hand, the long history of tension-filled relations with Nicaragua, along with a more general distaste for antidemocratic regimes, served to stimulate pro-Sandinista sentiment. On the other hand, many Costa Ricans clearly were concerned about the eventual impact of a possible Sandinista victory. Costa Rica itself had suffered a civil war in 1948 in which a central issue was communist influence in the government. Since the international mass media unceasingly spoke of Sandinista links to communism and Cuba, fears of the eventual establishment of a communist state to the north were not by any means irrational.

These cross-pressures were clearly evident in the fall of 1978. At that time, a survey of urban Costa Rican public opinion was taken. The sample, consisting of 201 respondents, was designed to represent opinion in metropolitan San José, as well as in the provincial capitals of Cartago, Heredia, and Alajuela. Approximately 36 percent of the country's population, and most of its urban population, are located in these areas.

Costa Ricans strongly believed in the justice of the Sandinista cause. As is shown in Table 19.1, 96 percent (adjusted) of all respondents who had an opinion believed that the Sandinistas were fighting for a just cause. It should not be assumed, however, that this overwhelming belief in the justice of the Sandinista cause translated into a demand for pro-Sandinista action, either on the part of the government or the citizens.

TABLE 19.1

JUSTICE OF SANDINISTA CAUSE

Question: In your opinion, are the Sandinistas fighting for a just cause or are they not fighting for a just cause?

	Relative Percent	Adjusted Percent	(N)
Just cause	87.1	96.2	(175)
Not just cause	3.5	3.8	(7)
Don't know	9.5	—	(19)
	100.0	100.0	(201)

We see in Tables 19.2a and 19.2b that the demand for action was considerably lower than the belief that the Sandinista cause was just. About two-thirds (65 percent) of the respondents believed that the Costa Rican people ought to help the Sandinistas. Only a little more than a majority (54 percent), however, believed that the government should take any action. Nearly 9 percent of the respondents offered no opinion on these items. If these individuals had sided with the "no action" position, then a majority would have been opposed to the government taking any action. Support for the justice of the Sandinista cause, therefore, did not translate into a mandate for government action.

TABLE 19.2

HELP FOR SANDINISTAS

Question 2a: In your opinion, the Costa Rican *people* ought to help the Sandinistas or ought not to help them?

	Relative Percent	Adjusted Percent	(N)
Help	59.2	64.7	(119)
Not help	32.3	35.3	(65)
Don't know	8.5	—	(17)
	100.0	100.0	(201)

Question 2b: In your opinion, the *government* of Costa Rica ought to help the Sandinistas or ought not to help?

	Relative Percent	Adjusted Percent	(N)
Help	49.3	53.8	(99)
Not help	42.3	46.2	(85)
Don't know	8.5	—	(17)
	100.0	100.0	(201)

Why were the "Ticos" reluctant to come to the aid of the "Nicas" in the latter's hour of need? One reason, as is shown in Table 19.3, is that 40 percent did not believe that armed struggle was the only way to resolve the problem. Costa Rican repugnance for violent solutions to conflicts obvious-

TABLE 19.3

JUSTIFICATION OF SANDINISTA VIOLENCE

Question: In your opinion, armed struggle is the only way to resolve the problems of Nicaragua, or is it not the only way?

	Relative Percent	Adjusted Percent	(N)
Armed struggle the only way	54.7	60.4	(110)
Armed struggle not the only way	35.8	39.6	(72)
Don't know	9.5	—	(19)
	100.0	100.0	(201)

ly played a role in forming this opinion. But we can also conjecture that there was some fear that violence in Nicaragua would ultimately affect Costa Rica, as indeed it did.

When it came to discussing specific actions the government of Costa Rica might take against Somoza, even the mildest was rejected by most citizens. In Table 19.4a, we see that only a little more than one-quarter (28 percent) of the sample was willing to break relations with Nicaragua in October 1978. Interestingly, and as an aside, there was much more support for having Costa Rica withdraw from the OAS if that organization did not impose sanctions on Nicaragua for violation of Costa Rican national territory, than there was for breaking relations with Somoza. In Table 19.4b, we see that just over half of the Costa Ricans interviewed would have wanted to withdraw from the OAS under those circumstances.

TABLE 19.4

SUGGESTED DIPLOMATIC SANCTIONS

Question 4a: In your opinion, Costa Rica ought to break relations with Nicaragua or should not break them?

	Relative Percent	Adjusted Percent	(N)
Break relations	23.9	27.6	(48)
Not break relations	62.7	72.4	(126)
Don't know	13.4	—	(27)
	100.0	100.0	(201)

Question 4b: Do you believe that if the OAS does not impose sanctions on Nicaragua (for violation of national territory), Costa Rica ought to get out of that organization?

	Relative Percent	Adjusted Percent	(N)
Get out	40.8	50.3	(82)
Not get out	40.3	49.7	(81)
Don't know	18.9	—	(38)
	100.0	100.0	(201)

Carazo evidently was quite successful in tailoring his foreign policy on this issue to the desires of the citizenry. As is shown in Table 19.5, 75 percent of the people thought that the government had acted "very well" or "well" in the conflict with Nicaragua.

What lay behind the fears of Costa Ricans which might have mitigated their support for the overthrow of a regime they obviously detested? A fear of communism was certainly one factor. In Table 19.6, we see that nearly one-third of the respondents thought that communism would follow a Sandinista victory in Nicaragua. It is also important to note that almost one-

TABLE 19.5

EVALUATION OF COSTA RICAN GOVERNMENTAL POLICY TOWARD NICARAGUA

Question: Overall, would you say that the government (of Costa Rica) acted very well, well, fair, poorly, or very poorly in the recent conflict with Nicaragua?

	Relative Percent	Adjusted Percent	(N)
Very well	20.4	20.8	(41)
Well	53.7	54.8	(108)
Fair	13.4	13.7	(27)
Poorly	8.5	8.6	(17)
Very poorly	2.0	2.0	(4)
Don't know	2.0	—	(4)
	100.0	100.0	(201)

third also had no opinion on this item, over three times the nonresponse rate of the other items. Obviously, many were unsure about the nature of the Sandinista movement (an uncertainty by no means confined to Costa Ricans). Likewise, as is shown in Table 19.7, although nearly one-fourth (24 percent) of those who held an opinion were willing to label the Sandinista movement as communist, over one-third had no opinion. It was obviously of crucial importance for the outcome of the revolution that for the most part, Costa Rican public opinion viewed the Sandinistas as either noncommunist or were uncertain as to what the movement really was.

TABLE 19.6

WILL COMMUNISM FOLLOW DOWNFALL OF SOMOZA?

Question: In your opinion, if Somoza falls, will communism follow (*se meterá el comunismo*) or not?

	Relative Percent	Adjusted Percent	(N)
Communism will follow	21.4	31.6	(43)
Communism will not follow	46.3	68.4	(93)
Don't know	32.3	—	(65)
	100	100	(201)

TABLE 19.7

PERCEIVED LINK BETWEEN COMMUNISM AND SANDINISTA MOVEMENT

Question: In your opinion, is the Sandinista movement communist or is it not communist?

	Relative Percent	Adjusted Percent	(N)
Is communist	16.4	23.5	(31)
Is not Communist	50.2	76.5	(101)
Don't know	34.3	—	(69)
	100	100	(201)

Had the movement been perceived as a communist movement by the bulk of the Costa Ricans, there would have been less support for it. Such a decline in support could have made a critical difference in the outcome of the revolution, perhaps leaving Nicaragua to follow what was purported to be the United States-backed plan of "Somocismo without Somoza."

Evidence for this contention is presented in Table 19.8. Looking at Table 19.8a, we see that those who perceived the Sandinista movement as linked to communism were much less willing to extend help to the Sandinistas. Whereas 56.4 percent of those who thought the movement was communist would have given either government or citizen assistance, over four-fifths (81 percent) of those who perceived the movement as noncommunist would have extended such help. We suspect that controlling for the respondent's attitude toward communism would have influenced his or her impression of the Sandinista movement being linked to communism, and this in turn would have affected levels of support for pro-Sandinista action. Such a contention is supported. As can be seen in Table 19.8b, the proportion of respondents who would give help to the Sandinistas steadily increased from 50 percent among those who believed that the Sandinistas were linked to communism and who held a negative evaluation of Costa Rican communism to 89 percent among those who believed that the Sandinistas were not communist-linked and who had a positive evaluation of communism. Of the two variables shown in Table 19.8b to have had an influence on the respondent's willingness to help the Sandinistas, the perceived linkage to communism was by far the more important. Hence, while the respondent's evaluation of Costa Rican communism only increased the likelihood of his or her willing to give help to the Sandinistas by an average of 12 percent, the respondent's perception of Sandinista links to communism increased the likelihood of willingness to give help by 26 percent. Nonetheless, it should not be forgotten that even among those who believe the Sandinistas were communist-linked and who held a negative evaluation of Costa Rican communism, 50 percent were still willing to give aid. We should caution, however, that the cell size in this table is quite small, and care needs to be exercised in drawing firm conclusions.

One final examination of the data permits us to study the linkage between socio-economic status and support for the Sandinistas. As we see in Table 19.8c, nearly four-fifths of the respondents who were classified as poorer in a dichotomization of an index of wealth (see note to this Table 19.8c) approved giving support to the Sandinistas, whereas, only 59 percent of those who are categorized as richer on our index approved giving such support. Such a finding is to be expected since many of the richer Costa Ricans probably identified with business interests which had benefited from the Somoza rule, although such support was tempered by the knowledge that even those Nicaraguan interests eventually withdrew their support for Somoza. The poorer Costa Ricans, on the other hand, could easily identify with the oppressed and impoverished majority of Nicaraguans.

TABLE 19.8

PREDICTORS OF ATTITUDES TOWARD THE SANDINISTAS

8a. *Cross-tabulation of Perception of Sandinistas Linkage to Communism with Approval of Help for Sandinistas.*

	Perception of Sandinista Linkage to Communism	
	Communist	**Not Communist**
Give help	56.4 (22)	80.6 (58)
Withhold help	43.6 (17)	19.4 (14)
	100% (39)	100% (72)

Tau b = .26   Sig. = .01 (X^2)

Note: Perception of Sandinista Linkage to Communism is the sum of the questions presented in Tables 19.6 and 19.7, collapsing the intermediate category with the "communist" category, the smallest of the three.

8b: *Cross-tabulation of Perception of Sandinista Linkage to Communism with Approval of Help for Sandinistas Controlling for Evaluation of Costa Rican Communism.*

	Linkage of Sandinistas to Communism			
	Linked		**Not Linked**	
	Evaluation of Communism		Evaluation of Communism	
	Negative	Positive	Negative	Positive
Give help	50.0 (8)	61.9 (13)	75.(27)	88.6 (31)
Withhold help	50.0 (8)	38.1 (8)	25.0 (9)	11.4 (4)
	100% (16)	100% (21)	100% (36)	100% (33)

Zero-order Gamma = .28   Partial Gamma = .38

Note: Evaluation of Costa Rican Communism is an index based upon a four-item semantic differential scale, in which the adjective pairs "good-bad," "just-unjust," "safe-unsafe," and "honest-dishonest," were employed. Each adjective pair was scored on a seven-point scale, and the scores for each item were summed and then dichotomized at the mid-point.

TABLE 19.8

PREDICTORS OF ATTITUDES TOWARD THE SANDINISTAS

8c. *Cross-tabulation of Wealth with Approval of Help for Sandinistas.*

| | Wealth | |
	Poorer	Richer
Give help	79.0 (64)	58.8 (57)
Withhold help	21.0 (17)	41.2 (40)

Tau b = .22   Sig. = .007 (X^2)

Note: Wealth is defined as a summated unweighted index of artifacts (television, refrigerator, electric iron, washing machine, floor polisher, hot water heater, telephone, sewing machine, automobile) owned by respondent. The index was dichotomized to divide the sample approximately in half.

Help for the Sandinistas was the sum of the questions used in Table 19.2 of this chapter. The intermediate category, containing the smallest number of respondents, was combined with the "give help" category. When left as a trichotomy, the Tau statistic does not change appreciably.

Conclusion

Scholars will long debate the causes of the Nicaraguan Revolution, as they have done for the several other major social revolutions of this century. Equally important, however, are the factors which led to the success of the insurrectionary phase of that Revolution. The long standing antipathy between Costa Rica and Nicaragua set the stage for the important role the former was to play in the success of the insurrection. Not only did Costa Rica provide a relatively safe haven for the guerrillas, but it also provided an important forum for the Junta-in-Exile in the last months of the war. However, more vigorous support was precluded by an ambivalence in Costa Rican opinion towards the Sandinistas, which, while supporting Sandinista goals, feared the revolutionaries' possible communist sympathies.

Notes

[1] This chapter is a revised version of a paper delivered at the Conference on "Central America in the 1980s: Options for U.S. Policy," held in El Paso, Texas, November 16-17, 1979. The public opinion data reported in the chapter were gathered by Miguel Gómez B. of the Universidad de Costa Rica as part of his ongoing assessment of Costa Rican public opinion. We would like to thank John Booth, Steve Ropp, Thomas W. Walker, and Robert Woodward for their helpful comments on the earlier version.

[2] Thomas L. Karnes, *The Failure of Union: Central America 1824-1975*, Rev. Ed. (Tempe: Center for Latin American Studies, Arizona State University, 1976), pp. 34-35.

[3] *Latin American Political Report*, Vol. 12, No. 10, (1978), p. 76.

[4] *Latin American Political Report*, Vol. 12, No. 28, (1978), p. 222.

Chapter 20

A Cuban Perspective
on the Nicaraguan Revolution

MAX AZICRI

In a period of only twenty years, from 1959 to 1979, Latin America was elated, as well as perplexed, by two authentic political and social revolutions occurring in its midst. Although the desire for radical change, deeply rooted in historical tradition and national ethos, served to motivate the populace into an unparalleled level of militancy, Cuba and Nicaragua had to overcome colossal obstacles in their struggle against domestic and foreign foes. Nicaragua in the early 1980s was facing internal and external threats against its stability and security very similar in nature to those confronting Cuba in the early 1960s. In addition to the task of painstakingly building a new social order, the major concern of revolutionary Nicaragua was centered on safeguarding the stability of its revolutionary Government of National Reconstruction. The fact that the Sandinist leadership had deviated from Cuba's Marxist-Leninist model and had chosen instead to pursue a controlled form of pluralism involving an alliance between classes had not entirely deterred the domestic and foreign enemies of the Revolution.[1]

Reacting to Nicaraguan developments, conservatives in Washington and elsewhere were apprehensive from the start, fearing that radicalism would run unchecked under the Sandinistas. As things worked out, the costly lessons gained from the excesses committed in the 1960s by the then inexperienced Cuban revolutionaries apparently exerted a sobering influence on the Sandinista National Liberation Front (FSLN). The fresh memories of the plight of a problem-ridden Cuba were instrumental in cutting down to realistic proportions Managua's immediate revolutionary goals. These included avoiding as much as possible a repetition of Cuba's defiance of an antagonistic United States and its inimical, anti-Cuban policies, as well as delaying until some time in the future defining the ultimate character of the Nicaraguan state. Thus a final decision on the pluralistic experiment now being implemented was postponed.

All in all, it seemed that a sense of timing and moderation was guiding the Sandinista revolutionaries. Policies were formulated and enforced keeping in mind what was practical and feasible; priorities also differentiated short-range from long-range goals. For the FSLN, this was not primarily a

345

question of preventing the disclosure of long-range plans which might have proven embarrasing or could have provided additonal grounds to the already existent opposition—although these are possibilities which could not be rejected altogether. More likely, what was happening was that the Sandinistas were allowing the process of revolutionary change to run its course, thus following its developmental stages in a sequential order. This strategy allowed for specific policies to be proven sound and viable, or rejected and replaced by new ones.

A comparative analysis of both revolutions, as briefly presented in this chapter, draws our attention to the remarkable absence of extremism displayed by Nicaragua during these founding years, in contrast to what happened on numerous occasions in Cuba during its early revolutionary period. From the outset, the Sandinistas by their words and deeds seemed closer to the mature Cuban revolutionists of the 1970s and 1980s, rather than the less experienced, and highly idealistically motivated, non-pragmatic Fidelistas of the 1960s.

Cuba's Early Radicalism
The behavior of the Fidelistas in the 1960s was motivated primarily by deeply felt emotions, and by their perception of the threats posed to the Cuban revolution by the existent constellation of international forces at that time. They feared that, in such a highly volatile and dangerous historical period as they were living, they might fall victim to a United States Central Intelligence Agency-organized invasion by exiles such as had happened in Guatemala in 1953.

Inasmuch as the Guatemalan experience heightened the sense of urgency and danger created by counterrevolutionary actions, Cuba's reaction was to become increasingly radicalized—in both its internal and international policies. In so doing, Cuba sought to surround itself with a protective shield that would guarantee its survival.[2]

In the early 1980s, after more than two decades of Cuban permanence and stability, it seemed plausible for Nicaragua to look forward to a lasting future for its own revolution. This time, however, the price of a relative degree of national security was moderation. It was precisely the example of an institutionalized and still successful Cuban revolution only ninety miles from an antagonistic United States that suggested to the Nicaraguans the practice of principled pragmatism rather than ill-advised radicalism. In this sense, Nicaragua's self-styled cautious approach signaled the feasibility of future moderate revolutions emerging in Latin America and elsewhere.

The FSLN's Political and Socio-Economic Pluralism
In Nicaragua, a radical leadership, the nine-member FSLN National Directorate, had skillfully performed a balancing act by providing enough room

for both the public and private sector and for the Sandinista mass organizations and the traditional and conservative political structures to exist side by side. Almost from the beginning, however, the new system came under attack from the right and sometimes even the left.

Nevertheless, this peculiar arrangement showed enough fortitude to sustain the triarchy formed by (1) the unified FSLN leadership, (2) the executive / legislative five-member ruling Junta of the Government of National Reconstruction, and (3) the Council of State, a 57-member legislative body which included a wide spectrum of mass organizations and other political, social, and economic interests. The successful performance and viability of the triarchy—proving that in spite of their differences these institutions could work together as responsive power-holding actors—constituted a valuable empirical indicator of the effectiveness of Nicaragua's revolutionary democracy. The actual political authority wielded by each sector of the triarchy had been previously determined by its status in the revolutionary hierarchy of power, with the FSLN sitting at the top.

The Reagan Threat

It seems proper to examine here some of the immediate and long-range dangers faced by Nicaragua. Obviously there were very serious implications for the present and future well-being of the revolution in the decision taken in Washington just a few days after President Reagan's inauguration to freeze the remaining $15 million of the $75 million loan granted during the Carter administration. According to Washington, weapons from Nicaragua had been smuggled into El Salvador destined for the guerrillas fighting the United States' supported military-Christian Democratic junta. At this juncture, the fear of another Cuba in Latin America, which had been haunting the United States for over two decades, was compounded by the additional fear of another Nicaragua in Central America.

The critical issue, however, was not really whether or not, or to what extent, Cuba and Nicaragua were engaged in the business of exporting their revolutions to neighboring countries. (In the case of Nicaragua it would be difficult to substantiate such a charge; regarding Cuba, its former policy of supporting guerrilla movements in Latin America in the 1960s was drastically reduced, if not practically abandoned after the early seventies.)[3] More properly, the issue lay in determining accurately how meaningful, if at all, these revolutions were to the peoples of Latin America.

In all likelihood, the Nicaraguan model with its controlled pluralism was probably more appealing than that of Cuba to would-be revolutionaries in Central America. The question was whether a moderate model could be retained if Washington's public displeasure with the Sandinistas materialized into a full-fledged financial destabilization campaign such as President Nixon had launched against Salvador Allende in Chile in 1973, or into covert or open warfare.[4] In fact, it appeared that hostile moves by the United States would very likely radicalize Nicaragua—as it did Cuba in the 1960s—and destroy its pluralist experiment and model.

The potential appeal of the Nicaraguan model was twofold in nature. Partly, it meant that the application of modified developmental strategies tested earlier in Cuba had produced a novel revolutionary experience. Also, Managua seemed to address itself more realistically, and less radically, to prevailing social and political problems, particularly if one considers what might have been attainable in the region at the time. This included the characteristics of different but related domestic conditions, and the pressures exerted by international political actors operating in Central America and the Caribbean, especially with a threatening hard-liner in the vicinity, as was the United States under President Reagan and Secretary of State Alexander Haig's antirevolutionary militancy.

Seemingly, striking an even balance in the course of the revolution was a cardinal principle for the FSLN during its initial period of revolutionary power. Hence Nicaragua's membership in the movement of nonaligned countries, the repeated presence of FSLN and other revolutionary leaders in every major celebration in Havana, and President Castro's visit to Managua on the occasion of the first anniversary of the Revolution were properly balanced with other relations in the international community without compromising its official anti-imperialist posture. These international policies included friendly relations with Western European socialist parties and governments, with the Soviet Union and other Marxist-Leninist states, and more critically, with the United States. Also, it continued its commitments in the inter-American system and its membership in the Organization of American States, which dated from pre-revolutionary days. Likewise, economic programs like Plan 80—the first year's blueprint for the reconstruction of the economy after the devastating insurrectionary war—guaranteed the private sector a vital role in this national effort.

The Cuban-Nicaraguan nexus represented a reservoir of experience accumulated after years of engineering radical approaches and techniques for socio-economic and political development. Some of these were tested first by Havana and, substantively modified and even improved, were then applied by Managua; i.e., the year-long literacy campaign launched less than a month after the overthrow of the Somoza regime, and the unique role played by the Sandinista trade union and different mass organizations in the FSLN's strategy. These organizations both worked and competed with nonrevolutionary social, political, and economic organizations and trade unions, and had done so even before the demise of President Somoza.

Thus the Latin American revolutionary tradition was still alive. Originating in Mexico, it had moved to Cuba and then to Nicaragua. And yet, in spite of such strong bonds, common background and goals, the Cuban and Nicaraguan revolutions were still quite different.

Conceptualizing Revolutionary Politics

For all the emotional reaction that a revolution seems to provoke, the contradictory meaning the term has had historically is paradoxical. The word "revolution" describes the rotation of celestial bodies following natural, fixed laws. This implies that once engaged in revolutionary motion, an object would return to its point of departure, rather than deviate or change its course of action. After the concept of change became related to the word "revolution," it was then applied to artistic, cultural, or industrial change. Politically speaking, the word was used first in a "reactionary context," denoting a regressive movement, the kind that would bring the restoration of a previously existent regime. Earlier, then, the term meant a rebellion, a renewal, or a restoration.[5]

It was not until the eighteenth century that "revolution" gained its contemporary denotation. Naturally, both the American and French revolutions provided timely historical material for the development of a meaningful vocabulary on this subject. Nonetheless, after all these years, the literature on this political phenomenon is not only rich but many times confusing as well. Even when the concept of change—political, social, or economic—is related to the problem under examination, available theoretical paradigms seem to conceptualize different realities. Since the concept of revolution is sometimes glorified and other times vilified in the literature, one wonders if a more accurate understanding of the term is more likely to come from those engaged in revolution-making than from those involved in revolution-explaining; that is, the revolutionaries rather than the theorists.

Hannah Arendt characterizes revolutions as modern political phenomena signifying a search for freedom through social change, while Sigmund Neumann understands them as basically totalitarian in nature. For Harry Eckstein and a group of social scientists from the Princeton University Center for International Studies, a revolution is a form of *internal war* attempting to "change by violence, or threat of violence, a government's policies, rulers, or organization." Peter Amman states elsewhere that a revolution is "a breakdown, momentary or prolonged, of the state's monopoly of power, usually accompanied by a lessening of the habit of obedience."[6]

Thus, according to Eckstein's and Amman's focus on conflict as the core component of the revolutionary process, violence brings changes in either the state's governmental structure (political institutions), the allocation of values (policies), or political actors (decision-makers). Likewise, it changes the long-established tradition of compliance by the people with the regime's authority. Even if indirectly, Amman is raising here the question of changes in the regime's legitimacy (authority), which provides the basis for the people's support or political consensus. This process includes two separate actions. First, the revolution would bring an erosion of the established authority, among other means, by questioning its legitimacy through undermining its political consensus. Second, it would provide the foundation for a new legitimacy—a new, revolutionary political consensus—which would sustain the authority of the newly established revolutionary government.

By centering his analysis on the concept of power and the way it breaks down during the revolutionary (insurrectionary) process, Amman indicates that the symbiotic power (government)-compliance (populace) relationship normally existing in a stable political system would have to be reestablished once the revolutionary (insurrectionary) stage is over. In this way, the newly established revolutionary government would gain the populace's compliance by holding and exercising power (force), and by building political consensus and authority (legitimacy).

Moreover, from Amman's theoretical perspective, a revolutionary government would no longer be in a revolutionary phase once it has established its own power and authority—i.e., effectively wielding sociopolitical control—as manifested by the populace's complying to the new government's policies. Notwithstanding its conceptual value, this interpretation runs contrary to prevalent thought in Havana and Managua on this subject. In actuality, it was understood in both places that the revolutionary phase would start *after* the revolutionary movement had gained power (and authority) and would proceed then to implement social changes with the people's support. The previous stage, the *internal war* in which the revolutionaries fight against the old regime, was considered to be the *pre*revolutionary or insurrectionary, phase.

Other authors have followed developmental or chronological categories in their fourfold classification of successive stages: (1) the rule of the moderates, (2) the accession of the extremists (3) the reign of terror, and (4) the Thermidor. Thus after the moderates were substituted—eliminated—by extremists and a period of terror ensued, the final stage would bring along a period of "convalescence from the fever of revolution." Here Brinton understands revolution mainly as a destructive process. Its main attraction would be that it would calm down eventually by releasing its own forces so things could go back to a certain normalcy. There seems to be a recognition in this approach, however, even if only implicitly, that some significant changes would take place throughout these four stages. In a more concise form, Alfred E. Meyer also follows a sequential process of three distinctive phases: (1) the destruction of the old regime, (2) a period of characteristic disorder, and (3) the creation of a new order or political system.[7]

According to Chalmers Johnson, seeking socio-political change through a revolution implies the acceptance of violence as part of the revolutionary change process. He provides a classification of revolutions: (1) the targets of the revolution (the regime, the form of government, or the community); (2) the identity of the revolutionaries (elite, masses, or elite-led masses); (3) the goals or ideology of the revolution (properly elaborated and specified ideas, or not), and (4) the timing of the revolution (a spontaneous, or a calculated uprising).[8]

Johnson's fourfold classification brings together such analytical categories as (1) the goals of the revolution (whether it is a political or social revolution, and the extent of the structural changes involved); (2) the personality of the actors (leaders, masses—whether their socio-economic background is upper-, middle-, or lower- class, and their psychological makeup and leadership qualifications; (3) the politico-philosophical values informing the revolutionary movement (whether it follows a chiliastic ideology ["a perfect final state of mankind"], a trial-and-error policy-making approach, or an eclectic posture of principled pragmatism), and (4) the conditions of the revolutionary occurrence in relation to its socio-political and ecological context (whether the revolution is triggered by an unexpected incident which puts an end to the balance of political forces under the old regime, or is the outcome of a premeditated action initiated by the revolutionaries).

Applying Theory to Revolutionary Reality

In some instances, the Cuban and Nicaraguan revolutions fit well into the conceptual categories mentioned above, while in others, they do not. Except for Brinton's and Johnson's, they permit the following generalizations: (1) both revolutions sought social justice and political freedom through social engineering approaches, while rejecting totalitarianism as a societal-political goal; (2) both revolutions changed violently the old regime's policies, rulers, and organization through an *internal war* (insurrectionary process); (3) both revolutions confronted instances of lack of, or poor compliance with, their policies, particularly from disaffected groups, after having broken the state's monopoly of power during the insurrectionary period; (4) both revolutions built, during the insurrectionary process, a new political consensus which supplied later political support and acceptability (legitimacy) to the authority of the revolutionary government; and (5) both revolutions signaled the initiation of the revolutionary phase, as distinguished from the previous insurrectionary stage, during the process of social change initiated after gaining power.

There are differences between Cuba and Nicaragua which become more apparent once they are examined according to Brinton's sequential stages of the revolutionary process and Johnson's fourfold classification, as examined below. In the following discussion, Brinton's four stages will be grouped into two separate categories.

The Moderates and the Extremists

From 1959 to approximately 1961, Cuba underwent its early period of radicalization. This initial set of events provided the foundation for what became known, according to critics of Cuba, as the "betrayal of the revolution." This was a charge raised over and over against Castro and other revolutionary leaders. During this first period, moderate leaders like José Miró Cardona, first Prime Minister, and Manuel Urrutia, first President, were replaced in their positions by Castro and Osvaldo Dórticos, respectively. After many of the first leaders—among them, members of the the then single governmental body, the executive-legislative Council of Ministers—had resigned, gone into exile, or were sent to prison or even executed, the brief initial reign of the moderates gave way rapidly to the ascension and dominance of the revolution by a more radical leadership.

Nicaragua also had difficult crises threatening its revolutionary political structure. The vulnerable balance of political forces integrating the broadly-based pluralistic framework of Nicaragua's popular democracy became an ideal target for individuals and groups opposing the revolution. This was an antagonistic response from some nonrevolutionary groups to the built-in tension present in what seemed to be a contradictory FSLN revolutionary strategy: "The maintenance of an alliance with the bourgeoisie, . . . [while] fomenting . . . mass organizations with a militant class perspective."

The actions and threats against the FSLN in particular, and the ruling political triarchy in general, were in reality aimed at the revolution as a whole—which, after all, was the major cause of the changes which were then taking place in Nicaragua. In this sense, the revolutionary leadership's commitment to changing the previous political and socio-economic structure known as *somocismo* proved to be a very demanding task. Likewise, the Sandinista social change model was too radical for some Nicaraguan conservatives. If these groups seemed to be going along with such changes, it was mostly a question of what they saw as best for their own survival in a fast-changing situation, and a repressed expectation that things might improve later if they changed back to the old ways.

In the spring of 1980, when Violeta Chamorro and Alfonso Robelo resigned their positions in the ruling Junta of the Government of National Reconstruction, in which they represented moderate to conservative political forces and the private economic sector, they provoked a chain reaction that could have led the Revolution into a radicalization process. This possibility was very real, regardless of whether Chamorro and Robelo had this in mind at the time of their resignations.

The logical outcome of such an event would have been that the Sandinista leadership would have reacted by moving away from its relatively moderate and conciliatory political scheme—at least such a development was, in all probability, desirable to opponents of the Revolution. Most likely, the expectation was that the regime would move toward more radical forms of social and economic relations at the expense of the existing controlled form of pluralism; i.e., the alliance between the FSLN and Sandinista mass organizations and the bourgeoisie and nonrevolutionary groups and political parties. This movement would have thwarted ongoing socio-economic developmental programs and policies and weakened the Revolution. Remarkably enough, confronted with this and other similar actions—provocations, really—the Sandinista leadership demonstrated prudence and self-control in its stewardship of public affairs. They simply requested new representatives from the same sectors and organizations for the vacated seats. The potential negative impact of this politico-economic crisis was significantly limited in this way to the personal domain and did not affect class interests as such. When, finally, Arturo Cruz and Rafael CórdovaRivas occupied the two unfilled positions, the crisis was deflated, preventing nonrevolutionary groups and leaders from becoming further alienated from the revolutionary process.

A similar crisis happened later, in the summer of 1980. This time, Robelo's Nicaraguan Democratic Movement (MDN) refused to join the newly organized Council of State. Later, instead of continuing its boycott of that broadly-representative deliberative and legislative body, the MDN decided to send its representative. And so did other political groups and the economic organizations constituting the Superior Council of Private Enterprise (COSEP). A more serious incident happened towards the end of 1980, however. It provoked a massive boycott of COSEP's six reprsentatives at the Council of State. The crisis originated when the acting chairperson of COSEP, who allegedly was involved in counterrevolutionary activities was slain by forces of the Sandinista People's Army responsible for combating the counterrevolution. Most of the circumstances surrounding this unfortunate incident were not clear at the time of this writing, so it was difficult to appraise the significance of specific details.

Nevertheless, what seems evident is that a pattern of social class conflict kept recurring in Nicaragua. It was not that the private economic sector did not have an important role to play, or that all kinds of political groups and organizations did not enjoy freedom of association or the right to express themselves freely in the press or through any other media. All of these individual rights and freedoms existed in post-Somoza Nicaragua as they never had before. Seemingly, the important qualifier in revolutionary Nicaragua was the prevalent bias towards popular democracy, which opposed allowing sectorial or individual interests to prevail.

Even that large sector of the business community which had never been favored by Somoza, and in many ways had been victimized by his unfair business practices in building an ever-expanding economic empire, found itself freer in pursuing its economic sectorial interests. This was possible in spite of the controls the revolution imposed upon the private sector. Such an apparent contradiction meant in reality that businesses enjoyed an officially recognized margin of profit, and that there was enough room for incentives leading to new initiatives and financial transactions. However, what the private sector lacked in the new Nicaragua was its traditional monopoly of political (and economic) power.

Now this political power lay primarily in the hands of the FSLN. The policies and legislation of the ruling Junta of the Government of National Reconstruction and the Council of State had to be approved under FSLN guidance and supervision. The rationale behind this phenomenon was that the interests of the people, as defined by the FSLN, had to be defended. And yet, the FSLN leadership included not only its national directorate and other leaders from the revolutionary stage, but also six Sandinista mass organizations, and they were not always in agreement with each other. As a matter of fact, the Sandinista mass organizations seemed very much to have minds of their own. Because of this, many concerns and ideas initiated at the grassroots level, found their way up to the FSLN national leaders, cabinet ministers, and others. The FSLN leadership seemed to welcome this vital and productive input. Both the activism and the mobilization capabilities demonstrated by the mass organizations in Nicaragua, and the welcome attitude by the revolutionary leadership for this participatory form of politics, resembled the Cuban experience. (From its first years, the Cuban revolution witnessed the activism and involvement of the numerous mass organizations in what was characterized as the politics of revolutionary mobilization.)[9]

Many private interests in Nicaragua found it difficult to understand and accept this new political reality. Thus the crises of legitimacy kept repeating themselves. This situation would continue as long as the authority of the Revolution remained unaccepted by some segments of the Nicaraguan society.

An interesting contrast between Cuba and Nicaragua is that in the former the dynamics of revolutionary actions and counterrevolutionaries' counteractions brought about the final radicalization of the revolution. This radicalization included its leadership, ideology, social and economic relations, and international posture. Later, during the institutionalization of the revolution initiated in the early 1970s, the Cuban state was organized in a final revolutionary form. Its Marxist-Leninist characteristics became formalized with corresponding legal and political institutions. These include the 1976 socialist Constitution, the legislative-administrative Organs of People's Power at the national, provincial, and municipal level, and the Cuban Communist Party (PCC), which was founded in 1965 in its present form. The government of the country was organized in the form of a pyramidal structure with the Council of Ministers and its Executive Committee at the top. These institutions functioned on the basis of, and practiced the tenets of, the dictatorship of the proletariat, the philosophical and socio-political foundation of Cuba's socialist democracy.

Meanwhile in Nicaragua, a radical leadership—the FSLN National Directorate and other leading members—struggled to safeguard an institutional arrangement which provided a balance between the private and public sectors, and between revolutionary and nonrevolutionary groups and organizations. An unanswered question was whether this was only a tactical maneuver by the FSLN, given the nature of internal and external circumstances, or if it was a more permanent, or perhaps even a final organizational blueprint for revolutionary Nicaragua. More likely, the final form of the Nicaraguan state would evolve from this early institutional arrangement. Whether it would be a state close to socialist Cuba's institutions was something that only the dyanmics of the revolution and the future would answer.

The Reign of Terror and the Thermidor

According to historical standards of what revolutionary justice is capable—Cuba and Nicaragua were noteworthy exceptions, although the latter was much more so than the former. Though the Cuban revolution avoided turning the people's legitimate desire for justice into a bloodbath, there were many executions in front of the *paredón*, particularly during the first year. Originally, the death penalty was applied to those members of President Batista's military and police forces who were directly responsible for murdering and torturing thousands of revolutionaries and innocent civilians—the latter usually bystanders who happened to be in the wrong place at the wrong time during the insurrectionary period. Altogether, during Batista's last seven-year period in power, from 1952 through 1958, thousands fell victim to his repressive methods.

After the death penalty was for all practical purposes suspended, once the initial phase of revolutionary justice was over, it had to be applied again. This time it was due to counterrevolutionary activities. Facing tremendous odds given the magnitude of the domestic and international campaign launched against the regime, the rationale behind the decision to apply the death penalty again was simply revolutionary survival. This ambivalent position of enforcing, then rescinding, then reinstituting such a stiff sanction as the death penalty was symptomatic of the general disarray that existed in the judiciary at the time. Much more significant than any counterrevolutionary actions, the underlying cause for such legal malaise was the close relationship established between the parallel processes of social and legal change. Although in practice they sometimes reinforced one another, by design the latter was meant to service the former. At that time, a primary revolutionary objective of the Cuban leaders was to transform Cuban society, not to establish a legal system.

Nevertheless, the first ten years of the revolution were decisive in setting the foundation for the final form of its judicial system. The Popular Tribunals' movement, which developed in the 1960s, provided grass-roots perspectives which were applied in the judicial reforms of 1973 and 1977. Although no longer in existence, the Popular Tribunals had such lasting influence as making the use of lay judges in the courts a permanent feature of the Cuban judiciary. However, from the standpoint of the complex problems faced by the revolution during its first years,

> The revolution's dilemma . . . was twofold in nature during this early period: to guarantee the survival of the regime . . . and to

proceed forward with a never-ending process of social change. The demands placed upon the regime were contradictory in nature: whether to respect the rule of law above all . . . or to apply its own sense of ethics, of revolutionary justice. . . .[10]

Nonetheless, the intensive change process pursued during the first decade was followed by the institutionalization of the state in the 1970s. From the standpoint of social transformation, this latter development could be seen as a Cuban Thermidor of sorts. Once the foundations of a socialist society had been established, the revolutionary regime set up new and permanent legal and political institutions. This time, the state's political and judicial structure truly mirrored the social changes accomplished in the intervening years.

All in all, the sequence of events followed by the revolutionaries paid off handsomely. Not only was Cuban society transformed thoroughly by the 1970s, but a socialist legal system was also established in those years:

The second decade of revolutionary rule stands out as a period of maturity and sobriety in the regime's demeanor; consequently, these years convey a qualitative difference in the character of social and legal change. In the 1970s, in contrast to the changes experienced in the 1960s, the regime pursued institutional permanence and political stability as primary goals.[11]

By the summer of 1980, a year after the Sandinista victory, there were approximately 8,000 political prisoners in Nicaragua. Most of them were either members of the National Guard, in particular its School of Basic Infantry—which had operated as a repressive elite force under the command of Anastasio Somoza III—or police informers. There might have been at least 10,000 more if they had not conveniently fled the country escaping revolutionary justice.

After forty-five years living under the Somoza dynasty, Nicaragua began a new era with what was expected to function as a fair and effective judicial system. The major and most immediate judicial problem facing the Sandinistas was how to deal with those responsible for the genocidal war waged for so long against the people in order to sustain the Somozas in power. Given the historical antecedents and the deeply felt emotions of the populace, the most surprising decision taken by the revolutionaries was to forbid the death penalty, even for the worst of Somoza's henchmen. But justice had to be done. Otherwise, the people would have sought revenge themselves. In the summer of 1979, six new Supreme Court justices were appointed, and by the end of the year, on December 17, new Special Tribunals were established with jurisdiction over these matters.

The criminal laws used under the Revolution were basically the same as existed before 1979. No significant new legal definitions of crime or penalties were added. There was important legislation in the public law area, however, This included the Statute on the Rights of Nicaraguans which guaranteed "all basic human and democratic rights, [and] reserve[d] to the Nicaraguan people the right to control the country's natural wealth and resources, and prohibit[ed] foreigners from intervening in the political affairs of the country."[12] Also, in the summer of 1979, the 1974 Constitution was suspended upon the installation of the ruling Junta of the Government of National Reconstruction, which, as one of its first decisions, proceeded to appoint the members of the Governing Council (cabinet).

The newly created courts, or Special Tribunal, resembled the Cuban Popular Tribunals of the 1960s. Besides having a **professional** judge—who had to be a lawyer or a law student—there were also two lay judges. The latter came from the people's ranks—housewives, factory or construction workers, clerks, and others—and were appointed by the government from lists submitted by the Sandinista mass organizations. The courts made their final decision by the majority, secret vote of the three judges. Three stages of appeal could be taken advantage of before a sentence became final. At any one of these points, or throughout his entire trial, a defendant could have an attorney appointed to defend him if he could not provide himself with legal counseling. As long as they worked full time, the judges were duly compensated for their work. To guarantee a fair degree of objectivity, recruitment for the judiciary avoided those individuals who were directly affected by Somoza's repression, i.e., someone who had a relative killed by the National Guard during the insurrectionary war.

Due process under the law was guaranteed, balancing the people's desire for justice and the defendant's rights. Pictures of and reports from those awaiting trial were published. Anyone with a legitimate grievance against a defendant could press charges at the nearest office of the Department of National Security. As established procedure, the charges were corroborated by the Office of the Special Prosecutor, which functioned under the Attorney General, Nora Astorga. If the charges were properly substantiated, they were presented in court by the people's prosecutor. On many occasions, defendants were released upon recommendation of the Office of the Attorney General. During the first year, in more than 300 cases, the charges did not warrant prosecution, or could not be substantiated and the defendants were released. On different occasions, representatives from international organizations visited some of the prisoners as part of an ongoing monitoring of judicial practices in Nicaragua.

The slowness of the courts caused a serious problem. Approximately **800 cases were resolved by the courts or the Office of the Attorney General** during the first year. If each trial were to continue to take between two and three weeks, it would take approximately six more years before the courts' backlog was cleared.[13]

As of early 1981, Nicaragua had avoided a revolutionary reign of terror, in the same way it had not allowed the accession of extremists to positions reserved for political moderates both in the Government of National Reconstruction and the Council of State. The Revolution, however, had not yet entered into anything resembling a Thermidor stage. Things had not calmed down. As a matter of fact, with all the backlash from the active conservative forces accepted in a pluralistic politico-revolutionary framework, the ongoing process of social change was a relatively recent phenomenon still in its formative stage.

Even if Nicaragua never moved into an extremist, radicalized position as part of a self-defense posture against domestic and foreign enemies—as Cuba did—a period of maturity, leveling off present imbalances and improvisations with more permanent institutions, still lay in the future. An institutionalization (Thermidor) stage would not only have been premature but also counterproductive at that time. It would have prevented the process of societal change from reaching its full potential. Thus, if domestic and international pressures and threats did not increase, but remained at the level of the first two years, the Nicaraguan Revolution would be in the long range a much less radical example of social transformation than Cuba. By the same token, Cuba's reign of terror, even if rather modest and limited by worldwide revolutionary standards, had been more severe than anything experienced in Nicaragua. Moreover, Cuba also knew how to wait for the proper time before launching its institutionalization drive. Hence a Thermidor period, which most likely would limit its present phase of societal transformation, was something that Nicaragua had wisely delayed.

Johnson's Fourfold Classification

Cuba and Nicaragua lived through a violent and bloody insurrectionary war against the corrupt and repressive regimes of Batista and Somoza respectively. In their struggle, the revolutionaries had faced more than just military might. Besides the internal support received by the two dictators from the local alliance of corporate interests—the traditional marriage of convenience between wide segments of Latin American bourgeoisie and socially-conservative and politically-repressive dictatorships—there were also the traditional, close, and friendly relations with the United States. Significantly, Washington tried to put some distance between itself and those regimes once the popular tide supporting the insurrection was practically overwhelming and, therefore, the end of the autocracies a foregone conclusion. In both cases, some sectors of the social classes and interest groups originally associated with the dictatorships also tried to separate themselves from these regimes.

This complex web of political and socioeconomic interests provided the setting for the revolutionary struggle in both the insurrectionary phase and the period of Revolutionary social change which followed. Consequently, the application of Johnson's fourfold classification to the Cuban and Nicaraguan experiences must be made in the face of the magnitude of this socio-political phenomenon. The challenge faced by the revolutionaries of accomplishing national liberation first, and socio-economic development later, was simply awesome.

The Three Targets of the Revolution

By including the full scope of the different targets for change involved in this category—the regime, the form of government, and the community—Cuba and Nicaragua constitute a comprehensive type of political and social revolution. Both Batista's and Somoza's regimes were eliminated; political institutions and socio-economic relations were modified, or completely changed. As of early 1981, political and societal changes were more extensive in Cuba than in Nicaragua.

Although some of the characteristics of the political and social changes included in this section have already been discussed in this narrative, the close association that exists between Cuba's decision in the early 1960s to radicalize the revolution and the kinds of political and social institutions which finally emerged from that process should be noted. In other words, once it was publicly announced, in May 1961, that the Cuban revolution would be socialist, and especially, in December, when Castro characterized it as Marxist-Leninist, the processes of social and political change moved in a clear direction. These announcements were an official recognition of what in reality had been in the making for a while. Thus Cuba's revolutionary transformation followed a sequence of developmental phases related to parallel processes of nation- and state-building which led to the organizational structure of today's society and state.

There was a parallel of Nicaragua's decision to limit the extent of its socio-political radicalization and its ability to balance interacting revolutionary and conservative social forces. Nicaragua's broad socio-political framework went back to the difficult years of the anti-Somoza struggle. In July 1978, progressive groups joined in a single bloc called the United People's Movement (MPU), including workers, peasants, women, students, and representatives from trade unions, political parties, and revolutionary groups. This significant consolidation of forces was the outgrowth of earlier anti-Somoza coalitions—i.e., the controversial Broad Opposition Front (FAO), the Group of Twelve, and the business and middle-class Democratic Union of Liberation (UDEL)—and led to the foundation later in 1979 of the revolutionary National Patriotic Front (FPN), which included as well grassroots movements such as the Civilian Defense Committees and other revolutionary forces. This time, all were united under an FSLN initiative aimed at offering an alternative to the power structure of *somocismo.*

Moreover, the MPU was preceded by such developments as the formation of the Permanent Commission for Human Rights (CPDH) on October 26, 1977. This group was supported by the women's (AMPRONAC) and students' (MES) organizations, which were protesting Somoza's widespread repression of *campesinos.* The assassination of anti-Somoza activist Pedro

Joaquín Chamorro on January 10, 1978, and the publicized imprisonment of revolutionary leaders like Marcelo Jaen and Tomás Borge added new impetus to the insurrectionary process.

In the summer of 1978, with the arrival from exile in Costa Rica of the group known as The Twelve and the extraordinary outpouring of anti-Somoza militancy expressed by the populace which turned out to welcome them, the process of integrating groups with diverse ideologies was reinforced. The fact that, upon their arrival, The Twelve proclaimed publicly their commitment to the ideological principles of *sandinismo* was equally significant. Two of the leaders of this group representing progressive-liberal sectors of Nicaragua's middle-class were Sergio Ramírez, who became the head of the ruling junta of the government of national reconstruction,[14] and Father Miguel D'Escoto, an upper-class Maryknoll priest, later Nicaragua's Minister of Foreign Affairs.

This analysis does not support the notion that a revolutionary regime would force a specific type of societal transformation in either Cuba or Nicaragua. Neither does the analysis support the notion that revolutionists must be conditioned, or predetermined, towards a single politico-philosophical choice which excludes any possible alternative ideology. Evidently, these are questionable and debatable positions. Furthermore, it does not imply, either, that the ensuing progression of events had to follow a unilinear, deterministic historical order. Decisions and policies, including the direction and identity of the revolution, were in many ways circumstantial, imposed to a large extent upon the revolutionaries by domestic and international political realities.

In this sense, the innumerable debates held among Cuban leaders on some fine points of Cuban socialism are publicly known. Among controversial issues were the recurring theme of moral versus material incentives, which would have an effect on the nature of social and economic relations (the reward system) and, as a derivative of the same issue, on the meaning and applicability of Ché Guevara's socialist man as an exemplary behavioral model to be emulated by the population at large.

The internal debate among the three different tendencies existing within the FSLN is another example of this problem. The termination of this controversy became official when the leaders of the three sections signed the "program of national unity" on March 8, 1979. This consolidation under a joint national leadership ended the internal divisions between the Protracted Warfare Tendency (GPP), the Proletarian Tendency (TP), and the Third Party (*Tercerista*), or Insurrectionary, Tendency. Although they had always thought of themselves as Sandinistas and bona fide members of the FSLN, the leadership of the three tendencies represented more than just divergent positions on the correct strategy for launching the revolutionary war against Somoza. Certain ideological underpinnings were attached to their positions as well. However, after unification in March 1979, the consolidation of the FSLN at the national leadership and rank-and-file level proved solid and durable; in many ways, it made the divisions of the past look more like an historical footnote than anything else.

More central to our discussion is the issue of when and why the Cuban leadership decided to embrace a Marxist-Leninist ideology and socio-political developmental model—a fateful decision so far avoided by the FSLN. This is particularly relevant to understanding not only the Cuban and Nicaraguan but also many other Latin American revolutions that may take place in the future under similar circumstances; i.e., El Salvador, Guatemala.

Another formulation of the same question is whether there were any alternative models which Cuba could have followed in the early 1960s, and which might still have been available, and relevant, to the Sandinistas. Evidently, the Nicaraguan model of government and societal organization was apparently feasible, even if still in the formative process. Was there any assurance, however, of its viability and permanence in the face of increasingly difficult challenges and threats?

The possible demise of the Nicaraguan developmental model might suggest their having to pursue an enduring successful model such as Cuba's, especially since a would-be Latin American revolution would encompass all the three targets of change discussed here. On the other hand, it was possible that a successful Nicaragua might turn itself into a new alternative, offering a workable revolutionary model available to others. In this sense, the survival of the Nicaraguan form of popular democracy would bring a new pluralism to the Latin American revolutionary experience as well.

The Identity of the Revolutionaries

Johnson's three indicators measuring the identity of the revolutionary leaders suggest that a revolution could be led by either the elites or the masses, or by both. Implicit in this analysis is the question of the socio-economic composition of revolutionary elites, or more properly of revolutionary leadership. This question is briefly examined here as it pertains to this comparative analysis of Cuba and Nicaragua.

Comparative studies of Latin American revolutions have espoused the notion that area revolutionaries are mostly of middle-class social extraction and that these are precisely the most effective of all revolutionary leaders. Other analyses take a somewhat divergent position upgrading the leaders' socioeconomic background, identifying them as the disaffected children of the upper social strata—the *enfants terrible* of the wealthy classes. The argument supporting the latter explanation is that their higher education, wealth, and free time available could turn them into more effective revolutionary leaders, if and whenever their vocations take them in that direction.

Revealing their elitist bias, neither approach has recognized in the masses in any kind of leadership capacity, or even included the masses in their analyses. This runs against what so poignantly was recognized by Ché Guevara regarding the Cuban revolution, and which could be equally said of Nicaragua:

> With clearly defined features, there now appeared in the history of the Cuban revolution a personage that will systematically repeat itself: the masses. The mass participated. . . . [I]t lived one of the most important definitions of modern times, and today it continues the work to build socialism.[15]

(The revolutionary leader was speaking of the role played by the Cuban masses during the revolutionary period, as distinguished from the insurrectionary stage.)

In actuality, by narrowing their scope to the middle and upper classes, the two approaches under consideration seemed out of tune with the historic socio-economic changes experienced in Latin America since the 1930s. At the time of the Great Depression, the traditionally dominant triarchy formed by the church, the landed aristocracy, and the military was apparently shaken up and forced to open up to new corporative power contenders such as the emerging middle sectors and organized labor. The obvious inefficiency of this refurbished pyramidal structure, however, in responding satisfactorily to the increasing demands of an expanding and restless polity made revolution not only an acceptable but a likely event in Latin America. Cuba and Nicaragua are two cases in point.

The two revolutions compared in this study offer some common characteristics in the socio-economic backgrounds of their leadership while exhibiting significant differences in the roles played by different social groups within the revolutionary process. Equally important is the urban-rural dichotomy and the question of which would be the ideal arena for launching revolutionary warfare. Depending on the one actually chosen, city or rural dwellers would find themselves in either a leadership or a rank-and-file capacity engaged in urban or rural guerrilla warfare.

Generally speaking, the different groups fighting against the Batista regime were of middle-class, urban composition. Castro's 26th of July Movement was originally formed with members of the youth section of the *Ortodoxo* political party (PPC) who had middle and lower socioeconomic backgrounds, coming from cities like Havana, Artemisa, and others, mostly from the western provinces of the island. The Havana University Student Directorate was formed by students of all classes who lived in Havana but came from various parts of the country. The Civic Resistance was an underground movement comprised mainly of urban middle- and upper-class professionals and small businessmen. The old communist party, the *Partido Socialista Popular* (PSP), had a mixed membership with working-class representation, but was mostly of an urban middle- and lower-middle class composition.

These groups established an underground network in every province throughout the entire country and in large and small municipalities. This was the bulk of the insurrectionary movement. Although many workers were in its ranks, it was not basically working-class in composition. Nor was there substantial peasant participation. Indeed, not until the days of Castro's guerrillas in the Sierra Maestra and the Student Directorate and PSP guerrillas in the Sierra del Escambray did the insurrection gain an agrarian perspective.

After December 1956, the Cuban insurrection had an increasingly rural character—even if this was not a noticeable feature to the city populations. During 1957 and 1958, the Sierra Maestra was not only Castro's rebel domain but the symbol of the struggle as well. This was the period when the insurrection turned from an urban underground to a rural guerrilla warfare. On the other hand, Santa Clara, the capital of Las Villas province (where the Sierra del Escambray is located), was the site of the largest battle for a major city. When Santa Clara was taken from the army by rebels under the command of Ché Guevara, the Cuban insurrection had gained more of the aspect of urban warfare. All in all, the Cuban insurrectionary phase, from the standpoint of Johnson's second category, could be classified as an elite-led mass type of revolution.

The insurrection in Nicaragua had a much broader urban and rural character than that of Cuba. The expansion of the insurrection into urban and rural areas was reflected in the all-out populist war of the final offensive, launched in early summer of 1979. The country was divided by the guerrillas into six "Fronts" or geographical zones which included both rural and urban areas.

The anti-Somoza leadership covered a wide political spectrum. The FAO (Broad Opposition Front) originally brought together an array of conservative and middle-of-the-road leaders and organizations. The political parties and groups, and their leaders, included the Nicaraguan Conservative Party, René S. Argüello; Independent Liberal Party, Eduardo Rivas; Democratic Liberation Union (UDEL), Alfonso Robelo; and Nicaraguan Social Christian Party, Roberto Ferrey. The Group of Twelve was a broader organization including professionals, academics, businessmen, and priests. In opposition to FAO's policies, The Twelve decided to quit this organization in October 1978. Also, this was the only group included in FAO's membership which had relations with the FSLN.

Most of these groups featured urban, middle-class leadership. Their opposition to Somoza was not necessarily addressed against *somocismo;* that is, they repudiated the man, not the system. Of all the groups affiliated at some moment with FAO, The Twelve represented the most progressive political organization, providing important leaders for the Revolution. Later in 1980, in order to muster political support for the Council of State and the revolution, the FSLN created the Patriotic Front of the Revolution (FPR) including the Nicaraguan Socialist Party (PSN), the Popular Social Christian Party (PPSC), and the Liberal Independent Party (PLI), a former member of FAO. Besides supporting the revolutionary regime, all three parties were anti-Somoza during the war. On the other hand, to the left of traditional political parties were groups like the anti-Soviet Communist

Party of Nicaragua.

In addition to the political organizations and parties mentioned above, many kinds of civic, labor, professional, student, and women's social groups and mass organizations were part of the insurrectionary process. However, the central revolutionary organization of the anti-Somoza struggle was the FSLN. During and after the insurrection it was the spinal cord of the Nicaraguan Revolution. Its membership, including its leadership and rank-and-file, represented an ideological diversity which was openly expressed through its three early tendencies, the GPP, TP, and Insurrectionist or *Tercerista*. Through the formation of the FSLN's Joint National Directorate, its final reunification was formalized. This collegial body balanced its membership with an equal representation of all three tendencies: Daniel Ortega Saavedra (*Tercerista*, and member of the five-member ruling Junta of the Government of National Reconstruction); Humberto Ortega Saavedra (*Tercerista*, and Commander-in-Chief of the Sandinista People's Army); Victor Manuel Tirado (*Tercerista*); Bayardo Arce (GPP); Tomás Borge (GPP); Henry Ruiz (GPP); Luis Carrión (TP); Carlos Nuñez (TP), and Jaime Wheelock (TP, and Minister of Agricultural Development).

Aside from this top revolutionary echelon, the FSLN gathered in its ranks many other important leaders like Father Ernesto Cardenal (Minister of Culture), whose brother, Father Fernando Cardenal, became coordinator of the National Literacy Crusade; Father Gaspar García Laviana, a Spanish priest who joined the Revolution inspired by the example of the Colombian priest, Camilo Torres; and the heroes of the National Palace attack on August 22, 1978—Eden Pastora (Commander Zero), Hugo Torres (Commander One), and Dora María Tellez (Commander Two).

Though both Nicaragua and Cuba fall under the revolutionary leadership category of elite-led masses, there were significant differences between the two. To a greater degree than in Cuba, the widespread insurrection in Nicaragua blurred the urban-rural dichotomy almost entirely. Also, the masses were central to the struggle. In cities and towns across the country, *los muchachos* challenged the repressive apparatus of the Somoza regime again and again, taking the initiative in the fight on innumerable occasions. In the countryside, the *campesinos* fought against Somoza to such an extent that they provoked repressive, genocidal policies, which served to unify the country in opposition to the dictatorship as never before. Finally, in the words of Commander Carlos Nuñez, the intimate connection between the FSLN and the people was recognized by the fact that "[t]he FSLN came to be and is the vanguard of the Nicaraguan people . . . for having clearly defined that the masses were the forces capable of moving the wheel of history."[16]

The Goals or Ideology of the Revolution

As discussed earlier, Cuba and Nicaragua represent political and social revolutions which aimed not only at overthrowing the old regime—its leaders and political structure—but at overhauling social institutions as well. It is precisely at this point that the question of what ideological blueprint for social change should be followed becomes central. The early Cuban radicalism moved the revolution from reformism to Marxism-Leninism. Some felt that Castro promised a political revolution—meaning a pluralistic, constitutional, representative republic—but in reality he delivered a fast and far-reaching social revolution, which meant turning the country into the first socialist state in the western hemisphere. Regarding Nicaragua then, what precisely is the Sandinista ideology, besides intensely nationalistic and anti-imperialistic? Is *sandinismo* a deterrent to social change as radical as was experienced in Cuba, or is it the proper foundation for a revolutionary political culture leaning towards some form of socialist development? That is, even if it became socialist, would Nicaragua search for its own socio-political arrangements based on Sandinista revolutionary ideology?[17]

Several significant facts could be verified upon examining the leadership and ideological makeup of the FSLN. Two thirds of the national directorate was comprised of Marxist-Leninist tendencies—the GPP and TP tendencies. The *Tercerista* Tendency, however, not only avoided identifying itself with any particular ideological label (other than, of course, being Sandinista), but attracted into its ranks a broad segment of Somoza's opponents with different professions and socio-economic backgrounds, and with political ideologies ranging from moderate to radical. Rapidly, it became the tendency with the largest following. Many of its members came to occupy positions in the ruling Junta, the Government of National Reconstruction, and the Sandinista People's Army, and to be responsible for carrying out major developmental programs.

The importance of such characteristics, at the highest level of the FSLN leadership, is manifold. For one, the reunification of the three tendencies was an effective reality which proved its viability in daily practice, and not as a mere formality. Second, early ideological preferences or discriminating labels were not an obstacle in effectively operating a decision-making body as important as the FSLN's joint National Directorate, nor in producing short- and long-range policies determining the course of the Revolution. Third, it seemed plausible that the reunification process had created a certain degree of ideological syncretism among former members of the three original tendencies. After all, in the words of Tomás Borge, FSLN's founder: "There were never serious ideological differences between us. The differences have been essentially of a political and strategic nature." Thus a unified revolutionary vision emerged, having the potential of being stronger and more lasting than an early philosophical bias. Even if one recognizes that the consensus among the FSLN leadership was to build a socialist society, it is clear that there was no qualifier attached to such socialism determining its final characteristics.

The vision of a future socialist society appeared to be widely shared by the population, notwithstanding the polarized negative reaction expressed by an entrenched right-wing opposition. Underscoring this fact was the Catholic bishops' historical joint pastoral letter of November 1979 addressed to the people of Nicaragua:

> If socialism implies that power is to be exercised by the majority and increasingly shared by the organized community so that power is actually transferred to the popular classes, then it should meet nothing in our faith but encouragement and support.
>
> If socialism leads to cultural processes that awaken the dignity of the masses and give them courage to assume responsibility and demand their rights, then it promotes the same type of human dignity proclaimed by our faith.
>
> Insofar as the struggle between social classes is concerned, we think that a dynamic class struggle that produces a just transformation of structures is one thing, while class hatred which is directed against individuals, and which radically contradicts the Christian duty to be guided by love, is another.[18]

Thus even though they conditioned and tempered their statement with a significant qualifier, the Catholic bishops found constructive possibilities for the ongoing class struggle and, moreover, for the possible establishment of socialism in Nicaragua. The Theology of Liberation had made its way into the ideology of the revolution by means of a religious faith representing close to 95 percent of the population. It seems that the Catholic Church had become "increasingly aware of the fact that the cause of the poor is her own cause."[19]

As in Cuba, a broadly based "ideology of the revolution" was developing in Nicaragua. However, in Cuba the Christian ideological components were not present in such a supportive role as provided by the Nicaraguan Catholic bishops. The influence exercised by Vatican Council II and especially the Latin American Bishops' Conference at Medellín (1968) and Puebla (1978) had not materialized into a "liberating" theology. But Nicaragua, like Cuba, based its revolutionary ideological paradigm on social egalitarianism and collectivism. How these egalitarian and collectivistic notions would finally be institutionalized in the state's sociopolitical structure would be decided by many factors, and not by ideology alone.

As Cuba had done, it was possible that Nicaragua might find that an ideology like Marxism-Leninism—along with its political, social, and economic determinants—might provide the proper foundation and operational framework for the type of social egalitarianism and collectivism espoused by the revolution. On the other hand, it seemed more likely that Nicaragua's social class alliance—and social class conflict—its revolutionary form of pluralism defining its people's power and democracy, would lead to different forms of socialist organization. At the heart of this problem was the question of whether the FSLN could lead an alliance with the bourgeoisie without sacrificing the interest of the Revolution and its longer-term objectives; that is, who would lead whom, and what the final form of Nicaragua's socialism would be.

At least in part, the answer to such a question could be found in the revolutionary process, since it was not the FSLN leadership alone but the masses who were responsible for carrying out the revolution. The San-dinista mass organizations provided the channels and nuclei for the people's participation (revolutionary mobilization): the Sandinista Workers' Con-federation "José Benito Escobar" (CST), the Association of Rural Workers (ATC), the Association of Nicaraguan Women "Luisa Amanda Espinosa " (AMNLAE), the Sandinista Defense Committees (CDS), the Sandinista Youth "19th of July" (JS), and the Association of Sandinista Child-ren (ANS).[20]

These mass organizations were the agents—channels—of an intensive socio-political mobility covering the entire country. Characteristically, revolutionary mobilization was breaking down the remnants of tradition which inhibited full political participation at all social levels. All in all, as in Cuba in the 1960s, revolutionary politics in Nicaragua became the politics of mobilization.

There were differences, nonetheless, between the Cuban and Nicaraguan context for revolutionary mobilization. The major differences lay in Cuba's revolutionary monistic framework, as distinguished from Nicaragua's revolutionary pluralistic system.

For example, while the central organization of Cuba's trade unions, the Confederation of Cuban Workers (CTC), was the only legal one, the San-dinista Workers' Confederation (CST) found itself coexisting and com-peting with five other trade union organizations: the Nicaraguan Con-federation of Workers (CTN), the General Confederation of Workers-Independent (CGT-I), the Action and Labor Union Federation (CAUS), the Confederation for Trade Union Unification (CUS), and the Workers' Front (FO). These labor organizations had different ideological orientations and their own political connections and interests. Some of them took positions against revolutionary policies, altering the orderly conduct of labor rela-tions and production ratios by demanding salary increases and creating work stoppages that the country's economy could not afford, ignoring the fact that such could lead into an inflationary spiral at the very moment the nation was recuperating from the devastation of the insurrectionary war. Trying to bring about labor discipline, as well as creating workers' revolu-tionary consciousness, were among the difficulties of the Sandinista Workers' Confederaton. In this sense, the problems confronted by the FSLN in its uneasy alliance with the bourgeoisie were extended to the working class as well due to the pluralistic, competitive context in which the Revolu-tion was functioning. Under these conditions, it became increasingly dif-ficult to create a revolutionary consciousness based on political consensus.[21]

It was within this peculiar Nicaraguan context that the revolution would eventually define its ideology and the final form of the state and society. As already mentioned, there were different currents within the revolutionary (Sandinista) ideological framework. As long as they were supportive of the revolution, in all likelihood they would have some impact in the formation of the country's revolutionary political culture. Whatever final form the ideology of *sandinismo* would take, it would be very much a reflection and a product of the ongoing revolutionary experience, its needs and aspirations. In this light, Cuba's commitment to Marxism-Leninism as a revolutionary ideology was a principled and pragmatic decision of a central politico-philosophical question: the recognition that Marxism-Leninism embodied as an ideological construct the political values and social goals of the revolution, in addition to offering a model for political procedures and institutions already established in other states. This was Cuba's choice. In due time, Nicaragua would make its own decision.

The Timing of the Revolution

Regarding the question of whether the revolutions were spontaneous or calculated uprisings, neither Cuba nor Nicaragua had short-term insurrections; instead they had long-term fiercely fought *internal wars* (against Batista and Somoza respectively). Besides first debilitating the dictators and later causing their demise, the revolutionary wars witnessed similar processes of political maturation whereby the leadership and the populace gained a broader and deeper revolutionary consciousness. It was not an historical accident that far-reaching political and social revolutions occured after protracted rural and urban guerrilla warfare. It was precisely during the insurrectionary years that strong bonds developed between the leaders and the masses; this was when the leadership firmly embraced long-held national aspirations, proceeding, after gaining power, to pursue and defend them with the people's support.

During the insurrection, immediate military priorities weighed heavily in the leaders' decisions. Pressing issues including both short- and long-range socio-economic and political objectives followed these concerns. After experiencing costly and painful insurrectionary wars, neither the leadership nor the masses could settle for a superficial approach in dealing with public affairs; more properly, they chose profound societal change. In many ways, the high price in human and material losses extracted from the peoples of Cuba and Nicaragua during their insurrections had practically determined that the ensuing revolutions would have the depth and scope that they finally did.

From Castro's attack on the Moncada garrison in the city of Santiago de Cuba on July 25, 1953, to Batista's political demise on December 31, 1958, there were revolutionary actions throughout the island. From an early urban warfare type of insurrection—centered on educational institutions and the underground, which challenged the might of the repressive police apparatus—the struggle moved to the Sierra Maestra, and the mountains of Oriente province. Later, the Sierra del Escambray at the center of the Island also became a site for guerrilla warfare.

Throughout these years, different groups took leading positions in the underground only to relinquish them to other groups. Included were such groups as Civic Resistance, and spin-off revolutionary cells from the *Auténtico* (PRC) and *Ortodoxo* (PPC) political parties. Also, by 1958, the old communist party (PSP) had positioned its own guerrillas in the Escambray mountains after having joined the underground in the cities, while some of its leaders had joined Castro in his Sierra Maestra headquarters. Batista's armed forces had their share of rebellions as well, i.e., Colonel Ramón Barquin's "conspiracy of the pure" (1956), and the Cayo Loco Naval Base uprising in the city of Cienfuegos (1957). However, it was not long before Castro and his 26th of July Movement became the leading actors in the insurrection—with Havana University's Student Directorate running a strong second.

This was perhaps the most lasting outcome of such a long, agonizing insurrection: first the supremacy achieved by Castro and the Sierra Maestra as the leader and the center of the rebellion; and second, the fact that the most politically and socially radicalized revolutionary leaders emerged from the rural-revolutionary experience in the Sierra Maestra. In retrospect, it seems natural that these radical revolutionists would gain the leadership and control of the ensuing revolution.

The Nicaraguan insurrection had a long history of urban and rural warfare. The insurrection spread originally throughout the countryside engulfing towns and villages. Cities like Estelí, León, Matagalpa, Chinandega, Masaya, Jinotepe, Granada, Ocotal, Managua, and many others, became revolutionary battle sites. Nevertheless, the most significant single development during those years was the close, and competitive interaction among the three FSLN tendencies, especially regarding which guerrilla strategy should prevail: rural warfare or urban insurgency. By the end, it was the war itself that brought the three tendencies and their strategies into a unified FSLN; this unity paved the way for the ultimate victory of the revolution.

The attack on the National Palace in August 1978, followed by the September offensive initiated in the city of Matagalpa, triggered the change in the position of the GPP and TP tendencies, which came out finally in support of the *Tercerista*'s urban strategy. By the time of the final offensive, in early summer 1979, there was already a unified command as well as an organized amalgamation of guerrilla tactics; the war against Somoza covered both the cities and the countryside. By then, the FSLN had gained the military and political direction of the revolution. As in Cuba under a radical revolutionary leadership, the FSLN, with its radical revolutionary leadership, was about to begin the socio-economic and political transformation of Nicaragua.

Conclusions

This comparative study of Cuba and Nicaragua reveals some significant similarities and differences in their revolutions. The fact that Nicaraguan revolutionaries gained power only twenty years after their Cuban counterparts (1979 and 1959) established the proximity, and affinity, of these two Latin American revolutions. Other characteristics of the Cuban and Nicaraguan revolutions are equally worthy of comparison (1) they involved far-reaching social and political upheavals in the immediate vicinity of the United States, the Caribbean, and Central America (2) they involved protracted violent urban and rural guerrilla warfare which culminated in the overthrow of corrupt dictatorships; (3) they had prerevolutionary bourgeoisies which by and large were supportive of, and supported by, the old autocratic regimes and their political and economic allies in the United States; (4) they had radical revolutionary leaders who positioned themselves during the insurrectionary war at the head, and in control, of the revolutions; (5) they attained a new political consensus which supplied political support and acceptability—legitimacy—to the authority of their revolutionary governments; (6) they experienced instances of lack of, or poor compliance with their revolutionary policies by disaffected social groups, after social transformation processes were intitiated; and (7) they constituted examples for other Latin American countries, and the Third World in general, of how to approach, and achieve, socio-economic and political development.

This comparative study shows significant differences as well: (1) while both revolutions espoused the values of egalitarianism and collectivism in their revolutionary political cultures, Cuba established Marxism-Leninism as its official ideology whereas Nicaragua chose to use the nationalistic and anti-imperialistic values of *Sandinismo* as its revolutionary ideology; (2) while the Cuban revolution experienced a limited reign of terror, especially during its initial period, when some of Batista's military and police officers, and later some counterrevolutionaries, were executed, Nicaragua refused to institute the death penalty; (3) while Cuba followed a radical path of social change which led to the establishment of a socialist, Marxist-Leninist state, the Nicaraguan people's power revolutionary democracy was based on an FSLN-led alliance of revolutionary leaders and mass organizations with the bourgeoisie and its conservative political parties and economic and social organizations, and included an economic arrangement whereby the public and private sectors coexisted; and (4) while both Cuba and Nicaragua became members of the nonaligned group of nations, developing relations with all sorts of countries—developed and undeveloped, socialist and non-socialist—Nicaragua followed a more open and less committed approach in foreign policy by avoiding alignments with either of the superpowers.

After twenty odd years, the Cuban revolution had not only gained permanence and stability, but also had achieved the institutionalization of the state. From 1979 onward, the Nicaraguan revolutionaries pursued transformation, sometimes applying policies and programs similar to those used earlier in Cuba, while at the same time adopting an innovative and autochthonous political form: a pluralistic, yet revolutionary, people's democracy. Of course the future was uncertain, but at least it seemed clear that, in Nicaragua, the process of social change, as well as the external economic and political forces impacting on the country, would determine the final form of the Nicaraguan state. What the characteristics of such a state would be—whether it would be socialist or not and, if socialist, whether it would also be Marxist-Leninist—only the future would tell.

Notes

[1] For a discussion of Nicaraguan exiles' military camps in southern Florida, training in collaboration with Cuban exiles, see Eddie Adams, "Exiles Rehearse for the Day They Hope Will Come," *Parade*, Mar. 15, 1981.

[2] Richard H. Immerman, "Guatemala as Cold War History," *Political Science Quarterly*, 95, 4 (Winter 1980-81), pp. 629-653.

[3] The literature on this subject has recognized the decreasing role played by Cuba in support of Latin American guerrilla movements, especially in comparison with its alleged involvement with such groups throughout the 1960s. The anti-Somoza struggle in Nicaragua was blamed by the Somoza regime partly on Cuba's "militant support" for the guerrillas. Historical facts seem to indicate that Somoza was intimately involved all along with anti-Castro groups and even played a central role in some instances. Meanwhile, Cuba gave moral, and in all probability military support to the groups opposing and fighting Somoza, particularly the FSLN. After the revolutionary victory in 1979, the charges of Cuban involvement in Nicaragua surfaced again. Publicly recognized by Cuba and Nicaragua is the fact that thousands of Cuban experts were helping the Sandinistas in different capacities, from the Literacy Campaign of 1979-1980 to a myriad of developmental programs. There were also Cuban military experts helping to train the Sandinista People's Army. For Cuba, this was proletarian internationalism in action, supporting a revolution close to the hearts of Cuban revolutionaries. This close cooperation was seen quite differently in Washington, expecially under the Reagan administration. However, it was the Carter administration which had decided to reinstitute, after stoppingit momentarily, economic aid and military support for El Salvador, allegedly due to Nicaraguan support for the guerrillas. The Reagan administration reported that documents demonstrating Cuban and Soviet involvement in El Salvador had been captured by the Salvadoran Christian Democratic-military junta. (The documents, the authenticity of which is open to question, were equally incriminating for Nicaragua since it was claimed that Nicaraguan soil was utilized to smuggle weapons into El Salvador for the guerrillas.) The obvious implication of this report was the need for further support—particularly military—to the ruling Salvadoran junta, and punishment—particularly economic—for Nicaragua. Thisand other developments underscored the increasingly confrontational nature of President Reagan's approach to such revolutionary groups as El Salvador's and governments as Nicaragua's and Cuba's. For the Reagan administration's position, see *Communist Interference in El Salvador* (Special Report No. 80), United States Department of State, Feb. 23, 1981, pp. 1-8. For opposing views, see James Petras, "Invented Red Menace—White Paper on the White Paper," *The Nation*, Mar. 28, 1981, pp. 353, 367-372, and John Dinges, "El Salvador—Documents Tell Different Tale," *In These Times*, Apr. 1-7, 1981, p. 9. For a general discussion of this political problem, see Alan Riding, "Reagan and Latin America: Region Viewed as Likely To Resist Closer U.S. Ties," *New York Times*, Feb. 13, 1981, p. 6. A sensitive analysis of Cuba's decreasing involvement in Latin American guerrilla affairs throughout the 1970s is provided by Jorge I.

Domínguez in "Cuban Foreign Policy," *Foreign Affairs,* Fall 1978, pp. 83-108. Regarding pre- and postrevolutionary Cuban-Nicaraguan relations, see William M. Leogrande, "Cuba and Nicaragua—From the Somozas to the Sandinistas," *Caribbean Review,* IX, 1 (Winter 1980), pp. 11-14.

⁴ For a discussion of President Nixon's policies towards Allende's Chile, and the persecution launched after 1973 by President Pinochet's DINA (secret police) against Chilean exiles, see John Dinges and Saul Landau, *Assassination on Embassy Row* (New York: Pantheon Books, 1980).

⁵ This analysis draws on Carl Leiden's and Karl M. Schmitt's discussion on revolutions in their *The Politics of Violence: Revolution in the Modern World* (Englewood Cliffs, N.J.: Prentice-Hall, 1968). Also, see John Dunn, *Modern Revolutions* (London: Cambridge University Press, 1972); Carl J. Friedrich, *Revolution,* Nomos VIII (New York: Atherton Press, 1966), and James C. Davies, "Towards a Theory of Revolution," *American Sociological Review,* 27, 1 (Mar. 1962).

⁶ Hannah Arendt, *On Revolution* (New York: The Viking Press, 1963); Sigmund Neumann, "The International Civil War," *World Politics,* 1 (1949); Harry Eckstein, ed., *Internal War* (New York: The Free Press, 1964), and Peter Amman, "Revolution: A Redefinition," *Political Science Quarterly,* 77 (1962), pp. 36-53.

⁷ Crane Brinton, *The Anatomy of Revolution* (New York: Vintage Books, 1956), and Alfred G. Meyer, "The Functions of Ideology in the Soviet Political System," *Soviet Studies,* 17, (1966), p. 275.

⁸ Chalmers Johnson, *Revolution and the Social System,* Hoover Institution Studies No. 3 (Stanford: Hoover Institution, 1964), 10, 24-28.

⁹ Max Azicri, "The Governing Strategies of Mass Mobilization: The Foundations of Cuban Revolutionary Politics," *Latin American Monograph Series,* No. 2 (Erie, Pa.: The Northwestern Pennsylvania Institute for Latin American Studies and Mercyhurst College, 1977), pp. 1-32; and Richard R. Fagen, "Mass Mobilization in Cuba: The Symbolism of Struggle," in Rolando E. Bonachea and Nelson P. Valdes, eds., *Cuba in Revolution* (New York: Doubleday, 1972), pp. 201-223.

¹⁰ Max Azicri, "Crime and Law Under Socialism: The 1979 Cuban Penal Code," *Review of Socialist Law,* 6, 1 (1980), p. 10.

¹¹ Max Azicri, "Change and Institutionalization in the Revolutionary Process: The Cuban Legal System in the 1970s," *Review of Socialist Law,* 6, 2 (1980), p. 178.

¹² "The New Nicaragua: National Reconstruction," *Nicaragua Fact Sheets* (Washington, D.C.: National Network in Solidarity with the Nicaraguan People, n.d.).

¹³ "Revolución Sin Paredón," (*Nicaragua Año 1*), *Cuadernos del Tercer Mundo,* IV, 39 (Aug.-Sept. 1980), pp. 41-42.

¹⁴ The other members of the ruling junta of the Government of National Reconstruction were Daniel Ortega Saavedra, member of the FSLN national directorate; Moises Hassan, a founding member of the United People's Movement (MPU); Dr. Arturo Cruz, a bank manager; and Rafael Cordova Ruiz who, together with Cruz, joined the ruling Junta in May 1980 representing the private sector and conservative political groups. Arthur S. Banks, ed., *Political Handbook of the World—1980* (New York: McGraw-Hill, 1980), pp. 337-340; Marifeli Pérez-Stable, "Nicaragua: Revolución Sandinista y Poder Popular," *Areíto,* VI, 23 (1980), pp. 4-9, and "El Mayor Logro: Haver Sobrevivido" and "Un Banquero en la Revolución," (*Nicaragua Año 1*), *Cuadernos del Tercer Mundo,* IV, 39 (Aug.-Sept. 1980), pp. 16-22, 36-40.

¹⁵ Bertram Silverman, ed., *Man and Socialism in Cuba: The Great Debate* (New York: Atheneum, 1971), p. 339.

¹⁶ Roger Burbach and Tim Draimin, "Popular Democracy: Taking the First Steps," *Nicaragua's Revolution, NACLA Report on the Americas,* XIV 3, (May-June 1980), pp. 29-30.

¹⁷ For a discussion of *sandinismo* as a revolutionary ideology and its centrality to the Nicaraguan revolutionary value system, see José Luis Balcarcel, "El Sandinismo, Ideología de

la Revolutión Nicaragüense," *Nicaráuac,* 1 (July-Aug. 1980). pp. 112-119. Also, see Sergio Ramírez, Ed., Foreward to *El Pensamiento Vivo de Sandino* (San José, Costa Rica: Editorial Universitaria Centroamericana [EDUCA], 1979), v-lxix.

[18] "The New Nicaragua: The Role of the Church," *Nicaraguan Fact Sheets* (Washington, D.C.: National Network in Solidarity with the Nicaraguan People, n.d.).

[19] Ibid.

[20] Roger Burbach and Tim Draimin, "Popular Democracy: Taking the First Steps," 22-23, and *Nicaragua: A People's Revolution* (Washington, D.C.: Epica Task Force, 1980), pp. 76-96.

[21] Ibid. pp. 84-86; "The New Nicaragua: Trade Unions," *Nicaragua Fact Sheets* (Washington, D.C.: National Network in Solidarity with the Nicaraguan People, n.d.), and Burbach and Draimin, "Popular Democracy: Taking the First Steps," pp. 25-28. For background information on these and other developmental issues faced by the Government of National Reconstruction and the FSLN leadershp and mass organizations, see *Datos Básicos Sobre Nicaragua* (Managua: Secretaría de Propaganda y Educación Política del FSLN, 1980).

Chapter 21

The Nicaraguan Revolution
and the Reemerging Cold War

SUSANNE JONAS

In the first year and a half after the victory of the Frente Sandinista de Liberación Nacional in Nicaragua, an intense drama unfolded in the highest circles of the U.S. government. Both the Carter Administration (in its last eighteen months in office) and Congress were locked in a fierce debate over U.S. policy toward Nicaragua, focusing on a proposed $75 million "aid" package. During the course of the debate, the House of Representatives twice went into secret session—for the first time in 149 years—to discuss Cuban influence and the possibility of "another Cuba" in Nicaragua. The highest officials of the Carter Administration and leading congressmen testified during the debate, and the President himself was instructed, as a precondition for releasing the aid funds, to verify every three months that Nicaragua was not aiding revolutionary movements in other countries. Because of this debate, the aid to Nicaragua was held up an entire year.

The Nicaragua aid debate, which pitted transnational bankers against right-wing militarists, was not an isolated phenomenon. It was a drama of the new Cold War which had been aggressively and deliberately revived by the U.S. ruling class in mid-1979. It was in many respects a compressed version of a larger debate in U.S. policy circles: how the United States should exercise its declining power in the world today—whether to continue pretending to wield unilateral power or to make certain pragmatic adjustments to the reality of eroded U.S. power—and how to pursue a Cold War interventionist stance in the hemisphere.

In historical perspective, particularly in the light of more aggressive and adventurist policies that the Reagan Administration could be expected to pursue, it would seem that the Carter Administration was moderate in dealing with the Sandinista government. Nevertheless, the Carter policy toward Nicaragua must be seen in the broader context of the revival of a Cold War U.S. foreign policy in 1979-80, which was a foreign policy of the entire U.S. ruling class. To be sure, the U.S. ruling class is not monolithic; it is composed of different blocs or factions, principally the transnational interests represented by the Trilateral Commission and President Carter, and a domestic faction tied into the military-industrial complex (although all factions rely on U.S. military power to achieve their goals). These factions

375

contend and cooperate in the formation of U.S. foreign policy. Although they diverge on a number of points, they appear to have been converging in 1979-80 in regard to the abandonment of detente, the revival of the Cold War, and some form of interventionism abroad, combined with the imposition of austerity policies within the United States.

This apparent convergence was a most dangerous development for the people of the United States, as well as for Latin America. A majority of the American people opposed Cold War interventionism after Vietnam, and recognized that overall such policies harmed more than they benefited the American people and the American economy. Therefore, if we use the term "U.S. imperialism" in reference to the Cold War policies of the U.S. government, we must be clear that this refers solely to the ability of the various factions of the U.S. ruling class to set foreign and military policy.

The Decline of U.S. Power and
the Consolidation of a New Cold War Policy

Let us begin by examining briefly the global situation of U.S. power.[1] The United States has seen its power seriously undermined since the late 1960s by internal and international capitalist crisis. By the 1980s, it is not the U.S. or any other *national* economy which is the principal locus of imperialism, but giant transnational corporations and banks. The dominant economic force is the drive for capital accumulation by these corporate giants that rule the capitalist world economy. The ruling class within a particular nation and its military arsenal may be used to serve transnational interests, but these transnationals know no single national constituency; their interest lies in their own capital accumulation, and comes into frequent contradiction with the needs of the national economy.

Thus the "international capitalist crisis" is a crisis not for the transnational corporations or banks, but in the national economies of the Western capitalist powers, most notably the United States. The crisis, which began in the late 1960s and gave rise to a full-fledged recession in the United States by 1973-5, was manifested concretely as a profit squeeze for large domestic industries. In order to restore their profit margin, these industries have moved to transfer their accumulation crisis to the U.S. working class through the imposition of austerity policies (long pursued in the Third World). Austerity for U.S. workers has meant a deliberate campaign to reduce the social programs and benefits returned to the working class from the taxes they pay, and more specifically, no real controls on price inflation, reducing real wages; layoffs and planned unemployment; and across-the-board cutbacks in necessary and basic social services.

The transnational corporations have responded to international capitalist crisis in their own way by restructuring the international division of labor[2] (for example, relocating industrial production from the "core" capitalist countries to the underdeveloped countries of the periphery and semiperiphery where, above all, they have access to unlimited supplies of cheap labor). This shift causes the proliferation of "runaway shops," and intensifies the crisis and the imposition of austerity upon the working class in the core countries.

Internal economic crisis has been matched by the decline of U.S. hegemony internationally, particularly since the U.S. defeat in Vietnam. This decline has meant, first, the intensification of inter-imperialist rivalry between the United States and the other Western capitalist powers (Western Europe and Japan). The fraction of the U.S. ruling class most deeply rooted in transnational capital has attempted to hold together the "Western alliance," for example, through the Trilateral Commission. Over time, however, the Trilateral alliance has been subjected to increasing strains, as the U.S. ruling class is less able to coordinate international capitalist interests or to maintain hegemony over its counterparts in Europe and Japan (who have their own priorities, including preservation of *their* detente with the Soviet Union).

Second, the direct challenge to U.S. power worldwide has come from escalating resistance by oppressed and exploited peoples in the Third World. The United States emerged from the Vietnam War drained, isolated, and defeated. Yet the potential for "more Vietnams" existed in many parts of the world, including Central America.

International decline has meant that the U.S. ruling class no longer has the power to set the terms of its relations with other countries unilaterally. U.S. options are more limited, and the United States is less able to force its will unrestrainedly on other nations through instant military interventions as it did, for example, in Guatemala in 1954, in the Congo in 1961, and in the Dominican Republic in 1965. Beyond Vietnam, the United States had to accept the overthrow of its long-standing puppet, Somoza, and the victory of a progressive, nationalist, Marxist-led revolution in Nicaragua, a country long viewed as "our own backyard." In other parts of the world as well, the United States had to make concessions.

Particularly since the U.S. ruling class has always regarded Latin America as its natural sphere of domination, the response to defeats elsewhere was an intensified effort to preserve U.S. hegemony in Latin America. The brutal overthrow of the Allende government in Chile was only the most extreme example. In numerous other countries, such as Guatemala and Argentina, U.S. imperialism has shown its shameless brutality in supporting, indeed instructing and training, the right-wing butchers.

After the U.S. defeat in Vietnam, with the lack of domestic support for foreign intervention, and with increasing isolation internationally, the U.S. ruling class had to make certain adjustments in its foreign policy. Tactically, the United States had to project a short-range policy of nonintervention and detente with the Soviet Union. At the same time, after 1976, Carter and Brezinski went on the offensive against the Soviet Union by criticising "human rights violations" there. But they could not call for "human rights" in the Soviet Union without making a show of advocating human rights elsewhere; hence, Carter's "human rights policy" in Latin America. In fact, this represented no real commitment to human rights; it was a tactical adjustment to new realities in the world—a short-range concession in order to preserve U.S. options long-range,[3]—and a platform for attacking the Soviet Union.

This shift and the years of detente did create, for a short time, a less dangerous, less interventionist international climate. In some sense, the Nicaraguan people benefited indirectly from this opening; they won their victory at a time when the United States was constrained from intervening militarily to stop the overthrow of Somoza. However, the ephemeral nature of this opening, and the fact that it was always tactical rather than long-range U.S. policy, became clear in the increasingly provocative policies of the U.S. government after mid-1979, the deliberate revival of the Cold War with the Soviet Union.[4]

An early sign of Washington's increasingly aggressive posture was the drummed-up "crisis" over the "discovery" of Soviet troops in Cuba in mid-1979—troops which, by Carter's own admission, had been there for at least several years. This became the pretext for an escalating program to reestablish U.S. military hegemony in the Caribbean and Central America. More broadly, it was an opening shot in the Carter Administration's global Cold War offensive. In October 1979, Carter provoked the crisis in Iran and used this opportunity to rattle the U.S. saber (as well as to override domestic opposition to U.S. intervention abroad by whipping up "patriotic" fervor).

Subsequently, the Carter Administration continued its deliberate provocations of the Soviet Union (new nuclear missiles in Western Europe, shelving of the SALT II Treaty, a greatly increased military budget, and so on). In addition, the United States continued to solidify an anti-Soviet alliance and "encirclement" policy with the People's Republic of China. These provocations threatened to elicit a less moderate response from the Soviet Union, which had previously pursued a policy of detente; concretely, they set the stage for the Soviet intervention in Afghanistan—which in turn gave the U.S. ruling class a new opportunity to heat up the war machine and to fan the flames of anti-Soviet hysteria.

Thus, Carter's foreign policy in 1979-80 catapulted the United States from an era of detente into an era of Cold War, an era of increasing instability, unpredictability, and brinksmanship. The "Carter Doctrine" reflected the U.S. government's desire to undertake an anti-Soviet offensive, and to assert U.S. power, *precisely at a time when actual U.S. power worldwide was declining.* Because U.S. power is in fact limited and declining, this offensive has been more provocative, less controlled, less predictable. Once again, the U.S. ruling class has been willing to intervene abroad and literally to threaten world peace, using the Soviet Union as a scapegoat.

The Policy Debate over U.S. Aid to Nicaragua

During the year and a half following the victory of the Sandinistas, U.S. policy toward Nicaragua was the subject of intense debate. After having their way for over forty years, the advocates of overt U.S. military intervention to keep the right-wing Somoza dictatorship in power were temporarily silenced in the summer of 1979—not out of any change of heart by the U.S. ruling class, but rather out of necessity, a necessity imposed by the military victory of the revolutionary Frente Sandinista over the Somoza dictatorship. These circumstances forced a reappraisal in Washington, and presented the opportunity for a different breed of interventionists to be heard—the soft-line interventionists. These officials, represented most clearly by former Assistant Secretary of State for Inter-American Affairs Viron Vaky, and his successor, William Bowdler, sought to prevent "another Cuba" in Nicaragua (and "another Nicaragua" in El Salvador) by giving conditioned U.S. economic aid. Elsewhere in Latin America, they advocated creating a "democratic opening" in the most repressive regimes. The goal of the soft-line interventionists was the same in all cases—to recoup or at least to minimize the losses of U.S. power; their principal weapon was not the machine-gun but the dollar.

The weapon of the dollar was particularly powerful because the Nicaraguan economy at the time of the Sandinista victory was in ruins, and required massive international aid. Somoza had maintained the country in a state of underdevelopment for years, and waged a brutal war against the Frente Sandinista which left a number of towns utterly destroyed and 70 percent of industry damaged or destroyed. Physical damage from the war was estimated at $600 million, with an additional $500 million or more in capital flight because of the war. When Somoza fled the country, he left barely $3.5 million in international reserves. Unemployment had reached 34 percent in Managua, higher elsewhere, with an additional 25 percent underemployment. Eight hundred thousand people, more than one-quarter of the population, needed daily food handouts.[5]

Clearly, the job of reconstructing a devastated country required massive international aid, and the Nicaraguan government sought $2.5 billion in aid from a wide variety of sources, including the United States.[6] The Carter Administration responded with various small loans and grants, and with a longer-range proposal of $75 million for Nicaragua as part of the overall foreign aid bill for Fiscal Year 1981. This sparked an intense, months-long debate within the Carter Administration and within the U.S. Congress.

Before tracing the details of this debate, let us see briefly who were the main players and what interests they represented. The Carter Administration was itself divided, with a number of State Department officials such as Vaky and Bowdler taking the "accommodationist" view toward Nicaragua, while others in the Pentagon and intelligence agencies took a "hard-line" approach. Behind the "accommodationists," on the one hand, was a significant chunk of transnational banking capital (which, as we shall see, had its own interests in controlling U.S. relations with Nicaragua) and the major Eastern newspapers (*New York Times, Washington Post,* and so on, which carried numerous editorials supporting aid to Nicaragua). Alligned with the hard-liners, on the other hand, was a vocal right-wing bloc in Congress, whose goal was to stop U.S. aid to Nicaragua altogether—or to impose so many conditions as to make U.S. aid unacceptable to the Nicaraguan government. As we shall see, they were able to make great headway toward achieving that latter goal.

Lest the intensity of the debate obscure the underlying unity of objectives, let us be clear from the outset: all parties were in agreement that the United States must preserve maximum control over Nicaragua (within the context of declining U.S. power worldwide); the debate was merely about *how* best to achieve that objective. Because the stakes were high, the tactical debate was intense, but at no time was this underlying objective ever questioned.

From the very beginning, an underlying issue in U.S. policy circles was not simply Nicaragua, but Cuba (and, by extension, the Soviet Union): how to stop Cuban assistance to Nicaragua, how to prevent Nicaragua from following the "Cuban model," how to counter Cuban training of Frente leadership, "Cuban troops" on Nicaraguan soil, and so forth. Or at least, so it seemed in the congressional debate; in fact the international bankers had other objectives as well.

Thus, when President Carter presented the aid request to Congress in late 1979, the right wing lost no time in launching a counteroffensive. In response to the dominant position within the Administration that the United States could only keep control over future developments in Nicaragua (and keep Nicaragua out of the Cuban-Soviet camp) by giving U.S. aid, the right wing argued that it was already too late for any real U.S. influence, and U.S. funds would only aid the consolidation of a pro-Cuban, Marxist regime; therefore, the United States must move directly to overthrow that regime, and certainly must send no aid.

After Carter submitted the request for $75 million in U.S. "aid" (of which $70 million was credits to buy U.S. goods, and only $5 million a grant),[7] the Senate Foreign Relations Committee approved the aid package, and the House Foreign Affairs Committee approved it after attaching a condition requiring Carter to cut off aid if Cuban or Soviet combat troops were found in Nicaragua.[8] The bill was approved on the floor of the Senate in January 1980. When it came to the floor of the House in February, the House convened a highly unusual two-hour secret session (for the second time since 1830—the first being in June 1979, also on Cuban influence in Nicaragua) to hear testimony on classified documents as to whether Nicaragua had become "Cuba-like." After this unprecedented session, the bill was passed in the House by a thin five-vote margin, and with several onerous conditions attached:[9]

First, it was stipulated in the legislation itself that 60 percent of the aid would go to the private business sector—the idea being to strengthen the influence of the private sector in the new regime and in the economy. Those funds would not go to the public sector, which was controlled by the popular government, but rather to private businessmen.

Second, the House added a stipulation making the aid conditional on Nicaragua's "overall human rights performance," and on the holding of elections within a "reasonable period of time." This, of course, could become a ready-made justification for cutting off aid and possibly intervening in the future. This stipulation calls to mind the Marshall Plan in Western Europe after World War II, in which U.S. "aid" was tied to the purges of elected socialists from office. In fact, one U.S. businessman spoke of Nicaragua's need for a "Marshall Plan."[10]

A third condition placed on the $75 million package was that the funds could not be used in facilities with Cuban personnel. This meant that, at a time when the literacy campaign was a principal national priority, no U.S. funds could be used in schools or educational facilities where there were Cuban volunteers or technicians—as would be likely, given Cuba's extended experience with such campaigns.

A fourth condition prohibited Nicaraguan involvement with "international terrorism or attempts to subvert other governments," or the presence of Soviet or Cuban combat troops in Nicaragua.[11]

The Nicaraguan government and people reacted angrily to these conditions. On the one hand, they needed approval of the aid—not so much because of the amount (which, as many have pointed out, was almost insignificant compared with Nicaragua's needs)—but because international banking sources were holding up some $500 million in additional international funds for Nicaragua until passage of the aid bill as a "signal of U.S. confidence in the stability of Nicaragua."[12] On the other hand, the conditions imposed amounted to blackmail. Junta member Sergio Ramirez contrasted U.S. aid with that of other countries:

> We think of the revolutionary generosity of that poor but proud
> people [Grenada], who gave us what they had. [If the U.S. were
> to offer a per capita equivalent, it would mean] not 75 million,
> but $7.5 billion—and without conditions.[13]

Twenty thousand Nicaraguans marched in the streets to protest the conditions on the U.S. aid. The Nicaraguan government indicated that it would study the aid package in its final form before deciding whether to accept it—and meanwhile negotiated new trade and technical agreements with the Soviet Union[14] and Eastern European countries, as well as with Western Europe—all of which was "absolutely without conditions."

In April, the situation took a new turn with the resignation of businessman and political "moderate" Alfonso Robelo from the governmental Junta. Conservatives in Nicaragua, consulting with the U.S. Ambassador,[15] seized the opportunity to renew their clamor for "pluralism" and representation for the private sector in the government. Conservatives in Washington seized upon the Robelo resignation and the Nicaraguan government's agreements with the Soviet Union and Eastern Europe to continue their efforts to stall or kill the U.S. aid bill; Speaker of the U.S. House of Representatives, "Tip" O'Neill, stated publicly that there was a concern about Nicaragua becoming a "Marxist state," and that Congress would not approve the Nicaragua aid bill "unless they have a bipartisan government down there"[16] (meaning, unless the private-sector representatives were appointed to the government). The State Department declared that Nicaragua's agreements with the Soviet Union "clearly signalled" a Soviet move to expand its influence in Nicaragua—while others went further, pointing to the agreements as evidence of "a Soviet plan to communize Central America and use that land bridge as a dagger pointing north and south. . . ."[17]

These pressures were somewhat relieved when the Sandinista leadership, while denouncing U.S. "blackmail," appointed two new "moderates" to the Junta. In Washington, the Senate accepted the House version of the aid bill with all the new conditions. The House voted to approve the measure, after President Carter had a top-level Congressional delegation visit Nicaragua; Speaker O'Neill, in his first foreign-aid speech in twenty-eight years, and Majority Leader Jim Wright pushed through the bill, after nine hours of debate on the House floor.[18] The final version of the bill required President Carter to report every three months "on the state of Nicaraguan democracy," and give assurances that Nicaragua was not aiding revolutionary movements in other countries.[19] In signing the authorization measure, Carter declared the U.S. intention to resist "interference" by Cuba "and others."[20]

However, only the first stage of the battle was over, for the funds still had to be appropriated by Congress. New pressures began building up for the Nicaraguan government to announce a date for "free elections." In July, the Republican Party platform directly attacked the "Marxist Sandinist takeover of Nicaragua," opposed the Carter aid program, and stated support for any movement to overthrow the Sandinista government.[21] In August, there were reports that conservative groups within the Carter Administration (the intelligence agencies and the Pentagon) were trying to stop appropriation and disbursement of the aid until after the November elections in the United States, when the whole aid package could be canceled by a Reagan Administration—and that these officials were deliberately leaking information (to the Evans and Novak column, published August 1, 1980), portraying Nicaragua as a "Soviet and Cuban puppet, supplying arms to Communist insurgents in neighboring El Salvador."[22] The Carter Administration complied with the Congressionally-required investigation, and on September 13, 1980, reported that the Nicaraguan government was not supporting violence or terrorism in Central America (as opposed to right-wing allegations that Nicaragua was shipping Cuban arms to other countries).[23] The path was finally cleared for Congressional release of the $75 million, and the final agreement releasing the funds was signed with the Nicaraguan government in October. Thus ended, at least temporarily, the year-long Nicaragua aid debate.

The Hidden Actors: The Transnational Banks

What were the goals of the pro-aid forces, the soft-line interventionists? And who were they, really? Throughout the debate, the dominant force in the Carter Administration argued that U.S. aid must be given to keep Nicaragua out of the Cuban-Soviet camp, and that the long delay in Congressional approval of the aid was having a "radicalizing impact" on Nicaragua.[24] On the surface, the goals of the soft-line interventionists in the State Department were the following:

—to shore up the political role of Nicaragua's "moderates" and businessmen and to assure a future political role for non-Sandinistas;

—to preserve the role of the private sector in the economy and maintain a "mixed economy," rather than follow the "Cuban model" of socialism;

—to prevent Nicaragua from lining up internationally in the Soviet camp;

—to exert pressure to get Cuban technicians out of Nicaragua.

To be sure, these political goals were important. But, as noted in the London *Financial Times,* there was another hidden force which provides the key to the Carter-Trilateral strategy: "Pressure on the Administration to help Nicaragua has come from a consortium of U.S. banks, which recently negotiated a refinancing of $600 million of Nicaragua's debt."[25] In fact, Carter released the U.S. aid only after Nicaragua reached an agreement with the private banks.[26]

Here, finally, we find the key to the mystery—the counterforce strong enough to resist the political and military right-wing forces. Just at the time that Carter was presenting the foreign-aid bill to Congress, this consortium of the capitalist world's largest transnational banks was beginning a long series of negotiations with the Nicaraguan government to reschedule payment on the staggering foreign debt left by Somoza. All in all, this was a debt of over $1.6 billion. More than $618 million was due by the end of 1979 (more than the total value of Nicaraguan exports), of which $444 million, or 70 percent, was owed to private foreign banks.[27] Seventy-five percent was owed to U.S. banks.[28] According to the U.N. Economic Commission on Latin America, Somoza had deliberately designed this private debt so that most of it could be drained from Nicaragua, rather than being invested there.[29]

Talks between the Nicaraguan government and a steering committee of thirteen bankers representing ninety creditor banks began informally in the winter of 1979-80. The meetings continued in March, with the Nicaraguan government attempting to obtain a grace period for repayments; and, in spite of pressures from the international bankers, to keep the International Monetary Fund (IMF) out of the picture; as one Nicaraguan official stated, "It is not for us to involve the IMF at this stage and to get involved in an austerity program;" in the words of another, ". . . we consider that the IMF has no role to play in the formation of economic policy."[30] (Later in 1980, the issue of the IMF did block an agreement between the Nicaraguan government and the "Paris Club," which represented Western governments to which Nicaragua owed most of its $250 million bilateral debt: the United States insisted that Nicaragua open discussions with the IMF, and Nicaragua refused to do so under such pressure.[31]) After nine months of talks (and a last-minute ploy by Citibank of New York, the largest creditor, to push for annual debt-service payments, beginning in 1980, of more than 30 percent of Nicaragua's 1980 export revenues !), an agreement was reached in September, rescheduling the $582 million due in 1980 for repayment at commercial rates over the next twelve years.[32] Nicaragua had succeeded in keeping the IMF out of the agreement and gained a five-year grace period, but the banks had Nicaragua's agreement to repay all of the Somoza regime's debts, at commercial, not concessionary, rates.[33]

Now it is clear why the banks had pressured the Carter Administration not to bow to right-wing political pressure to delay U.S. aid until after the November election:[34] just at the moment when they were successfully completing their own negotiations with Nicaragua, the banks had a great stake in not allowing the apple cart of U.S. aid to Nicaragua to be upset.

Why did the transnational banks care so much about their negotiations with Nicaragua? First, they saw the issue as much larger than Nicaragua itself, as a kind of test case: they wanted to establish a clear precedent of a revolutionary government not defaulting (in contrast to Cuba some years earlier), and of agreement to pay the debt at commercial rates, even under the outrageous circumstances of a staggering debt accumulated by Somoza, primarily for his own gain, and on which he had defaulted after the fall of 1978. Such a precedent would serve them well in their negotiations with other countries ranging from Bolivia, Brazil, and Jamaica to Poland, Sudan, and Turkey. As one banker stated, the Nicaragua settlement "could make it more palatable for other countries to go the rescheduling route."[35]

Second, the banks and their political spokesmen had a special strategy for Nicaragua. In a situation where the Nicaraguan government began with only $3.3 million in international reserves, whatever paltry reserves could be accumulated through international aid would have to be used for paying off the international banks for loans made to the Somoza regime, rather than for meeting Nicaragua's domestic needs for the coming years—reconstruction of a devastated economy, creation of 90,000 new jobs, stimulation of economic growth, and reduction of the annual inflation rate from 60 percent to 20 percent. The Nicaraguan government accepted this intolerable burden for one simple reason: without doing so, they would have faced closed doors for all short- and medium-term credit from international banks in the capitalist world. (In fact, the banks did refuse to extend any new credits to the Nicaraguan government until the rescheduling negotiations were concluded.)[36] This would have left no option other than massive aid from the Soviet bloc—and it is questionable whether the Soviet Union would have undertaken such a responsibility for a second time in the Western hemisphere.

This unspeakable situation had political ramifications as well: it meant that the Sandinista government was forced into the position of imposing austerity upon the Nicaraguan people as the price of their liberation—of asking the Nicaraguan people, who had fought and died for a better life, to suffer and sacrifice still more, so that the international banks could be paid off. As soon as the government made its first move in this direction, by limiting the end-of-year bonus for workers to $150 at the end of 1979, the middle class had its golden opportunity to begin its protest against the government. (Now we can see why the Nicaraguans so strongly opposed IMF involvement, which would have meant a *formal* austerity plan.)

More broadly, and over a longer range, this situation gave the international bankers a lever to exert pressure upon and squeeze the new government—and then to wait for the discontent bred by the necessary austerity measures to erupt into antigovernment demonstrations (along the lines of the middle-class women's "March of the Empty Pots" against Allende in Chile) and eventually perhaps a Chile-style counterrevolution.

Thus, transnational capital may be seen to have adopted a strategy which *appeared* less direct than the militarists', but which was every bit as hostile in attempting to undermine and destabilize (and eventually to "moderate" or get rid of) the Sandinista government. The new gnomes of international finance capital are indeed the *patient interventionists*—but not one whit less interventionist than the shrill right-wing Congressmen in Washington. Their concern—and it was clearly communicated to Carter, we may speculate, via the Trilateral Commission—was above all to assure that U.S.-Nicaraguan relations were not interrupted too early, which might prompt the Nicaraguan government to pull out of the debt renegotiations and refuse to repay Somoza's loans.

This, then, was an important source of the policy of the "soft-liners" in Washington, who were arguing publicly that the U.S. must maintain good relations with Nicaragua, aid Nicaragua, and so on. Underneath the Carter position lay the determination to get hard cash repayments, and politically, over the long range, to undermine and destabilize the Sandinista government through austerity policies which would turn the middle class against the government.

Thus the transnational banks presented Nicaragua with a serious political problem. In a situation where either compliance (paying off the huge Somoza debt) or resistance (resulting in no new credits or aid) would result in austerity for the Nicaraguan people, why did the Nicaraguan government play the game of the international bankers, and what other options did it have? As the Nicaraguan government knew only too well, there was no easy answer: this was the dilemma that Cuba had faced nearly twenty years earlier; this was the vise which ultimately brought the Allende government in Chile to its knees (the U.S.-transnational bank credit blockade, which laid the groundwork for austerity and the 1973 *golpe*). Other than transnational capital, there was only the Soviet bloc (the option chosen by Cuba), or a larger bloc of Central American-Caribbean-(eventually) Latin American nations, once they were liberated. The last is, of course, the "domino" spectre that haunts the U.S. ruling class—which is precisely the reason for the phobia about Nicaragua aiding revolutionary movements in other countries, and the reason, even as he signed the Nicaragua aid measure, Carter also increased U.S. aid to El Salvador to $73 million, to prevent "another Nicaragua" there.[37] Clearly the future options of the Nicaraguan Revolution would be profoundly affected by the struggles in other countries, especially in Central America.

Conclusion: Prospects Under the Reagan Administration

While the Carter Administration was forced to accept the Sandinista victory in July 1979—it was too late to do anything else—no wing of the U.S. ruling class necessarily accepted the Sandinista regime, long-range. Particularly if we remember the history of solid U.S. support for the Somoza dictatorship for nearly forty-five years (primarily under Democratic Administrations), and U.S. opposition to the Sandinista victory up to the very last minute (attempting to preserve the National Guard, to send an OAS "peacekeeping force," to form a "moderate government" and isolate the Frente), we must expect the U.S. government to make trouble in Nicaragua, secretly or openly, directly or indirectly. All the more so under an openly hostile Reagan Administration.

On the eve of the Reagan Administration (December 1980), it was not yet clear exactly what the United States could or would do in Nicaragua, but there were some indications. First, it seemed relatively clear that the Reagan Administration would not continue U.S. government aid to Nicaragua; also in question was future aid from U.S.-dominated multilateral agencies. The Republican Party platform in the summer of 1980 had stated opposition to the Carter Administration aid program to Nicaragua, and subsequently this position had been maintained, with Reagan spokesmen stating that aid to Nicaragua would do the U.S. no good, as it would not really go to the private sector nor diminish the dominant role of the "Marxist Sandinistas."[38]

Second, the Republican platform stated, "We will support the efforts of the Nicaraguan people to establish a free and independent government."

Even before the U.S. election, Reagan representatives are reported to have held discussions with possible leaders of a movement to overthrow the Nicaraguan government. Third, simultaneously, the Reagan team planned to greatly increase military aid to right-wing governments surrounding Nicaragua, in El Salvador, Guatemala, and Honduras. In the wake of the Reagan victory, right-wing forces throughout Central America went on an all-out offensive. Reagan advisers talked openly of a regional "Truman Doctrine solution" for Central America, using as a model U.S. policy toward Greece after World War II (i.e., massive economic and military aid to Guatemala and El Salvador, possibly combined with sending U.S. military advisors).[39] Exactly what this would mean for Nicaragua was not clear. At the very least, it would mean militarily strengthening the hostile neighboring government to "contain" Nicaragua's influence. At worst, it could portend aid to Somocista exiles in neighboring countries,[40] and(or) an overt move to overthrow the government, similar to the overthrow of the Arbenz government in Guatemala in 1954. In this regard, there was also the question of what would be the effect on Nicaragua of a possible U.S. intervention in a neighboring country (most likely El Salvador).

Despite these initial indications of Reagan policy, the Reagan Administration in office would have to deal with the real constraints on U.S. power, the same constraints that faced the Carter Administration. For one thing, a number of Western European governments, including the formerly staunch U.S. ally Western Germany, had moved toward an open break with U.S. policies in Central America: the European-based social democratic movements had refused to go along with U.S. maneuvering to keep Somoza in power and had aided the revolutionaries; and in 1979-80, they continued to pursue their own interests and policies in Central America, which did not coincide with those of the United States.[41] In addition, some Latin American governments, primarily the Mexican, went on record warning the United States not to intervene in Central America.[42] Although this would hardly constitute a military deterrent to U.S. action, it did raise the political issues which were likely to become the subject of debate within the Reagan Administration: What would be the political costs of an isolated U.S. intervention in Central America?

In addition, there were political considerations stemming from the situation within Nicaragua. The Nicaraguan people were organized and armed; unlike Allende's Chile, the army was in the hands of the Revolution. If the United States were to send the Marines or attempt some other form of military intervention, the Nicaraguan people could and would defend their revolution. Moreover, the net result of such intervention would most likely be to radicalize the Nicaraguan Revolution and to hasten the march toward socialism (similar to the overall effect of the U.S. Bay of Pigs invasion of Cuba in 1961). Indeed, even the talk of U.S. intervention as a possibility, in the wake of the Reagan victory, could only serve to further polarize an already unstable situation within Nicaragua.

Finally, Reagan would face problems of anti-interventionist sentiment within the United States. A June 1979 poll indicated that two-thirds of the American public opposed the Somoza regime; and an October 1980 poll showed that 60 percent of all men and 68 percent of all women "opposed the use of U.S. military force in trouble-spots in developing countries."[43]

Thus, the Reagan Administration faced a complex situation in Nicaragua, with many of the same constraints that Carter faced still operative. And within the Reagan Administration representatives of the Trilateral Commission (e.g. Vice President Bush) were jockeying for power with the more vociferous right-wing militarists. Certainly, the international bankers who worked so hard to get an agreement with Nicaragua on debt repayments were not likely to agree readily to adventurist policies, and could be expected to play some role in moderating Reagan policies. For all these reasons, it would be an oversimplification to draw a sharp line demarcating Carter policy from Reagan policy. The Carter Administration, as we have seen, was bitterly divided, with "hardliners" playing a significant role at times. As a number of dissidents within the Carter foreign policy apparatus stated in their November 1980 "Dissent Paper" (they were speaking of El Salvador, but their words held true for all Central America): "Should President Reagan choose to use military force in El Salvador, historians will be able to show that the setting for such actions had been prepared in the last year of the Carter Administration. . . ."[44]

Nevertheless, whatever the continuities between Carter and Reagan, and despite the fact that Reagan policy would not be a "180-degree turn" from Carter policy, there were also likely to be important differences. Carter policy, with its rhetoric of human rights and its actual emphasis on regional security, was contradictory and hypocritical. However, the very contradiction of "human rights" policy boxed in the Carter Administration and forced the United States to denounce its allies (even Somoza, eventually) in Central America. The rhetoric of human rights became a fetter on the policies of hemispheric security. This was a fetter which would not bind the Reagan Administration. And with this political constraint removed, the Reagan Administration had at least several degrees more freedom to intervene directly or follow aggressive policies in Central America, including Nicaragua. Such a prospect was cause for serious concern on the part of the workers' movements and all progressives opposed to U.S. intervention abroad, both in the United States and in Central America.

Notes

[1] The following draws from the analysis developed by Marlene Dixon at the Institute for the Study of Labor and Economic Crisis in San Francisco. See, for example, "Responsibilities of the U.S. Working Class to Latin American Revolutionary Movements in a New Cold War Period," Introduction to *Contemporary Marxism*, 1 ("Strategies for the Class Struggle in Latin America"; Spring 1980).

[2] See Susanne Jonas and Marlene Dixon, "Proletarianization and Class Alliances in the Americas," in *Synthesis*, Vol. III, No. 1 ("Contradictions of Socialist Construction"; Fall 1979).

[3] See, for example, James Petras, "U.S. Foreign Policy: The Revival of Interventionism," *Monthly Review*, Feb. 1980.

[4] For the following analysis, see *The Rebel Worker News Journal* and insert, "Plain Speaking," Vol. 4, No. 1 (Feb. 1980).

[5] See *Miami Herald*, Dec. 11, 1979, and *New York Times*, Feb. 3, 1980. Note: These and most of the newspaper articles cited below were found in Information Services on Latin America (ISLA), a monthly clipping service which follows major English-language newspaper coverage of Latin America. 464 19th St., Oakland CA 94612.

[6] *Financial Times*, Dec. 5, 1979

[7] *Miami Herald*, Dec. 14, 1979

[8] *New York Times*, Dec. 12, 1979

[9] See *Wall Street Journal*, Feb. 29, 1980

[10] *New York Times*, Oct. 9, 1979

[11] *Miami Herald*, Mar. 17, 1980

[12] *Wall Street Journal*, Feb. 29, 1980

[13] *Miami Herald*, Mar. 2, 1980

[14] *Miami Herald*, Mar. 20, 1980

[15] *Miami Herald*, May 8, 1980

[16] *Washington Post*, May 21, 1980

[17] *Los Angeles Times*, May 17, 1980; *New York Times*, May 16, 1980

[18] *Washington Post*, June 6, 1980, *New York Times*, June 10, 1980

[19] *New York Times*, June 10, 1980; *Washington Post*, Aug. 8, 1980

[20] *Miami Herald*, June 1, 1980

[21] *Washington Post*, Aug. 8, 1980

[22] *Washington Post*, Aug. 8, 1980; *Miami Herald*, Sept. 6, 1980

[23] *New York Times*. Sept. 13, 1980

[24] *Washington Post*, Sept. 13, 1980

[25] *Financial Times*, Sept. 16, 1980

[26] *New York Times*, Sept. 13, 1980

[27] *New York Times*, Nov. 27, 1979; *Miami Herald*, December 11, 1979

[28] *Financial Times*, Dec. 18, 1979

[29] *Miami Herald*, Sept. 5, 1979

[30] *Financial Times*, Mar. 18, 1980: June 28, 1980

[31] *New York Times*, Dec. 25, 1980, *Inforpress Centroamericana* (Guatemala), 421 (Dec. 4, 1980)

[32] *Latin America Regional Reports* (Mexico / Central America), Aug. 15, 1980; *Latin America Weekly Report*, Aug. 15, 1980; *Financial Times*, Sept. 16, 1980

[33] *New York Times*, Sept. 9, 1980; see also Terri Shaw in *Washington Post*, Oct. 5, 1980; *Latin America Weekly Report*, Sept. 12, 1980

[34] *Financial Times*, Sept. 16, 1980

[35] *New York Times*, Sept. 9, 1980

[36] *Journal of Commerce*, May 9, 1980

[37] *Washington Post*, Sept. 13, 1980

[38] *Latin America Weekly Report*, July 18, 1980; *Miami Herald*, Aug. 24, 1980

[39] See Susanne Jonas, "Reagan Policy for Guatemala," (manuscript: Institute for the Study of Labor and Economic Crisis, Dec. 1980)

[40] *Latin America Weekly Report*, Sept. 36, 1980

[41] *San Francisco Chronicle*, Sept. 17, 1980; *Latin America Weekly Report*, Aug. 22 and Aug. 29, 1980

[42] *Latin America Weekly Report*, Nov. 14, 1980; *New York Times*, Jan. 4, 1981

[43] "Dissent Paper on El Salvador and Central America, DOS, Nov. 6, 1980, pp. 19-20

[44] "Dissent Paper," pp. 1-2.

The Editor and the Contributors

The Contributing Editor
THOMAS W. WALKER is Associate Professor of Political Science at Ohio University, Athens, and a former Director of Latin American Studies at the same institution. He holds a B.A. in political science from Brown University, an M.A. in Latin American studies from the University of New Mexico and a Ph.D. in political science, also from U.N.M.

Professor Walker is the author of *The Christian Democratic Movement in Nicaragua* (University of Arizona, 1970), *Nicaragua: The Land of Sandino* (Westview Press, 1981), and a number of articles, chapters, and so forth on Latin America in general and Nicaraguan politics in particular.

The Chapter Authors
MAX AZICRI is Professor of Political Science at Edinboro State College, Pennsylvania. He holds M.A. and Ph.D degrees from the University of Southern California, a Doctorate of Law from the University of Havana, and a Manuel Marquez Sterling professional journalist degree from the Havana School of Journalism.

Professor Azicri has written extensively in the areas of Cuban legal and political change, social and political mobilization, the women's movement, and international relations. Presently, he is working on two book-length projects concerning the Cuban socialist legal system and the community of Cuban-Americans in the 1980s. His other research in progress includes the present state of social and political change and the relations among Caribbean nations.

ALEJANDRO BENDAÑA has the rank of Ambassador and is the Alternate Permanent Representative of Nicaragua to the United Nations. Until 1979, he was a teaching fellow in History at Harvard University.

Professor Bendaña has published numerous articles on Nicaraguan politics, including the NACLA issue "Crisis in Nicaragua" (September-October, 1978).

He holds a B.A. and M.A. from the University of New Orleans and a Ph.D. from Harvard University.

THOMAS JOHN BOSSERT is Assistant Professor of Government at Dartmouth College; Research Associate in Community and Family Medicine at Dartmouth Medical School, and Research Fellow in International Health at Harvard School of Public Health. Previously, he was Assistant Professor of Political Science at McGill University and Swarthmore College.

Professor Bossert has published in the area of political science, Latin

American Studies and public health. His articles and reviews have appeared in *Latin American Research Review, Social Science and Medicine,* and *Latin American Perspectives.*

He holds an A.B. from Woodrow Wilson School at Princeton University and an M.A. and a Ph.D. from the University of Wisconsin at Madison.

PHILIPPE BOURGOIS is a doctoral candidate in anthropology at Stanford University.

In 1980, M. Bourgois worked for the Nicaraguan Agrarian Reform Institute, among the Miskitu Amerindians.

He holds a B.A. from Harvard College and an M.A. from the Food Research Institute of Stanford University.

WILLIAM J. CARROLL III is a Ph.D. candidate in political science at the University of Arizona. He holds an M.A. in Latin American Studies from the same institution.

Mr. Carroll served as a U.S. Peace Corps Volunteer in rural Nicaragua in the mid-1970s and returned there late in 1978 to conduct research. Presently, he is Project Director of the Partnership for Productivity Program in Honduras.

RICARDO E. CHAVARRÍA teaches sociology at the Universidad Centroamericana in Managua and is Personnel Director for Nicaragua's National Energy Institute (INE).

Professor Chavarría holds a B.A. and an M.A. from the Universitá Gregoriana in Rome and an M.A. from Ohio University. He is also a Ph.D. candidate in Latin American studies at Tulane University, and is currently writing his dissertation on the Nicaraguan Revolution.

MICHAEL DODSON is Associate Professor of Political Science at Texas Christian University.

Professor Dodson has published extensively in the area of religion and social change in Latin America. His research articles have appeared in *Polity, The Journal of Latin American Studies, The Journal of Inter-American Studies and World Affairs,* and *Latin American Perspectives.*

Professor Dodson holds a B.A. degree from the University of South Dakota, an M.A. from the University of New Mexico, and a Ph.D. from Indiana University.

EDMUND V. K. FITZGERALD is Professor of Development Economics at the Institute of Social Studies, The Hague. Until 1979, he was Assistant Director of Development Studies at Cambridge University.

Professor FitzGerald has published widely on problems of the state, capital accumulation, and Latin America. In August 1979, he was appointed as Economic Advisor to the Nicaraguan Government of National

Reconstruction, working at the Ministry of Planning in Managua.

Professor FitzGerald holds an M.A. from Oxford University and a Ph.D. from Cambridge University.

STEPHEN M. GORMAN received his Ph.D. in political science from the University of California, Riverside, in 1977. He is presently on the faculty of North Texas State University and has formerly taught at Purdue University, Dickenson College, and SUNY-Fredonia.

Professor Gorman has completed several research projects in Peru, Nicaragua, and Mexico. His recent publications include articles in *Government and Opposition, Journal of Inter-American Studies and World Affairs, Inter-American Economic Affairs, Economic and Social Studies,* and *The Journal of Latin American Studies.* He is also coauthor of the *Yom Kipper War: A Case Study in United States Crisis Decision Making* (University Press of America, 1981).

SUSANNE JONAS is a Research Director of the Institute for the Study of Labor and Economic Crisis in San Francisco and a coeditor of the Institute's journal, *Contemporary Marxism.* Over the past twelve years, she has written extensively about Central America, particularly Nicaragua and Guatemala. In particular, she wrote her dissertation and coedited a book on Guatemala, wrote the February 1976 issue of NACLA's *Latin America and Empire Report* on Nicaragua, and continues to write on Central America.

She holds a B.A. from Radcliffe College, Master's degrees from Harvard University and the Massachusetts Institute of Technology, and a Ph.D. in Political Science from the University of California, Berkeley.

DAVID KAIMOWITZ is a Ph.D. candidate in agricultural economics at the University of Wisconsin, Madison. He has followed the Nicaraguan agrarian reform closely since its inception as part of a broader interest in noncapitalist agricultural models in Third World countries.

Mr. Kaimowitz received his B.A. at the University of California, Berkeley, in 1979.

WILLIAM M. LEOGRANDE is Director of Political Science at the American University, Washington, D.C. Until 1978, he was Assistant Professor of Government at Hamilton College, Clinton, New York.

Professor LeoGrande has published widely in the area of Latin American politics. His articles and reviews have appeared in *Foreign Affairs, Latin American Research Review,* and *The New Republic.*

He holds B.A., M.A. and Ph.D degrees from the Maxwell School, Syracuse University.

VALERIE MILLER is a Ph.D candidate in adult education at the Center for International Education at the University of Massachusetts and worked as a planning advisor to the Nicaraguan Literacy Crusade and the Vice-Ministry of Adult Education (Managua) during 1980 and 1981. She has spent over twelve years working with Latin Americans as a programming and evaluation consultant in the fields of education, health, community development, and human rights.

T. S. MONTGOMERY is a political scientist; her primary research interests are the churches and social change in Latin America and the Central American region. She has carried out field research in Mexico, Nicaragua, and El Salvador, and has published on Latin American Protestants, as well as U.S. policy, the Popular Organizations, and the Church in El Salvador. Her book, *El Salvador: Profile of a Nation in Revolution*, is to be published in 1981. She is a Senior Research Associate at the Center for Socioeconomic Investigation and Analysis (Centro de Investigación y Asesoría Socio-Económica, CINASE) in Managua.

JOHN SPICER NICHOLS is Assistant Professor of Journalism at the Pennsylvania State University and a specialist in international communication and comparative foreign journalism.

He is the collaborating author of *Keeping the Flame: Media and Government in Latin America*, and the author of a forthcoming monograph, "Organization, Control and Functions of the Cuban Mass Media." His articles on world communication have appeared in *Gazette, Journalism Quarterly, International Development Review, The Quill, Studies in Third World Societies* and other academic and popular publications.

Professor Nichols holds B.A., M.A. and Ph.D. degrees in journalism and mass communication from the University of Minnesota.

MARIFELI PÉREZ-STABLE is Instructor in Political Sociology in the Politics, Economics and Society Program at the State University of New York, Old Westbury.

Professor Pérez-Stable has published articles and reviews on Cuba in *Latin American Perspectives, Cuba Studies / Estudios Cubanos* and *Latin American Research Review*.

She holds a B.A. from Rosemont College and an M.A. from the University of Florida. Her doctoral dissertation will be on the Cuban working class in the Revolution.

SUSAN E. RAMÍREZ-HORTON is Assistant Professor of Latin American History at Ohio University.

Professor Ramírez has recently finished a book on land tenure and the political economy of Peru. She has published articles and presented papers related to these general themes and ethno-history.

Professor Ramírez holds a B.A. from the University of Illinois at

Urbana and M.A. and Ph.D. degrees from the University of Wisconsin at Madison.

MITCHELL A. SELIGSON, Associate Professor of Political Science at the Unviersity of Arizona, completed his chapter while a visiting professor at the University of Essex, England. Among his publications are several recent books, including *Peasants of Costa Rica and the Development of Agrarian Capitalism* (University of Wisconsin, 1980), *Political Participation in Latin America*, Vol. I and II (Holmes & Meier, 1978 and 1979) and *Maquiladoras and Migration: Workers in the Mexican-United States Border Industrialization Program* (University of Texas, 1981). His present research is focusing on a comparative study of support for democratic regimes.

Professor Seligson received his B.A. from Brooklyn College, City University of New York; his M.A. from the University of Florida; and his Ph.D. (Political Science) and Certificate in Latin American Studies from the University of Pittsburgh.

LUIS HECTOR SERRA is Professor of History at la Universidad Centroamericana in Managua. He is also a member of the "Popular Education Team" of the Agrarian Education and Promotion Center (CEPA), also in Managua.

Professor Serra holds professional law and history degrees from la Universidad Nacional de Buenos Aires, Argentina, and Master's degrees in Latin American Studies and Political Science from Ohio University.

JOSEPH R. THOME is Professor of Law at the University of Wisconsin, Madison and a Research Associate of the Land Tenure Center of the same university.

Professor Thome has published widely on land tenure and agrarian reform in Latin America and is currently helping to organize a collaborative research program between INRA and the Land Tenure Center.

Professor Thome holds a B.A. from the University of California at Los Angeles and a LL.B. from Harvard Law School.

HARRY E. VANDEN is Assistant Professor of Political Science and Latin American Studies Coordinator at the University of South Florida, Tampa, Florida. A former Fulbright Scholar, he has extensive field experience in Latin America.

His articles have appeared in the *Latin American Research Review* and the *Journal of Interamerican Studies and World Affairs*. His books include, *José Carlos Mariátegui: Influencias en su formación ideológica*, and *Marxismo Nacional: penasamiento y praxis de Mariátegui*. Currently he is working on a bibliography of Latin American Marxism and a study of Marxist voluntarism in Latin America.

Professor Vanden studied at the University of Madrid, and holds an M.A. and a Certificate in Latin American Studies from the Maxwell School of Syracuse University and a Ph.D. from the New School for Social Research.

ERIC A. WAGNER is Associate Professor of Sociology at Ohio University. From 1974 to 1978, he chaired the Department of Sociology and Anthropology at Ohio University, and in 1979-1980, was President of the Midwest Association for Latin American Studies.

Professor Wagner has published more than a dozen reviews and articles on Latin America and the sociology of sport, and has presented a number of papers on these topics.

HARVEY R. WILLIAMS is Assistant Professor of Sociology at the University of the Pacific. From 1973 through 1976, he was a Fulbright Latin American Teaching Fellow at the Universidad Centroamericana in Managua, Nicaragua and served as a consultant to several post-earthquake recovery programs.

Professor Williams holds a B.A. from the University of California, Berkeley, and M.A. and Ph.D. degrees from Vanderbilt University.

INDEX

Action and Labor Union Federation (CAUS), 143, 367
Afghanistan: Soviet invasion of, 324–25, 378
Africa, 48, 322
Agrarian Institute, Nicaraguan, 228
agrarian reform, 223–37; goals and policies of, 227–30; and land distribution, 227–31; problems of, 230–31 (*see also* Association of Rural Workers; Agrarian Reform Institute, Nicaraguan)
Agrarian Reform Institute, Nicaraguan (INRA), 209, 228–31
Agricultural Council, National, 232
Agricultural Workers Committees, 232
agriculture: exports of, 235; and government credit, 228–30, 233–35; importance of, 203–4, 236–7; income from, 225, 236, 237; labor in, 224–25, 227; and poverty, 225–26, 235; productivity in, 231, 237; and unemployment, 224–25 (*see also* coffee; cotton, sugar)
AGROINRA, 229
AID, 268 (*see also* USAID)
ALFALIT, 167, 175
Allende, Salvador, 25, 53, 347, 377, 385, 386
Alliance for Progress, 2, 3, 16, 17, 72, 276
ALPROMISU (Alliance for Progress of the Miskitu and Sumu People), 312–13
AMNLAE (*see* Association of Nicaraguan Women)
AMPRONAC (*see* Association of Women Confronting the National Problem)

ANS (*see* Sandinist Children's Association)
APP (*see* People's Property Area)
Arce, Bayardo, 188, 248, 364
Argentina, 92, 377
Argüello, Alexis, 295
Argüello, Álvaro, 177, 178
Argüello, René S., 363
armed forces (*see* National Guard; Sandinist Front of National Liberation)
Army to Defend National Sovereignty, 43, 44
Association of Nicaraguan Women "Luisa Amanda Espinosa" (AMNLAE), 95, 98, 154–56, 259, 266, 287, 367
Association of Rural Workers (ATC), 95, 96, 106–7, 127, 138, 170, 226, 234, 254, 260, 266 (*see also* agrarian reform)
Association of Women Confronting the National Problem (AMPRONAC), 31, 105, 151, 153–54, 359
ATC (*see* Association of Rural Workers)
Azicri, Max, 345–73, 391

banks, 207–12, 383–86, 388
Barcenas Meneses-Esguerra Treaty, 14, 325
Barricada (*see* newspapers)
baseball, 291–300
basketball, 292–93, 297, 299, 300
Batista, Fulgencio, 25–26, 358–59, 369
beef, 204, 224, 226, 235, 324
Bendaña, Alejandro, 319, 327, 391
Bolivia, 325; democracy in, 9, Ché Guevara in, 4, 115–16; revolution

F1528 .N4 1982   c.1
                   100105   000
Nicaragua in revolution / edit

3 9310 00044356 2
GOSHEN COLLEGE-GOOD LIBRARY